Wild Life
in the Far West

Author as a Comanche

Wild Life in the Far West

The adventures of a hunter, trapper, guide, prospector and soldier

James Hobbs

Wild Life in the Far West
The adventures of a hunter, trapper, guide,
prospector and soldier
by James Hobbs

First published under the title
Wild Life in the Far West

Leonaur is an imprint
of Oakpast Ltd

Copyright in this form © 2009 Oakpast Ltd

ISBN: 978-1-84677-964-0 (hardcover)
ISBN: 978-1-84677-963-3 (softcover)

http://www.leonaur.com

Publisher's Notes

In the interests of authenticity, the spellings, grammar and place names used have been retained from the original editions.

The opinions of the authors represent a view of events in which he was a participant related from his own perspective, as such the text is relevant as an historical document.

The views expressed in this book are not necessarily those of the publisher.

Contents

Introduction	7
Birthplace	9
A Raid on Mexicans	22
McIntyre's First and last Bear Hunt	38
The Pursuit and its hardships	53
James Kirker	66
Visit Bent's Fort	82
Volunteer for Duty	102
Return to Chihuahua	112
The Regiment Starts for Home	133
Visit to My Uncle	141
Peace Declared	149
Engagement with an English Mining Company	160
An Attack of Gold Fever	175
A Hunting Expedition	184
An Uprising	196
A Hospital Established	209
History of Lozado	225
Taken Prisoner	237
Surrender of Maximilian	257
I Resign My Captaincy	270

My Uncle's Massacre by Moromons	284
Death Valley	294
The Execution	308
The Last of the Gang	315
The Attack	323
Amalgamation Process	337
Sunday Amusements	355
A Brutal Dogfight	367
Deserted by Our Guide	378
A Visit to the Comanches	389
Decide to Settle Down	400
Robbery of a Mule train	409
Conclusion	422

Introduction

In presenting this work to the public, it is not the intention of the publishers to add another to the already numerous histories of the parts of country which are the scene of the adventures herein recited, but to give what the title page promises, an account of the personal adventures of the author during a long and wild life in the far West. He belongs to that class of pioneers and trappers, now become nearly extinct, of which the famed Kit Carson, who was for many years the companion of the author, has been considered the most perfect type.

In addition to his experiences as a hunter and trapper, we have an account of his life as a prisoner among the powerful and warlike Comanches, his adventures as a trader in Mexico, his services as interpreter and guide, under Doniphan, in our war with Mexico, and with the Liberals in the Franco-Mexican war as Captain of artillery, as well as his experience in mining in the days of the "forty-niners" in California, and elsewhere.

Probably no man living has passed through so varied and exciting a life as this one. At times he has seemed on the high road to fortune, when by a turn of the wheel he would find himself penniless. But in whatever condition he was, he was always ready to respond to any call for aid from the famishing emigrant train who were lost on the great plains, or the settlers who were in peril from the remorseless cruelty of the savages.

In writing out the incidents of this strangely eventful life, no attempt has been made to put them in glowing colours, but we have the account in few words. There are many incidents and descriptions that occupy but part of a page, which could easily have been spread over several pages; but the fact is there. Had as many words been used to say as little as there are in many books, it would have required several volumes the size of this to have contained the account of the author's experiences.

One thing the author wishes distinctly understood; he has in no case "drawn upon his imagination for his facts." There are a few incidents given upon what he considers reliable information, and they are so designated; but nearly all is from his own experience. As he never contemplated the publication of his adventures, he kept no diary or record of events, but relies entirely upon his memory, which prevents his giving exact dates in all cases. But this does not affect his own acts, and as has been stated, this is not intended for a history.

The Publishers

CHAPTER 1

Birthplace

I was born on the 10th of May, 1819, in the Shawnee Nation, on the Big Blue creek, a tributary of the Missouri river and about twenty-three miles from Independence. The place then known as Indian Territory is now better known as Jackson County, Missouri.

Being one of a pair of twins, the chief care of me devolved on a faithful old Negro nurse who was one of my father's slaves. My twin sister, who was brought up on her mother's breast, after weaning, looked so much whiter than I that my tanned and sunburnt complexion has been the occasion of many a joke from friends who laid it to my nursing from a negro.

My mother died in 1825, when I was about seven years of age. My father married his second wife when I was about thirteen years old, and she, being quite a young woman and high-spirited, commenced to rule the house after she had introduced the first one of a second crop of children. This made matters very uncomfortable for me, but I contrived to amuse myself for three years longer at home or till the age of sixteen, when I struck out for myself, pretty much on my own hook,, resolved to hunt for furs with some company, or hunt Indians, or do anything else that would pay.

While working on my father's plantation I had become familiar with the rifle and shot gun, and indeed had to provide nearly all the meat for the family; but game was plenty and that was an easy task, much easier than pleasing the mistress who took no pains to give me any educational advantages. Though young, I was nearly full grown when I found an excellent chance to join a fur company that had just started out from St. Louis, under the lead of Charles Bent, and were going out to a fort and trading-post called Bent's Fort, some three hundred miles south of Pike's Peak on Big Arkansas River. The party consisted of about sixty men. The more prominent hunters were Charles Bent, Guesso Chauteau, William Savery, and two noted Indian trappers named Shawnee Spiebuck, and Shawnee Jake. Some of the party were agents of, and interested in, the Hudson's Bay fur company, having their head-quarters at St. Louis. This was in 1835. As I shall have considerable to say of some of this party, a brief description of them may be of interest to the reader.

Charles Bent, the leader of the party, and a manager of the fur business at Bent's Fort, was a native of St. Louis, Mo., and a brother of the famous Captain Bent who originated the theory called the "Thermal Gateways to the Pole." At the time I joined his party, he was about thirty-five years of age, light complexioned, heavily built, tending to corpulency. In all my acquaintance with him I always found him perfectly upright in his dealings, both with his party and the Indians. He commanded the confidence and respect of all the tribes he dealt with, and his honourable treatment of them prevented violence on their part.

Savery, who was next in interest to Bent was a French Canadian a few years younger than Bent, and like him was a very fair and honourable man in all his dealings. These two men were well calculated for Indian traders, for they were respected as honest men, and would never furnish intoxicating liquors to the Indians for the purpose of making more advantageous bargains with them.

Spiebuck was a noble looking Indian, full six feet high, had a high forehead, Roman nose, malicious looking black eye, and was rather lighter coloured than most of the Shawnees who composed the party, who were all large, well-built men. He spoke English fluently, having been educated at a mission-school in Missouri. He retained, however, many of the Indian peculiarities, among them his fondness for liquor and his roving disposition, so that we never could keep him at one thing long at a time. He was the best shot with a rifle, at long range, I ever saw.

The Shawnees of the party wore buckskin pants and hunting-shirt, with fringes of buckskin strings along the seams of the legs and sleeves. They nearly all could speak English, but when by themselves they usually employed their own language. They were quiet and peaceable except when under the influence of liquor: then they needed just such a man as Bent to restrain them and keep them within bounds.

Most of the white trappers wore a dress similar to that of the Shawnees, on account of its great durability, as it would last from three to four years, notwithstanding the very hard usage it received.

The prospect to me was very pleasing. We were all mounted on horses, having some led mules and half a dozen one and two-horse carts to haul our provisions and bring in our furs, &c. It was a wild and lonely tramp. Before us were the vast plains, unbroken except here and there with a belt of timber, and we were following a mere trail, never seeing a house after leaving Independence. My capacity in the company was that of hunter, to provide fresh meat we needed on the route. John Batiste, a boy about my age, was mule-packer.

We had proceeded, without adventure, until the night after crossing Pawnee Fork, between live and six hundred miles from Independence, our point of departure. We crossed the fork, staked out our animals and, after supper, lay down in the tall grass that covered the valley. I stood guard from two till half-past three in the morning, and when one of the company named Spencer had taken my place, the six on guard had all been changed. About daylight, while the camp was wrapped in slumber, I was startled out of my blanket by a yelling, stamping of horses' feet, cutting tent-ropes, and then came the click of two arrows against a water bucket by my side.

We sprang to our feet and seized our rifles, amazed to discover that three or four hundred Pawnee Indians had crept through the long grass, surprised our guard and made a fierce assault with a view of running off our animals. We were not slow in returning their fire and soon the savages were driven into a corner where a precipitous ledge prevented their retreat. Finding it difficult to create a stampede among our horses and mules, and seeing us all well armed, the Indians took to the river in front of us and swam over. I broke one redskin's back with a bullet as he was climbing the opposite bank, and three others were killed.

Our party were more frightened than hurt, though one or two were pierced with arrows. At that early period guns and ammunition had not been freely sold by Indian agencies to these hostile western tribes, and their principal weapon was the bow and arrow. After this our party kept a stronger guard and looked out for night surprises.

I had little difficulty in keeping the company supplied with meat, as there were great numbers of buffalo, antelope, deer, elk, &c, on the plains at that time.

After travelling about one hundred and twenty-five miles further, we met at Big Coon creek a party of about three hundred Sacs with twenty-five or thirty Americans. These Sac Indians were friendly, and were taking one hundred and fifty buffalo calves to Missouri to raise for English purchasers. These calves had been given to cows whose calves had been killed to make room for these hump-backed strangers. Besides these calves the party had young grey wolves, elk, and antelopes.

We camped and feasted together four days, fishing for trout in Coon creek, hunting deer, &c, and at night carousing around, drinking liquor, and having a good time generally.

The reader must bear in mind that the men who engaged in expeditions of the kind we were on, were not noted for their total abstinence, any more than the representative sailor, having the same roving and frolicking nature.

Their party was under the direction of Mr. Fitzhughes, and he had taken the Sacs as a protection to his American party. . He warned us that there were signs of Indians before us, though he could not say what tribe. About four days after leaving our friends we arrived at the "*Caches*," a camping place on the banks of the Big Arkansas river, deriving its name from the fact that a number of wagons had been broken down in that neighbourhood and the provisions and goods "*cached*," or stored there for safe keeping till they could repair damages.

The next morning after leaving this camping ground, our attention was attracted by a distant smoke among some sand hills on the left side of the Arkansas. Our suspicions were that the smoke proceeded from Indians and was, perhaps, a hostile signal to notify other Indians of our approach.

We continued on our route and as our party moved slowly, only fifteen miles per day, and as I hunted on horseback, it gave me plenty of time. I killed three buffaloes that day, one of which, being old and tough, was abandoned after our boys had skinned him. The last one I shot was a fat buffalo cow which ran across the trail in front of our train late in the afternoon. I dashed after her wounding her with my pistols, and she swam across the river in the direction of the smoke. I started to the rear of the train for my Hawkins rifle, the men laughing at me for letting the cow escape.

"Don't try to follow that cow," said Bent, "she is going straight for that smoke and it means 'Injun' and no good in 'em either."

"But I'll get her," I answered, for I was mad on account of some of the boys laughing at me.

"Get your pack mule," said I to my young friend, Batiste, "and we'll fetch that buffalo back."

"All right," he answered, and we crossed the river. I went ahead, and about three miles from the train came up with the cow. She turned and showed fight. I galloped around her several times, finally getting in a good shot which killed her. Jumping off my horse I began cutting off the choice pieces for use in camp, young Batiste helping me and loading his mule until, suddenly, it was dusk and we were in doubt which way to return to our train. It was very soon pitch-dark, so we could not discern the tracks by which we had come, nor could we see the few Cottonwoods that lined the river, relieving the barren plain, and only at intervals could we see the stars.

"John," said I, "this running around the buffalo has bewildered me, but I think yonder is the way back."

"No," replied John, "I know the way I came, follow me," starting off in a different direction from what I proposed.

We travelled in this dismal fog and darkness, occasionally stopping to hear, if possible, some signal from our friends who we vainly hoped would be out looking for us. Nothing but the sound of a distant wolf, or night owl screeching, to break the stillness, when we stopped about ten o'clock, and said I, "John, we are going wrong. We have come at least ten miles and the best thing we can do is to stay here all night."

It was September and we slept comfortably enough, except being disturbed in the middle of the night by grey wolves, who, snuffing our meat from a distance, came prowling around us. We had kindled a fire, very luckily, before going to sleep, and knowing the habits of these "varmints," I made them scatter by flashing powder in our fire, and we were left in peace the balance of the night.

About sunrise we awoke and looking around for our train, to our amazement, could not even see the Cottonwoods that marked the bank of the river up which our train was moving.

We had been going away from the river on account of John's injudicious advice and want of experience. So we turned and retraced our steps as rapidly as our loads would permit, and were travelling along cheerfully, when a large herd of buffalo appeared and dashed along towards us, passing us at a fearful rate, as though terribly frightened.

"That means hunters or Indians," said I, and still they came thundering past, probably two thousand in number, filling the air with dust, and we discovered that they were closely followed by Indians, shooting arrows into them and piercing them with lances.

"To that little hollow, to that little hollow," I exclaimed to John, "throw away the meat and make for that hollow we just passed."

Batiste didn't need any urging, but we both wheeled and rode for the hollow, hoping to reach it before we were seen.

Descending the little ravine we looked back to see if we were safe and were astonished to see nine "Comanches" close behind us.

"How d'ye do?" said a stalwart chief in good English.

"How d'ye do" I replied for politeness' sake, but the state of his health was a matter of little concern to me just then.

"Texas?" (They hated Texans and it was well I answered,)

"No, friendly, going to establish a trading post with the Comanches and other Indians."

"Friendly? Better go with us awhile, though. Got any tobacco?"

I had a little old clay pipe and Batiste had another, which we gave them with some tobacco, and they took us in tow, starting for their camp where we arrived late that afternoon, our escort having swelled from the nine who captured us to about a thousand. They gave us some cooked buffalo meat and afterwards escorted us to the head-quarters of their tribe, introducing us to "Old Wolf," the head chief.

"Old Wolf" was a large and very tall Indian, with a Roman nose, high forehead, and hair falling down to his hips, braided in plaits, and ornamented with rings an inch wide, put on at intervals. These rings were ornaments peculiar to him, as no other member of the tribe ever wore them. When he wished to make an unusually rich toilet, he wore on his breast a large, highly polished, copper plate, which glistened in the sunlight and of which he was very proud.

Batiste had a bottle of brandy hanging on the horn of his saddle and with a view to conciliate the old chief, I suggested to John to give him a dram. He was suspicious and would not drink. I drank some and he looked me steadily in the eye. I then handed the bottle to him but still he doubted. Batiste took a horn cup and pouring out some so the chief could see what he drank, poured down a good "swig." The chief looked at him steadily fifteen minutes, then taking the bottle drank down its contents, like water, to the last drop. He was, immediately, the happiest Indian I ever saw.

We had travelled forty or fifty miles that day, close-watched and guarded by our captors, but without any fear of bodily injury, as the Indians acted quite friendly. The chief of their tribe, "Old Wolf" always staid at home, moving only at such times as the tribe travelled bodily, to attend the annual feasts with friendly tribes, or to follow the buffaloes as they migrated north or south, for he was an old man.

He had a son called chief and another called second chief. Both were married to white girls, captives, named Brown, who were captured in Texas, near San Antonio. They were sisters and in the same Indian village were their two brothers, captured at the same time, one named Henry, about twelve years of age, and little Jim, hardly seven years old. They had been taken about four years before, when their father, mother and two elder brothers were murdered.

The girls were now about eighteen and twenty-one years of age. I made many attempts to talk with them but was always frustrated by savage watchfulness. The little boy could only say Yes or No in English, though he could speak good Indian, as could his brother and sisters. I was also forbidden any conversation with the boys, but I learned they had lived near Fort Alamo, the scene of Davy Crockett's death.

A council was held, soon after our arrival, to decide on the disposition of John and myself; but it was necessarily adjourned till the next morning, because "Old Wolf" had drank too much of our brandy and talked himself to sleep in the midst of the council, and was not competent to hear the report of our captors. As the result of the deliberations, next day, the captive, Henry, was instructed to inform us that if we were not Texans and would be good and not run away, they would not kill us but let us stay with them.

They, however, pointed to some dried scalps and informed us that about three weeks before, three Mexicans, captured by them and set to mind their stock, had attempted to escape. They were pursued with the intention of bringing them back, but it was finally decided, after having a long chase, to bring only their scalps, and they should feel compelled to do the same by us under similar circumstances. These remarks were made with such grave earnestness that we decided our best course was to keep quiet and stay with the Indians, for it would be madness for such boys as we were, with no knowledge of the country, to attempt to reach Fort Bent or to return to Missouri.

John was particularly faithful. I went out with the Indians, and hunted, and learned to catch trout with their bone fish-hooks. But John never stirred from camp, for he was afraid of mistakes; he might be going from camp with the best intention to return, and lose his scalp, as the Mexicans did.

Our hosts did not like John very well, though they regarded me very favourably. The Comanches are the most powerful of all the tribes of North American Indians. Their dress differs but little from that of the Shawnees, a description of which has already been given,—the men wearing a buckskin hunting-shirt reaching to the waist, buckskin pants so made as to require a breech-cloth, as the pants do not cover the small of the back, and moccasins.

The women wear a buckskin petticoat and dress, reaching to the knee, pants like the men, and buckskin moccasins. The dress is usually fringed and the moccasins ornamented. The more favoured often add a handsome blanket to their costume. The Comanches are superior to all other tribes in horsemanship, and a very large portion of their lives is spent on horseback. They have a remarkable fondness for horses, and, as might be imagined, are the most accomplished horse-stealers in the world, often making daring raids, the replenishing of their stock being the principal object, as will be seen in the following pages.

At the end of three months, they were making up a war-party to go against the Pawnees, and requested Batiste and me to go and help them fight. He declined, but I accepted the invitation. My Hawkins rifle was returned to me, and we started, going over the same route we had come to their camp. We even passed

WARLIKE EXERCISES OF COMANCHES

the very spot where I had been captured, and also where I killed the buffalo. I saw tracks of shoe clad feet showing that our white friends of the train had searched for us, and must have seen from the Indian footprints, that a party had either captured or killed us, and so, giving up the search, had gone on their way. This I afterward ascertained to be the case, and that I was returning in the right direction when captured by the Indian hunters.

My reflections, when passing these familiar spots, were anything but pleasing. Snatched so suddenly from the companionship of friendly white men, who had begun to look upon me, though a mere youth, as an important and valuable assistant in their fur business, I realized that I had lost a good opportunity to become a wealthy fur-dealer and trapper. They were men who did a heavy business, and I had hoped to prove serviceable to them, and obtain an interest in the profits. Now my hopes were blasted. My friends would consider me dead or a captive, and no effort would be made to find me by my relatives or anyone else. How far these disappointments, or how much this ill-luck has influenced my after course or made me the roving adventurer that I have been, I leave the reader to judge.

Our force moved onward rapidly to the Big Arkansas River, just a little below "The *Caches*," where we surprised about two hundred Pawnees, who were camped in a wild-plum thicket. They feared the Comanches, and undertook to escape by swimming the river. I had an old grudge against the Pawnees for their attack on our fur-train previously; and, nerved with a desire to show our Comanche braves that I was interested somewhat, and wanted a hand in, I drew a bead on a Pawnee who was out in the middle of the stream, and, with a yell, he went to the bottom. The Comanches rushed into the river, secured the body, took off the scalp, and returned to their village, as the river was high, and they did not choose to ford it at the risk of their lives. Several of the Pawnees were drowned in the attempt to escape across the river; but the only trophy secured in the way of a scalp came from the head of the Pawnee who happened to be in range of my rifle.

Upon our arrival back in camp, "Old Wolf" helped me off the horse himself, hugged me, and said I had a big heart, but John had a little heart, because he would not go and fight. A procession was formed, and the Indian who had the Pawnee scalp led off, while I was second, the chiefs following, with the warriors in the rear; after which there was a big dance and pow-wow. "Old Wolf" brought out his daughter, a really beautiful Indian girl about my own age, with whom I had become slightly acquainted, and offered her to me for a wife!

Of course I consented; what else could I do?—and the wedding was arranged to take place instanter. The old priest, whose age was over a hundred by the moons he had notched on his cane, united us in the bonds of matrimony at once. He repeated the marriage ceremony, which was unintelligible to me, and, placing on my finger a ring made of buffalo horn, and a similar ring on her forefinger, bade us change rings.

And thus "Spotted Fawn" became my wife, and proved loving and affectionate; and I have no doubt she remains faithful to me to this day, though I have not seen her for years. All their marriages are by consent of the chief; and then women are loyal and obedient, considering their marriage vows sacred and binding till death shall part them. The men are also true to their wives, as a general thing, and any breach of good morals is punishable by whipping, and sometimes, where the offense is aggravated, the criminal is cut to pieces with knives. Their notions of virtue and morality are, in some respects, in advance of more civilized communities.

About three months after my marriage, six Negroes were brought into camp as captives. They had run away from their Cherokee masters, and were trying to reach Mexico when the Comanches picked them up. Five were on horses that were too wretchedly poor for crow-baits, and one Negro on foot. When they came into camp under guard, they were so badly scared as to turn ashy pale! Seeing me, they called out, "For God's sake, massa! Please don't let 'em kill us!" I promised them they should not be hurt. These Negroes were a great curiosity to "Old Wolf," who had never seen one of that race before. He came to me for an explanation.

"What kind of people are these?" said he; "what black 'em for? What swinge hair for?"

"Not blacked," I answered; "hair not swinged; born so." This he would not believe till he had rubbed his fingers over their faces, and then examined the ends of them, to the amazement and terror of the poor captives. He also plucked at their wool, in the endeavour to ascertain how it got so kinky. The whole nation flocked to see these human curiosities, and crowded around them, raising uncontrollable terror in the minds of the Negroes.

When they saw them coming, old "Josh," their leader, cried out, "Now they's gwine to kill us sure! Please don't let 'em, massa! Gorra mighty! Ise afraid of 'em!"

"No," I replied; "they will not hurt you. This is the old chief, a greater general than any in the United States, and what he tells you, you can depend on; and I am his son-in-law." That satisfied them.

On the eighth day after their arrival, "Old Wolf" told them they had rested long enough, and must leave. He gave them buffalo robes to sleep on, a supply of buffalo meat, fresh horses to ride, and an escort of eight Indians; and my wife gave old "Josh "a pair of moccasins, for which he stuttered out many thanks. The Negroes seemed to have more confidence in me than in their escort; but I calmed their fears, and they started. Four days afterward, the escort returned, having conducted their charge into the main road to Mexico.

CHAPTER 2

A Raid on Mexicans

About two months after the incidents related in the last chapter, I accompanied a war-party of four hundred Comanches down on the Rio Grande, to a place called Monclova, over three hundred miles from where our Comanche nation were encamped. We had a battle with the Mexicans; after surrounding and attacking the town of some two thousand inhabitants, forty or fifty Mexicans were killed and twenty scalps taken.

Attending our party, and foremost in this fight, was a young girl of our tribe, selected for her purity, and looked upon by these superstitious warriors as an angel of good or ill luck. Mounted on a fast horse, she was first in our charge, or in advance (as soldiers say) of the line of battle. She was skilled in the use of the bow and arrow and handling of her horse, and to her boldness and cool daring our success was partially attributed.

We lost four of our warriors. We returned with nine Mexican women and children prisoners, and captured fourteen hundred horses and mules, making a clean sweep of all such animals in that section of country. On our return, we picked up, at the Nueces River, a youth of seventeen years, named Nathan Martin. He was out hunting for runaway stock, and, being discovered by some of our party, was pursued and brought in, terribly frightened.

On finding that I could speak English, he became more calm, and, in answer to my questions, stated that he was from San Antonio, Texas. I instantly warned him not to let that be known, for our tribe hated the Texans, and would be sure to show him no mercy, if they knew he was from Texas. I told him how to represent to them that he was from the same place I was, and to show no signs of fear, as they would be much more likely to spare him, if he appeared brave. He followed my advice, and was treated kindly by the tribe during his stay with them.

This was one hundred miles north of the scene of our battle, and to this place the four dead warriors were brought, that their remains might be laid to rest within the boundaries of their own nation. The funeral ceremonies hindered us here half a day. The departed were wrapped in buffalo robes, and placed on scaffolds made in trees as high as we could go. Their bows and arrows were laid beside them, buffalo meat put under their heads, and finally their horses were killed at the foot of the trees.

Then the warriors, falling on their knees, with hands uplifted and joined, with eyes raised toward the sun (which is their God, or Great Spirit), murmured in low tones their prayers to the sun, to take the bodies of their departed friends up to his bosom, and happily revive them in the heavenly hunting-grounds. This is the best idea they have of anything spiritual. They believe their departed brother, with his bow and arrows, sitting astride the horse at the foot of the tree, will ascend to the sun, bearing the provisions placed under his head, which is thought sufficient to last him through his upward journey, at the end of which he is expected to find plenty.

After the lapse of a hundred years, he will return to his nation, with the same bow and arrows, riding the same horse! All their dead,—men. women, and children,—after meeting friends in the sun and enjoying happiness there, must return at the end of a hundred years, and thus keep up the population and power of the tribe. All the Comanches worship the sun, morning and evening. At sunrise the men, on their knees, with their faces toward the sun, hands elevated and joined, pray for health and prosperity in hunting. At sunset the women pray in the same manner for the same blessings. This was the daily custom year after year, and probably is continued to this day.

Upon reaching our head-quarters, the chief, my brother-in-law (the commander of the war-parties), gave orders for the men to assemble at his father's tent, "Old Wolf's" lodge, the next morning, for the purpose of making our report, as well as to have a jollification over the scalps and prisoners we had captured. Our expedition had occupied several months, being delayed by hunting and branch raids in different directions. Our report to "Old Wolf was made somewhat as follows;

All of the war-party sat in a circle in front of the chief's tent, so that the door of the tent was within the line of the circle. "Wolf sat in the doorway on a buffalo robe, and by his side his son, the war-chief. The medicine pipe passed around for good luck, and .then, in a loud voice, so that all the four hundred warriors could hear it, every event was narrated by the war-chief, from the setting out of the party till its return. During this narration there was the most profound silence. When he concluded he asked the warriors if he had stated the events correctly. These reports are meant to be very accurate, but, if any mistake is made, the warriors correct it.

After this ceremony was ended, three amputations were made by the chief's surgeon. Two of our war-party had each a leg shattered and one an arm. They were brought back to camp from the scene of our late tight on buffalo robes, bolstered up on horses that were led by others, and must have endured much suffering, but nothing compared to the final amputation, which was barbarous. The old surgeon, with a butcher-knife and a saw made of a piece of hoop-iron, cut off the limbs, seared the stumps with a hot iron, and bound over them a poultice made of a pulverized bark, somewhat resembling oak or slippery elm, which they always carry with them.

The victims of these rough operations each held a bullet in his teeth, convulsively hugged one of the Indians holding him, and gave vent to some slight groans, but, on the whole, bore it man-fully. They all recovered in due time. After the surgical operation was over, there was a general carousal over the scalps, and a council held to make a proper disposition of our prisoners.

The women and children captured were finally disposed of by being adopted in various lodges through the tribe.

I had now been with the Indians about a year. Cold weather was again approaching, and we began preparations for winter. The squaws sally forth in the fall, gathering acorns and pine-nuts. The acorns, being pulverized in stone mortars to the fineness of meal, make a kind of mush when boiled, which goes very well with their meat. In summer they secure wild currants, gooseberries, plums, and cherries, which they dry for winter use. They have vessels for cooking and carrying water, made out of clay and baked in kilns by the squaws.

The fruits and nuts having been provided, and the season for buffalo hunting being at hand, some of the squaws accompany the warriors out to assist in buffalo packing, &c. These animals move southward in large droves in the fall, naturally dreading the deep snows of the plains. Our tribe of Comanches were often very successful in the hunt, sometimes killing a thousand in the fall. They went out, armed with bows and arrows, mounted on their best horses or mules. There was a precipice several hundred feet high on the bank of the Little Red River, and back of this precipice was a plain which was often covered with buffalo. By surrounding a drove, getting them into a panic, and heading them for the river, they would rush over this high precipice in crowds.

Our squaws would assist in skinning them, cut up the meat into strips, salt it (with salt gathered from several natural salt-springs and deposits in the vicinity), dry it in twists, with a streak of lean and fat together, and put these twists into square bales for packing. They scraped the hides with the rib-bone of a deer or elk, and dressed them with the buffalo brains. There were always more or less deer, elk, and antelope crowded over the precipice with the buffaloes, and the meat was preserved and skins dressed in the same way. The buckskin is dressed for clothing by them in such a manner that wetting does not stiffen it.

Fish are also caught in the fall and salted or dried for winter use. For this purpose a hook is used, made of a small short bone about an inch long (for trout), baited with a grasshopper, and hung in the centre. They also shoot them with arrows. I taught them how to catch fish with a seine, which greatly pleased them, and for this purpose we used buffalo hides stitched together, with innumerable holes cut in them.

This they thought splendid fun, hauling in enormous quantities of bass, trout, perch, &c.

About Christmas, a party of five hundred Comanches went down into Mexico and attacked the Apaches, who, being friendly with the Mexicans, retreated about sixty miles to the Mexican village of Passo del Norte. Some Mexicans were killed, and the party returned toward spring, after an absence of three months, with four or five Mexican women and children, one young Apache squaw, and eighty Apache scalps. They also brought over a thousand head of mules and horses. This was a grand triumph for our tribe, and they danced over it a week. I did not go with them on that trip, but, judging from what they told me, the distance was about three hundred miles.

We spent the remainder of the cold season in hunting buffalo and other animals in small parties. Among the winter sports are wrestling matches, running foot-races, jumping, and horse-racing. At their horseraces, they frequently stake their horses, and their stakes, whatever they are, are always paid without any grumbling.

The young Comanches (oftentimes the lads not over fifteen years of age) were educated and trained for the war-path in an amusing way. Two deer or wolf skins—sewed together, and cut somewhat in the shape and about the size of a man—are stretched on bushes, one such image on each side of the track to be raced over.

Mounted on horses fleet as the wind, these boys go back three or four hundred yards. The horses are started, and come down the track at full speed, and, in passing the target, the young warrior must shoot an arrow through it, by throwing himself on the side of his horse, his weight held by his heel against the rear projection of his saddle. His left arm, with a shield on it, is thrown over the horse's neck, grasping the bow, with the arrow in his right hand; he must send the arrow through the target while passing. This is practiced in shooting with both the right and left hands. Bets are made on the young warriors, as to excellence of shooting. Right and left thrusts with lances are practiced in the same way.

The women of the Comanche tribe are busy in the winter months at various kinds of employment. They cook, and wash, and make up garments with great skill,—for needles using awls made of thorns or sharp bones; for thread they procure their material from a species of wild flax, which is pounded and rotted and twisted into thread, though they often used the sinews of wild animals. They were dexterous in the manufacture of clothing for themselves, their husbands, and children, making them up from skins they had dressed or tanned themselves, often ornamenting them with beads procured from the Mexicans or shells found in the river bottoms. They were generally a good-looking, hardy set of squaws, and made good, faithful wives.

Their good health and toughness of constitution may be inferred from their system of midwifery, which was very simple, and not at all like that of our delicate American ladies. When the eventful period arrives, the Comanche squaw proceeds alone to a clump of willows or bushes by the banks of a stream, and, entirely unattended, performs all the necessary offices or duties, goes into the water and bathes herself and infant, wraps the babe in a wolf or other skin, and carries the little stranger back to camp, suspended on her back by a strap which passes over her forehead or around her neck.

There is a use made of looking-glasses sometimes in battle that was rather ludicrous. A Comanche will give a horse for a piece of a mirror. This he fastens in a shield, and is often able to dazzle the eyes of an enemy taking aim at him, and thus cause his shot to go harmlessly wide of its mark. In pillaging the houses of people living out on the frontier, such relics were often obtained and brought home as very valuable trophies. If an unlucky trapper or emigrant, who happened to fall into their

Comanches moving

hands, had a hand-mirror for shaving and a silver watch, the mirror was prized as much the most valuable, for its wonderful reflecting properties; while the watch would, perhaps, be broken up, and the pieces made into nose or ear ornaments for the squaws and papooses.

In June, our chief told us we were all to meet the Arapahoes and Cheyennes, at the annual feast usually held in common by these three tribes. Then commenced the operation of moving; a long pole strapped to each side of a horse or mule, with a platform made on the parts dragging behind, sufficed to transport our tents and children. The squaws packed the horses and mules, and carried all that was not transported on the platforms. Many of the dogs belonging to the squaws are also made to do service, in "moving time," a small platform being arranged in the same manner as for the horses. Some of them will not submit to this treatment, and worry those that otherwise would, and many fights, often including the squaws who side with their respective dogs, are the result.

The warriors, who ride on the flanks of the procession, leaving the pack-train to the care of the squaws, always appear to enjoy these little differences very much. Then the whole tribe of twenty thousand men, women, and children got ready to move. (The number of the tribe is, of course, much less now than at that time.) This required but little preparation, for Indians do not scatter out and leave themselves exposed to raids and attacks. They build their villages compactly, setting their tents thickly on the borders of some stream, keeping the old people in the centre. These old men and women provide fuel, and busy themselves making bows and arrows for the use of the warriors.

We had about one hundred and twenty miles to go to reach the feasting ground, which was on the Big Arkansas, between the point where that river is crossed by the Santa Fe road and Bent's Fort. John Batiste went with us, of course; but this was the first time he had left camp since his capture. On the first day after we started, his horse threw him, which created a general laugh, for the Indians all despised him, and would have taken his scalp long before, if they had not been so attached to me. John was still unmarried, having never asked for a wife; for he well knew that none of the squaws would look with favour upon him, as he was such a coward.

As we expected, we met on the Big Arkansas about twenty thousand Arapahoes and Cheyennes, these two tribes being very friendly and mixing together. To me it was a lively scene, as I gazed on forty thousand people assembled in one grand mass meeting, with their tents and animals spread out over an area several miles in extent. We took a large quantity of provisions with us, killing some game on the way, and sent out daily hunting-parties, to provide food during the feast.

The favourite dish of the Arapahoes and Cheyennes was dog, gelded and fattened, which they cooked in covered pits in the earth, the bottoms of which were covered with burning coals and red-hot stones. The Comanches do not eat dog at home, but with these two friendly tribes, at their feasts, they partake. I never tried the flavour of the animal.

Upon our arrival, "Old Wolf" introduced me to the Arapahoe chief, telling him I was his son-in-law; said I was a brave fellow, reciting the killing of the Pawnee and the trip to Mexico; and then, pointing to John, said he had a little heart and never stirred out of camp. Kit Carson and I have since had many a laugh at John Batiste about his little heart; for we three had many an adventure after that on the plains together.

The feast continued ten or fifteen days, and was enlivened by running horse-races, foot-races, and by playing ball. In these races and games, the Comanches bet horses against the Arapahoes and Cheyennes, and almost always win, so that, by the time the great feast is over, those two tribes are afoot! But "Old Wolf," always gave them back a number of horses to go home with, and the different tribes went each their way in good humour and the best of spirits.

The game of ball was played with crooked sticks, and is very much like our "shinney." The players are dressed with a simple breech-cloth and moccasins, and the game is always played with enthusiasm, and affords much amusement. They choose sides, and put up stakes on the result of these ball-games, as well as on the foot-races. As a spectator among these ignorant savages, I was highly amused and interested by these harmless festivities.

The eighth day of the feast, I saw a white man coming toward our chief's tent, in company with a number of Cheyennes. "John," said I to Batiste, "they are bringing in a white man." They came to "Old Wolf," and the stranger, seeing me, opened a conversation, which I translated to the chief. The newcomer said his name was Kit Carson. He was mounted on an Indian pony, and was a man of slight build, small in stature, with long flowing hair, light complexion, with a piercing grayish eye, inclined to blue; and altogether his appearance was such that I took a natural liking to him.

Afterward, in my long acquaintance of twelve years with him, I noticed that other men, even the Indians, were favourably inclined to Kit at first sight. I found, also, that he was a superior shot with his rifle and a remarkable rider, being familiar with many feats of horsemanship learned only among the Indians. Either he or I could with ease pick up a silver dollar from the ground, when going at full speed, mounted on the swiftest pony. We often, in idle hours, amused ourselves by one shooting apples held by the other on a sharp stick two or three inches in length.

Carson said he was an old friend of the Cheyenne chief, and wanted to be friendly with the Comanches. He was a member of a trading company that were encamped not far from Bent's Fort, and he said he had beads, trinkets, and all sorts of merchandise for sale. "Old Wolf" was evidently suspicious and disposed to be hostile. He did not like to have me converse with Carson; but I got a chance to tell him privately, in the course of the two or three hours that he stopped in our camp, that he might say to the people at the fort, that John and I who were lost at "The *Caches*," were captives there among the Indians. He said he had heard about our being missed from a trappers' train, and that we were considered as dead or captives among some Indians.

To see us alive and well once more, was a very agreeable surprise. Kit soon left our camp, and returned to his trapping company, from seventy-five to one hundred miles from us, up the Big Arkansas. Before he left, he stated that "Peg-leg "Smith, a noted trapper, so called from his having a wooden leg, and Shawnee Spiebuck, one of the party I left home with, were in his party, and he had left them back in camp, to come here and see his old friend, the Cheyenne chief, and, if possible, to trade for furs.

At the end of the feast, the three chiefs—Comanche, Arapahoe, and Cheyenne—held a council, in which they laid plans for the ensuing year, marking out routes for hunting and war parties, so they should not come in collision with each other, and arranged for the next feast, to be given on Comanche grounds to the Arapahoes and Cheyennes. Then our whole party started down the Big Arkansas.

At the mouth of Ash creek, two hundred miles from the place of our late feast, we encountered a war-party of Pawnees, scalped twenty-three, and took all their horses. Thence, going up to the head of Ash creek, we encamped, sending out war-parties occasionally. After we had been in camp here about a month, we had a battle with the Sioux Indians, and here the Comanches were again victors. There were about four hundred engaged on each side, and we lost twenty-one of our warriors, but took about eighty scalps, while some of their dead were carried off the field.

After burying our dead, we spent about two months dancing over the Sioux scalps and doctoring our wounded. After they were well enough to move, we went with a large war-party, one hundred and fifty miles, to the foot of the Rocky Mountains, where we had an encounter with the Crow Indians, but suffered small loss ourselves. We remained in that vicinity about a month, when we started for our old home, travelling slowly, and killing meat on our way, reaching home in November.

After laying up sufficient provision for the winter, a war-party of five hundred was organized to make a raid into Mexico.

"Old Wolf" asked me to go; but I excused myself, and urged Martin, our young captive, to join the expedition. He consented, and they gave him a horse and gun, when he departed with the warriors, after smoking the medicine-pipe all around. I had some suspicion that he would find some way to escape.

On the return of the warriors, two months afterward, they reported that, at Cerro Gordo, some five or six hundred miles distant, they were in the midst of a fight with Mexican troops, into which Martin had rushed with the rest, when suddenly they missed him, and afterward found his horse among their own. They supposed him to be killed; but such was not the fact, for, within a few years, I have seen him in Los Angeles County, California, where he is keeping a hotel. In that fight, our Comanches fought the Mexicans about even, but whipped them, and brought home a lot of horses, brood mares, guns, ammunition, and several Mexican prisoners.

We spent the remainder of the winter in the usual sports and in hunting, and in June the Arapahoes and Cheyennes came over to our village, on Little Red River, to hold the annual feast, according to agreement. At this feast there was a show of scalps taken during the year, and our tribe had the most, our chief showing over a hundred; while the other two tribes could only show about half that number. This feast and grand carnival lasted twenty days.

At the usual chiefs' council, at the expiration of the feast, the Cheyenne chief advised "Old Wolf" to go to Bent's Fort and trade with the white people. He had done so, and liked them; showed some presents he had received; said they were good people,—not like the Texans, but like me, and were of the same party as myself. "Old Wolf" agreed to go and have a talk with Bent the next year, when he should come around to feast with the Cheyennes; for the camp of the Cheyennes was not more than a day's travel from the fort. At this feast the Cheyennes complained of bad luck and a scarcity of horses, and "Old Wolf" made them a present of three hundred head, saying he knew where to find plenty more.

During the ensuing year, we made some important raids into Mexico, and had a number of fights, travelling a large circuit with the entire tribe, sometimes with good success and sometimes quite the contrary.

At the June feast among the Cheyennes, when I had been with the Comanches nearly four years, "Old Wolf," went with their chief, by invitation, to visit Bent's Fort, about twenty miles distant. Bent had learned from Kit Carson that John Batiste and myself were with the Comanches, and offered to buy us of "Old Wolf." He replied, that he would be willing to sell John for a Jews-harp, but could not spare me, unless I was dissatisfied, and wanted to leave them. He sent a warrior back to our camp, saying we were wanted at the fort.

While saddling our horses, my wife began to cry, but assisted in our preparations and finally decided to go with us to the fort, telling me repeatedly on the road that she wanted me to stay by her and not forsake their tribe.

At the fort I met Kit Carson, Peg-leg Smith, and most of the men that belonged to the train with which I engaged nearly four years before.

Peg-leg Smith, as has before been stated, received this name from the fact of his having a wooden leg. He was a stout built man with black eyes and gray hair. He was a hard drinker, and, when under the influence of liquor, very liable to get into a fight. When he found himself in a tight place, his wooden leg proved very serviceable to him as he had a way of unstrapping it very quickly, and when wielded by his muscular arms it proved a weapon not to be despised.

His love of liquor was his ruin, as he died about the year 1868, in a drunken fit, in Calaveras County, California.

The whole party were much pleased to welcome John and me from our captivity, and, as might be imagined from previous descriptions of the leading men of the party, whisky occupied a prominent place in the rejoicing. Peg-leg Smith, at this, our first meeting, showed me what to expect of him in future, whenever he and whisky came together, and John and I found our heads hardly able to stand the many toasts drank to our good health.

The whole party, "Old Wolf," and his companion, the Cheyenne chief, got very much elated; and nearly every person in the fort smelt the whisky, if they did not get their feet tangled with it. About midnight a messenger came inside, stating that a thousand warriors were gathering around the fort. They demanded their leaders, fearing treachery; they desired to know why their chief had not returned.

I went out and explained that we were among good friends. They insisted on seeing "Old Wolf" himself. He, and my wife, and myself showed ourselves to them, and the chief made a speech, telling them that he and the Cheyenne chief were among good men who were friends to the Indians and presents would be given out the next morning.

The warriors were pacified with these assurances, though they did not leave the vicinity of the fort. Next morning Bent gave our chief eight yards of curtain calico for John Batiste, and took possession of his property at once. "Old Wolf," made many objections to disposing of me, but I was finally ransomed from the Indians for the trifling consideration of six yards of red flannel, a pound of tobacco, and an ounce of beads.

My wife, who sat looking on was greatly distressed, cried bitterly, and would have gone with me if the chief had given permission, but he refused, saying he preferred to keep her, and that I could visit her often, if I chose, as I promised faithfully to do. I tried to comfort her by rigging her out gaily, giving her a variety of beads and a red dress, but this, although very pleasing to her Indian taste, hardly reconciled her to the separation.

I took "Old Wolf" in charge and with a lieutenant, showed him all over the fort, letting him see the rifle port holes, and explaining how the fort could stand a siege against thousands of Indians. Finally we went out on the parapet where there was a six pounder at each angle. "Old Wolf" inquired how they could shoot that thing. By my request a blank cartridge was put in and the piece fired. The chief sprang back in amazement; my wife came up to see what was the matter, and the Indians on the outside, under the walls, knowing nothing of what was going on, ran away as fast as their legs could carry them, convinced that "Old Wolf" must be dead now, and their own safety depended on flight. The chief and I sprang up on the wall and signalled and shouted to them and they returned, asking in much astonishment, what kind of a monstrous gun that was.

About noon, trading commenced. The Indians wished to come into the fort, but Bent prohibited the entrance of any but chiefs. At the back door he displayed his wares, and the Indians brought forward their ponies, buffalo robes, and deer and other skins, which they traded for tobacco, beads calicoes, flannels, knives, spoons, whistles, Jews-harps, &c, &c.

He sold them whisky the first day, but it caused several fights among themselves before night, and he stopped its sale by my suggestion and with "Old Wolf's" consent. Indians do not waste time in fighting with their fists, but use knives and tomahawks, and a scrimmage among themselves is serious. There was considerable difficulty the first day, with drunken Indians outside the fort, and two or three deaths resulted.

The trading continued eight days and Bent reaped a wonderful harvest of what would turn to gold when shipped to St. Louis. "Old Wolf" slept in the fort every night except one, and every time he did, his warriors aroused him during the night and compelled him to show himself on the walls to satisfy them of his safety.

On the morning of the ninth day the chiefs met and told Bent they were going home and would send out hunting parties, collect more skins and furs and come to trade with him every two or three months. "Old Wolf" told Bent that his goods were splendid, his whisky excellent and he should furnish him with all the horses and mules he wanted by sending out parties and making raids into Mexico. Bent offered to give him the market price for all such stock, and had no conscientious scruples about the way the Indians obtained them.

I reported to Bent concerning the two American girls and their two brothers I had found in camp when I was captured by the Comanches, and he made "Old Wolf" liberal offers for them, but the chief would not hear to anything of the kind. He replied that he was glad that he had got rid of John Batiste, for they were tired of supporting him as he had never killed any game or been useful. But he could not think of parting with the wives of his sons, and the little Brown boys, who were as wild, active, and expert as Indians.

I now had to part with my wife and little son, three years of age, which "Spotted Fawn" had brought along to the fort, probably as an inducement for me to remain with her. She had also brought with her from camp a fine bay horse which she knew I valued highly. This horse she left with me; and picking up our child, with a tearful embrace, with a look of sorrow bordering on despair, and one wild, mournful shriek, she was gone from the fort, her grief at the separation caused the poor woman to lose prematurely her second child, as I have learned since.

When "Old Wolf" bade me goodbye he presented me with two mules, and to John Batiste he gave a pony. He liked his fare and treatment at the fort very much indeed. The variety of cooked dishes suited him, but the bread he disliked, saying it would be good to make a smoke-fire with to colour their buckskins.

About three months after I was ransomed the chief's eldest son was killed during a raid into Mexico and the elder of the two American girls, who was thus made a widow, was sold to Bent and is now living in San Antonio, Texas. Matilda Brown, the younger sister, was sold to Bent, but the chief would not let her little half-breed son accompany her; so after stopping at the fort three or four days, she declared herself unfit to live among white people, and returned to the tribe where she is still living or was a few years ago; and her two younger brothers never could be induced to leave the Comanches.

CHAPTER 3

McIntyre's First and last Bear Hunt

It was in 1839 when I was restored to the company of hunters and trappers with whom I had started out nearly four years before. It surprised me that the party had changed so little; in fact the principal men were all here at the fort or out on a hunt and would soon be with us. Trapping for beaver and hunting game, &c, was the chief occupation of these traders and fur dealers whose head-quarters were at Bent's Fort. About one hundred trappers were in the employ of Bent and his partners, and sometimes one half the company were off on the hunt; sometimes more; leaving a small force at the fort for its protection, though a military company was constantly stationed there with a small battery, which was considered sufficient for its defence.

When a company of trappers returned to the fort from a successful hunting trip, they were very jubilant and usually staid at the fort playing cards, drinking whisky and carousing, till a new party would organize and start off on another tramp, to be gone for several months, perhaps.

I staid at the fort some three months and then went out trapping under the lead of Kit Carson, with Peg-leg Smith, Spiebuck, Shawnee Jake, and other Shawnees, with some hunters I had not seen before; in all the party numbered forty or fifty.

Our destination was Picket Ware at the foot of Taos Mountain, ninety or a hundred miles from Bent's Fort. In the region about "Picket Ware" and along Beaver creek we trapped and hunted four months. Altogether we captured over five hundred beaver and put up a great deal of bear bacon and bear's oil.

Spiebuck and Shawnee Jake, with myself, were the principal hunters for meat. Out hunting one evening, between sundown and dark, I wounded an elk. Being so dark I could not see my rifle-sights clearly, I shot it too far back. It was so late I let it run and returned to camp. It ran up a ravine which opened out a mile and a half from camp. Knowing that a wounded elk invariably takes to the water and stays by it till he dies, I was satisfied that I should find my game in the morning near one of the sloughs or small pools of water scattered through the ravine.

On my return to camp I enjoyed a luscious supper of Shawnee cooking, being a mixture of turkey, grizzly bear, beaver tails, and buffalo, all cooked together in the same pot. I may as well say here that bread forms no part of an Indian's diet, and in my four years of captivity I had lived on meat altogether, and had lost my appetite for bread.

Perhaps the reader may never have heard of such a dish as beaver tails; but I consider them the best meat that I ever fed on, when properly cooked. After supper, while lying around on our buffalo robes, smoking, I told my companions that I had wounded a splendid elk, close by, which I assured them I should be able to bring into camp the next morning. I also told them that grizzly bears were very thick in that part of the country, and we stood a good chance of finding one by the elk in the morning.

I had a friend in camp, named John McIntire, who proposed to go with me. I accepted his proposition, though. I had some doubts as to his fitness for a bear hunt, for he was perfectly green. I cautioned him of the danger in hunting grizzlies, but he had no fears, and insisted on going with me.

The next morning I buckled on my tomahawk and hunting-knife, took my gun and dog, and accompanied by McIntire, I started to see about the elk. On arriving at the ravine I instructed my friend to cross over to the opposite side and climb the hill, but by no means to go into the hollow, as the grizzlies were dangerous when they got a man on the downhill side. I went directly to where I presumed the elk would be found, if he had died by the water-side, and as soon as I approached within a short distance I saw that a large grizzly bear had scented my elk and was making his breakfast out of him.

He was in thick, scrubby oak brush, and I made my dog lie down while I crawled behind a rock to get a favourable shot at the animal. I shot him but he only snapped at the wound made by the bullet and started tearing through the brush, biting furiously at the bushes as he went. I reloaded my rifle as rapidly as possible to get in a second shot, but to my surprise I saw the bear rushing down the hollow, chasing after McIntyre who was only about ten steps in advance of the beast, and he was running for dear life, and making as much noise as a mad bull. The truth is McIntire was scared and I hastened to the rescue, first sending my dog forward to help him.

Just as the dog reached the bear McIntire darted behind a tree and flung his hat in the bear's face, at the same time pointing his gun at him. Old grizzly seized the muzzle of the gun in his teeth and as it was loaded and cocked it went off either accidentally or otherwise and blew the bear's head open, just as the dog fastened on his hind quarters. I ran to the assistance of my friend with all haste, but he was out of danger, and had sat down several rods away with his face as white as a sheet and as badly frightened a man as I ever met. I commenced laughing and he became indignant, saying it was no laughing matter; and I never got McIntire out on any more bear hunts. He would cook or do anything, but said he never intended to make a business of bear hunting. He had only wished for one adventure, and this one had perfectly satisfied him.

After McIntire had recovered from his fright and bewilderment, I told him to go to the camp and bring me the pack mules while I skinned and cut up my bear and elk. He returned shortly with four of the strongest pack mules there were in camp, and several. Mexican packers. The bear being extraordinarily large, weighing probably one thousand pounds, and the elk of average size, they made a good load for each mule; and when we returned to camp all hands were collected to enjoy a hearty supper.

The adventure I had with McIntire was too good to keep, so I explained to Carson and the rest of the company what a narrow escape and terrible fright McIntire had, and they laughed at him so much that he declared he had no intention of hunting grizzly bears in future.

Beaver and game now began to get scarce and we were ready to move again. We concluded to send twenty loads of furs and meat to Bent's Fort in charge of our packers. The Shawnee, Spiebuck, said he had been out and found a place where there was a plenty of game and lots of beaver, &c. It was at a place called Bald Buttes, about thirty miles north of us. We started off our pack train for the fort, giving them directions where to find us on their return. We arrived at Bald Buttes the second day after, and found it an excellent hunting ground for buffalo and trapping beaver, as Spiebuck had told us.

We had a green Irishman, named O'Neil, who was quite anxious to become proficient in hunting and it wasn't long before he got his first lesson. We instructed him that every man who went out of camp after game was expected to bring in meat of some kind. O'Neil said he would agree to the terms and was ready to start out that evening. He picked up his rifle and started for a small herd of mountain buffalo in plain sight, only three or four hundred yards from camp.

We were all busy fixing up our new camp, some of us putting up tents and some cooking supper, when we heard Mr. O'Neil's rifle in the distance, and shortly after the gentleman came running into camp, bare-headed, without his gun, with a bull buffalo close after him, both going at full speed, and O'Neil shouting like a madman,

"Here we come, be Jasus. Stop us! For the love of God, stop us!"

Just as they came in among the tents, the bull not more than six feet in rear of the Irishman, who was frightened out of his wits and puffing like a locomotive, his toe caught in a tent-rope

Bringing meat into camp

and over he went into a puddle of water, head foremost and in his fall capsized several camp-kettles, one of which contained our supper. But the buffalo did not escape so easily, for Shawnee Jake and I jumped for our guns and dropped the animal before he had done any further damage.

We all laughed heartily at O'Neil when he had got up out of the water, for a party of trappers show no mercy to one who meets with a mishap of this kind; but as he stood there with dripping clothes and face covered with mud, his mother wit came to his relief and he declared he had accomplished the hunter's task, "For sure," said he, "havn't I fetched the mate into camp, and there was no bargain whether it should be dead or alive, at all, at all."

Upon asking O'Neil where his gun was—

"Sure," says he, "that's more than I can tell you."

Next morning Kit Carson and I took his tracks and the buffalo's, and, after hunting an hour or so, found O'Neil's gun, though he had little use for it afterwards as he preferred to cook and help around the camp to exposing his precious life in fighting buffaloes.

One morning Kit Carson and I discovered some fresh signs of Indians while we were out on a tramp prospecting the chances for trapping. On our return to camp we warned our partners to keep a good lookout for them and not to stray away from camp without due precaution.

The next day while out with a company, including Kit Carson and Spiebuck, we discovered that otter and beaver were plenty in the neighbourhood; before night we made an interesting capture of an old "Crow" Indian squaw, who was over one hundred years old. We took her into camp, fed her, and gave her a blanket to sleep on. None of us could converse with her except Peg-leg Smith, and he having lived among the Crow Indians could talk with her some, and gain a little information, though she was too old and timid to be very chatty with him even.

Next day we divided into two parties for setting beaver traps, hunting game, &c, and at night one party reported in camp that they had discovered eight Crow Indians that day at some distance, but had no communication with them. Peg-leg Smith, who lost his leg among the Crows several years before and was acquainted with their habits and language, said he should like to hunt them up, and, taking only Shawnee Jake for a companion, sallied forth the next morning to visit the Crows; though we offered to send an escort, they refused, thinking there was no danger.

The rest of us were busy all day in hunting game and skinning our beaver and otter, having caught in our traps by the river side, seventy-six beaver and a dozen otter, which we thought good luck for the first night's trapping. At night all of us were gathered in camp except Peg-leg Smith and Jake, for whom we had fears, but concluded to wait another day for them to come in, and if we saw nothing of them, to then go in pursuit. The second night we had only caught fifty beaver and five otter, but on returning to camp we espied ten Indians near where we found the old squaw and they were apparently looking for her.

After watching them awhile, Kit Carson advised us to show ourselves, as we might have some communication with them. On discovering us they started to run; but Kit placed a white handkerchief on his ramrod and made other friendly signs which induced them to stop, and one of their number cautiously approached to meet Kit, previously laying down his bow and arrows as Kit threw down his gun. After they had conferred alone, chiefly by signs, the Indians advanced to meet us, and after a good smoke all round they had confidence enough to go with us on our return to camp for they saw from our game that we were simply friendly hunters. When they saw the old squaw they were much pleased, and one Indian who looked about sixty years of age, said she was his mother and appeared very thankful that we had given her a blanket.

Kit Carson said to us that as Peg-leg and Jake had not returned, we might keep these fellows as hostages and take their scalps, if they should not return.

He felt so anxious that Spiebuck and I concluded to go with

him to hunt up our missing comrades, and we finally found them returning to our camp in company with the Crow chief and four warriors. When we got in, there was great joy among the Indians to meet their chief.

Smith declared the Crows rather treacherous, but he had a wife among them and lost his leg fighting for them, which would be a sufficient guaranty of our safety so long as he remained with us. The chief staid in camp till next day and Peg-leg Smith proposed to take his people to Bent's Fort to trade with Bent; but the chief declined as it was dangerous for the Crows to leave their mountain country, and get down among the Cheyennes, Comanches, and Arapahoes. But the chief was desirous to trade with the whites if they would bring their goods up there. Carson immediately started a Shawnee Indian with a letter to Bent's Fort, over two hundred miles, with instructions to send him some goods on our pack mules, which had been sent down with furs.

After the Indian and his letter had started to the fort, the chief and his warriors left, mostly on foot; but before going he assured us that none of us should be hurt and promised to come back in about a month to trade. Smith furnished the Indian with a pack mule to carry his mother home and he returned with it in four days, according to promise.

We kept on trapping and hunting there until the pack mules arrived with the goods from the fort. Bent sent four or five hundred dollars worth of goods and we traded them to the Crows for three or four thousand dollars worth of furs. Then we all returned to Bent's Fort with our train heavily laden with furs and buffalo-robes.

We stayed two or three weeks at Bent's Fort, recruiting up and having a good time with old friends. Bent was highly pleased with our trip. Trappers always have many thrilling yarns and funny stories to tell each other when they meet at head-quarters, and we had our share. Often did we have a good laugh over the adventures of McIntire and O'Neil.

Bent proposed that we should go back to the Crow nation

and establish a post among them, but Carson objected on account of furs being scarce up there, and he considered that we had drained that market already, and he thought there were other places where we could do better.

In a short time, we were ready for another hunt. Kit Carson, Peg-leg Smith, and myself, with a number of our Shawnee Indian trappers, started for New Mexico, going over what was called the Taos Mountain. We stopped in Santa Fe some two or three weeks, meeting there Colonel Owens, Nicholas Gentry, and other traders from Independence, Mo. Soon after (in December, 1840), a report came that Albert Speyers's train was snowed in on the Cimarron creek, about two hundred and fifty miles from Santa Fe, and that over four hundred of his mules were frozen to death.

He had seventy-five wagons and ten mules to the wagon. All the American mules died, and the Mexican mules sustained life by eating off the manes, and tails from the dead carcasses. The snow was two feet deep, and the teamsters could make no fire, except by tearing up their wagon-boxes and side-boards, as the buffalo chips were all covered up, and the nearest timber was about ten miles off, at Cottonwood Grove. The storm had come on suddenly, and the cold was so intense that the animals had frozen, and their bones remain there to this day, which gave that place the name of Bone Yard.

Colonel Owens came to me, when the report of this disaster reached Santa Fe, and, knowing I had been among the Comanches, he begged me to take charge of a relief train and start off immediately. As the route lay through a part of the Comanche country, and I spoke their language, he offered me a good price to go, and I consented. The train was fitted up with dispatch, and the mules, oxen, and provisions were soon ready. We had ten Mexicans to drive the loose oxen and mules, and teamsters to drive the wagons.

A Mexican in the employ of Mr. Speyers, who had come in with the news, returned with us as guide. We were twenty days in reaching the perishing train, and found them in an awful situation. They had driven what mules remained alive to the cottonwood grove, ten miles away, and, loading part of them with wood, had taken it back to camp. They had also cut down immense quantities of the cottonwood trees for shelter, and the mules lived on the buds and bark. If the storm, which lasted several days, had not come on so fiercely and suddenly the first night, they might have saved the whole train, by starting at once for this grove.

My trip for their relief was through a wild country, and, as we encountered deep snows, our progress was necessarily slow. We had four hundred mules and sixty yoke of Mexican cattle; but it was hard work to move the heavy train of Mr. Speyers back to Santa Fe, for the starving mules, barely saved alive from the hunger and cold, could not pull much. The oxen were yoked in Mexican fashion, the yoke being lashed to the horns with rawhide, and the different yokes in the same team connected with rawhide ropes. They were driven by a man on each side, with a long stick or pole, having a sharp nail or spur on the end, which was used instead of a whip.

We travelled slowly, enduring much suffering, and at times nearly freezing, till we reached Las Vegas, where we got more men and animals and were much relieved, making the balance of our journey into Santa Fe much easier. Our arrival produced great excitement, and our old friends were all glad to meet us and to learn of our safety.

Speyers, if living, must now (1872) be quite an old man. He has done a heavy business in Kansas City, purchased largely in real estate, and, the last I heard of him, he had acquired a large amount of property. He was of German descent, tall and spare, with keen eyes, and his language, though somewhat broken, was always polite. He had a good reputation as a fair trader, and, at the time he was snowed in at Cimarron creek, the merchants of Santa Fe manifested the liveliest sympathy for him and his men, and showed the respect in which they held him, by doing everything in their power for his relief. During my long acquaintance with him, I found him in all respects, a gentleman.

On my arrival at Santa Fe, I went to hunt up my friends, Kit Carson and Peg-leg Smith, finding Kit in a Mexican hotel, and he gave me a cordial welcome. He said Smith was probably in a saloon nearby, and that he had seen him drunk nearly every day since I left. Going over to the saloon, we found Smith in a fracas with two or three Mexicans, and, having un-strapped his wooden leg, he had knocked one Mexican down with it, and was hopping around on one foot, determined to knock down the others.

Our arrival put a stop to his warlike demonstrations, and, after he had buckled on his wooden leg, we escorted him to our hotel. There we made him drink a cup of tea, and locked him up in a room to get sober. He was nearly dead with the horrors; but we kept him confined there four days, during which he kept up a yelling that would have astonished a wild Indian. We took him in food and liquor in small quantities, and, at the end of four days, let him out, and kept an eye on him, to prevent the Mexicans killing him.

We amused ourselves here attending several dances, or *fandangoes*, with Mexican ladies. The last *fandango* was a terribly exciting affair. At this ball, there were sixty or seventy Americans, most of whom were pretty hard customers,—teamsters, &c. We had hired two Mexican musicians to play all night for three dollars. One of them had a "fiddle" of his own manufacture, and the other an instrument he called a "guitar," but it was big enough to float a man.

About midnight, the Mexicans, becoming jealous of the attentions of some of our party to the ladies, and exasperated by the manner in which the attentions were received, attempted to remove their lady friends and close the ball. By this time several of the party were in no condition to be dictated to by any one, and, as the result of this attempt to remove the ladies, the room was quickly cleared of the indignant Mexican gents, the ladies willingly remaining, and the door placed in charge of one of our party. The dance then proceeded for a while, the "music" being furnished by a half-way "tiddler" named George Stilts, who afterward married Kit Carson's daughter.

After the ejected Mexicans had made an unsuccessful attempt, by the aid of a number of soldiers, to gain admission to the hall, they went to Governor Armijo (governor of the State of New Mexico), who resided at Santa Fe, with a complaint that the Americans were making a disturbance, and they could do nothing with them. The governor, with a strong bodyguard, soon appeared on the scene, and demanded admittance, which was granted, on condition that he should leave his guard outside, only bringing his servant in with him. On entering the hall, he was warmly received, and, after partaking of the hospitalities of the party (mostly whisky), he felt in a dancing mood himself, but did not like our music, and so sent for his own musicians.

By the time the music arrived, it was nearly four o'clock, and, as the presence of the governor was considered an event which required many pledges of esteem, the whole party, including the governor and ladies, was in a sad condition, and the dancing was anything but graceful. The doors were not opened till nine o'clock, when those who could retired.

There was a wicked joker in the American party, named Gabe Allen, who, when the governor yielded to sleep, had him carried to a room adjoining, and laid on a bed between two women, who were in the same condition. About nine o'clock, the governor's wife, attended by two soldiers, came in search of him, fearing he might have received some bodily injury at the hands of the revellers. When her anxiety was at the highest pitch, she was conducted by Allen to the room where her husband lay in his drunken stupor. On seeing him and his companions, her anxiety changed to rage, and she "went for" him in a manner that was very pleasing to Allen, in his half-tipsy condition. After some words between the governor and his wife, Allen and I escorted him to his residence, where we left him to the tender mercies of his wife, who would listen to no explanations by Allen, tending to establish the innocence of her husband.

Gabe Allen, the perpetrator of this practical joke on the governor, was a tall, slim, light-complexioned man, always ready for

Fandango

a joke or a perilous adventure. I was associated with him much of the time for a number of years. He has acquired considerable property, and is now living at Wilmington, Los Angeles County, California.

A few days afterward, two hundred Mexican troops came from the State of Chihuahua as an escort for a specie-train of pack-mules, in charge of a conductor, which money was delivered to the governor of New Mexico, our friend of the fandango. Two or three days after their arrival at Santa Fe, they called on the governor for payment for their services, which he objected to giving. The soldiers formed on the square, and said they would have their pay or blood. The governor offered them a draft on the State of Chihuahua, which they refused to accept, as their orders were to collect pay from him for whom the service was rendered.

There were about one hundred and seventy Americans then in Santa Fe, and the governor called on them for assistance. I asked Kit Carson's advice on the matter, and he replied that he thought it was fair to help the governor out of this scrape, as he had befriended us in our difficulty with the Mexicans at the *fandango*. We all gathered our arms, excepting a few men left as a guard for our teams, wagons, &c., and presented ourselves to the governor, ready for action. By the time we reached the palace, the Chihuahua soldiers, on the plaza in front, were drunk and fighting among themselves.

Our American friends, about one hundred strong, formed in line in front of the palace, in connection with about the same number of the governor s troops. The governor now sent word to the officers of the Chihuahua troops that he was ready to fight any time they were.

Gabe Allen and Kit Carson now interfered, and advised a compromise, which was agreed upon, the governor agreeing to advance ration-money sufficient to take the Chihuahua troops home, and to pay thirty-seven and a half cents per day to each soldier for eighteen days of service, which money was immediately distributed, and they were ordered to leave town instanter, or they would be put out. After some little delay and difficulty in the distribution, they moved off, out of the place, toward home, and the governor, being highly pleased, remarked, "It 's now my treat." We were all called into his grounds; wines and different kinds of liquors were set out, and a jolly time commenced. Peg-leg Smith, hopping around on his wooden leg, with his rifle on his shoulder, got drunk as usual. As we all had our rifles, it was a mixed scene, warlike and yet convivial.

Mr. Speyers finished recruiting his teams, repairing his wagons, &c, and, in the spring of 1841, started his train for Chihuahua. Myself and all the Shawnees were engaged by him, and went on with his train; but Smith and Carson returned to Bent's Fort, in company with other trappers.

Chapter 4

The Pursuit and its hardships

We met with no particular adventures, after leaving Santa Fe, until we had travelled about one hundred and fifty miles, to a small village on a tributary of the Rio Grande, when, one morning while driving in our mules and preparing to start the train, a band of Navajo Indians attacked us, for the purpose of creating a stampede among our mules. They did not succeed in getting any of our animals, and one of the Indians paid the forfeit of his life, as Spiebuck shot him at long range.

We had no further trouble till we reached Dead Man's plain, some two hundred and fifty miles from Santa Fe. This desert is ninety miles wide; and we rested on the border of it over one day, to rest our mules and provide water, preparatory to the terrible trial, as we were to travel night and day till we should strike the Rio Grande again. The morning we were to start across the desert, I was on guard with eight others, and, just before daylight, nine Apaches made a raid on us, stampeding our mules, running them over three or four of the guard, and breaking one man's ribs. In our train were seventy-five wagons, ten mules to each wagon, and there were about seven hundred of the mules run off. It was all done by the nine Apaches, who ran in among the mules, rattling buffalo hides and stones in gourds, scaring the animals fearfully.

We were now in a bad predicament. Nearly all our mules were scampering over the plain, and our camp thrown into terrible confusion. As soon as possible, I mustered a party of eighteen, saddled our best remaining mules, and, taking some bacon and bread, started in pursuit; feeling rather sore that the mules should be run off while I had charge of the guard, and determined to bring them back, or leave my scalp with the Apaches. In our party I had James Littleton and several other Americans, with Spiebuck and some of the best shots among the Shawnees,—all picked men.

We followed the tracks to the Rio Grande, and found the mules had crossed by the help of other Apaches, who had here joined the raiding, thieving Indians. The river was high, and we had to stop and hastily construct a raft to carry us over with our rifles and provisions, swimming our horses alongside. This detained us all day, and at night we slept on the opposite bank, wet and chilly, but determined to give chase as soon as it became light enough to see the tracks. Spiebuck took the lead, and we followed as rapidly as possible. The fourth day, our bacon and bread gave out, and we had nothing to eat. The fifth day, the largest game we saw was jack-ass rabbits, of which we killed two and divided among the company of eighteen persons.

On the sixth day, I shot a wolf, but its flesh was so poor and bad-flavoured, that we could not eat it, but lay down that night, hungry and nearly discouraged. The sixth night, we held a council to decide whether to return or go forward, which was decided in favour of going ahead to the next mountain, and then, if no smoke appeared, or other signs of Indians, we would return. The seventh day, upon reaching the top of the hills, we found one of the mules with a leg broken by getting into a crevice in the rocks.

"Here is my off-wheel mule, Poor Old Ned," said Enoch Barnes, one of the Americans in our party. We killed the mule and took off all his meat, packing it on the rear of our saddles, and proceeded down the other side of the mountain to a green flat, or "bottom," where we found good water and plenty of grass for our jaded animals. There we feasted on sweet mule-meat, without salt. Spiebuck said he was confident we should soon overtake the Indians, as the tracks were fresh. With only three hours' delay for feeding our animals and refreshing ourselves, we proceeded on our way, and just before sundown found two more mules that had given out.

Spiebuck noticed that the animals were sweating, and remarked that the Indians were near. We took an early start the next morning, and soon arrived at the spot where the Indians had just broke camp, probably not two hours before. There was still fire burning, and remnants of a mule which had furnished their breakfast. Spiebuck, after closely examining the signs, said there were less than twenty-five Indians in the party. After going five miles further, we came in sight of our animals feeding.

As the feed was good, the Apaches had stopped, and some of them were watching the stock, while nine were lying down in a hollow, apparently asleep. Dismounting from our mules, we advanced very cautiously, without being discovered, till we arrived on the bank above the sleeping Indians, when, each picking his man, we fired and killed or wounded the whole of them.

At all events, we brought away nine scalps; but there were ten or twelve more Indians on the other side of the ravine, who fled up the hillside and escaped, though we fired at them and pursued them a short distance. Then we gathered our animals together and started back as quickly as possible; for we were within one day's travel of the Apache nation, and it was unsafe to stay long.

We started back with more animals than we lost, for we gained several mules from the Apaches whom we killed. We were pursued and fired upon, just as we arrived at the Rio Grande, by two hundred Apaches. The river having fallen, we forded it quickly, and were not pursued beyond the river, for they knew we were prepared to give them a warm reception. We reached our camp safely with the mules, after an absence of two weeks, and found that our friends had given us up for lost, knowing the light stock of provisions we had taken and the extreme danger of the enterprise.

There was great joy in camp when we returned. That evening we carried out a plan we had formed while on our return, to give those who remained in camp a taste of what we had encountered in the pursuit. They came around us as we were unsaddling our mules, and, seeing what remained of Barnes's Old Ned, asked what that was. We very soberly told them it was venison,—the remainder of a fat buck we had shot. As they had been living for some days on bacon, beans, &c, they were all very anxious for pieces of it.

We very generously supplied them, and soon a number of fires were started and the meat put down to roast. They all declared it to be the sweetest meat they ever tasted. After they had finished eating it, we disturbed their stomachs somewhat by telling them they had been feasting on Old Ned, whom they all knew very well, when some of them were disposed to resent it, but finally called it a good joke.

Mr. Speyers, having given us up for lost, had gene back to Santa Fe, to purchase a fresh supply of mules, and we immediately started a messenger to inform him of the recovery of his animals. He had not completed any purchases, and came back at once. Upon seeing us safe, and hearing of the perils of our expedition for the recovery of his mules, he was highly pleased, and paid us liberally, besides promising us one hundred dollars for each of the nine Apache scalps when we should arrive at Chihuahua, which promise he faith-fully kept.

Owing to the jaded condition of the mules, Mr. Speyers sent several wagons back ten miles to a Mexican settlement for corn, and we rested five days, herding the mules under a double guard, day and night. On the sixth day, we started to cross the ninety-mile stretch of desert, where there is not a drop of water or a stick of wood. We started at 3 o'clock in the afternoon, and travelled till the next morning at 9 o'clock, when we were compelled to lay by on account of the extreme heat.

We resumed our march in the evening, and thus travelled for three nights. The second day, we were overtaken by two Mexican mail-carriers, who were nearly in a perishing condition, for want of water and provisions, and we supplied them. The next night, while I was driving the forward team, I became very sleepy, and got off and walked alongside to keep awake. Suddenly I stumbled over a man lying in the road, and fell, with my hand striking his face, and my flesh crept on my bones when I discovered that his head and face were mashed and bloody.

I stopped the train, and Mr. Speyers, who rode in a carriage, drove up, and was considerably frightened when he saw, by the light of his lantern, that the body was that of one of the Mexican mail-riders, who had been fed by us the day before. We found, a few feet distant, the body of the other unfortunate carrier, and both were fearfully gashed by tomahawks.

Speyers ordered Spiebuck and a party of our Indian companions to go forward, and proceed cautiously, for fear of a surprise by the Indians. We picked up the dead men and placed them in a wagon, and gathered up the mails, which were scattered over the ground, taking them along with us. I didn't feel sleepy any more that night. We arrived at the Rio Grande the next morning, where we found a splendid camping-ground, and concluded to stop over one day, as there was plenty of grass, with wood and water. Here we buried the two mail-carriers.

The Shawnees went out for game, and succeeded in killing four deer. They reported that they saw fresh tracks of Indians, and advised us to be careful. We were so apprehensive of an attack, that we took extra pains to secure our stock, and made a Mexican boy sleep among the mules, holding the bell-mare. This was a grayish spotted mare, that all the herd would follow. That night, after changing the guard, the camp was alarmed by the report of a gun, and by this Mexican running in with his mare. We inquired of him who fired the gun, and one of the guard, a Dutchman named Charlie Mayer, said he discharged his piece at an Indian who was skulking out beyond the mules, and said he, "Follow me, boys, and I'll show you the Injuns."

A party went with him, and, discovering an object that, in the darkness, resembled an Indian, they fired into it; but, as it did not move, they went up to it, and discovered that it was only a black stump, and they returned to camp badly sold. Mr. Speyers, noticing the stump, the next morning, with two bullet-holes in it, said it was good target-practice for night-work.

Next day we proceeded to a place called Dona Anna, where Mr. Speyers reported to the authorities the deaths of the two mail-carriers, and delivered their mail, or what there was left of it. He decided to rest there that day, and bought feed for his stock of the Mexicans. I had the ill-luck that day to break the main-spring of my rifle, and, as I was to have charge of the guard that night, Mr. Speyers gave me a double-barrelled shot-gun, which I put in order and loaded with fifteen buck-shot to each barrel.

Our animals were turned into a field that had no fence on one side, next the river, for it was a bluff bank, four or five feet high. The Mexicans told us to beware of certain Indians who were lurking about, stealing horses, &c, while they pretended to be friendly. My guard came on duty at midnight, and, after placing them at favourable points to protect the mules, I took my station on the river-bank, near a cottonwood-tree.

Soon after I had thus taken my position, I saw a mule looking across the river as though some object attracted his attention. Turning my eyes in that direction, and looking sharply, I noticed a shadow approaching the river from the other side, which I soon made out to be an Indian, advancing silently into the water. The mule, becoming more alarmed at this, snorted.

"What's that?" whispered Amos Hambright, one of my guard, a few steps distant from me.

"Keep still," I answered in a low tone, moving toward him, and keeping the cottonwood-tree between me and the Indian.

I cocked my gun, and got down behind the tree, as I knew the fellow would come up the bluff by the path, which would cause him to pass within a few feet of the tree. When he had got half-way across the river, he was alarmed by the mule snorting a second time, and paused for some minutes, but finally came over and began crawling up the bank toward me.

When he had got within two or three lengths of my gun, there was another snort from several mules in the vicinity, and the Indian stooped down, with his back toward me and his face near the ground, to listen. I thereupon poured into the small of his back fifteen buck-shot, which killed him instantly. At the noise of my gun, I heard a clatter of hoofs on the opposite bank of the river, and a "What's the matter?" from Hambright, who came running up.

"Matter enough," I answered; "I've just killed an Injun, and there are plenty more on the other side."

The mules stampeded, and the Mexican bell-boy, who had foolishly tied the bell-mare to his leg, and laid down for a nap, was dragged some distance over the field, with the frightened animals trampling on him. Not hearing from him, we went in search, and found the poor fellow insensible, with his face mashed and his ribs broken in. He was untied and taken to a wagon, where he remained some time before coming to, and he was on the sick-list for a good while after. The bell-mare was led into our corral, which was formed near the road on the outside of the fence, by ranging the wagons in a circle, with the wheels tied together by ropes, and an opening at one side like a horse-shoe. The mules all followed the mare into the corral.

"Who fired that gun?" inquired Mr. Speyers.

"I did," was my reply.

"Did you shoot another black stump?" was his next question.

"No," I said; "I didn't shoot a black stump, but I shot a mighty black Indian."

"I would rather see him than to hear tell of him," said he.

Several of us took a mule down to where the Indian lay, and, tying a rope around his neck, we fastened it to the pommel of the saddle, and dragged the man into camp.

"Mr. Speyers, here's your stump," I said, with a laugh.

"Not much stump about that fellow," said he, gazing at him in surprise.

"Will you have him scalped, or take him as he is?" I asked.

"He will do as he is," said Speyers.

The Indian was scalped, however, and dragged off and thrown into a hollow. The mules were let out of the corral again to feed in the field, as soon as we saw there was no more danger; while I reloaded my gun, and went back to my station, seeing no more thieving Indians that night.

At breakfast, next morning, Mr. Speyers told me he thought he should raise his price for the scalps of such Indians as that, and this one was worth about one hundred and fifty dollars. He was the biggest Apache I ever saw, measuring full six feet four inches; but usually the Indians of that tribe are rather under size.

That afternoon, while we were moving down the Rio Grande, nearly one hundred Apaches appeared on the other side of the river, and made signs and called to us in Spanish, that they were friendly, and wanted to make peace with us. Spiebuck shot one of them, at the same time calling out, that was the peace he had for them. They then dispersed, and we saw no more Indians for some time. The third day after this, we arrived at the Mexican town of Paso del Norte, a place of some eight thousand inhabitants.

The crossing of the river here is dangerous, as its bed abounds in quicksands. We had to double teams to each wagon, and cross one at a time, keeping in motion; for? if allowed to stop, the wagon and mules sink immediately. Notwithstanding our precautions, one of our heaviest loaded wagons halted in the middle of the river, and at once sank, till all the goods were wet, and we had to pack the load ashore on our men's backs, before the wagon could be drawn out.

We remained at Paso del Norte six days, recruiting our mules and drying our goods. We spent the time very pleasantly, among other pleasures attending several fandangos. The place is handsomely built up. Fruits and grain are abundant, and the land is rich and well-watered by irrigation. At this point, the river becomes the boundary between New Mexico and Chihuahua.

The seventh day after our arrival, we renewed our journey down the right bank of the river, and made about fifteen miles, when we camped. Spiebuck said, as we were pretty well out of danger now from the Apaches, he would go out and get a deer. Some half an hour later, we heard several shots in the direction he had gone, and ten of us mounted and started off to see what was the matter, and, after travelling a short distance, we saw about twenty Apaches, armed with guns, bows, and arrows, fighting with Spiebuck, who was nowhere to be seen. The Indians ran when they discovered us, and we, fearing they had killed Spiebuck, commenced a search for him, finding him in a little cave barely large enough for him to lie down in, the mouth of which was nearly closed by a large stone.

He could load his rifle while he lay on his back as well as standing up, and, using the rock at the mouth of the cave (which was a good protection for his head) as a rest for his rifle, he could pick off the Apaches at a long range. He had killed three of them in this manner, and escaped with slight injuries himself, though around the rock were battered bullets and an armful of arrows. He had got one eye full of sand, but thought the three scalps he took off the Apaches' heads a good thing, and better than so many deer. He went into camp with the scalps elevated on a pole, and attracted much attention. Mr. Speyers complimented him for his bravery, and promised him three hundred dollars for the scalps at Chihuahua, from the authorities.

We travelled one day more down the Rio Grande, and then, leaving the river, took a southerly direction straight for Chihuahua, arriving at Sacramento, about fifteen miles from Chihuahua, the fourth day after leaving the river. Here we discharged and "*cached*," or concealed, four wagon-loads of contraband goods, to escape seizure at Chihuahua, and left four of our Shawnees to watch them. The next afternoon, we arrived, with our train, before the custom-house at Chihuahua, and an officer and ten privates watched our wagons, to see that no goods were taken out till we had paid the duties. The next day, we were allowed to discharge our freight, and the first thing Mr. Speyers did was to establish a store for trading purposes.

Some six days after our arrival at Chihuahua, an American named Riddle volunteered to bring in the concealed goods left back at the "*cache*," saying he could do it without danger. Mr. Speyers told him to bribe the custom-house officer, and he consented. So did the custom-house officer consent, for he had been bribed before. I was detailed to assist in bringing in these goods to the city. The customs official instructed us as to which side of the city to come in, agreeing to meet us a mile from town. He met us, with a file of ten soldiers, about midnight, and escorted us secretly to a room, where our goods were discharged, and the official was paid one hundred dollars, which he said was a good night's job,—far better than he expected, and more than he could make in a month out of government! His soldiers were each presented by Mr. Speyers with a dollar, a pair of shoes, and a bottle of whisky, the last of which they could fully appreciate.

We stayed in Chihuahua some two months (November and December, 1841), enjoying ourselves very much among the Mexicans of both sexes, who were remarkably friendly, as we had plenty of money.

Being out of employment, and ready for an adventure, I was selected, with several others of the party, to go with a train of wagons loaded with goods for the fair at San Juan, which place is very central and convenient for people to meet from all parts of Mexico. This trip occupied eighteen days. This fair is the worst place I ever saw, for thieving, gambling, and vice of all sorts.

The rich people play a game called *monte*, at which they sometimes stake thousands of dollars; while the lower classes indulge in bullfights, cockfights, and all sorts of low gambling. The place is situated near the San Juan river, under a hill, and there are not over four thousand inhabitants when there is no fair. This great carnival lasts from fifteen to twenty days, and is thronged by Mexicans, Americans, French, Germans, Spanish, and all sorts of people, to the number, perhaps, of fifty thousand. At the close of the fair, which is intended for trading purposes mainly, we started on our return.

One morning, while we were on our homeward journey through the state of Durango, moving quietly along, the train of seventy wagons being stretched along some two miles, I, being in advance, discovered a body of about four hundred Indians. On their approach, the alarm was passed along to the rear of

A COMIC BULLFIGHT

the train: "Corral your wagons and teams! Fix for a fight! The Indians are coming!"

Putting a white flag on the ramrod of my gun, I made directly for the Indians; for, by certain peculiarities, I knew they were a war-party of Comanches, who were on a Mexican raid. One of the party advanced to meet me, in response to signals I had made, and, after each had dropped our arms, we advanced for a friendly greeting. All my friends were calling out to me to come back, or I should be killed. They were not aware of my acquaintance with the Comanches, nor of my being able to speak their language.

Upon meeting the Indian, he knew me in a moment, jumped from his horse, and embraced me. He inquired if those were my teams, and I replied that they were. I asked after my wife and child and other friends in their tribe. He said they were well, but that my brother-in-law ("Old Wolf's" son), the first chief, had been killed, and that he was chief in his place; also, that Henry Brown, the next in command, was back in their war-party. I told him to wait for me, and I would go and get them some presents.

I soon returned, with pipes, tobacco, flannel, and handkerchiefs for the Comanches, and, meeting the chief again, we went back to where he had left his warriors formed for battle. Upon arriving among them, they all knew me, dismounted, and formed a ring for smoking. I saw Henry Brown, and had a sociable smoke with him and the chief. Henry could not be told from an Indian, except by his long red hair, which hung in plaits over his shoulders.

They asked me if I knew where the Mexicans had any horses. I answered that there were horses in almost every direction, probably; but the country was new to me, and I was on a peaceable trading expedition. We then mounted our horses, and they told me not to be afraid of them, but turn our mules out to feed at night, and they would not molest them. Then, with a rousing war-whoop, they darted away over the plain.

On my return to the train, our owners and teamsters all

gathered around me, asking what the Indians had said. I told them not to be uneasy; that I spoke the Comanche language, and they were friendly Comanches, with a captive American among them, who was second chief. They inquired how I came to know their language, and I explained by telling them of my four years' experience among them. They were so thankful for this providential escape from the Indians, that they made up an extra purse of one hundred and fifty dollars for me on our return to Chihuahua.

CHAPTER 5

James Kirker

Soon after I returned to Chihuahua, I was informed that a white man, named James Kirker, a Scotchman, was chief of the Apache nation, and that the governor of Chihuahua had offered a reward of nine thousand dollars for his head. The Apaches had stolen great numbers of mules from the State of Chihuahua and sold them in New Mexico, through Kirker's agency. He had sold the property and put the money in his pocket intending never to return to the Apache nation.

Kirker was a blue eyed, gray haired and gray whiskered man, about fifty years old, short and stout, weighing probably about one hundred and seventy-five pounds. He was a very hard drinking man, which may have had some connection with his mysterious death, as he was found dead in his cabin at Mount Diablo, California, in 1852. He died poor, as his habits were such that he could never keep what he acquired.

After the governor offered the reward for his life, Kirker desired to treat with him, and proposed to help him kill off the Apaches, as he knew their traits, and would turn against them if the governor would co-operate with him and spare his life. This proposal, which was sent by a friend, was accepted, and he soon same down to Chihuahua for a conference with Governor Trios.

He stated that he had been taken prisoner by the Apaches while trapping; that he had no sympathy with them, but had taken the part he had to save his own life; and that this was the first chance he had to escape from them.

Mr. Kirker then came to ns Americans and Shawnees, who had come from, various quarters as teamsters and guards, and were now out of employment. Spiebuck was at the head of the Shawnees of our party, and they numbered about seventy, and of the Americans there were nearly a hundred in the city who regarded me as their leader, now, as Kit Carson was absent at Bent's Fort.

Take the party all together they were a fearful set to behold. But the Shawnee trappers and guards harmonized very well with our teamsters and hunters, as a general thing, especially when any danger was feared, or an expedition planned against the savages. Then all hands were united as one common brotherhood.; and we would fight certain tribes of Indians for the fun of the thing, and for common humanity, even if we were not offered a reward for every scalp.

Mr. Kirker asked us, when we were mostly assembled together, whether we wanted to go out on an expedition to fight the Apaches.

Spiebuck, speaking for his band, said if the government of Chihuahua would give him fifty dollars for each scalp, he would go along with us, and risk but what he could clear his expenses. This proposition was accepted, the rest of us consenting to the arrangement, with the *proviso* that we were to have all the animals we should capture.

We at once commenced organizing our company in the "Bull Pen," or place for bull fighting. Here we stored our arms, ammunition, and accoutrements for our mules until our company was fully organized and equipped for service, which did not take long, as we were all anxious to be on the road.

We got a job, sooner than we expected, which promised to be a good thing. There was a rich Mexican in Chihuahua who sent his pack train of sixty or eighty mules every year to the Mexican coast for goods. On its return this year, 1842, every man accompanying the train, excepting one, was killed within ten miles of Chihuahua, by the Apaches, and the mules and goods taken away by them. The single person who escaped came into the city and reported the facts of the massacre and robbery, when the proprietor of the pack train came directly to us and promised that he would give us half of all the mules and goods we could recapture from the Indians.

That night we packed our provisions, mounted, and started off. We requested Mr. Pores, the owner of the train, to send the escaped Mexican to show us where the murders were committed. Spiebuck said all he wanted was to get on the track and he would soon fix the Indians. In the morning we arrived at the place of massacre, and found nine dead bodies horribly mutilated, and scalped. We were cooking breakfast when men, sent by the Mexican authorities at the request of Mr. Pores, arrived to take the dead bodies into the city. After a hasty breakfast, we took the tracks of the Indians, with Spiebuck leading our party, and after going four miles found a dead mule. Tin's mule was loaded with sugar, and had given out and been lanced and left by the Apaches. We took off the pack saddle and the sugar, putting it on an extra mule of our own.

That night we reached the Indian camping ground of the first night, finding rice, coffee, and sugar scattered about. We stopped there for rest and feed, and, starting early, proceeded ten miles further the next morning, where we found several more mules which had given out and been left to perish with their valuable loads strapped to their backs, the Indians having no means of saving the freight. We secured this property, leaving a guard to watch it, and pushing ahead with all the speed we could muster out of our tired animals, we overtook the rascals the third day, and Spiebuck, who was in advance, bade us stop, so that he could reconnoitre and find out the force of the enemy.

When he returned he reported that the Indians were all drunk. They had travelled as they supposed beyond danger, and having found a quantity of liquor in their capture, were enjoying a good spree. There were forty-three of them, some dead drunk and some asleep, so we concluded that from their tipsy condition they would be an easy prey.

We opened out, dividing into two squads, so as to attack from opposite sides, and reached them before they noticed our approach. They were so completely taken by surprise that but few guns were discharged, the most of them being killed with knives and tomahawks. The Shawnees immediately scalped the whole lot, and Spiebuck took charge of the ghastly trophies, giving them a little dressing of salt, to preserve them till we saw the governor again and got the money for them.

We recovered sixty mules belonging to Mr. Pores, and captured besides forty-three Apache horses and mustangs. We camped on the spot that night, as some of our numerous company of Americans and Indians were about as fond of liquor as the Indians we had killed; and finding some choice wines and liquors in some of the mule packs, they soon were in no condition for travelling, and it was difficult to find enough sober men for a guard for the animals.

As we were within two days' march of the principal village of the Apaches, we decided to secrete our goods, which were mostly of a valuable character, and leave behind us such animals as we should not need, with a guard over all, and with about one hundred and fifty men all told, push on and destroy the village, securing what scalps we could. Nearly every man was armed with a rifle and pair of six shooters, and we were confident of the result. We were guided by Kirker and a Mexican half-breed, who had lived among the Apaches when Kirker was their chief, who were in advance with Spiebuck.

After two days' travel we approached the main Indian camp, and Spiebuck bade us halt our train while he went forward to take a look at their position and learn their strength. He returned saying they were over a thousand in number, counting the women and children, but did not fear the result. However, he made Kirker go forward and reconnoitre with him, and they both returned confident that the odds were in our favour. We moved our stock into a low ravine about a mile and a half from the village, and left six men to watch them. The balance of us went up on the top of a hill, where we could look down into the village with-out being discovered.

The view was splendid. The sun was just setting. Their lodges were thickly spread out in a pine grove close to a lovely lake some six or eight miles across. The sheet of water, so beautifully smooth, resembled a mirror among the hills, and there was scarcely a sound to break the stillness that reigned throughout their camp.

Presently, a little after sunset, we discovered a war party of seventy or eighty Apaches returning to the village, from the direction of Sonora; and as they came around the edge of the lake, we saw that they had scalps, and made up our minds that if we let them alone till daybreak we should do better; for, no doubt they had made a capture of liquor, and would have a drunken war dance that night, which proved to be the result. Spiebuck suggested the delay, and his advice was always respected by Kirker and the rest of us.

We lunched on some provisions we had brought, and then all laid down to get a little sleep till the guard should call us, at three o'clock in the morning. Then we jumped up, and, forming into two parties, made preparations for the attack.

The day was just breaking; and Spiebuck, who had been down looking at the enemy from a short distance, said they were nearly all overcome with liquor, and most of them asleep. Three or four, however, were staggering around a camp fire, and it was important that we proceed very cautiously. Kirker led one of our parties around on one side of their camp, while Spiebuck and myself led the other and posted it on the opposite side of the camp. Kirker had a whistle, which he was to blow when all was ready, and then we were to rush in with yells, shoot all we could at the first discharge, and then finish up with our knives and tomahawks.

There was a huge negro in our company, named Andy, who had loaded his musket with buckshot. I placed him not far from me, and close to one of the outside lodges, giving him orders not to fire until he heard Kirker's whistle.

Soon, an Indian came out of the lodge near Andy, and he

blazed away, without waiting for orders. He must have put a handful of buckshot in his gun, for the savage was fairly riddled. The negro was lucked over backwards by the gun, and the barrel flirted out of the stock. Upon this alarm, both parties rushed into the fight.

I had been looking at two Indians, sleeping in a lodge not ten steps from me, and I jumped for them, levelling my rifle at one, while the other ran on all fours, between my legs, as I stood in the doorway, rising with me on his neck. I managed to slip off his back in a hurry, and was going to knock him down with the gun, but he ran a little distance and undertook to shoot me with an arrow, but a slug from my rifle hitting him between the shoulders, his arrow fell at my feet, harmless. The other Indian escaped from the opposite side of the tent just in time to save himself from a charge out of my revolver.

Spiebuck got into a lodge where there was a drunken warrior asleep among three or four squaws and papooses. He shot the man, and tomahawked the women and children. By this time our forces were hotly engaged all over the camp, making every shot tell with fearful effect on the drunken and affrighted savages, who were running in all directions. Our Shawnees fought like devils, with their knives and tomahawks, after they had discharged their guns; while our Americans, using their rifles and revolvers, were fast driving the miserable Apaches into the lake, or pursuing them across the valley.

I was reloading my rifle, when I noticed the negro, Andy, had caught up his gun barrel and was chasing an unarmed Indian. He threw the gun barrel with all his force after the Indian, and it struck him in the back of the head, knocking him down. Before he could arise, the negro was on him. With an old butcher knife he then undertook to stab the Indian, but the knife struck a rib and glanced off. It was a tierce tussle, and might have resulted badly for Andy, if one of our party, named Robert Fry, had not rushed in and clubbed the Indian with his gun, after which Andy dispatched him easily.

Many of the Apaches sought refuge in the nearest mountain,

while others rushed into the lake and were drowned or shot. We lost the chance of taking a great many scalps, from bodies which sunk in the lake, but as it was, we took one hundred and thirty-nine, and should have got many more if the brave but stupid negro had not discharged his gun prematurely.

The Apaches had their animals in a bottom, or flat, near the lake, and they started to run them off. They were followed by the Shawnees, who forced them to abandon the attempt, and they had to flee for their lives, while the Shawnees gathered together nearly a thousand horses, mules, and mustang ponies. Truly, a valuable prize.

The Indian chief, "Cachese," had recognized Kirker as the leader of this attacking party, who had made such fearful havoc with his tribe, and when he had reached the top of the hill with some of his followers, who were fortunate enough to escape, he turned around to look at the destruction of his camp. Kirker was gazing at him; and when the Apache chief saw Kirker, he asked him what he meant by fighting them in this manner. Was he not their war chief? And had they not treated him like a brother always? And was he no longer their friend?

Turning to flee, with the feeble remnant of his once powerful tribe, he declared in a loud voice, intended for many of us to hear, that Kirker was the last white man he would ever put any confidence in. Kirker felt the rebuke keenly, but allowed the broken-hearted chief to escape.

Kirker ordered me to take twenty men, at once, and go and bring in our animals, and the six men, which we had left behind in the ravine. This I did without delay, for there was some danger of their being captured by the retreating Apaches. When we had got them united with the thousand animals taken from the Apaches, we were all ready to start on the return trip to Chihuahua, provided our Shawnees had finished scalping the Apaches.

On my return to the grove, among other startling and singular spectacles, was our negro Andy, tied to a tree, and groaning, and calling loudly for help. Kirker and Spiebuck took this method of punishing him for firing his gun too soon. By my advice, the poor fellow was released; but not till after Spiebuck had threatened his life if he ever disobeyed orders again. He said the reason he did not scalp him then was because his kinky, woolly scalp would not fetch a cent.

Among the slain, was found the body of our Mexican half-breed guide, who had assisted in piloting us to this place. He had got frightened when the fight commenced, and started to run, when a Shawnee had thrown a tomahawk at him, which struck him on the head and killed him.

"Here," said Spiebuck to some of his Shawnees, "scalp that fellow."

"No," we replied, "he is our guide."

"No difference," answered Spiebuck, "he is dead now; he won't know it; and his scalp is worth fifty dollars, and is as good as any."

So they scalped our friend, to please Spiebuck.

At this fight, we rescued a number of Mexican women and children, and made prisoners of nineteen young Apache squaws. In scouting around the head of the lake, on the opposite hillside we found about three hundred head of sheep and goats, which the Apaches had no doubt stolen from the Mexicans, and we took them to camp and gave them in charge of the Mexican women and children.

We found, close to this lake, on a small stream of water, some ancient ruins,—the cement walls and foundation stones of a church; and a *lignum vitæ* cross, which seemed as sound as ever it had been. We also found remains of a smelting furnace, a great quantity of cinders, and some dross of silver and copper. From the appearance of the ruins, it seemed as if there had once been a considerable town there. The lake was the head waters of the river Yagui.

Gabe Allen, who was in our company, found in a hollow, a piece of gold, nearly pure and weighing ten ounces. That afternoon we met in council, reporting to Kirker the finding of the ruins, the gold specimens, etc. He said that there was extreme danger of having two or three thousand warriors down on us if we staid there long enough for the whole Apache nation to be aroused. He therefore counselled the utmost haste in leaving the country, even if it abounded in gold specimens. We had a flock of sheep to hinder us in travelling, and a large drove of other animals to attend to. So we packed up at once for Chihuahua, thinking we could return at some future day, with a larger force, and dig gold.

We left the country with regret, for it possessed marvellous beauty, fertile soil, and had every indication of rich, mines, unworked, probably, by civilized man, to this day. Besides the remains of furnaces, we saw old mine shafts, that had been worked, apparently long before, by Mexicans. Specimens of gold, silver, and copper ore that we took to the mint at Chihuahua, were assayed and pronounced very rich.

For the information of the public, let me state more, particularly, that this lake is on the westerly side of the Sierra Madre (Mother Mountain), between the States of Sonora and Chihuahua. The valleys in the vicinity are broad, and the soil well adapted for cultivation. Around the lake were growing large quantities of wild Indian tobacco.

On arriving at the place where we left the property of Mr. Pores with a guard, we found it all safe as we had left it; the animals, it will be recollected, had already been joined with ours. Considering our extraordinary luck, Kirker thought it best to examine the goods, and see if there was not a little good liquor left; and as a consequence, most of our force got drunk, for they found nearly twenty gallons of choice whisky in bottles among the goods.

The next morning, while on the march, a man named John Spencer, being ahead, saw a deer asleep on the side of a hill, with his head laid over on his side. He dismounted, and was slipping along to get a good shot at the deer without alarming him, when Spiebuck, who was just behind him, cocked his rifle, and about the time Spencer was going to shoot, burst out with a tremendous war whoop, and as the deer jumped up to run, shot him, while Spencer stood silent and amazed.

"Go and get your deer," said Spiebuck, sternly, "and never take advantage of a poor animal, while he's asleep."

Spencer secured his deer, and it made a capital supper that night, for some of us, but Spencer looked bluish, and didn't relish the reproof, as it reflected on his skill with the rifle.

Late in the afternoon, just before we camped, I was made the victim of misplaced confidence, and in a way which did not tend to raise me in the estimation of Spiebuck.

I was at the rear of the train, riding carelessly along in company with the young squaws, and some of the Mexicans we had rescued. On coming to a small stream of water, one of the squaws made known by signs that she wanted a drink. I dismounted, drank myself, and told one of the Mexican boys to carry her some water in his gourd, while I fixed my saddle, which had got loose, laying my gun down for that purpose.

The whole train was ahead. The squaw seeing her chance for an escape, broke the gourd over the boy's head, drenching him with water, and wheeling her horse, she was off in a twinkling. Although we expected to realize the same sum for the squaw prisoners as for the scalps, I could not think of shooting this young girl, for she was barely sixteen years of age, even if in addition to her own scalp, she did take away one of our horses. I went forward to Kirker, and reported that one of the squaws had escaped, and gave the particulars.

Spiebuck was quite indignant, and said he would have shot her if he had been in the rear of the train, and there would have been a scalp and a horse saved. Before we started next morning, Spiebuck mounted all the squaws on the poorest animals we had, so they could not get a chance to run away.

The next day we readied the Mexican settlement of San Andreas, where we laid over two days, on account of our pack mules having very sore backs. We then resumed the march, and in three days more arrived in Chihuahua, having travelled slowly, on account of the sheep and goats. Our arrival was anticipated; for Mexican couriers had gone ahead and reported to the governor that we were coming, with many prisoners, scalps, and a large drove of captured animals.

Five miles out of the city, we met the governor, with a band of music, his wife with him in a carriage, and hundreds of people, who had come out to greet us with a cordial welcome.

The governor pronounced us a brave set of men, and inquired how many men we had lost. We reported that the half-breed Mexican, who went out as our guide, and two Shawnees were killed, and two or three slightly wounded.

Spiebuck, who had charge of the scalps, which were packed on a mule, ordered the driver up to show them to the governor.

"What d'ye think o'them fellers?" said Spiebuck, triumphantly, to the governor.

The governor asked him how many there were. Spiebuck replied that there were one hundred and eighty-two; besides a good many sunk in the lake before he could get them off. Also, eighteen good scalps on the heads of as many squaws we had brought along as prisoners.

This declaration amused the governor very much, and he ordered the liveliest music while we were being escorted in. When we arrived at the plaza in front of the palace, three cheers were given by the great crowd around, for Captain Kirker and our party. The scalps were then counted and delivered to the governor, and a receipt taken. After this receipt was given, Spiebuck brought up the Indian girls, and said, "Here's eighteen more." The governor refused to receive them as scalps, or to pay for them at any price, when Spiebuck said if all he wanted was to have their scalps taken off, it was but a small job; and taking out his hunting knife, started for one of the girls, who ran screaming and terrified towards me for protection. The governor then called out to him to hold on, for he would pay for them as scalps. He took charge of them, and locked them up in a room by themselves.

After this part of the business had been transacted, Kirker brought forward the rescued women and children, and delivered them, stating that we looked to the authorities to send them home. For our part, we made them a present of the sheep and goats, and looked to the citizens of Chihuahua to come forward liberally with gifts of clothing, etc., as they were very destitute. The governor cheerfully promised to assist them.

We now went to the Bull Pen, and deposited our arms and accoutrements, discharged our cargo, sent our animals to a pasture, under protection of Mexicans provided by the governor, and went to a grand dinner Which had been gotten up in our honour, and served in the palace. It was splendid, and enjoyed by all of us; and after dinner we were invited, by the governor, to attend a ball, which he said he had prepared for us, to come off that evening. Spiebuck responded that he was no dancer, but he could drink his share of wine and whisky; which we knew to be the truth.

The ball commenced at eight o'clock, and we amused ourselves previous to that hour, by marching around town, visiting our friends; for everybody was anxious to entertain the Apache company.

Kirker and I went to see Mr. Pores, the owner of the train we had recaptured from the Apache robbers. He was overjoyed at our success, and we arranged to divide everything the next morning, except the whisky. That, we told him, would be impossible, for what the Apaches didn't drink up, our party had finished. This he laughed at, and thought we deserved much praise for what we had done towards wiping out that miserable Apache nation; and promised to assist us in any further military movements. We appreciated his offer, for he could do a great deal for us, as his property in Mexico was reported to be worth two millions of dollars.

Leaving our friend Pores, we went around to Mr. Speyers's store. He was glad to welcome us back, and presented Mr. Kirker and myself with a new suit of clothes, in which to attend the ball. The hospitality of the saloon keepers in the city was so great, that our Shawnee friends were very much elated, and went whooping and yelling over the town, like wild men.

At eight o'clock we went to the ball. Not more than ten of

our company attended, as most of them were too much intoxicated to get there. Soon after three o'clock in the morning, we returned to our barracks in the Bull Pen, and slept till noon. Rising at the call of a messenger, we found an invitation for several of us to attend a complimentary dinner at Riddle & Stephens's hotel.

After dinner, we went to Mr. Pores's, and with him and his son, proceeded to the division of the recovered property, dividing equally all the mules that bore his brand. And we also turned over to him half the goods. After this was done, he gave us a bill of sale of our share of the property; thus showing himself to be a gentleman, as well as a man of business.

A day or two after this division, we went to Mr. Potts's mint with our metallic ores, which we requested him to assay. He found them very rich in gold, silver, and copper. We had some virgin copper, apparently pure metal, that assayed twenty-five *per cent.* gold.

Next day we visited the governor, to talk over matters relating to our agreement. He said he had not funds to pay us for over forty scalps, but would settle for the balance soon. Kirker, Spiebuck, and myself were present. Spiebuck said that was no way to do business. It was not the way the United States Government did their business, for they always performed their agreements. We received the pay for forty scalps ($2000) and asked the governor how long before he would pay the balance. He answered that all the tobacco in Mexico belonged to the government, and as fast as he could sell it he would pay us. We left the palace, and went up to the Bull Pen, and calling together all hands, reported what had taken place.

This Bull Pen, as we called it, was the amphitheatre, where they had bull fights, and made a very convenient head-quarters for our noisy, reckless party.

The money received by us for the forty scalps, was then divided equally among the party. Spiebuck was very indignant at not receiving his money, and said he would not work anymore for such a government. Kirker and I advised him to join with us in an expedition to the region we had just visited. It was the richest country in the world, Kirker thought, and if the government was too poor to pay us for scalps, we could make our fortunes digging gold.

The matter had been under discussion three or four days, when one day the Mexican boys who had charge of our animals, came in and reported that there were Mexicans at the pasture claiming the horses and mules we had taken from the Apaches. Kirker went and had a conference with the governor, reminding him of the contract that we were to have all we could take from the Indians, besides fifty dollars a scalp. He found several parties of Mexicans talking to the governor, with their branding-irons in their hands, and saying it was their property, and they had a right to take it wherever they could find it.

"Governor," said Kirker, "you knew, when you made this written agreement, that animals recaptured by us from the Indians, were liable to be claimed by various owners, but you promised it should be ours. Otherwise what pay do we get for risking our lives in recovering mules, &c. If your government is so weak and rotten that you can't sustain yourselves, and keep your promises, then let us know it."

"It is their property," replied the governor, "and the law gives it to them; therefore, they can take it, though I am sorry that any of the animals should be claimed, after your party have done so nobly."

Kirker returned and reported what had taken place at the palace. Spiebuck immediately commenced arming his Indians, saying he would just as lief scalp the governor of Chihuahua as anybody else. We asked Spiebuck what it was best to do in the matter. He said he was going out to take charge of the animals, and if any one claimed the property he would suffer for his interference. He went to the pasture, and found a Mexican riding around among the mules, looking at them.

Riding up to him, Spiebuck struck him on the back of the head with the flat side of his tomahawk, knocking him off his horse. Alter the Mexican got up, he told him to leave; if he ever caught him there again he would scalp him. The Mexican left in a hurry.

Then Spiebuck went to the Mexicans who had been furnished with orders to take away their animals. He ordered them all to leave instantly, or his Shawnee warriors would show them no mercy. They left at once, and reported to the governor that Spiebuck and party were dangerous fellows; had called them thieves, and ordered them to leave the place.

Learning that the governor had taken sides against us in behalf of these pretended owners of the stock, our whole party became infuriated, as they saw six or eight hundred soldiers collecting, by order of the governor, at the barracks near the palace. Spiebuck put a strong guard over the animals, then went to the Bull Pen, put on his feather cap, painted his face, took a large drink of whisky, and started for the governor; with Kirker and myself, besides a number of his Shawnees, following after him to prevent any collision, or open rupture.

He rode straight to the governor's door, passing through a file of soldiers, who vainly tried to stop him. The sergeant of the guard said the governor was busily occupied, and could not be seen. Kirker and Spiebuck insisted on going in, and soon the door was open for them to enter. The governor promised that none of the animals should be taken away at present; but said he understood that Spiebuck had knocked a man off his horse, and advised him to be less violent. Spiebuck was a little better satisfied, and we all returned to the Bull Pen, for a consultation. He sent down instructions to the guard over the mules, to shoot the first Mexican that came skulking around after the animals.

"Mr. Kirker," said he, the morning after these occurrences, "if you want to stay in such a country as this is, you can do so, but I am going to take my portion of the animals, and leave. Tomorrow or next day the governor will come down on us with six or eight hundred troops, and then we can't do anything but submit to his infamous treachery."

Kirker insisted on his staying, saying that even if we lost a portion of the animals, our organization should be kept up. It would be advantageous in the end, and a large additional force could be speedily got together to go with us and work the mines we had discovered; but it was useless to argue the case with Spiebuck, for nothing but a separation would satisfy him. The whole force was therefore called together, and a fair division made of the property.

I told Kirker I would take my share of the animals with Spiebuck, and the Shawnees took charge of their portion, as well as mine. Having concluded to go along with Spiebuck's party, I was soon packed up, saddled, and ready for a start for New Mexico; our party now numbering only about seventy men.

The whole city was aware of our departure, but no attempt was made to detain us, or to get possession of our stock; probably for prudential reasons, for they knew we would fight for them. We afterwards learned that they took most of the ponies and mules that remained with the other party.

As we rode out of the place, bidding good bye to Kirker and all our friends who remained, Spiebuck remarked to Kirker that he had but one regret on leaving Chihuahua, and that was that he had not the governor's scalp to carry along with him.

We travelled fast, and reached Santa Fe in eighteen days, where we stopped a week to recruit our animals. I sold to a party of traders there, all of my animals, except the two mules presented me by "Wolf" and the horse given me by my wife. These were prized by me as keepsakes, and I had taken the best care of them, and money could not buy them. The others brought me about $2500.

In Santa Fe I had the great pleasure of meeting my friend John Batiste. I inquired after Kit Carson and Peg-leg Smith. He told me they were probably at Bent's Fort. This was in the year 1843, and as over three years had elapsed since I was at the fort, I felt quite anxious to see our old friends, the trappers, and as John was staying in Santa Fe for a few days only, on business for Bent, and would return soon to the fort, we agreed to make the trip together.

Chapter 6

Visit Bent's Fort

After spending a week very pleasantly at Santa Fe,—for we found many old friends there,—Spiebuck concluded to go to Bent's Fort, with John Batiste and me, taking along with him most of his Shawnees. Thinking it best for me to revisit my Indian home among the Comanches, as soon as I had stayed a while at the fort, I laid in a stock of presents for my wife and child, father-in-law, and others in the tribe. I then informed Spiebuck and Batiste that I was ready to start the next morning for the fort, and would advise that we go by way of Taos mountain, which was agreed to.

On our way over the mountain, at a place called the Moro, the Mexicans stole in the night some eight or ten of Spiebuck's animals. There were four of the thieves, and we tracked them, killing two, the other two escaping in the mountains, but the animals we recovered. After four days' travel, we arrived at Bent's Fort, where we were received with many demonstrations of joy. Bent and Savery purchased all the mules that Spiebuck and his friends could spare, at good prices,—about seventy-five dollars a head.

The Shawnees were delighted to receive so much gold for their animals, and, before they got away from the fort, some of it was spent for choice brandies, wines, whiskies, &c. They intended to make a short stop only at the fort, as they were on their way to their old homes, on the Shawnee reservation, near Westport, Mo. However, they stayed here several days, feasting and carousing. Bent was fitting up a large train, to take over forty thousand dollars' worth of furs to Independence, Mo., thence to be shipped on steamboats to St. Louis. I was requested to take charge of the train. I told him of my plan to see my old Comanche friends, and visit my wife and child; therefore I could not accommodate him. Finally, Mr. Savery decided to go himself with the train, and they engaged Spiebuck and his band to escort the train till it was out of danger.

When the train was ready, it consisted of twenty-four ten-mule teams, loaded with furs and provisions. I went with them to the crossing of the Big Arkansas river, some four days' travel, and on my route to the Comanches. There I took out of a wagon the presents I had bought at Santa Fe for my family, and two bottles of whisky (which I knew "Old Wolf" was fond of), and, mounting Limber Bill, the horse my wife had given me, and leading my two mules or jacks (Brigham Young and Heber Kimball, as I had called them), I bade my companions farewell, and started across the country alone, for the only spot on this broad earth that I could call my home.

The Shawnees had tried in vain to persuade me to go along to Missouri with them, and see my father and relatives; but the painful recollections of my boyhood prevented. I did, however, send a letter to my father, by them, which they promised to deliver, in which I told him of my health and prospects, and sent my regards to my relatives and friends of my childhood. Spiebuck was the most urgent of all for me to continue with them. He even called me crazy, to start alone on such a visit, though he knew I was familiar with the country.

The first night out, I came near being eaten up by the gray wolves. They caused one of my mules to break loose, and I had a great deal of trouble getting hold of it in the morning. There were eight or ten wolves around me in plain sight, growling, snuffing, and whining, and I could not sleep, fearing they might cut my rawhide ropes with their teeth, and let all my animals loose. I scared them off, by throwing powder into the fire, and they did not return. The smell of powder is dreaded by all wild animals. My camp-fire was made of buffalo-chips and little wild cherry-tree bushes. I had to fasten my mules to this small brush, though I often carried iron stakes to drive into the ground when there was nothing strong enough growing in the way of trees or shrubbery.

I rode hard next day, and in the afternoon was sadly disappointed, on arriving at the old Comanche camp, to find it moved. I unsaddled and staked out my animals, studying what to do. I made me a cup of coffee, and roasted a piece of buffalo-meat, and just at dark I crowded down a little supper; but, though I was faint and weary, my emotions and melancholy reflections deprived me of appetite.

Fortunately, I picked up my rifle and started off for a little hill, where I could see down the Little Red river, and there appeared the smoke of various campfires, some three or four miles off. I returned, and, saddling up, mounted and rode for the fires, for I knew they were the fires of the Comanches. After travelling two miles, I came into a great drove of horses and mules, feeding, and rode a mile or two further, through animals thickly scattered over the plain, till I came to the first lodges of the Comanche camp.

Here I gave a regular Comanche war-whoop, and the Indians, jumping up, wanted to know who it was. I answered that it was their friend Hobbs. An Indian ran out, shook hands with me, and, when I asked where "Wolf's" lodge was, he said about the centre of the camp, half a mile below, and he went with me to show the way. Another Indian tore off at full speed, to announce to "Wolf" and my wife that I had arrived. As we went along through the lodges, the crowd around me increased, and they made such a noise that the whole camp seemed aroused. They remarked that I was a true friend to them now, or I never would have returned to them.

When I reached "Wolf's" tent, he and Henry and my wife and child were outside, waiting to receive me. I was pulled off my mule, and nearly squeezed to death with joyful embraces. They then unpacked and unsaddled my animals, and took care of them. I commenced taking out my presents for my wife and child, and took out one of the bottles of whisky which I had brought for "Wolf's" special benefit. He said he wasn't afraid to drink that, as he was the first we had given him years before. Among the presents which I gave "Wolf" were a nice butcher-knife and a beautiful tomahawk which had a hollow handle, a pipe on the back and a mouth-piece to screw on the handle; also, a quantity of tobacco, lots of red flannel, calicoes, beads, trinkets, &c. The beads and the flannel I told him to give his wife, my mother-in-law.

Then I got out the presents for my wife and child, which were numerous and valuable, consisting of shawls and dress-patterns, ribbons, beads, mirrors, knives and forks, thread, &c, the whole filling one of the pack-saddles, and enough to last her for years. I knew she appreciated the liberal gifts, though she said but little. Occasionally, as she looked at me and then at the presents, her eyes would till with tears, and, if she spoke, her voice would tremble and indicate her deepest gratitude. I could see that she had almost despaired of my ever returning to her, fearing that I had been killed in some of my expeditions. My return was a joyful surprise to them all.

"Wolf" called me to come and sit down by him. He commenced crying, and told me about the death of his son, my brother, as he called him. But he said he was satisfied that the sun, his god, had taken him up, and he would be back some day. He said he had another brave son in his place, who was fast learning to be a brave chief. He said Henry had told him that he had seen me down in Mexico, with a large lot of wagons and teams. Henry stood by, listening, and appeared desirous to hear me converse with the old chief; for he, as well as many other of the principal warriors, appeared to think as much of me as though I was in reality in command of their tribe.

His little brother Jim came around to see me. He had even forgotten the "yes" and "no" which was all the English he could speak when I left the Comanches. My little boy was about seven years old, and as wild as a deer, and it was a good while before

I, assisted by his mother's talking to him, could get him to come to me.

My wife told me she had a lodge of her own we could go to, though, since I had left, she had stayed all the time with her father and mother. We moved into our lodge about 12 o'clock that night, and I rested, for the first time in four years, after every manner of privation and hardship, in the bosom of my family, without any fear of wolves, robbers, or Indians.

The next day, "Old Wolf" had a long tale to tell me about his particular friend, the Cheyenne chief, being taken by Bent to Independence, Mo., and to St. Louis and New Orleans, whence he had brought presents of all kinds, some of which he had given to "Wolf." The accounts given "Old Wolf" by his friend, of the treatment he had received at the different places he had visited, gave him a very high opinion of the people of the United States,—much different from that they had of the Texans. Probably one great reason of the tribe's dislike to Texans was the fact that they had given them their first lesson in the power of revolvers.

"Old Wolf" laughed heartily when he related the experience of the Cheyenne chief, when he first went on board a steamboat at Independence. He was leaning over the side of the boat, when the engineer blew off steam on that side, and the frightened Indian jumped into the river. He swam out, and dry clothes were put on him; but it was some time before they could get him on the boat again, for he declared it was the devil. "Old Wolf" told him he was foolish to get scared at a thing before he knew what it was; but he thought if "Wolf" had been with him on the boat, he would have jumped too.

"Wolf" wanted to know if I had seen "Little-hearted John," as he called him. I told him where I had seen him, and he said he had also seen him once since he sold him.

Bent's kindness to the Cheyenne chief was part of his policy, by which he shipped thirty or forty thousand dollars' worth of furs every fall to St. Louis or Independence.

It pleased "Wolf" and my wife that I had taken care of the

mules and horse they had given me. The second day after my arrival, the old chief said his whisky was gone, and he would like to have another drink. I told my wife, who had taken it in charge, to hand him out the other bottle, informing him that it was all I had brought.

I stayed in camp, hunting buffalo and amusing my-self with the Indians, for about a month, when, much to their surprise, I informed my wife and father-in-law that I was going to Mexico again. When I told them, as a reason for my going, that I had left money there, and was going to return for it, they could not understand why I need go on that account. "Old Wolf" asked what need I had for money; hadn't he everything we needed? I explained to him that, among the whites, purchases were made with money instead of skins and furs, and therefore it was very useful to me.

I then told my wife that I had left orders at Bent's Fort, so that, at any time her father went there to trade, he could get all the clothes and other articles for her and the child that she needed.

"Wolf" said, if I must go, he would send out and prepare some nice buffalo-meat for me to take with me. This was soon done. They prepared some buffalo-tongues and fleeces or large flakes cut from the back and sides of the buffalo, well salted and cured over the fire, and also some dried venison-hams. "Wolf" then inquired which route I wanted to take, and I replied the straightest to New Mexico, which would be by way of Cimarron creek. After looking at my two mules, he said they were weak and poor, and advised me to take some better ones, for I could have all the animals I wanted. I picked out six fine riding and packing Texan mules and another fine saddle-horse, besides taking the bay Limber Bill, given me by my wife when I left them the first time.

I bade them all goodbye, parting sadly and reluctantly from the lovely and affectionate "Spotted Fawn," who hung upon my neck, and almost refused to let me go. This daughter of "Wolf" was far above the average of Indian women in looks and intelligence, and was nearly white. Her amiable ways, during the years of my pleasant sojourn among her people, had so endeared her to me, that I could not leave on this occasion without promising her that I would return again soon to stay permanently. How well I kept that promise, the reader will see hereafter.

My little boy, Jimmy, though wild and afraid of me a few weeks before, now came up to say goodbye to me and give me a parting kiss. The old men and young warriors of the camp also gathered around to say farewell and wish me good-luck. Mounting my horse, and waving a final *adieu*, I started off, escorted by Henry Brown, the assistant chief, and twenty-four warriors, who were detailed to take me to where there would be no danger from any unfriendly Indians. "Wolf" directed the escort to see me safely into the Mexican settlements, and for that purpose they carried plenty of provisions.

On the fifth day after leaving "Wolf's" camp, we struck the main Santa Fe road from Independence, about ten miles above the bone-yard where Mr. Speyers's mules were frozen to death. Here we came upon a train of eight wagons, eight mules to each, with the necessary number of teamsters, &c, who had halted here to recruit their mules. As soon as they saw us, they prepared for a fight, part of the men starting for their animals.

When I saw they considered us a hostile party, I halted my escort and rode forward to reassure them. I told them they need have no fears, as the Indians were friendly and under my command. On inquiring for the leader of the party, I was introduced to Mr. Calvin McCoy, from Westport, Mo. I now signalled to Henry, who came up with the warriors, and, by my direction, proceeded to stake out their animals to feed, and make a camp near our friends.

In this train I found an old acquaintance named James Prewitt, who was moving his family, who occupied one of the wagons of the train, from Missouri to New Mexico. His wife was a Spanish woman, and they, with their children, had been several weeks on the road from Westport, Mo. Seeing her afraid of the Indians, I spoke to her in Spanish to have no fear of us. She was surprised, and inquired where I learned Spanish. I told her in Santa Fe and the lower part of Mexico, when she informed me that Santa Fe was her native place, and that she was a relative of Governor Armijo.

I asked McCoy if he had met Bent's fur-train going east, under escort of a party of Shawnees. He replied that they did meet them, at Walnut creek, and, to get feed, laid by with them one day. Said he, "I suppose you are the man Hobbs they told us had left them at the crossing of the Big Arkansas to go to the Comanches." I told him I was the man, when he informed me he was well acquainted with my father's family, and that they considered me dead, until Mr. Prewitt told them he had met me in Santa Fe, and that I had been ransomed from the Indians. On inquiring about my father and other friends, I learned they were all doing well, and were much surprised and pleased to hear of my being alive and well, after having given me up as lost for so long a time.

We had a hearty supper, and spent most of the night talking of old friends. I called in Henry, and told the strangers that this was an American boy, but he had become a principal man and chief among the Comanches. McCoy asked him if he would prefer to live with the Americans hereafter. He said no; he would rather be with the Indians.

The next morning, I told Henry that he and his Indians might go back, and they could tell "Wolf" that I had met friends to go into Santa Fe with, and I was perfectly safe. Then procuring a bottle of whisky of Mr. Prewitt, which I sent to my old friend "Wolf," I thanked Henry and his party for their great kindness in escorting me thus far on my journey, and bade them goodbye.

Mr. McCoy agreed to haul my provisions and pack-saddles into Santa Fe, and give me a hundred dollars apiece for my mules on arrival there. With the aid of my strong mules, our train reached the first Mexican settlement in seven days. There I left Mr. McCoy, took my two horses, and went on through the Mexican settlements to Santa Fe. McCoy bought corn, recruited his animals, and got into Santa Fe fifteen days after my arrival there. He sold part of his goods, and paid me six hundred dollars for my six mules. I visited Governor Armijo, and introduced McCoy to him; his acquaintance proving very useful in getting the goods through the custom-house.

By my advice, McCoy left Santa Fe, as the market for such goods as he had was easily glutted, it being a small place of not over eight thousand inhabitants. I told him that Chihuahua was a city of over thirty thousand people, and lie requested me to go there with him and show him the way. As he was short of means, and would have to feed all the way down, I drew money I had on deposit at Scully's (a large mercantile house), and loaned it to him. to be repaid when we reached Chihuahua.

We arrived there in twenty-four days from the time we left Santa Fe. There I met my friends, James Kirker, John Spencer, Gabe Allen, and others, who were on the expedition against the Apaches. They were all "dead broke." Kirker said if he had done as Spiebuck and I had advised, he would have made much more money. In answer to my inquiries, I found that he had succeeded in getting enough money from the governor, on account of the scalps, to barely live, and that, shortly after we left Chihuahua, the Mexicans took all the animals recovered from the Apaches, besides stealing all their own riding-mules.

I told him how Spiebuck and his men sold all their mules to Bent and took their horses to Missouri, while I had sold my mules at Santa Fe; and we had all got good prices, and got the cash, which was better than to have stayed in Chihuahua and lost them.

He went on to tell us how the Apache girls we brought in as prisoners had all run off, after being distributed as servants among the rich people by the governor. Dr. Duvas, who married a sister of the governor, was persuaded by him to take one of the squaws into his family as a nurse, and one day, when Mrs. Duvas went across the street, leaving her infant of a year old in the arms of this nurse, she took the child by the heels, smashed its brains out against the door-jamb, and then escaped, and was never caught.

Kirker further said, that, since our raid, the Apaches had been killing people all around Chihuahua, and had even ventured into the city, murdering citizens in the suburbs. The governor had called on him and the Americans there for help; but their reply was that there was an old contract unfulfilled, and they declined to furnish aid till that was settled.

Being now out of business, and meeting an agent of an English manufacturing company, located in Zacatecas, who was looking for someone to take cotton from Chihuahua to their factory, I determined to try my luck as a freighter. For this purpose, I bought of Mr. McCoy four wagons and thirty-two mules, and hired a number of our old Apache hunting-party as teamsters and guard. As the country through which we were to travel was infested by various hostile tribes of Indians, I joined my force with those of three other freighters, named Henry Cappilard, Robert Carlisle, and Samuel Miller. Cappilard was a Frenchman, and the other two Missourians. Our party were all well-armed, and in due time we started our train for the south.

The fifth day after leaving, we were surprised by about fifty Apaches. We were travelling through a thick brush, or thicket, when they jumped suddenly out upon us, and killed a teamster named Harvey Gleaves and six of our mules, and wounded Mr. Cappilard in the head, the bullet glancing upward from his forehead. By this time, we had all got ready for action, and poured into the savages a well-directed succession of shots, which caused them to flee, with the loss of several killed and wounded, which they carried off the field with them.

Unharnessing our dead mules, and putting our dead teamster in a wagon, we continued our march. On arriving at El y St. Bartolo, twenty miles further on, we laid over a day, and buried our friend Gleaves. Next day we bought six mules, and resumed our journey, meeting with no unusual adventures till we reached our destination.

After unloading my freight, I went toward the southern part of Mexico, my destination being San Luis Potosi. There we loaded with blankets, sugar, and other groceries,—about onehalf of which was freight and the other my own venture,— and returned to Chihuahua, where I sold out everything I had bought at a hundred *per cent*, profit. I continued in that business, making three or four trips, until the year 1846, at which time I had enough money to purchase ten wagons and teams, and was making trips with my own train, doing business on my own account and hiring all my help.

In the midst of my success, when I fancied that I was on the road to a fortune, hostilities commenced between the United States and Mexico. In February, 1847, the Mexican authorities seized my wagons, teams, and all the property I possessed, impressing it for the use of their army. War had been declared in 1846, but only vague and unreliable rumours had reached us in that far-off region of Central Mexico.

We had heard a good deal of talk about the disputed boundary between Mexico and Texas, and the $18,000,000 debt due from Mexico to the United States, which Mexico refused to pay, and it was manifest that war, at no distant day, was probable. I, with others, continued trading, however, because we were acting under a treaty of commerce between Mexico and the United States, which gave us the right to trade in that country freely; and we knew that our government, in any event, possessed the power and the willingness to protect our property.

We could take care of our interests better by remaining, as any attempt to get out of the country would be destructive to our interests as traders, and I had considerable property to risk. Of course, our lives were in danger, but we took all such chances, relying on our wits and courage to carry us through. Many other American traders came to the same decision, and, by remaining too long in Mexico, lost all their property after the war commenced.

The first official report that United States troops had crossed the Rio Grande gave us much alarm. I was at San Luis Potosi when I heard that Santa Anna was marching, with fourteen thousand troops, to meet General Taylor at Buena Vista, and was levying indiscriminately on the property of Americans and Mexicans. I was loading up my teams and settling up my business, which would require about ten days, and I made all haste to get out of his way.

I had got on all my goods, passed the custom-house officers, and was hurrying out of the city, when I saw coming up behind me about fifty mounted Mexican lancers on a full gallop. I knew at once their business. When they came up, I was ordered to return by the officer in command of this advance-guard of Santa Anna's army. He said his orders were to impress all the property and stores that he could find for the use of the Mexican army. I had to return with them! Now all my hopes of trading and becoming wealthy in that line of business were blasted.

I demanded of the officer who took charge of my property something to show as a voucher for what he had taken from me. He said he had no authority to give me a receipt; but I could see General Santa Anna, who would be along in a day or two, and lie would doubtless give me one.

The next day, Santa Anna, at the head of his army, marched into the city, on his way to Buena Vista, which was about two hundred and twenty-five miles from San Luis Potosi. It was two days before I could get an interview with Santa Anna, When I did gain an audience with him, he inquired my business, and I told him I desired some document to show that he had taken my property from me. He thought there was no necessity for it, as he was going down to give the Americans a thrashing, and wanted me to go along with him and haul some artillery.

He offered to pay me and give me back my teams, if he was successful. I had less confidence in his whipping the Yankees than he had; at all events, I did not feel willing to help him fight against the flag of my country, nor to stand up to be shot at by American infantry and artillerymen. So I refused to go, after politely telling him that I was a Missourian by birth and could not conscientiously go against my nation. He said he thought I would be safer with him than anywhere else, for in a short time he should issue an order that any American found in the country, after twenty-five days, should be shot.

I insisted on a receipt for the goods seized, and told him how many Mexicans I had rescued from Indian tribes, where they were held as captives, and stated the part I took in the expedition against the Apaches, and the shabby treatment I had received from the governor of Chihuahua, He finally promised to give me the receipt, saying he had heard of me before, and gave the urgent necessities of his poorly supplied army as the only excuse he had for holding my property. He directed me to make out a written statement of all my effects that had been seized, which I did, as follows: eighty mules, with ten wagons loaded with leather of various kinds, blankets, saddle-trees, sugar, coffee, rice, and other groceries, giving the items in detail.

He said, before he could give a receipt, he must see the officer who made the seizure, and have the account verified, which was done at once. I asked the general if he wouldn't be good enough to leave me my goods, even if he took the mules and wagons; but he objected, on account of his troops being short of provisions. I took my receipt from the general, and bade him goodbye.

I now had nothing left out of twenty thousand dollars' worth of property, except my horse and saddle and five hundred dollars in money, which I had saved to pay expenses on our way back to Chihuahua. I called up my teamsters, after I got back to the hotel, and paid them what I owed them. These teamsters were all Mexicans, and I had been stripped of nearly all I had by the commander-in-chief of the Mexican army; but, so long as I had enough to pay them the wages due, I felt bound to do so. I told them I was a ruined man, and could not take them back to Chihuahua, as agreed; but if they wished to return north, they could probably do so under the army wagon-masters, as drivers of the same wagons, which I believe they did.

I had only one hundred dollars left, after paying the teamsters,, I then went to a Mexican store, and bought me a large wide-brimmed straw-hat, with rolls of cotton covered with silver lace wound around it, and a regular Mexican "Greaser" costume,, being buckskin over riding-pants, white drawers and buckskin leggings, a buckskin roundabout, and shoes with Mexican spurs. The over riding-pants are made to button up on the outside of the leg, instead of with a seam, so that in riding they can be opened to relieve the knees.

This change of dress was all that saved me. I spoke Spanish fluently, as well as any of the natives and better than the common classes. I had been smoked yellow in the wigwams of the Comanches, tanned by my out-door life and exposure since, and I could not now be told, with my new rig on, from a native Mexican. I saddled my horse, and started for Zacatecas. This was one hundred and fifty miles distant.

On my arrival, I met some of my friends,—Mr. Kirkford, Dr. Jenkins, and Humphrey Gentry; the latter an American and the first two Englishmen. They informed me that Colonel Doniphan's regiment was expected to arrive soon at Santa Fe. I informed them of my bad luck at San Luis Potosi, at which they expressed much sympathy, and offered me the loan of any money I needed.

The next day, the order of Santa Anna was issued in Zacatecas, that every American who was not out of the country within twenty-five days should be shot. Then I went to Mr. Gentry, and asked him what he thought of doing. He replied that he would be protected with the English in the mint at Zacatecas. I then called on Dr. Jenkins for fifty dollars, which was handed over to me at once. He inquired what I thought of doing, and I told him I was going to the city of Durango. He said he could give me some useful letters to some English friends of his working there at the iron-works.

I accepted one letter, and immediately started for Durango, arriving there in a week. Proceeding directly to the iron-works, I presented my letter to the principal man, Solomon Houck, from Booneville, Mo. He said he was sorry to hear of my bad luck, and that I could stay there as long as I wished, and he would give me a good berth to oversee a party of Mexicans, who were working in the minerals for him. He also informed me that some of our friends had been put in prison the day before by the Mexicans. I asked who they were, and he stated that they were two brothers, James and Samuel McGuffin, from Kentucky, and Samuel Wetherhead, a friend of Mr. Houck, from Booneville, Mo., and a Scotch tailor named Joseph White.

These men I had known for some time, and felt a strong desire to help them, when I heard of their misfortune, and so informed Mr. Houck. They were all wealthy men. The twenty-five days were about elapsing, and the Mexicans were in haste to get hold of their property. They fined these four men twenty-five thousand dollars, and gave them twenty-five days more to leave the country. They dared not start with any means, for that would insure their robbery and murder on the road.

About this time, news came that Colonel Doniphan's famous regiment, with over eight hundred men, besides a park of artillery, was on the march from Santa Fe to Chihuahua, and also that our old friend Bent, of Bent's Fort, was acting-governor of New Mexico, with a force of four hundred men. Governor Armijo had not stopped for an interview with Doniphan, but had cleared out of Santa Fe in haste.

Mr. Houck had a Mexican servant-girl, in whom he placed all confidence, who used to carry the provisions to prison for these four men, by consent of the jailor. The provisions were examined every time she passed the jailor. Mr. Houck wrote a note to the men, and inclosed it in a loaf of bread, also a small inkstand, pen, sheet of paper, &c. The letter informed them that Colonel Doniphan had taken Santa Fe and was marching into Mexico, and there were hopes for them.

They found the writing materials, and replied that Doniphan was a personal friend of the brothers McGuffin, and they thought, if they could get word to him of the danger they were in, he would make a strong effort to save them, as they believed the Mexicans intended to secure their property and then kill them. They wished him, if possible, to procure a messenger to take a letter from them to Colonel Doniphan, and send them paper to write it on.

Houck succeeded in getting more paper to them, and a note, in which he informed them that I was stopping with him, and had volunteered to take a letter from them to Colonel Doniphan, notwithstanding I well knew the risk I ran, and that, from what he knew of me, he believed I could get safely through with it. This encouraged them; they wrote the letter and sent it past the guard, by the Mexican girl, to us.

I took the letter, rolled it in thin linen cloth into a cylindrical shape, then sewed around it a piece of oil-cloth, loaded a double-barrelled shot-gun with buckshot, and down upon one of these charges rammed the letter, which was made to fit closely like a cartridge. If examined too closely, I meant, as if by accident, to shoot the letter away.

I saddled my horse and started on my journey, which proved to be one of three hundred and eighty miles or more, to the place where I met Doniphan's regiment. I travelled day and night, sometimes off and sometimes on the road, being well acquainted with the country and the direction. Twice on the road I was examined by the Mexican authorities, for they kept a close watch on all strangers, whether Mexicans or foreigners. But they did not find my letter. The weather was fine, warm, and clear, with starlight nights, which was quite an advantage.

When I had travelled some two hundred and forty miles, I began to get into towns and settlements where I was well known, from my former travels up and down. Then I left the road, going through woods and mountains, till I arrived within fifty or sixty miles of Chihuahua, travelling one day and night during this time without eating anything. Here I came in sight of a place called St. Pablo. In this town lived a friend of mine, named James Hill, an American, from Clay county, Mo.

This was about 3 o'clock in the afternoon. I rode into a thick belt of timber, near which was good grass for my horse, took off my saddle, spread down my blanket, hobbled my horse, laid down, and, being very sleepy as well as hungry, fell asleep, while studying how I should get something to eat without being seen. I slept until dark, and then got up and saddled my horse.

My friend Hill lived near the edge of the town, where he had a grist-mill. I made my way to his house, riding very slowly, and keeping a good look-out. On my way, I met several Mexicans, but excited no suspicion, for they took me for a Mexican. I had no fear of them, as my horse had considerable speed, and I had a double-barrelled gun and six-shooter. Guided by the dim lights in the scattered houses in the suburbs, I arrived about 8 o'clock at Hill's house; dismounted, and went in cautiously.

Mrs. Hill did not recognize me in my "Greaser" dress until I made myself known. I inquired for her husband. She told me that she did not know where her husband was. He and another American, a friend of his, from Clay county, Mo., named Milton Favour, had gone into the mountains, fearing the Mexicans, who were very hostile, would take their lives. The wives of both Hill and Favour were Mexicans. Mrs. Hill told me I must be very careful, and I had better put my horse in the stable before he was seen, as a great many Mexicans were prowling about and were looking for Hill, and that I had better hide in a private room. I stabled the horse, fed him hay and grain, and then went into a private room as directed by her, where she brought me food, as I told her I was perishing with hunger.

I remained secreted till midnight, and then proceeded on my way, being furnished by her with cold meat and bread for my next meal. Notwithstanding her friendly hospitality, I told her no secrets, for my life depended on my extreme caution. Silently I saddled and rode away by the light of the moon, feeling much relieved and encouraged to think my mission would be successful.

All the remaining hours till morning, my way was through the roughest kind of country, and I found my horse fast failing, his feet having become sore, so that it was with difficulty I could urge him out of a walk. I found I was approaching the position of a large Mexican force, which was stationed at the foot of the mountains to bar the progress of Colonel Doniphan's regiment toward Chihuahua. I had gone around to the right of Chihuahua, and was going up the point of the mountain between Chihuahua and Sacramento, a sort of "cow *ranche*," fourteen miles from Chihuahua, and near the place where we had previously "*cached*," or secreted, some goods we took from the Apaches.

The Mexicans were intrenched at Sacramento, and I could hear their drums and the occasional tiring of a gun. By the time I had got half-way up the mountain, travelling through the scrubby brush away from the road, the blood was running from my horse's feet, and it was evident that I could get him along but a little further. I watched the failing attempts of my faithful Limber Bill, and resolved to abandon him; for, indeed, I had been walking and leading him an hour.

Fortunately I saw in the path before me a Mexican, coming toward me, riding a horse and leading a fine one in his rear. I hailed him, and inquired how he would trade horses, telling him I would give him boot-money. He said he would not trade, and inquired where I was going. I told him I was going over to help Governor Trios whip the Americans out of the country. He asked me where I was from, and I answered from Lower Mexico.

I now demanded that he should trade horses with me anyhow, and, cocking my gun, told him to get down and change with me. He looked at me, and asked if I was in earnest, when I replied that if he didn't do it mighty quick I would convince him. He alighted, and I took hold of the hair-rope by which he led his animal, while he took off my saddle and bridle and put them on his horse. When arranged to my satisfaction, I led his beast a few steps up the mountain and sprang into the saddle. The Mexican gazed at me with astonishment, and I asked him, as I looked back,

"Aint you going to fight for your country?"

"No," he replied.

I started off at a gallop, feeling that it was lucky indeed that the Mexican had come along, for I saw I had exchanged for a good horse. The Mexican felt that I had cheated him, for he shouted after me to return and pay the difference; but I had only time to refer him to a warmer climate for satisfaction.

Travelling about four miles further, I came to the brow of the mountain, where I had a good view of the valley below, and discovered, just at the foot of the mountain, the Mexican army. I got off my horse, fastened Mm back in a secluded place, and went forward where I could see the whole encampment of the Mexicans and judge of their strength. The idea suddenly seized me to sketch their position as well as I could for the use of Colonel Doniphan.

Having some loose paper and a pencil in my wallet, I made a hasty drawing of the whole force. They were drilling, and I judged their number to be about five thousand, besides eighteen pieces of artillery; but not over five hundred were regulars, as I could see by their uniforms. The rest were raw country volunteers. I could see the red flags on the lances some of them had. They proved to be poorly armed, and, though some had lances, many of them expected to fight by throwing the lasso, the only mode of warfare with which they were acquainted.

After finishing my rough map, which I knew Colonel Doniphan would appreciate, I remounted and picked my way along the mountain, with a view of going around the Mexican camp, so as to avoid being seen by them. After three or four miles' further travel, descending the mountain and turning a point among the hills, suddenly and unexpectedly the cheerful sight of the star-spangled banner burst on my vision.

It created in me the strongest enthusiasm. The reaction in my feelings was such that I could hardly control myself. The weary days and nights of anxiety and fear were now over; and there, on the plain before me, stood my countrymen, my friends, their bright guns glittering in the sunlight, and their proud banner,—the glorious old Stars and Stripes,—waving in the breeze. It was the same old nag I had often gazed at in admiration as it unfolded in the wind over the walls of Fort Bent, when I was returning there to greet my old trapping friends after a long absence.

And farther back, even, in my early childhood, I had seen it borne aloft by some military company, and my young breast heaved with patriotic emotion when older persons explained to me that it was the emblem of my country's freedom, and a guarantee of protection to its citizens. Ye who have been brought up in the lap of luxury, in the midst of the refinements of society, who know nothing of the weary tramps, the dangerous expeditions, the thrilling adventures among savages, the privations, exposures, and hardships which it had been my fortune to endure,—ye can know nothing of my joy, nor can be expected to appreciate my feelings, when, after losing all my property by the Mexicans, I had now accomplished an important mission, which might result in the defeat of our enemies and the liberation of my friends.

CHAPTER 7

Volunteer for Duty

Putting spurs to my horse, I dashed down towards Doniphan's regiment, for I saw it was preparing to move forward, and I was anxious to put my sketch of the Mexican position in his hands before he should become engaged. The mountain was so steep in some places that my horse slid on his haunches. Getting through the brush and emerging on the open plain, I approached at a full gallop, Doniphan's advance guard of fifteen mounted men. They quickly surrounded me, and one of them, named George Skillman, with whom I was acquainted, having met him as one of Speyers's teamsters, when I rescued them from the blockade at the Bone Yard, rode up to me with his gun cocked, asking me in Spanish who I was, where I came from, &c. I answered in Spanish, that I was from Durango, and bursting into a laugh, shouted out in English:

"For heaven's sake, Skillman, don't you know me?" He lowered his gun, came up closer, and recognising me, said he took me at first for a "Greaser" spy. I inquired for Colonel Doniphan, and they said he was back at the head of his regiment. I informed Skillman that I had a letter for the colonel, from some of his friends who were in Durango, in prison, and I had come to see what I could do for them. He asked if I had come anywhere near the enemy, and I replied that I had seen them all. "But," said I, "I have no time to talk; I must go and see the colonel."

I galloped on, to the head of the regiment, where I met Doniphan, and very quickly explained my business. Pulling out my ramrod, and putting the screw to it, I drew forth my letter, ripped off the cover, unfolded it, and handed it to the colonel. He asked me where I was from, and I told him from Durango.

By this time, a large number of men had collected around us, all eager to know who I was. Samuel Owens rode up, and I spoke to him, calling him by name. He looked at me for some time before recognising me, in my fancy dress. Said he:

"For Christ's sake, Hobbs, is that you?"

I had known Owens when a boy, in Missouri, and had met him several times, in my wanderings, he being the one who fitted me out when I went to the relief of Speyers's train; and I had done business after that with him, in Mexico. He was always known as Colonel Sam Owens, having received that title years before, in Missouri. He was not directly connected with the regiment, but was a merchant, having a store at Santa Fe, and had several wagon loads of goods with the regiment. In the battle, he had command of a company formed of the teamsters, and others, who were not enlisted men.

By this time, Colonel Doniphan had read McGuffin's letter. He said he was sorry for our friends, but all depended on the battle which was just coming off. If we gained it, we gained them; if we lost it, we lost them; which was all he could say in their behalf.

Then Colonel Owens, addressing me, said: "Hobbs, come this way with me."

I went with the colonel to the left of the regiment. Then he called my brother John, and said to him:

"Here's your brother James, that you considered lost so long." As I had no idea that my brother was with the regiment, and he knew nothing definite of me, this meeting, after a separation of twelve years, was a joyful surprise to us both. Without waiting long for congratulations, we went together to Colonel Owens's carriage by the colonel's invitation, when his negro servant, Andy, made himself useful by producing the colonel's private demijohn of brandy and some drinking cups.

We dismounted. I could see that Colonel Owens was greatly

excited, and appeared to be in deep trouble. As we raised the cups to our lips, I noticed that Colonel Owens's was filled to the brim. Drinking it off, he said: "This may be our last drink together, and probably is enough to carry me to perdition." I remarked to him that we should keep cool, as we were close to the enemy.

I excused myself to Owens, telling him I had further business with Colonel Doniphan, and I rode back to him, and producing my drawing, told him I had a rough sketch of the enemy's position, made an hour before, when I was on the mountain, where I had a full view of them, and their intrenchments. The colonel, after examining it carefully, seemed much pleased, and said he: "I see you have here the form of their intrenchments, and the position of their artillery. If I can rely upon this as being correct, we have an easy task before us."

"Colonel," said I, "to show you that I know what I am about, if you will look with your field-glass at yonder hillside, as we get a little further on, you will see a twenty-four pounder, or a large gun, mounted just above the brush at the edge of the plain, and manned by about a dozen men, so posted as to pour a raking fire into you, when you storm their intrenchments."

"Very well," said he; "I have need of the services of such men as you."

Just then we heard some shots exchanged between our advanced guard and the Mexicans. Our force was then ordered to march; and they did march as though they were going to a Fourth of July celebration.

Colonel Owens rode up and asked Doniphan the time of day, and added: "All I want is to get in among the Greasers." "Keep very cool,': said Doniphan, noticing that Owens was excited with liquor.

Here two of the advance guard "came back and re-ported that they had killed one Mexican, and that we were close upon the enemy, for they were just over the knoll, half a mile distant.

Colonel Doniphan immediately ordered our troops into line, and rode out in front with me, when I showed him the position of the twenty-four pounder gun. He noticed at once that the hillside was too steep to enable them to turn the gun to fire upward, and asked me if I couldn't take some of my old mountaineer friends, for he had learned that several in the regiment knew me, and go around above and come down on the gun and capture it. I answered that I was at his service, and would do the best I could.

Although not an enlisted man, I felt like doing something for my country against the good-for-nothing, rotten government of Mexico. At this reply of mine, many of the troops became boisterous in their applause, and were anxious to go with me. He immediately instructed an officer to detail twenty-five men, most of whom I had been in hard places with before, and I started with them, leaving our horses, because they could not ascend the hill.

When we had got in the rear of the gun, we saw that our troops were marching directly up in front of the enemy, and the Mexicans commenced firing. Two or three cannon balls went whizzing over the heads of our troops; at the same time a large force of Mexican lancers were making a circuit, to get in the rear of Doniphan's men. Lieutenant Chauteau, who was one of the hunting party I left home with twelve years before, and Doctor Waldo, ran out two pieces of flying artillery, and discharging a few shells among the lancers, they turned and tied back.

By this time we had crawled down through the brush close to the piece of artillery, the attention of the gunners being in front. We ran for the gun, shooting one of the gunners; another one undertook to spike it with a rat-tail file, and he was shot. Colonel Doniphan seeing we had the gun, ordered his men to charge the redoubts.

Having driven the Mexicans from their gun, we trained it so as to get it in range of the enemy, and finally got in a shot, when it kicked itself off its mountings, being terribly overloaded, with all manner of deadly missiles. As we abandoned the gun, and ran to the assistance of our comrades, I saw Owens dash in front of his men up to the redoubt, killing three or four with his six shooter, receiving himself a ball in his thigh, while another killed his horse, and she fell with him. At the same time, a Mexican sprang, out and run him through with a lance. Captain Jackson coming up, shot the Mexican as he was getting back into the redoubt. Owens was urged to be calm, and not expose himself foolishly, but family trouble made him desperate, and he threw his life away.

Our men had now got possession of the intrenchments, killing a great number in their charge, producing a regular stampede of the Mexicans. The Mexican colours were captured, and our nag put in its place with three cheers; one old sailor shouting, "Stand by, boys, she's all oak, and iron bound."

Lieutenant Sproule was out on the plain, with his cavalry, pursuing the Mexicans, and cutting them to pieces; while our flying artillery, which was under the command of Major Clark, made great havoc among those in retreat.

The Mexicans had a wagon loaded with $75,000, in specie, which they undertook to save, running their mules at full speed, pricking them with lances to urge them faster, when Lieutenant Chauteau, of the artillery, thinking something valuable aboard, sent several shells after the wagon, one of which knocked the for-ward wheels and axle loose, and the wagon fell down, the driver also being killed by the explosion, and the specie fell into our hands.

The Mexicans saved but little. Four hundred head of cattle, any quantity of sheep, and fifty cart loads of hard bread and dried meat were captured, besides eighteen pieces of artillery, with many small arms, and what ammunition they had, which was but little. There were four hundred of them killed and wounded, while our loss was very small.

We took several hundred prisoners, among whom were six officers. Encamping on the ground that night, it was dreadful to hear the cries of the Mexican wounded. Our dead and wounded were cared for first. Colonel Owens's body was laid in his carriage, and afterwards taken to Chihuahua. After our wounded were seen to by the surgeons, the Mexican prisoners brought in their wounded for attention, many of them needing amputations.

Colonel Doniphan issued an order that night, that as some men friendly to our cause were imprisoned in Durango, and suffering all manner of cruelty, he should shoot the six Mexican officers and as many more prisoners as he thought necessary, if his friends were not released immediately, and delivered, with all their property, to him at Chihuahua. The prisoners selected one of their number to start at once with the order to Durango, and the messenger was soon on his flying trip.

Next morning, we loaded the wounded into wagons and on animals, as well as we could, and started on the march for Chihuahua. The specie was loaded into another wagon, and properly guarded, as it was considered a capital prize.

When about four miles from the city, we met a man named Jose Cordaro, a great friend of the Americans. He inquired for the commander, and was referred to Colonel Doniphan. He informed the colonel that the men, generally, had escaped from the city, fearing the Yankees. A few Americans were left, at the Mint, and some old people, and a few friendly Mexicans; but the city, with its population, mainly composed of women and children, was entirely at his mercy.

Colonel Doniphan halted his troops, and ordered that any man guilty of burning, sacking, or destroying private property, or disturbing any family, or stealing the effects of the Mexicans of that place, would suffer death. We then marched into the city in good order.

The troops were disposed of at several stations, and the prisoners placed in my old quarters, the Bull Pen, or amphitheatre, with a strong guard over them.

Colonel Doniphan was notified that many convicts were starving to death, in the underground cells of the city prison, for the authorities had run off with the keys, and the poor wretches could not be got out. He ordered our quartermaster, Lieutenant Lee (a nephew of General Lee), to send a wagon load of provisions, which was done forthwith, the colonel going himself. It was impossible to get the doors open, until powder was picked into the lock and exploded. Even then, a sledge-hammer was required to finish the work.

The prisoners were ordered to march out. Some had been underground so long that they resembled corpses. After they were all formed in front of the prison, Colonel Doniphan told me and Gabe Allen to tell those Mexicans, in Spanish, that he didn't know what they were in there for, but he didn't suppose it was for any good, at all events, he was going to give them their freedom; but before doing so, would read his laws to them, and they must be very particular in their obedience. His instructions were short:

Any person stealing the value of five dollars, or under, would receive four hundred lashes.

Thefts over that amount would be punished by hanging.

Any crime worse than stealing, as aforesaid, would certainly be punished with death.

He said he was ignorant of their former laws, but those were his laws, and they might rely on their being enforced.

"All right," shouted the Mexicans. "Hurrah for our new Governor!"

The colonel told me and Mr. Allen to say to them that there was a wagon load of provisions which would be divided among them, after which they must go immediately to the scene of the late battle, put all the dead in ditches, cover them up, and return and report to him. They got their provisions, and started off, under guard, and the colonel returned to his quarters.

During the day, Colonel Owens was buried, with military honours, in the Catholic cemetery. The second day, in the afternoon, the burial party returned, and formed in front of Colonel Doniphan's residence, some being dressed in the clothes of the dead soldiers, and wearing soldier caps. They had picked up considerable specie, that was scattered about in the road.

They reported that they had buried all the dead, in good shape, and wanted to know what to do next. They told Allen and me to say to Colonel Doniphan that if they could be supplied with arms, they would fight for us. The colonel told me to say that he should have thought better of them if they had not made any such proposition to light against their own nation, as he despised all traitors; but he would give them employment, temporarily, at cleaning the streets, bringing in wood and water for the army, and other various kinds of work, and their wages should be fifty cents per day, but they must be sure not to steal anything.

A few days after this, a Mexican returned from Durango, bringing a letter from James McGuffin, stating that they had been liberated before the messenger arrived there, news having come that the Mexicans had been defeated at Sacramento. Everything belonging to them had been returned to them, and they would soon arrive at Chihuahua. The same Mexican brought a letter from the authorities at Durango, to the officers that we had taken prisoners.

Next day, those officers called on me to interpret for them, and asked me if I would see Colonel Doniphan and request him to liberate them. I did so, but the colonel objected. He gave me orders, however, to go to the Bull Pen and turn out the Mexican soldiers, and read to them, in Spanish, the same law I had read to the convicts, and bring their officers down before him.

He told the officers they could stay in a room adjoining his, considering them men of honour. They could go out, and come in, but must lodge there till the four men from Durango arrived.

In about two weeks after Colonel Doniphan's entry into Chihuahua, two of the thieves he had let out of prison, stole some blankets from one of his soldiers. When the articles were found with them, they were taken at once to two ash trees near each other in the public square. The law was administered, four hundred lashes being laid on to each. One of the criminals died at the foot of the tree, and the other the second day after.

Six days after this, the artillery horses were in a clover field on the opposite side of the river Chihuahua. Nine Mexicans stole nine of the horses, and started for the mountains. Doniphan had with him eight Shawnee trackers,—among them, my old friend, Shawnee Jake. They were called on, and immediately struck the track. The second day they overtook the Mexicans, in a valley in the mountains. Eight were asleep, while the ninth watched the horses. He started to run and was shot dead by one of the Shawnees; the others were taken prisoners, put on the horses, their feet tied under the horses' bellies, by the Shawnees, who returned with them and reported the killing, the arrest, and the recovery of the horses.

Colonel Doniphan told me to ask them if they did not understand his laws. They said yes, and if he would pardon them, they would observe them. He told them they would not violate any more laws, because they had only one hour to live. A two-horse wagon was immediately brought out, and horses put before it. The prisoners were placed in the wagon, each with his hands tied behind him and a rope about his neck. The doomed Mexicans now asked leave to confess their sins to their priest. The colonel told them he had no priests in the city; they had all run away, and there was no time for such a ceremony, under the circumstances.

The wagon was then drawn to what was called the Alameda, a kind of park. A long, heavy stick of timber was securely placed in the crotch of two trees, overhead, the wagon driven under the timber, and while the culprits stood up, the ropes were firmly fastened to the timber, about two feet apart. The teamster cracked his whip, and they were left hanging in the air. There was no more stealing heard of in Chihuahua, while Colonel Doniphan remained there.

Finding that Colonel Doniphan would not allow their property to be injured, people commenced returning to the city, and brought wood, hay, grain, fresh meat, and everything desirable for the army.

I was at the Quartermaster's department, one day, when I saw the Mexican I had swapped horses with so unceremoniously on the mountain, driving up with a load of hay. As soon as he got his hay unloaded, I spoke to him.

"My friend," said I, "do you know me?"

After looking at me carefully for some time, he replied:

"No, I do not."

As I had left off my "Greaser" dress, and got on a citizen suit, this was not to be wondered at.

"Do you recollect trading horses with, a man, out here on the side of the mountain ?" I asked.

"Yes," he replied, "I recollect the trade, but you do not look like the man."

I satisfied him, by repeating the conversation, that it was me he traded with, and inquired of him how my old favourite Limber Bill was, and found that he still owned him, and that he had fully recovered. As I had become much attached to the horse, and prized him very highly as a gift from my wife, I proposed to trade again, offering him his horse and ten dollars if he would bring mine with him next time he came into town. This he did, a few days after, and was as much pleased as I was at the turn the trade had taken. I saw him several times, afterwards, and laughed and joked with him about our horse trade.

The ensuing week, my friends arrived from Durango. They were happy to see me and the other Americans. So grateful were they for my services in carrying their letter, that they made up a purse of five hundred dollars for me, begging me to accept it, offering to increase it to a thousand, if I was willing. I declined any further contribution, though I accepted a present of a splendid pair of Colt's revolvers, from Mr. James McGuffin.

Chapter 8

Return to Chihuahua

A rumour reaching us from central Mexico, that a large body of troops were coming against Colonel Doniphan, to drive him and his force out of the country, the colonel called on Gabe Allen and me, knowing us to be acquainted with the language and ways of the Mexicans, to go as spies, and find out the truth of the report. We consented, and went about two hundred and fifty miles below Chihuahua, travelling chiefly by night, and away from the roads.

We learned some facts of importance, from friendly sources, and as we were about to return, we met an American travelling on the road with a train of wagons, who appeared to be posted up on war matters, who said that no troops had been organized, as yet, to operate against Colonel Doniphan, but that the country around there, especially the States of Durango and Zacatecas, had been drained of all the able-bodied Mexicans, to recruit General Santa Anna's army, which was being badly whipped and demoralized by General Taylor's army. We returned cautiously and safely to Chihuahua, and reported accordingly, to Colonel Doniphan.

Soon after, the colonel decided to send an express to General Taylor, and detailed twelve of his best men, under the lead of Sergeant James Collins, for that purpose. They started across the country, with a friendly Mexican guide, travelling nights, with orders to reach General Taylor's head-quarters as soon as possible.

The day after their departure, Colonel Doniphan told me he had important dispatches which he wished taken to Governor Bent, at Santa Fe, and asked if I would undertake the task of getting through with them. I consented, on condition that he furnished me a picked saddle mule, and two of his Shawnees, who should be similarly mounted, and a pack mule loaded with provisions; for I did not dare to go near any Mexican settlement on the way up. These arrangements suited, and all was in readiness by dark that evening. We started off well armed and in good spirits, and had no trouble on the journey, as we avoided public roads, and travelled nights only. We made the best time on record between the two cities, reaching Santa Fe in nine days.

Governor Bent gave us a cordial reception, remembering me well, from our long acquaintance, years before, at Bent's Fort, and elsewhere. He said that the dispatches were very important, and required an answer, which we must take back to Doniphan; and I told him I was ready to return after laying over a day or two, for rest and to recruit our animals. He further stated that Price's regiment was on its way to Santa Fe, from Missouri, and would be there in about a week.

During my interviews with him, I noticed that he was unusually gay and cheerful, telling me many funny stories about his recent experience in his new character of governor over that semi-civilized community. After giving me dispatches to take back to Colonel Doniphan, he told me he had received an invitation to attend a Mexican feast, at a little town some twenty-five miles east of Santa Fe, at the foot of the mountains; and as it was the birth-place of his wife, who was a Mexican woman, he had about concluded to attend, as it would make him more popular among the Mexicans

I had doubts about the expediency of his going, knowing the treachery of the natives, but left him, simply cautioning him to be on the lookout for danger. I had no particular fear for his personal safety, but that the garrison would be surprised during his absence.

I soon returned to Chihuahua, accomplishing the distance in

eleven days, carrying the dispatches to Colonel Doniphan, and making my report. The colonel complimented me for my speed and trustworthiness, remarking that we had made extraordinary time. The usual time of mule trains over the road was eighteen or twenty days.

The eighth day after my return, a courier from Santa Fe came into Colonel Doniphan's head-quarters, with the news that Governor Bent had been assassinated at the Mexican feast before referred to, by the treacherous Greasers. About the time of the assassination, Price reached Santa Fe with his regiment. He was so enraged that he at once executed nearly four hundred Mexicans, by way of retaliation for the murder of Governor Bent, and reported the facts to Colonel Doniphan, who sent back orders that he (Price) should assume the Governorship now vacant.

About the time of Bent's assassination, Colonel Doniphan sent for me, and wished me to take dispatches to Fremont, which had reached him, to be forwarded, from the lower part of Mexico. Fremont was at this time on his exploring tour in California, in which he had difficulty with Governor Castro.

I left camp alone, for this trip of four hundred miles, mounted on my Comanche horse, Limber Bill, and leading a pack mule, carrying my provisions and a very few cooking utensils. As I had been through this part of the country before, and knew the habits of the Indians who ranged over it, I managed to avoid them till I had nearly reached my destination. To do this, required the greatest caution. Towards night, I would build a fire and cook what meat I needed for my supper and to last me till the next night, make a cup of coffee, and eat my supper, while my animals were feeding; then I would mount my horse and ride several miles before stopping for the night, for fear the smoke of my fire might have been seen, and would bring hostile Indians upon me. I sometimes made a little fire, enough to boil coffee, in the morning, taking great care to make but little smoke.

Although I saw a great many signs of Indians, some of them very fresh, I had no trouble until the ninth day out; when, as I was leading up my pack mule, preparing to resume my journey, I was fired on by a party of four Navajo Indians, one shot striking my mule in the neck, killing him instantly. I saw that my only chance was in a running fight, and so put my horse to a gallop, abandoning my provisions, blankets, and cooking utensils.

The Indians followed some three or four miles, exchanging shots with me frequently. Fortunately, I received no injury, but succeeded in hitting two of my pursuers, one of whom I saw fall from his horse. Finally they left me and returned; probably to look after their prize,—the mule and his pack. Two days after this fight, I came up with Fremont, having eaten nothing in the meantime, but two rabbits I had shot and roasted.

On my presenting the dispatches to Fremont, he remarked that I must have had a dangerous and lonely trip to reach him, and asked me if I thought I could make my way back in safety. I replied that I thought I could, by taking a different route. During my stay in camp, he showed me every attention, and did all he could to make my stay pleasant.

Here I met my old friend, Kit Carson, who was acting as guide to Fremont. As I had not seen him for about four years, as may be imagined, we had a great many adventures to relate to each other.

The fourth day after my arrival, Fremont gave me the reply to the dispatches; fitted me out with another mule, and provisions, blankets, &c, and I started on my return Chihuahua, where I arrived without any particular adventure, after an absence of about four weeks, thoroughly jaded and worn out.

In a very short time after my return from Fremont, Sergeant James Collins and his squad returned from General Taylor's camp, bringing orders for Colonel Doniphan to march forthwith to Saltillo.

As soon as he could regulate his affairs in Chihuahua, and get into marching order (which only delayed three days), the little army was on the move to join General Taylor.

I was appointed interpreter for the Quartermaster's department, doing general service with Lieutenant Lee, the quartermaster; and it was my duty to provide, somewhat, for the regiment, going in advance with a strong guard, for foraging purposes, &c. My friend, Gabe Allen, had an easier berth; his duty being to act as interpreter for Colonel Doniphan, and assist him in his business dealings with the Mexicans on the route.

Colonel Doniphan, before we left the city, requested me to hire four Mexicans to assist in taking care of the artillery mules. I engaged four of the most honest-looking chaps I could find, but they turned out rascals. We had been on the march only three days, when these Mexicans stole eight of the best mules we had, and started back for Chihuahua. I was ordered to take six Shawnees, and go in pursuit.

After a fifteen mile chase, we lost the track; but the leading Shawnee going back a short distance, found where they had turned off the road into a thick forest, and we pursued them about three miles further, when we overtook the rogues. Two of them we shot; and the other two begged for their lives, which request we granted just long enough to get our rawhide ropes ready to hang them to the trees.

One of them resisted when he saw our preparations, whereupon a Shawnee pulled out his knife, and stabbed him, killing him instantly. The other met his fate very meekly, and we left him hanging to the tree. After securing the stolen mules, we hastened back to the army as rapidly as possible. We met them at a pass in the chain of mountains, where they had halted for dinner. I reported to Colonel Doniphan that we had got all the mules back, and he inquired what had become of the runaway Mexicans. I replied that that we left three on the ground where they wouldn't steal any more mules; the fourth we had elevated on a tree to keep guard over his comrades. The report was entirely satisfactory to him.

While I was lunching with the colonel, he remarked that one of his best men, Captain Reid, who had been wounded in the thigh by a copper ball, at the battle of Sacramento, was rapidly failing in health, and he feared he would die. The poison of the copper had been checked, at the hospital in Chihuahua, though the ball could not be found, and moving him in the ambulance was causing inflammation which the surgeons pronounced dangerous; but we dared not leave him on our march, neither would he be left with the Mexicans, fearing hard usage. He also said that his advance guard had reported that they had seen tracks of horsemen, and he feared guerrilla bands might give us some trouble. He requested that as soon as my dinner was finished I would select some of the best Shawnee trackers, and go ahead, examine the signs closely, and report.

With eight Shawnee Indians I started on,—the regiment following slowly,—and we discovered tracks of a number of mounted men, probably guerrillas; but our Shawnees, who were expert on the trail, said they were three or four days old, and there was no danger at present.

Travelling on till sunset, we came to a large Mexican stock *ranche*. As soon as the Mexicans saw us coming, they started to run. I called to them in Spanish, to come back, as there was no danger. Stopping them, I rode up and asked for the owner of the *ranche*. They pointed to a large *hacienda*, or country seat, a mile ahead, where they said lived the owner, a rich Castilian Mexican. Going up to this mansion, with my Shawnees, I found the gentleman badly frightened. I told him I wanted five beef cattle killed, and should need a hundred bushels of corn for our army in the rear, offering to pay for such supplies as we needed. He said: "With a great deal of pleasure; anything you want, you can have."

He asked if I was a Mexican. I answered that I was an American, but from my long experience among Mexicans, I spoke Spanish as well as English; or if I was among Indians, I could speak five of their languages. I was soon in an easy conversation with him, when he learned, in answer to an inquiry, that Colonel Doniphan was in command of the regiment which was just then coming in sight. He said he had heard of his defeating five times his own number at Sacramento, and expressed great admiration of his military ability.

He then requested me to assure Colonel Doniphan of his personal regards, and say that the beef and corn should be furnished at once; and to invite him and his staff to spend the night at his house. I thanked him, and gladly rode back with the message, reporting to Colonel Doniphan that I had provided everything necessary for the troops, and had an invitation from the Mexican for himself and staff to stay at his house, and partake of his hospitality. Also reported that all was quiet in the neighbourhood, the old Mexican having assured me that all the able-bodied men about there had gone to join Santa Anna's army.

The colonel and I, with several officers, rode forward to the mansion, the proprietor coming forward to greet us with a hearty welcome. He had the beeves killed immediately, and the corn put out in the yard, where it was handy to use as wanted. The colonel asked if he could furnish a room for a sick officer, and he said: "Certainly; with pleasure, Colonel."

Captain Reid was carried into a room, and placed on a comfortable bed. He appeared to be sinking rapidly.

The regiment encamped near the house, the meat was distributed to them, and the corn issued; in fact, everything furnished that was necessary. The gentlemanly Castilian tapped a keg of first-class wine, and invited the colonel and all the officers to take supper with him. The invitation was accepted; and all the officers who were not on duty, were called in about ten o' clock. The supper was splendid, and the wine flowed freely. Colonel Doniphan sat at the head of the table, with his officers around it, and the Castilian and his lady insisted on the privilege of waiting on them.

We had a fine drum corps with us, and while we were eating, they played several of our national airs, which was the first time the host and his lady had ever heard such pieces as "The Star Spangled Banner," "Yankee Doodle," "Red, White, and Blue," and the like. He was so pleased, that after we were through, the band was invited in and treated to a plenty of wine.

After supper, comfortable beds were provided for the officers, and Captain Reid was the recipient of every attention, Doctor Waldo and three soldiers staying in his room all night.

We all had a comfortable night's rest. We had arranged to start the regiment the next morning at eight o'clock. Just before starting, Colonel Doniphan sent me to our host, to ask for the amount of our bill, and directed the quartermaster to pay whatever was agreed upon. Upon asking the Castilian his price, he was surprised, and said: "Nothing at all."

Colonel Doniphan, on hearing this, rode up, and said: "Sir, this is not the way I do my business; I always pay my way."

"Well," replied the Castilian, "that's more than the Mexican troops have ever done. They have been here often, but they took what they wanted, and never said anything about pay."

It was soon arranged that we should pay only a low price, *viz.*: seven dollars a head for the beeves, and fifty cents a bushel for the corn; which prices he was well pleased with. On parting, he thanked Colonel Doniphan for the pleasure of his company, and remarked that he should prefer the American government, to the miserable rule of the Mexican, but he was placed in a delicate position, with his extensive property, that compelled him to keep still. Captain Reid was then placed in an ambulance, and the troops resumed the march.

We had twenty-four miles to travel that day, without water. Captain Jackson, with a mounted guard, was ordered to go in advance, with me and the Shawnees, to provide for the regiment, and if any roving bands of Mexicans were seen, to report to the colonel. We reached Mapimi, a lead-mining village about three o'clock. The Mexicans were much alarmed when they saw us approaching. I let them know that there was no danger, and inquired for the judge of the village. I found him at last, the biggest, blackest, ugliest Mexican I ever looked at. I told him I wanted five beeves, and a hundred bushels of corn. He said he had no such property, but I told him his friends had, and he must furnish them, as they would be paid for. He sent out among the villagers immediately, and ordered the beeves and corn to be furnished.

We went to a cottonwood grove nearby, where there was a stream of water, and selected a good camping ground for the regiment, and then going back to Colonel Doniphan, I reported that everything necessary was provided. This was good news to him, as some of the troops were nearly exhausted, and Captain Reid was failing rapidly.

We arrived at the camping ground at half past four o' clock, and Captain Reid died at sunset. The weather was hot, and mortification had caused his death.

We laid over here the next day, for rest, and to bury the captain with military honours, for he was universally respected as a splendid officer and a brave man. The Mexicans who witnessed the burial scene were favourably impressed, as they saw the soldiers of the burial squad, after each had put a handful of dirt in the grave, fire a salute over it.

Next morning, after settling our bill for the supplies that were furnished us by the citizens, we resumed our march, arriving towards evening on the bank of a river, where we encamped. The next day we crossed the river, and proceeded to the cottonwoods of Parras, or Alamo de Parras, where were some salt works. Here we were informed that we had for our next day's march, a long distance without water. I started before daybreak, with Captain Jackson, Gabe Allen, and a squad of eighteen mounted troops, who had been detailed to accompany us, to a place where the Mexicans had a famous well, with a huge trough, eighty yards long, and holding water enough for an entire train.

The water was raised by a Mexican reel, or a wheel with leathern buckets attached to it, and worked by a mule. Here we were to make preparations for the regiment to camp that night. On arriving at this place, we found one principal residence and a number of shanties. Surrounding the large house was a wall, ten feet high, pierced with port holes, for defence against the Indians. The wall was built of adobes (sun-dried brick, about eighteen inches long, six inches wide, and three or four inches thick), and was about a hundred yards square.

We went within the walls, and gave orders for beef and corn to be brought, and water to be drawn, which the owner said would be accomplished as soon as possible. We arrived there about eleven o'clock in the morning, expecting the regiment at evening.

While I was receiving corn, which was being poured out on rawhides, inside the walls, Gabe Allen and all the soldiers (except one who stood guard over the arms and equipments of the escort) laid down for a short sleep, as the sun was uncommonly hot, and our men were tired, as we had travelled nearly thirty miles that morning.

I was busily engaged, measuring the corn, when a little Mexican boy, the son of the woman who lived within the walls, came running in, crying:

"Oh, mother! the Indians are here !"

"What Indians ?" I asked.

The mother and son were frightened; but I went to the gate, and looking out, saw about eighty of the "Hickories" tribe of Indians, with some four hundred horses and mules, at the watering place. One of the savages was whipping the man who had charge of the mule at the reel, to make him work faster, as they were thirsty, and had travelled a long distance without water.

It was a very hot day, and to secure shelter, a stray ox had gone into a deserted grass shanty, near the watering place. For sport, the Indians had shut the door, and set the shanty on fire, and the poor beast was being roasted alive, making a terrific noise. I ran and shook Gabe Allen, and told him the watering place outside was surrounded by a host of Indians and animals. He partially waked, and asked, "Mexican guerrillas?"

"No," said I, "Indians!"

Captain Jackson, who was busy seeing to the dinner, which was preparing for us, immediately called up his troops, and running to a porthole, looked out, and saw what the Indians were about.

"Hobbs," said he, turning towards me, "you and Gabe Allen are older Indian lighters than I am. How had we better light them, on horseback or afoot?"

We said on horseback so we could capture their stock.

Fortunately our horses were inside the walls, and we were

soon in the saddle. By this time, four Mexican stock-herders and men-of-all-work, who had gone after beeves for Doniphan's regiment, came galloping into the inclosure, badly frightened, one of them with an arrow sticking in his back. It had penetrated two or three inches, and was extracted without much injury. The Indians had driven them in, and taken from them the stock they were driving up for us.

We asked these Mexicans if they would take part in the light, to get their stock back, and help us capture the horses and mules of the Indians, telling them we would do the heavy part of the fighting. They agreed to our proposition, and the Mexican owner of the *ranche* saddling his mule, we mustered a force of twenty-six men. We ran our horses out of the gate, yelling and firing on the Indians, who, having no idea of our presence, were taken by surprise. Some were at the trough, crowded among their animals, in their eagerness to get water, with their guns, bows and arrows resting against a fence.

Many did not have time to get hold of their arms. We killed six at the trough, and the rest fled to the top of a rising piece of ground nearby. They had killed one Mexican at the trough, and had captured two or three Mexican boys and girls. These children had sense enough to run inside the walls as soon as the firing commenced. The boys, however, with the aid of the Mexicans and several of our mounted soldiers, drove nearly all the stock of the Indians inside the walls and shut the gate.

The Indian chiefs hardly ever dismount at short stoppages; consequently their chief was able to get ahead of his scattered warriors, most of whom were now on foot and unarmed. He rallied them on the hill and formed them in position for defence; but, knowing their helpless condition, we charged directly through them, killing a dozen or more. Captain Jackson received an arrow in his upper lip, which penetrated between two teeth. An arrow also stuck in the collar-bone of one of our guard, Michael McLaughlin. He jerked it out, exclaiming:

"Be Jasus! quit sticking your broom straws into me."

Gabe Allen's horse was badly wounded. The Indians cried

out, "Americans!" and running into a hollow about three hundred yards distant, hid among the brush, and prepared to defend themselves. The chief was on a hill a little way from his men shouting his orders to them. Gabe Allen and I ran in between him and his warriors and cut him off. He tried to escape on his horse, but I gave chase and he, turning in his saddle, discharged several arrows at me.

When I got near enough I shot him in the thigh. He turned his horse to rush past me and connect with his men, when Allen shot him through the breast. He fell from his horse, and, turning on his back as I came riding up, discharged an arrow which struck my favourite horse, Limber Bill, and I felt him sinking under me. He was wounded fatally, the arrow penetrating the stomach, and I sorrowfully abandoned him. I sprang for the Indian's horse, which was an excellent one, while Allen finished the fallen chieftain with a shot through the head from his revolver.

Our men by this time gathered around us, and one of the Mexicans dragged up an Indian whom he had lassoed; and, mounted on my new horse, I led the party back to the watering-place, the Mexican dragging the Indian through thorny brush over rough ground full three hundred yards to the door of the wall. There he stopped, thinking, of course, the Indian was dead; but the latter jumped up, and would have got loose, if he had not been struck down by one of the Mexicans. A few paces back was found the Indian's sheath-knife, which he had probably pulled out to cut the lasso which was dragging him; but the rough, jolting motion, peculiar to that mode of travelling, knocked it out of his hand.

We found, after scattering the Indians, that we had killed eighteen, besides the one we lassoed and killed, and at the *ranche* we found two prisoners that we had saved from their clutches. One was the wife of a Mexican lawyer; the other the son of a Castilian, living four miles south of Parras,—a very wealthy man named Manuel Evarro, who had loaned General Wool one hundred thousand dollars to aid in the prosecution of the war

Combat with Indian Chief

against his adopted country.

The unfortunate lady, who was firmly tied to her horse, was overjoyed at her rescue. The Indians had tried to run her off, when they retreated, and, failing in this, had attempted to shoot her, one arrow having pierced her clothing. She stated that she and her husband, while travelling in a carriage the day before, had been attacked by these Indians, and her husband and two servants accompanying them were killed and she taken captive. She was suffering terribly from the inhuman treatment she had received. She was young, good looking, the daughter of a rich Saltillo merchant, and had been married only a month. She was kindly cared for by the lady of the *ranche* and next day taken to Parras.

The Mexicans gathered the bodies of the slain Indians, from the different parts of the field, and laid them in a row, by the wall of the *ranche*. The chief we had killed wore a beautiful cap, made of hawk's feathers, turkey tails, red bird's feathers, and some purple feathers from a crane belonging to that country. Two horns from a buffalo-calf pointed up from the sides of the cap. His bow and arrows were well made, the latter being in a quiver made of a panther's skin, with a long tail hanging. The cap, bow and arrows, hunting-shirt, and moccasins belonging to the chief, I secured, and presented them on his arrival to Colonel Doniphan, who forwarded them to Washington, where they are still preserved.

This Indian chief's horse, which I appropriated to my own use, was pure white, with a tail that reached to the ground, and a long mane; and, in substituting him for my faithful Limber Bill, I had the consolation of knowing that he was a showy animal. We learned from the Castilian boy that he was out that morning with a servant driving a lot of horses and mules to water, when they were surprised, the Mexican killed, and he captured with all the stock. They had brought him twenty-five miles.

While we were conversing with the boy, about twenty-five or thirty Mexicans came galloping towards us, and the boy exclaimed, "There is my father," as he ran to meet him. When the father saw him he sprang from his horse, gathered him in his arms, and shed tears of joy. The father had been educated in New York, and spoke English fluently.

We told him we had captured nearly all the animals brought there by the Indians; and, from what his son had said, he must be the rightful owner of many of them, and told him where to find them within the inclosure. He said the animals were of very small consequence to him, in comparison with his child. However, we insisted, and he selected his own, and sent them home by his men, expressing his gratitude to us for our services. He and his son remained to see the regiment when it should arrive.

The Mexicans then went to butchering stock, to be in readiness for the regiment when it should arrive. Toward evening the troops came in sight, and were all pleased to find the water drawn, the beeves killed, and the corn ready for the animals. Colonel Doniphan and his officers, when they approached the *ranche*, and saw the corpses of the Indians laid along by the wall, were astonished beyond measure, and wanted to know the whole story, which was soon told; and the colonel declared that such success in Indian righting was remarkable, and complimented us on our bravery.

Every man in the regiment filed past the Indians, gazing at the dead savages with pleased countenances. The colonel, usually very serious, had to laugh when Michael McLaughlin observed, "Sarved um right, colonel; see what one of the miserable bastes did to me," pointing to the wound made by the arrow in his shoulder.

Soon after the regiment arrived, we introduced Don Manuel Evarro and his son to the colonel and officers. The wealthy Mexican begged the privilege of arranging the dead bodies in a heap and burning them, which was granted. That evening Colonel Doniphan had a long conversation with Don Manuel Evarro, who told him he was well acquainted with Generals Wool and Taylor, who had stayed at his house sometime when they marched through his section by way of Monclova.

Next morning Mr. Evarro requested Colonel Doniphan to march his troops to his place, on the road to Saltillo, where the army would be provided with everything comfortable. This arrangement suited the colonel, and the troops were put in motion. The Mexican lady we had rescued was put into Major Clark's carriage and conveyed to Mr. Evarro's place, where his wife could make her comfortable. On the march Mr. Evarro and son, with myself, went ahead with an advance-guard, arriving at Mr. Evarro's place about 2 o'clock. We hurried forward, on account of his anxiety to relieve his wife of her great trouble on her son's account. Her joy at seeing her husband and son returning safe was very affecting.

Mrs. Evarro was an American lady, whom her husband had married in New York. Immediately a splendid dinner was prepared for the officers, with all manner of fruits and wines. Mr. Evarro, upon arriving, ordered beeves and hogs to be killed, wood prepared for cooking, and everything necessary to be got ready for the troops, who arrived about 4 o' clock.

Upon the colonel's arrival, he found a handsomely furnished room fitted up for his occupancy, and rooms prepared for all the officers who could occupy them. We were entertained with a late but sumptuous dinner, after which we passed a very pleasant evening.

The mansion and its surroundings were very fine: there was a large vineyard, which furnished a stock of wines and brandies; a fine orchard of orange-trees and bananas, and many other tropical fruits; also a thou-sand acres in cultivation, besides an extensive stock-*ranche*. There was a village adjoining the place, of some five hundred people, most of whom were tenants and in the employ of Mr. Evarro. Our host insisted on Colonel Doniphan's laying over the next day, as the animals and men were nearly worn out on the march, owing to the heat and scarcity of water in that country. The colonel gladly consented.

About 10 o'clock, after the officers had all partaken of a hearty breakfast and been furnished with the choicest wines and cigars, the whole party were in fine spirits, and Mr. Evarro asked the privilege of treating the whole regiment, and the request was granted by Colonel Doniphan with great pleasure. In front of the mansion was a grove of ash-trees. Out in the shade of these were rolled four barrels of liquors, being old wines and grape brandies. Mr. Evarro informed Colonel Doniphan that there was no danger of any surprise from the Mexicans, as all who lived about there were quiet, or inclined to favour the American cause.

So the whole regiment went in for a good time. The barrels were placed on their ends, the heads knocked in, and a supply of glasses and cups set out for the regiment, when they were marched up by companies and drank freely. I had got wine enough in the house, but drank a swallow, out of compliment to our host; then climbing into the forks of one of the shade trees, I was amusing myself by getting a bird's-eye view of the festive scene beneath me, as file after file and company after company marched to the barrels, drank their fill, smacked their lips, drank again, and then went off to lie down in the shade of the beautiful grove, thus making room for their comrades.

The Mexicans had driven some of Mr. Evarro's cattle into a corral nearby, in order to take from it such beeves as they needed to kill for the regiment. Among them was a very wild vicious cow, which, for safety, had the ends of her horns sawed off. As they commenced butchering near the corral, lassoing and hauling out beast after beast, this cow, smelling the blood, became furious, and, jumping the fence, made with all speed straight for our drinking crowd.

There was a big Irishman named Johnny Murphy standing near one of the barrels of liquor with his back to the cow, and holding up a glass of liquor. He had just commenced a toast to the health of our good friend and host, Mr. Evarro, when the cow caught him between the legs on the stumps of her horns, tossed him up, and he descended head foremost into the barrel of brandy, which was about half full. She then butted the barrel over, with Mr. Murphy's limbs sticking up out of it, which was fortunate for him, otherwise he would have strangled. The troops around, though they laughed heartily, did not like the spilling of so much good liquor, and, drawing their revolvers, riddled her with balls, killing her at once.

Pulling the frightened Murphy out of the barrel, it was some time before he recovered his breath, when he exclaimed: "By the holy St. Patrick! it's the biggest drink of liquor I ever had in my life !" The poor fellow was more scared than hurt, and he didn't hear the last of that cow till his term of service expired and he was out of Mexico.

We remained at this place till the next morning, enjoying ourselves finely, when we resumed our march for Saltillo. We left the rescued lady with Mrs. Evarro, as she was acquainted with her family in Saltillo, and would send her there as soon as she should be able to travel.

Two days after leaving Mr. Evarro's we arrived at Buena Vista (Good Sight), a plain between the mountains, with only two or three houses in sight, and distant from Saltillo three or four miles. It had deep gulches in places, but there was neither brush, shrubbery, or rocks. Here we laid over a day, awaiting further orders.

General Wool, who was quartered on the Mexicans in Saltillo with about fifteen hundred troops, came out with his staff to see Colonel Doniphan. The troops were ordered in line to receive the general. It was an odd-looking line, for no two were dressed alike. Most of them were in buckskin hunting-shirts and trowsers, and many had their trowsers' legs torn. Some were mounted on donkeys, some on mustang ponies, and others on mules.

One officer on Colonel Doniphan's staff had on the cap ornamented with feathers and horns taken from the Indian chief. Colonel Doniphan had the left sleeve nearly torn off his coat. The drill of the regiment compared very favourably with its uniform—as they had not the least idea of precision in any of their movements, or of the silence which is expected of regular troops.

The general and staff were dressed handsomely. He pulled his feather-adorned chapeau over his eyes, and turned away his

A HORN TOO MUCH

head, smiling. Then a salute to the general was fired by the flying artillery, which was managed with mules. The general pronounced the troops the healthiest looking men he had seen in all Mexico. He and his staff dismounted and went to Colonel Doniphan's tent to partake of some refreshments.

While in the colonel's tent, the general was startled by a loud report in the rear of the tent. He started to his feet, and inquired of the colonel what that could be, and was much surprised when he replied that he thought it must be some of the boys' foolery. That kind of "foolery" in camp was something new to the general.

It appeared, on inquiry, that a box of ball cartridges, for the artillery, had been wet and the powder caked hard, so that they were considered useless. These had been taken from the wagon and thrown in a pile in the rear of the tent, and nearby a soldier, called "Dutch John," was cooking his dinner. He threw a shovelful of live coals on to the cartridges "just to see if they would go," as he said. He found out.

After dinner, the volunteers gathered around to see General Wool, talking very freely with the colonel, some of them calling him "colonel," some "Doniphan" simply, while others, to abbreviate it, called him "Bill." One of them looking straight at General Wool said:

"Old man, I hearn you had a purty d—d tight fight down yander somewhere."

The general's adjutant standing by, said:

"Please address him as 'General;' that is his title."

"Wal," said the man, looking up undauntedly at the adjutant, "he is an old man. I reckon he can't deny that."

I never saw such a set of men. There was nothing on the face of the earth, or in the depths below, that they wouldn't fight. Colonel Doniphan thought a great deal of them, chatting familiarly with them very often. At the battle of Sacramento his battle cry was, *Now, boys, every man for his turkey*! They understood that, and went every man independently, and the result was the Mexicans were soon routed.

Colonel Doniphan was a lawyer, from Clay County, Missouri. He was very tall, handsome, and well-made, with a rather dark complexion, black hair and black eyes, and always shaved clean.

General Wool ordered Colonel Doniphan to turn in all his cannon, arms, ammunition, and commissary stores to General Taylor, on our arrival at Monterey. He then took Colonel Doniphan, myself, and a number of officers to the battle-ground of Buena Vista, in which General Taylor had defeated Santa Anna over three months before. There were some skeletons of Mexicans and of animals which had dried up on the battlefield. He showed us where the Indiana Posey County men had run, and the position they occupied when Jeff Davis reformed them and got them back to fighting.

General Wool also showed us where General Taylor stood at the time of the battle, and where he shook hands with Jeff Davis, telling him he now considered him worthy of his daughter with whom he had eloped, this being the first acknowledgment of the son-in-law by the father. General Wool also told us that General Taylor's adjutant had twice reported, after riding down the whole length of the line, that our troops were whipped. "I know it" General Taylor had replied; "but the volunteers don't know it. Let them alone, and see what they will do."

The general and staff then left for Saltillo, and we returned to our camp.

CHAPTER 9

The Regiment Starts for Home

The day following our visit to the battle-field, we marched to Saltillo, where we remained two days, after which we went on to Monterey, about thirty miles distant, starting early in the morning and arriving there late in the evening of the same day. General Taylor was encamped about a mile and a half east of Monterey.

Colonel Doniphan called on me that night to come to his tent. He showed me a list of everything to be turned over to General Taylor. The list embraced artillery, wagons, commissary stores, mules, equipments, &c. He requested me to go and carry a letter to the general, that he might be prepared to receive everything on our arrival. I started next morning for the general's head-quarters, and found a lot of teamsters hitching up some wagons.

Noticing a white-haired, short, thick set, common looking man, without uniform, except a military cap, riding a fine gray horse about among the wagons, whom I took for a wagon-master, I asked him if he could tell me where General Taylor's tent was. He said it was just around a point of the woods, and I started for it. He rode directly after me, inquiring if I had business with the general. I replied that I had a letter for him. He looked at my buckskin hunting-shirt, and with a good-natured twinkle in his eye, said:

"I suppose you belong to the buckskin regiment of Colonel Doniphan."

CITADEL AND TOWN OF MONTEREY

BATTLE OF BUENA VISTA

I told him I did, and he said he was the man I was looking for. On arriving at his tent, he said to his *mulatto* man, "Jeff, get out the bottle of brandy, and fry some ham and eggs. This fellow looks dry and dusty, and has come a long ways." The general sat down, and, pulling out my papers, I gave him a list of the things to be turned over to him, and a letter from Colonel Doniphan. He looked at them, and then, calling his orderly, sent for the quartermaster, captain of artillery, and a wagon-master, and gave them orders to receive what Colonel Doniphan was bringing to turn over to them, and stated that the colonel would be there shortly. Having received these orders the officers retired.

After breakfasting with the general, we mounted, and started to meet the colonel and our train, which was close by. I introduced the colonel, and then the general went along toward the rear of the train, looking closely at everything, especially the artillery, of which we had twenty-four pieces, eighteen of them being captured at the battle of Sacramento. The other six were flying-artillery which had been brought around from Fort Leavenworth. He said he would do all in his power to have the eighteen pieces that we captured presented by the government to our regiment. It was subsequently done, and the cannon remained in St. Louis until the opening of the great Rebellion.

Doniphan's regiment were sitting on their donkeys, mules, and horses, in the road, under the delusion that they were drawn up in line. The general passed along the line with his handkerchief to his face to hide his smiles. When he had got about halfway down the line, Dave McCoy, a big, long, awkward-looking Missourian, sitting on a donkey, cried out:

"Well, old man, what do you think of this crowd?"

This broke down the good-natured general, who was trying hard to maintain his gravity, and he burst into a hearty laugh.

"You look as though you had seen hard times," he remarked to McCoy.

"You bet" was McCoy's reply.

The general rode slowly on his return, chatting with Colonel Doniphan, and went on to where the men were turning in the military property from Doniphan, and asked them if everything had been received. They said it had, and he told them to make out an account of it so he could give a receipt. He asked Colonel Doniphan, the quartermaster, myself, and one or two others to go to his tent and partake of refreshments. There the general receipted for all that had been de-livered.

Our regiment had been enlisted for six months, and they had served three months and more over their time. We were ordered to march to Camargo, on our route homeward. We marched some twelve miles that day, arriving at a small *ranche* where we encamped. Next day, at noon, we reached Seralvo, where there was an encampment of Texan rangers. They had just come in from a fight with Mexican guerrillas, in which they had killed fifteen and captured one, and we stopped an hour, during which they took the prisoner out and shot him. He exhibited good pluck; for, after calling for a priest to whom he made confession, he put a cigar in his mouth, stood up boldly against a wall, facing with calm eyes those who shot him.

That night we stopped at Mier, near the Rio Grande. It was here that, while fighting against Mexico, when Texas was struggling for independence, some Texan rangers were captured by the Mexicans, some two hundred in number. These prisoners were taken to Mexico. On the road to Mexico some were dragged after horses till they died. The remainder, on reaching that city, were required to draw a life-and-death lottery. One bean in ten was black. He who drew this was shot, and the others were sentenced to work with ball and chain. One of the latter was with our troops.

Among these Texan rangers was a young, good-looking man, Johnny Lewis, who drew a black bean. While standing before his executioners, waiting to receive their *lire*, a handsome Castilian lady about his own age, a comparative stranger to him, stepped in front of him and offered the officers ten thousand dollars for the young man, which proposition was accepted. She took him away, and, as her parents were dead and she very wealthy, they were married and now live in the city of Mexico.

To those poor men who drew white beans and were working on the streets, this lady and other Castilian ladies sent provisions and blankets, to render them more comfortable in their lodgings in the castle of Chapultepec. This castle is partly a barracks for soldiers, and partly a city penitentiary. It was an old Spanish castle, built very strongly, with stone walls six or eight feet thick, and cells underground.

But to return to our regiment. From Mier we marched to Camargo, on the river. There was only one small boat there, and Colonel Doniphan, who was taken sick, went aboard with a few soldiers and the rest of the regiment started down the river by land for Matamoras.

About ten miles from Camargo one of our men, who strayed from the regiment a short distance, was shot down by Mexican guerrillas. The Shawnees and twenty-five or thirty men were detailed to follow the guerrillas. The dead man, named John Wells, who had a wife and four children in Missouri, was placed in a wagon and taken with the regiment. We buried him about ten miles below at Reinosa, where were stationed some two hundred of General Taylor's troops.

While engaged in burying our comrade, the Shawnees, who were keen on the trail, and whom nothing could escape, returned with the volunteers, they having followed the guerrillas through *chaparral* and thick brush and across a plain to a *ranche* where they captured nine of them. They found their horses covered with sweat, and one of the guerrillas had the rifle of the dead man.

We took the nine Mexicans for trial before Captain Cook, who had charge of this place. He was an old-fashioned soldier, having been many years in the army. He said he knew these Mexicans as they had brought beef into the United States storehouse here. He acquitted all but the man with whom the gun was found, and he was ordered under arrest. We said to Captain Cook, "All right; turn the acquitted men loose."

Not one of these men got four hundred yards from the depot. We were satisfied with the evidence against them, if Captain

Cook was not. The tracking of them up, the sweating horses, and the gun of our friend (whose death we sincerely mourned, for he was a fine fellow), was strong evidence enough. I was standing by a corner of the fence when one of the acquitted guerrillas came riding by. I shot him, Gabe Allen shot another, and the Shawnees shot the remainder.

The regiment was excited, and joined with us, when we went down to the guard-house, took out the remaining Mexican, and hung him to a tree in sight of Captain Cook. The captain ran out to defend him, when our boys told him he had better dry up; that he had struck the wrong crowd, and the best thing he could do would be to leave, or they would hang him on a tree.

We continued our march, and on the fourth day after leaving Reinosa depot, arrived at Matamoras, where we found our colonel, who had improved in health. We reported what we had done to those Mexicans. He said he had got a horrible letter from Captain Cook, calling us assassins, and giving a dreadful account of our proceedings. We explained, stating all the circumstances in full, just as they occurred, and then the colonel wrote a letter to Captain Cook, expressing his regret that the regiment had not hung him too.

We remained in Matamoras four days, and the day before leaving on our journey, Colonel Doniphan, who wanted to see the battle-ground of Resaca de la Palma, where General La Vega was captured, invited Gabe Allen, myself, and some others to accompany him. We went, and looked at the palm-tree grove from which that portion of the battle-ground derives its name. Many of the trees were cut down by cannon-balls. Thence we went to the *ranche* nearby, called Palo Alto, where the battle commenced. Colonel Doniphan sketched down a plan of the battle-field, and we returned. From the point of attack at Palo Alto, the Mexicans had retreated and fought for four miles to the place where La Vega was taken. He was a brave and talented officer, and left Mexico to reside in the United States, when the war was concluded.

On our return to Matamoras, complaint was made against a

soldier named Elijah Mann for drunkenness, worthlessness, and theft. The colonel issued an order for drumming him out of camp. He was accordingly marched out behind a drum and fife, playing "The Rogue's March," and the ceremony completed with a kick.

The next day our mules and horses were all put across the Rio Grande into Brownsville, whence the animals were to be taken through Texas and the Indian territory to Missouri, with an escort of fifty men, besides the eight Shawnees. We then started for Brazos Island, eighteen miles below, at the mouth of the Rio Grande, there to take vessels for New Orleans. Most of the regiment went down in boats. The remainder were transported in government wagons and ambulances. We arrived at Brazos Island the same afternoon. An old government boat lying there was used as a hotel, and there were a few frame houses.

The second day after our arrival, the regiment, with their arms, blankets, &c, were embarked on three schooners for New Orleans. Two of the schooners arrived at the lighthouse, at the mouth of the Mississippi, the seventh day after; the third vessel made the light the next day. We were taken in tow by a steam-tug and soon arrived at New Orleans. Our barracks, near the depot of the Lake Pontchartrain railroad, were ready for us, and we proceeded thither.

Colonel Doniphan was warmly received in New Orleans. He was placed in a carriage with ladies, and escorted to the St. Charles Hotel by the military and fire companies. The pleasing ceremony of paying off the regiment was the next thing in order. They were all paid for the entire time of over nine months they had been in service, and were allowed mileage to take them home. An invitation was received from Colonel Doniphan for the regiment to meet him the next day in a large hall for the purpose of hearing a parting speech and having a final interview together. That evening, the men, having received their pay, threw away their old buckskin suits, got washed and properly barbered up, put on new suits, appeared once more in style on the streets.

Gabe Allen, myself, and about twenty-five others went to a masquerade ball in the Third Municipality Market Hall, a large three-story building close by the depot of Lake Pontchartrain railroad. We all took our knives and pistols. The doorkeeper said we must leave them with him till the ball was over, and that we ought to wear masks, &c. We told him that was played out. We preferred to appear in our true character with our arms with us. He said it was against the law, but we replied that we had a law of our own, and as we had tickets we pushed the doorkeeper aside and went up into the hall where they were dancing.

There were a great many hackmen and cab-drivers in the hall, and what were called the "Sidney Ducks of New Orleans." About 12 o' clock there was a "row" raised by the roughs, who felt aggrieved by the marked favour with which our party was looked upon by the fair sex. During the fracas one of the cab-drivers was thrown headforemost out of the window. The hall was soon cleared of the troublesome ones, and all promised to be quiet.

Soon after, two policemen appeared and very quietly entered the hall, and immediately found themselves locked in. We told them it was impossible for them to take any of us out, or to get out themselves—so they might as well accept the situation and enjoy themselves. This they proceeded to do, and at the end of an hour were in as bad a condition as the fiddlers and most of the dancers.

The ball closed about 4 o'clock, when we left, taking the policemen with us. The next morning they were arraigned for not arresting the whole party and lined ten dollars. As we knew they did the best they could, under the circumstances, we did not wish them to suffer on our account, and so paid their fines, and they departed with a severe reprimand.

CHAPTER 10

Visit to My Uncle

It was now time for the regiment to assemble for the last time in the hall, to hear the parting words of our beloved colonel. After we had been in the hall some time, the colonel arrived, accompanied by the proprietor of the St. Charles Hotel, the Mayor of the city, other distinguished persons, and the firemen. After taking the stand, the colonel looked over the crowd, and said:

"I'm not certain whether these are my men or not. They look very differently from their yesterday's appearance; and the fact is, as I have a new coat, I am not sure that I know myself."

This sally was received with roars of laughter; but, continuing his speech, he thanked them for their valuable services, their uniform good conduct on the march, in camp, or in the fight; for no men could be braver, or more obedient. He expressed his regrets at the disbanding of the regiment, but as they had successfully accomplished their mission, it was now time for them to return to their homes and families.

Towards the conclusion of his eloquent and pathetic speech, which brought the moisture to all eyes, he took occasion to pay a high compliment to me, stating that my map of the Mexican position at Sacramento was of great value to him, and that I had been serviceable in so many ways that the government was under strong obligations to me.

At the conclusion of the speech, he stated that the next day, at ten o'clock, two government boats would leave for St. Louis and

Independence, Missouri, and lie hoped all the men would be ready to accompany him home. That evening, the theatre would be free for the entrance of himself and his regiment, by special invitation, and he hoped all would attend. After other kindly words and good advice from the mayor, and one or two distinguished citizens, the hall being filled with spectators,—many of them the first ladies of the city,—the soldiers received many hearty shakes of the hand and friendly congratulations, and an hour or two of delightful intercourse passed quickly away.

Just before the assemblage dispersed, the quartermaster stationed at New Orleans came to me and asked me to step around with him to his office, where he paid me eight hundred dollars for my services, saying he would risk getting it allowed to him. (The government afterwards allowed it to him on his pay-roll.) This was a present, and was in addition to my pay of one hundred and fifty dollars a month as interpreter and spy, or scout.

When night came the streets were illuminated, the regiment, without arms, formed in procession, with the firemen on each side, and Colonel Doniphan with the mayor and principal citizens in advance in carriages, and thus marched from the St. Charles Hotel to the St. Charles Theatre, taking a circuit around one or two squares for display. The stage was arranged for Stickney's Circus in the early part of the evening, after which it was raised, when Booth concluded the performance with Richard the Third. The whole entertainment lasted from nine o' clock till midnight. The next morning every man was at the boats.

I intended to remain at New Orleans with my uncle.

Going on board the boat on which my brother was embarking, I delivered to him the receipt given me by General Santa Anna for the property seized by the Mexican government. Colonel Doniphan told me that after a short visit among his Missouri friends, he should go to Washington, to report in full his operations in Mexico. I told him I should depend on him to get the receipt placed legally among the claims against Mexico. He promised to do so, and afterwards performed his duty, to my entire satisfaction, so that my brother drew the money, not without considerable delay, however, as Mexico was backward about paying claims of that nature.

Before leaving on the boat, Colonel Doniphan and Lieutenant Lee each gave me a flattering letter to the quartermaster-general at New Orleans, commending my services performed for the United States.

As the boats steamed away up the river, leaving me among comparative strangers, and separating me from officers and men whose society had been very agreeable and pleasant, I retraced my steps to the St. Charles Hotel with no very comfortable reflections. In my last interview with my brother on the boat, I declined to accompany him home, but instructed him to report to my friends, both my good and bad luck in Mexico, and my connection with the regiment, &c.

Having a desire to visit my uncle, whom I had not seen since my childhood, I went around to the quarter-master-general's office, left my letters, and drew out my money which I had deposited with him, amounting to twenty-five hundred dollars. He told me he should probably soon stand in need of my services if I wanted another berth. I got a carriage, and went down to my uncle, Henry Hobbs, with my money, and asked him if he would be so kind as to take care of that money for me, not letting him know who I was. He had been there many years, with a cotton press, and become wealthy in the business. He took the money and put it in the safe, and as I started to go out, he said,—"Sir, you had better take something to show that you have left this money with me.": I told him that I needed nothing. He looked at me in amazement.

After enjoying eight days of uninterrupted pleasure and excitement, I went down to my uncle's office and told him who I was. He said he thought it very singular that a stranger should come and leave that amount of money,—twenty-five hundred dollars,—and take no receipt. He told me to cut up no more pranks with him to test his honesty, or he should pay me off in my own coin. I rehearsed to him my adventures and wandering experience, and the result was that I had to stay at his house three weeks, visiting, having a splendid time, and going with the family somewhere every evening.

About this time, General Taylor arrived in New Orleans, from Mexico. The unexampled success of our raw volunteers and unpracticed regulars, in fighting the flower of the Mexican army, under the lead of Old Zack, had created a furore of excitement in this country. The day of his arrival in the city was a gala day for New Orleans. He landed in the Third Municipality, just above the market, with no accompanying troops, nor escort, except his staff. Salutes were fired as he came up the river.

When he landed, he was met by the mayor, principal citizens, and all the military and firemen of the city. A procession was formed, and he was escorted to the St. Charles Hotel. The crowd to see him was so great on the low, flat, market roof, that it fell in, impaling one man by the chin on a butcher's hook, and injuring several persons severely.

While the procession was moving, the general saw a soldier whom he had sent home with an amputated leg, standing in the crowd with his crutch. The general at once ordered the carriage stopped, and took the crippled soldier into the carnage with him, saying he was his kind of man. He afterwards took him to the hotel, and arranged for him to get a pension.

The general's negro, Jeff, was mounted on Old Zack's favourite white horse, which horse had been wounded several times. This faithful mulatto servant had been all through the Florida war, and saved General Taylor's life on one or two occasions; and, when the general died, it was found that, by his will, this servant inherited a liberal share of the property.

That night the city was brilliantly illuminated, and grand fireworks lit up the public squares. There were also two ships anchored in the river, opposite each other, that blazed all over in gaudy colours, every outline of hull, mast, and spar, glowing in fire, while the noise of mutual bombardment, and the bursting of shells in brilliant colours of flying stars, showed the semblance of war. Another fiery scene represented the words—"Live Zachary Taylor forever."

GENERAL TAYLOR

From the hotel the general and staff went to the St. Charles Theatre, accompanied by a host of friends. The performance was similar to that when Colonel Doniphan was there. Dan Rice played Clown, and during the play he asked the ringmaster if he knew why the city dandies of New Orleans were like the Mexican army. The answer was that they ran from the Taylor.

The general remained four days in New Orleans, and then started for home. The yellow fever was raging in New Orleans, and I had a slight touch of the disease. As soon as I got strong enough, I concluded to go up the river to Missouri, and see my friends and relatives. When I went to the quartermaster-general to bid him goodbye, he said he had been inquiring for me three or four days, to take charge of a vessel loaded with mules to be taken to General Worth's division, at Vera Cruz. I told him I was hardly able, but would try it.

There were ninety-five mules, and twenty-five teamsters to be taken. The day after my interview with him, I received my rations and forage, and started for the mouth of the Mississippi. I carried a letter of orders, instructing me to report, immediately on my arrival at Vera Cruz, and deliver the property under my charge, to Quartermaster Maston. In twelve hours after leaving New Orleans I was out at sea. The second day, the teamsters reported to me that they could not eat their rations of weevil bread and stinking meat. I examined the provisions and found them to be as they stated. Knowing that I had sound provisions on the vessel, I asked the steward for an explanation.

He replied: "The captain bought some damaged provisions from the government, and he is putting them on your men and saving those furnished, for himself."

I then kicked in the head of a barrel of fresh crackers, and opened a barrel each of beef, pork, and pickles, and told the steward to serve out these provisions to the men. Turning to the mate, I asked the meaning of these proceedings, and he referred me to the captain. I went to that officer and told him I wanted no more of that conduct towards my men. Sound provisions had been provided for the men, and it was my duty to see that they got them. He became very angry, and said I had better take charge of the vessel, and that he would report me at Vera Cruz. I told him to go ahead; we would see whose report would be relied upon. I ate on deck afterwards with the teamsters, and fared better than the captain.

The third day out we had a severe gale, which lasted twelve hours, with such severity that I expected it would be necessary to reduce the top-heaviness of the vessel by throwing the mules overboard. The storm abated, however, and on the eighth day after leaving the mouth of the Mississippi we arrived safely at Vera Cruz, with no damage except the severe rubbing of our mules against the stalls, caused by the rolling of the vessel.

The captain immediately lowered his boat and went ashore to report me, giving me no chance to go in the boat. I hired a boat and followed to report to the quartermaster my arrival with the men and property. When I arrived at the quartermaster's department I found the captain standing in the office reporting me! I took out my orders and requested the quartermaster to send out a steamer to bring ashore the teamsters and mules, the latter being in bad condition, owing to the rubbing and chafing caused by the storm. As far as the captain was concerned, I would attend to his case afterwards.

"Captain," said the quartermaster, "here are this man's orders; he has charge of all the water, provisions, and forage. Did he go outside of this to interfere with your vessel?"

"Yes," replied the captain, "he put on a good many airs."

"Mr. Maston," said I, "let me have the order to get my mules off the vessel, and I will come tomorrow morning, with my witnesses, and attend to the captain's case."

The quartermaster gave me the order; I saw the captain of the steamer, who brought ashore the men and mules, and by sunset the animals were all well cared for, and the men provided with quarters.

The next morning I called on the mate and steward to come around to the quartermaster's office with me, when I proved, to the satisfaction of the quarter-master, that I had done my duty.

Then said I (as Captain Smith of the vessel was present), "Mr. Maston, as the captain has gone so far, I will go further. I don't think he is capable of taking charge of a vessel, on account of his constant intoxication. If it had not been for the mate, the vessel would have been lost."

The quartermaster then told the captain he had no more use for him. If he had anything aboard, he ordered him to bring it ashore, and he directed the mate to take charge of the vessel.

The quartermaster told me that as soon as my mules got rested, I was to take them, with my teamsters, and twelve wagons, and break them to work. This was to be done on the beach, and this very comical labour I commenced on the fourth day after arriving at Vera Cruz. About the time of my arrival at Vera Cruz, General Scott, having captured Mexico and conquered a peace, was recalled to the United States, and I began to fear that my military services would soon have an end.

Chapter 11

Peace Declared

About this time, December, 1847, peace was declared between the United States and Mexico, and orders issued for the withdrawal of our forces from the country. After about two weeks patient labour, I had got my mules so they would work, and had a train of twelve wagons made up. A little incident now occurred which made an important opening for me. Captain Emory, of Mississippi, who was wagon-master for all the trains between Vera Cruz and the city of Mexico, for the divisions of Generals, Scott and Worth, had sold two wagons and two six-mule teams belonging to the United States government, and appropriated the money to his own use.

General Twiggs ascertained the facts, and sent him to the United States in irons. This left a vacancy in the office of head wagon-master. Train inspection was ordered on the beach, by General Twiggs, of five trains which were wanted to go to the city of Mexico, for the purpose of carrying provisions to all the stations on the road, and bringing to Vera Cruz, on the return trip, all the baggage and equipments of General Worth's division. My train of twelve wagons was drawn up on the beach, at the head of the other four trains. General Twiggs rode out on the beach, for inspection, in company with Quarter-master Maston.

Riding up to my train, he inquired who was the wagon-master there. I replied that I was. Said he: "Of course you have a jack-screw, and I wish you to take a wagon wheel off, to see whether your axles are greased, sir." This was soon done, and finding my wagon axle greased, and noticing that everything was in good order, he pronounced my train all right. I then rode with the general to my twelfth wagon. I told him it was my last wagon, and the rest belonged to different trains.

The train adjoining mine was made up with mustang mules, whose backs were sore from their harness not being properly fitted, and the wagon covers were torn. He ordered the wagon-master to take off a wheel, and finding the axle dry, he was very indignant. The general, who was a regular martinet, then continued his inspection till he had examined all the trains, finding none of them satisfactory; when he returned to the head of the train, where I was sitting on my horse, and said:

"Colonel Maston tells me you have letters of recommendation from Colonel Doniphan's regiment,—that buckskin crowd! I lack a head wagon-master, and I wish you to take charge of these five trains for a trip to the city of Mexico. You find a man to take charge of your train, and then report to Quartermaster Maston, who will give you your general orders."

I went, after inspection, to my camping place, and selecting one of my teamsters, named William Sharp, who had come from New Orleans with me, put him in charge of my train, and hired another man as teamster in his place, then reported the changes thus made to Colonel Maston, giving their names, &c, and told him I awaited his orders. General Twiggs, who was in the office, was very social, and asked me a great many questions about Colonel Doniphan's travels and his regiment; and, said he: "You've got a hard set of wagon-masters to deal with. They have been used to dealing with a miserable thief, whom I have sent home. In government affairs we must be very strict, and must accomplish orders at all hazards, sir."

He directed me to get everything necessary to fit up the train, from Colonel Maston, and undergo a general examination; then report to him, and he would give me an escort of fifty men, who would obey all my orders. Colonel Maston selected an officer to go with me to call a meeting of the wagon-masters, and present me to them as head wagon-master; after which I requested each wagon-master to go through his train, examine it thoroughly, and find out what was necessary to put them in condition. Some wanted wagon covers, others lacked harness, and some wanted blacksmith work.

These matters were attended to, all needful supplies furnished, and the next day we loaded up with provisions and forage, with orders to leave certain specified quantities at each station from Vera Cruz to the city of Mexico, for the use of General Worth's returning division. Then reporting to General Twiggs that I was all ready for the trip, he called an officer, directing him to take fifty men and go with my trains to see them safe through, and compel obedience to my orders from the men under my charge.

The day following we started on our way, travelling slowly, and camping at a station called Santa Fe, about twelve miles from Vera Cruz. There I left what provisions and forage were necessary, as per order. The second night we camped and left supplies at San Juan, a place belonging to General Santa Anna, where a small American force was camped. The third night, at Plan del Rio, where Santa Anna blew up a bridge to obstruct General Scott's march, thus gaining time in fortifying at the battle ground of Cerro Gordo. The fourth evening we camped at the National Bridge, and at each station left provisions and forage.

After travelling a few miles, the morning we left the National Bridge, we discovered a dismounted twenty-four pounder cannon in the road, and near it, many bones and skulls; also, fragments of clothing, &c. This was the field of Cerro Gordo; and Captain Wilson, who commanded my escort, having been in that battle, showed me the positions of the contending forces; also, where General Worth had drawn up his artillery over a rough mountain side covered with brush, and too steep for animals.

At this place a road was cut through the brush, men scaled the steep mountain a distance of a hundred and fifty yards, or more, and drew up the cannon by ropes, requiring a force of two hundred men to each piece. When daylight appeared, General Worth had flanked the Mexicans and had his cannon planted and frowning in their faces, while General Scott was upon them in the rear. Santa Anna was surprised and defeated; escaping in disguise by wearing only his drawers and shirt, while another officer, wearing a uniform, was eagerly pursued and taken prisoner under the impression that it was Santa Anna. Captain Wilson also showed me a precipice of a hundred feet, over which many of the panic-stricken Mexicans threw themselves.

The fifth night we arrived at a small station called Toluca, supplying the station; and the following evening found us at Jalapa, which is quite a city, where a force of American troops were stationed, for the security of trains between Vera Cruz and Mexico. Here, also, we left supplies. This region has a delightful climate, and is rich in coffee, oranges, and bananas.

We next camped at Perote; then at a small village where fancy Mexican spurs, saddles, bridles, and knives are made; and the night after at the city of Puebla. There we found five hundred of our men stationed, who were greatly relieved by the stores we left them. The next station to be furnished was Rio Frio, at the Sierra Madre (Mother Mountain); then Pinal Blanco, six miles from Mexico, where we left the last of our loads, and arrived, with our wagons perfectly empty, in the city of Mexico in twelve days from Vera Cruz.

After I had encamped my trains in the city, I took my letters from General Twiggs and repaired to General Worth, to report my arrival. He gave me a requisition on the quartermaster-general for all provisions, forage, &c, needed by my train, and informed me that he should not be able to close up his official business so as to leave in less than eight days.

He immediately issued an order, announcing to the authorities of the city that he should remain only a week longer, and it would be necessary for them to organize a home-guard for the preservation of good order after the United States troops had left the country; also, that if they had not arms sufficient, he would furnish a supply for that purpose. There was at once organized a force of eight hundred men, called the National Guard of the City of Mexico, to whom the general issued arms, ammunition, and everything else necessary.

General Worth's army had lost eight officers at the taking of the city of Mexico, and orders were issued to me for the removal of their bodies from the cemetery, in order that they might be embalmed, preparatory to my taking them to Vera Cruz in a wagon detailed for that purpose. This duty was attended to properly, and I afterwards saw them safely placed on board the steamer at Vera Cruz.

A few days before we left the city, the general notified the Mexican authorities of the day of his departure, inviting them to assemble their troops, and meet his on the public *plaza*, for the purpose of tiring mutual salutes on the hauling down of the American and raising of the Mexican flag. On the morning appointed, the recently organized National Guard, with a band of music, appeared on the *Plaza*, and were met by General Worth, with his army.

While the American flag was being lowered, and the Mexican raised, the bands played appropriate airs, and when the Mexican flag reached the topmast, it was saluted by the artillery of our army. The Mexicans showed their respect for the American flag by cheers and an infantry salute. This impressive ceremony was witnessed by a very large portion of the people of the city.

Immediately after the close of this ceremony, the word was given to march, and our troops, accompanied by the Mexican guard to the limits of the city, their band playing a farewell air, started for Vera Cruz, the immense crowd thronging the streets, and very many of them expressing regret at our departure, as they felt that General Worth's administration had been very favourable to poor people.

It was late in the afternoon before we got out of the city, and we only made six miles that day, stopping at the station of Pinal Blanco, the first station on the return trip.

I had a very different freight now from the provisions and

The Greaser's Mistake

forage I left Vera Cruz with, and my trains would remind one of moving day in New York. There were tents, and camp equipage of all kinds, saddles, old harness, blankets, and quartermaster stores, disabled guns, and some ammunition; also, a fair sprinkling of crippled soldiers riding on top of each load, resembling, in some respects, an omnibus overloaded with outside passengers.

The second evening after leaving Mexico, we arrived at Puebla, where we were delayed two days, breaking up the camp of our troops there, and loading their equipage, General Worth also assisting the city government in raising a military force for its protection, after our departure.

After leaving Puebla we pushed on for Vera Cruz, stopping at each station along the road which I had supplied with forage and provisions, and picking up our troops, who were rejoiced to leave the country and get away from the many diseases that were now operating like a scourge among them. Before we reached the place where I had seen the dismounted twenty-four pounder in the road, the general sent forward machinists, with proper tools, and had about a foot of the muzzle sawed off, which he placed in one of my wagons, to be forwarded to Washington as a trophy.

On the route we saw where Santa Anna had blown up a bridge to delay General Worth's division; and General Worth showed me where he threw a pontoon bridge across the creek, or river, in two hours. It was the plan of the Mexican general to retreat rapidly enough to blow up the National Bridge, but he failed to do it. This is a very large structure, built of solid masonry laid in cement, by the Spanish government, and the piers and abutments are probably one hundred feet high.

General Worth's haste in laying the pontoon bridge across the creek at Plan del Rio, enabled him to pursue the retreating Mexicans to the National Bridge, where they found holes drilled ready for blasting and destroying a section, but the Mexicans being compelled to leave suddenly, our troops crossed the bridge in safety. The day before we arrived at Vera Cruz, in the valley of Santa Fe, we met General Twiggs, with his brigade of soldiers. General Worth inquired as to the prospect of vessels to take his men home. General Twiggs replied that it was very poor, and his men were dying at Vera Cruz, from sunstroke, fevers, and other diseases. He was losing more men by sickness than he had on the battle-field. After counselling together, General Worth said that if such were the facts, he thought it best to leave the men outside of Vera Cruz, where the air was purer, until vessels could be obtained to take them home.

General Worth encamped his men in a pleasant grove in the Santa Fe valley, near a stream of pure water. All the wagons were overhauled, and such things taken out as the troops needed, after which I took the train into the city, had all the wagons unladen at the government warehouse and loaded up with provisions and forage, to return to camp, thus keeping the army supplied till they could be shipped home from Vera Cruz.

In an interview with General Twiggs, to whom I made my report, he said he was very glad I had no trouble with the wagon-masters, as he feared they had learned some bad lessons from my predecessor. He ordered me to keep my trains at Vera Cruz, but to transport all needful stores to the camp, eight miles distant, as often as necessary, and to come to him for orders if I stood in need of anything.

The day after my interview with him, General Twiggs caused a gallows to be erected on the beach, to hang a Texan Ranger who was a member of Colonel Jack Hays's regiment of six hundred men, and who had been arrested for shooting an inoffensive Mexican.

This was really a case of injustice, as I was an eyewitness of the affair, as it happened when I was in the city after forage, and I was called upon as a witness at the trial. The facts were, that as the Texan was walking on the street with a bundle of fodder under his arm, a drunken Mexican ran out from a grocery and said he would kill one Texan before they got out of the country, at the same time drawing a long knife from his legging. I shouted a warning to the Texan, who sprung to one side, threw the bundle in the Mexican's face, and drawing his six-shooter, shot him dead. General Twiggs did not like the regiment, for, as has been said, he was a martinet, and the material of this regiment was such that they did not take kindly to his strict ideas of discipline.

The gallows was prepared for the execution to take place the ensuing day at eleven o'clock. The Texan was taken out on the beach to the gallows, and walking boldly up, seated himself on the drop. The regiment of Texan Rangers rode up, surrounding the gallows, and with their pistols and carbines loaded, ordered the man to "come down off of that," which he did. He mounted the horse of a comrade, arms were given him, and then the regiment went into the city, got to drinking, and commenced tearing through the streets like madmen, inquiring for General Twiggs, and threatening him with instant death.

It was nearly dark, and Twiggs, who had no troops in the city except a small body guard, was secreted in the Custom House, which stood at the edge of the mole, near the castle, so that vessels could land at its side. The gates of the Custom House were closed, to keep out the crowd. Twiggs crawled through a window facing the sea, got into a boat, and was taken by United States marines on board the steamer *New Orleans*, which was anchored about a mile from the Custom House.

The following morning General Twiggs sent orders to Colonel Maston to send the Rangers to Texas immediately. After some delay, occasioned by the regiment demanding transportation for some of their lady friends who wished to accompany them, they were finally embarked. After they had gone, the general came on shore, feeling much relieved to find the town free from the unruly regiment.

That afternoon, four government transport steamers arrived, and the next day the general put mules, horses, and all government property under the hammer, selling it for what it would bring, and started me with my trains out to where General Worth's division were encamped, to bring in their baggage and stores. When my trains arrived and were unloaded, they were also sold at auction as they stood on the beach, with the mules in harness. Wagons brought twenty-six dollars each, mules fourteen to twenty dollars a pair, and some fair horses sold for two dollars and fifty cents each!

The men were then embarked on the steamers with all haste, on account of the deadly ravages of disease. A pontoon bridge, which cost the United States a very large amount, was abandoned and left lying in the quartermaster's department grounds, where I suppose it rotted down or was cut up for firewood. Haystacks, and much other property, were left without selling at all. Some Americans could not resist these opportunities, and staid to speculate.

The day before the troops embarked, I was paid off, and decided to stay in Mexico. I accompanied Generals Worth, Twiggs, and Kearney (who previous to this had been laid up sick at Vera Cruz) on board the vessel to see them off, and was urged by them to go to the United States, but declined, and bade them farewell, thinking I could do better in Mexico.

After continuing in Vera Cruz about a week longer, I had a desire to visit the Castle of San Juan de Ulloa, which is a prison as well as defence of the harbour, and obtained permission through a justice of the peace. He said it was customary for visitors to take a basket of provisions for the prisoners, and that was looked upon by the jailor as a sort of ticket of admission. I procured the provisions, hired a boat and went to the castle, which is built in the sea, about a mile from shore, and was cordially admitted.

There were fifty or sixty prisoners, and I was surprised to see that nearly all of them were as white as sheets. The light of the sun never penetrated with its cheerful rays into those cells. I went through the entire prison, giving a portion of my basket of provisions to each criminal. The cells run ten or fifteen feet below the level of the sea, and there are four ranges of cells, in circular form, one above another, and the lower tiers are very damp.

In high tide the sea runs within a few feet of the top of the castle. The light that struggled down through the thick glass sky-light lighted up the two uppermost tiers well enough, but the third was darker, and the lowest absolutely in pitchy darkness. In the lower tier were prisoners who were guilty of murder and other high crimes, and were confined for life, and they saw absolutely nothing, except twice a day, when the jailor, with his tallow candle, carried them their miserable rations.

These cells receive no ventilation, except by a sail-cloth and suction-pipe. The corpse-like appearance of the prisoners in the dark cells was truly frightful. There was one man there eighty-five or ninety years old, whose head was white as snow, and finger nails an inch long. The jailor said this prisoner was committed for the murder of his wife and four children. Other prisoners looked wretchedly, but this old man was the picture of misery and despair.

On coming out of the prison, I mounted the outside walls, and saw some places which appeared to have been damaged by the bombardment by our fleet, the year previous. The wall was from five to eight feet thick, and the whole protected by break-waters. I left the castle and went ashore, feeling truly thankful that I could breathe the free air of heaven and mingle with society.

CHAPTER 12

Engagement with an English Mining Company

The city of Vera Cruz is situated on a sand plain, and lies nearly on a level with the ocean. Commencing at the mole, a wall built of rock and cement fifteen or twenty feet high, extends entirely around the city to the water's edge at the opposite side, being like an immense horse-shoe in shape. A mole is built along the entire front, and at each end of it is built a strong fort, where heavy guns are mounted. The wall around the city is about three feet thick, and has portholes at intervals, for infantry to fire through.

There are only three gates, one of which opens to the northwest, being the road to Mexico. Another gate opens to the southwest, the road leading to the city of Orizaba, and the south-east gate is the entrance for all the vast trade from the country about Tabasco, from which district comes the greatest variety of tropical fruits, as well as cacao-nuts, from which chocolate is made in large quantities and shipped from Vera Cruz.

All the gates are kept locked at night, to keep contraband goods from going out or coming in, and for the city's defence. No person resides outside of the wall, which, as well as the forts at its ends, and the castle of San Juan de Ulloa, were built by old Spain. To this wall, and the filth of the city, I attribute the ill-health of Vera Cruz. The wall prevents ventilation, for no breeze ever reaches the city except in one direction, from the sea. Turkey buzzards in the streets of Vera Cruz are as tame as chickens, and any person hurting one subjects himself to a fine of ten dollars. The streets are very narrow and dirty, and the people remarkably filthy, and there is no drainage. The natives are very dark-coloured, being a mixture of a little of every kind of breed.

The dress of the ladies is rather primitive, most of them wearing a linen chemise, a silk handkerchief around the neck, a petticoat fastened at the waist, stockings and slippers, tortoise-shell combs in their hair, necklaces of pearls, and jewellery in their ears and on their lingers. The men of Vera Cruz wear such a variety of dress that there is no need of any description; but they uniformly wear a. broad-brimmed straw hat, called a "*Sombrero,*" a jacket, and loose pair of coarse trowsers.

I was soon employed again, for a wealthy merchant named James Saratusa, owning a stage line from Vera Cruz to Mexico, requested me to take a train of seventy-five wagons, loaded with goods, to the city of Mexico, which I agreed to deliver to a rich Castilian in that city, named Kitania Ruby, for the sum of seven hundred dollars. With a strong guard of mounted men I started the train for the city of Mexico, stopping at the castle of Perote, laying by there two days to rest my teams.

By permission of the authorities I examined the castle, which is strongly built of rock and cement, and protected by a double wall around it: the intervening space of twenty feet between each wall is spanned by a drawbridge, which is let down or drawn up by a windlass, this being the only means of access to the castle. Between the inner wall and the castle, which is three stories in height, there is a space of about ten feet all around. At the rear of the castle, outside the walls, stands a great wooden cross full of holes, and surrounded by men's bones. It is asserted that during the struggle of the Mexicans for independence, this was the place for the execution of Spanish prisoners. At the foot of the cross is an iron chair, very conveniently arranged for the unfortunate victim who is sentenced to die by the garrotting process, instead of by the bullet.

From Perote we went forward to Puebla, which is one of the

handsomest cities in the Mexican Republic. It is in a beautiful valley, surrounded by a thickly settled country, and in plain sight and not far to the east is the snow-capped volcano of Orizaba.

When the weather is clear there is usually thick smoke seen rising from the crater of this volcano, and the snow ever glittering on its summit is seen by the mariner out at sea long before he sees the land, though the volcano is inland some seventy miles. The great chain of mountains, running northward into Russian America, seems to start with this volcano for its base; though to the south the chain commences again after a little stretch of level country, and extends down through Guatemala and Central America.

To the south-west of Puebla is another volcano called Popocatepetl. It lies between Puebla and Mexico; and on the side towards Mexico, a large glacier extends down from which ice is easily obtained in sufficient quantities to supply those two cities. The western side, so glassy in appearance, glitters beautifully in the rays of the setting sun.

Within sight of Puebla, in the same lovely valley, is the village of the Publanos, a remnant of the ancient Aztec race. They are peaceable, industrious Indians, and have orchards and farms. They burn charcoal, make chairs, and haul wood, besides getting a good living off their farms. There are no half-breeds among them, for they will mix with no other tribes of Indians, nor with Mexicans.

Our way led over the mountains, in which is the volcano of Popocatepetl. Ascending ten miles over a rough road, and descending nearly as many on the opposite side of the mountain, we passed through heavy forests of pine, sugar-pine and fir-trees. Before Juarez time it was a harbour for thieves, who infested this forest and attacked the stages almost every time they passed. On the summit is the station of Rio Frio, called after a little stream running down among the hills, which is so cold that it is difficult to drink freely of it.

I arrived with my train and escort at the city of Mexico, and turned over to Mr. Ruby the wagons, teams, and merchandise entrusted to my charge by his partner at Vera Cruz. He wanted me to stay with him and run his trains regularly between the two cities; but I declined, telling him that money would not tempt me to go back to Vera Cruz. He paid me off, and I remained in Mexico about two months, examining the curiosities of that ancient city, and interesting myself in learning its manners and customs.

The city is almost an island, being surrounded by a lake and a canal, and entered by only four roads. At the museum, which I visited first, there were many wonderful things on exhibition. One was the "Mammoth rib," which is so large as to require four men to lift it. There was beside it a great tooth which, probably, came from the same animal, and its decayed hollow would hold a peck of corn. Standing on the ends of its four roots, it was about as high as the seat of a common chair, and a person could sit on it comfortably. The Mexican account of the finding of these bones is, that some men were digging for limestone on the further side of the lake opposite the city, and found them imbedded in the soft limestone.

I saw a stuffed serpent there, said to be from Montezuma's museum, which was six and a half yards in length, with two distinct and perfectly formed heads. The point of separation was about four inches back of the nose. In the middle it was as thick as an ordinary man's body.

In a large glass bottle were preserved a pair of Indian connected baby twins. The connection was similar to that of the Siamese twins; but the birth of these had been premature, and they were only six or eight inches long.

In the centre of the museum was the bronze statue of a horse, called the "Trioya Horse," on which was the statue of Charles the Fourth, looking through a spy-glass. It is a wonderful piece of work, and was made by some unknown artist, so long ago that there is no record of his name; still, there is a legend that he was shot for possessing supernatural powers.

The horse is shod, and one foot is raised. The bridle, the veins in the skin, the mouth and eyes, are perfect, and in size it is much larger than any common horse. In his side is a door, which, when shut, cannot be seen, but when open, a man can enter and sit inside. I went into it myself. The statue is moulded on a pedestal, and the whole work, including the pedestal, is cast in one piece. England offered thirty thousand dollars for it, and General Worth tried hard to get it to take to Washington. The Trioyas are said to be a tribe of Aborigines who were exterminated by Montezuma.

I went next to see the "Church of the Virgin Mary," three miles east of the city of Mexico, at the foot of a small mountain, and, I suppose, one of the richest churches in Mexico. The ornaments and altar decorations were elegant and costly; but what attracted my notice was a statue of the Virgin Mary, about the common size of a woman, standing on a moss-covered rock within the altar. She had a crown of gold on her head, angel's wings, a shining corona all around her, and was covered all over with gold-stars and spangles. The natives believe in an old legend which makes the origin of this angelic figure very miraculous, and the construction of the church is also considered miraculous by those deluded people.

From the church I went to look at "The Arches of Water." This is the aqueduct that supplies the city of Mexico with water from a reservoir eight miles distant. It is built of rock and cement, supported by arches and piers of the same material, and is so high above the ground in some places that a man cannot throw a stone over it. The reservoir is also built of rock and cement, and supplies the city with all the water they need. It is a very ancient work and is supposed to have been built at about the same time as the old castle of Chapultepec.

On returning to the city of Mexico, I found about one hundred Irishmen, who had deserted from the United States army and fought on the side of the Mexicans, on account of the Mexican religion being Catholic. They were part of two or three hundred Irishmen who deserted from General Scott's army on his way to Mexico, went ahead and joined the Mexicans, aiding materially in making the battle of Molino del Rey, a short

GREAT SQUARE MEXICO

distance from Mexico, almost a disastrous affair for us. This one hundred escaped, though numbers were killed and thirty taken prisoners.

Those thirty General Scott hung to the limbs of cottonwood trees as soon as General Worth planted our flag on the battlements of Chapultepec. Now, I saw before me this band of one hundred Irish deserters enlisted as a guard for the city of Mexico, under the name of the St. Patrick's guard, and commanded by an Irish soldier named Riley, who had deserted before the war commenced, and, instead of suffering death, as in time of war, had been let off with the letters, U. S., branded on one cheek.

I had heard a great deal of "Montezuma's Stone Almanac," and, having leisure, went to see it. It is a rock in the form of a cube, fifteen feet thick, lying close by the door of St. John's church. On one side more than a hundred new moons and over a hundred stars are engraved. On the opposite side are engraved lizards, snakes, toads, and different kinds of animals. On another side were ancient letters. I understand Spanish and half a dozen Indian tongues, but could make nothing of these curious signs. On the other side were cut full-sized representations of Montezuma and his wife. I could not see what was on the top for I could not get up there. Such were the contents of this celebrated Almanac.

During my stay in the city we had two shocks of earthquake. The most frightful of all scenes was presented. The waters of the lake were fearfully thrown up and agitated, overflowing the streets of the city. In many places the Mexicans gathered, and knelt, and prayed till the excitement was over. I was in a square close by the Cathedral. The bell-tower of the church was split by the earthquake, and through the opening the bell, weighing over two tons, was cast out and fell in front of the church, narrowly missing the head of a man standing in the door. This bell is supposed to be a third silver and gold, is quite large, and the ringing of its clear notes can be easily heard nine miles from the city.

I was not willing to remain unemployed for any length of

time, and was soon offered the conductorship of the same train of seventy-five wagons that I had brought through from Vera Cruz. This was in the spring of 1849. A wealthy English firm, McIntosh & Co., who owned mines in six Mexican States, had purchased the train of Ruby & Co., and desired me to go with it to Guanaxuato, about one hundred and sixty miles north-west of Mexico. That was the head-quarters of the mining company.

On my arrival there with the train, Mr. McIntosh employed me to haul his immensely rich silver ore from the mine, six miles away, to Guanaxuato, where they refined it. I made a trip with the seventy-five wagons every day, except Sundays, for four months. Besides my wagons there was a train of pack mules making daily trips. The vein of metal was an immense one—nine feet thick, and of great depth—being worked with many shafts and drifts. It had been worked since the time of Old Spanish Dominion, and is now yielding large profits.

During my stay there I had an escort of fifteen English soldiers with every day's trip, who guarded our freight with as much care as if it were pure silver. If a Mexican succeeded in stealing a hatful he got a hundred dollars. The Spanish name of this mine was the "*Luce*," (Light in English). I may here notice that this range of mountains called the Sierra Madre in Mexico, and Sierra Nevada in the United States, are, in my opinion, the richest in the world, as they abound in silver and quick-silver, as well as gold, copper, and iron occasionally.

The Mexicans employed in the mine were great thieves. There was much virgin silver found, usually in thin flakes in crevices of the rocks. Before going down into the mine, the labourers strip off all their clothes to a simple breech-cloth, and hand them to a person appointed to take charge of them. When they come out they often have strips and pieces of virgin silver worth from two to five dollars shoved under their hair, or secreted in their mouths, or hidden under their breech-cloths.

There is a great deal of mud in the mines which facilitates stealing. Upon coming out of the mine their breech-cloths are taken off and shaken, and they are then allowed to put on their clothes. There were five hundred men employed in the mine day and night. Under the law, when a man is found with metal secreted about him, he receives fifteen to twenty lashes with a cowhide on his naked back, and is sent back into the mine to work without pay for a week.

The mine is ventilated with air shafts three and a half feet square, to the number of twenty, and several of them are five hundred feet in depth. Without these shafts the air at such a distance from the surface would be impure and dangerous. An extraordinary occurrence at one of these shafts showed the extreme hazard to which a Mexican thief will expose himself.

One day a labourer was missed at roll-call by the overseer of his department. Fred Glenning, the assayer and general manager went directly to the door-keeper.

"Here's his clothes," said the door-keeper. "He never went out this way."

He must have gone out this way," was the remark of the assayer. "There is no other way, and yon must account for him."

While thus talking, some persons who had been sent out to hunt the Mexican, came up with him, naked, except a blanket around him. They also brought twenty-five pounds of virgin-silver and ore worth at least two hundred and seventy-five dollars, which they found tied up in his breech-cloth, and which he had accumulated and hidden in the mine. They found him standing by the gate with his plunder, for, as the mine is surrounded by a smooth stone wall, fifteen feet high, with sentry boxes on top, the man had no means of escape, except he slipped out with some wagon. Finding he had to go to jail, the Mexican confessed, saying:

"Don't blame the door-keeper. I'm the only one to blame. I didn't come out that way."

"How, then, did you get out?" inquired the manager.

"I will show you," replied the Mexican, taking him to a shaft over four hundred feet deep.

" Impossible," cried out the manager. "If you will go down into the mine the usual way, past the door-keeper, and then come up through this air shaft, bringing twenty-five pounds of ore, I will let you off from punishment, and give you the ore you bring up and the twenty-five pounds already brought up."

The Mexican went into the mine as directed, and after some time had elapsed, was seen working his way up, putting his toes and fingers on opposite sides of the shaft into the little indentures left in blasting, where a slip of half an inch would have been irretrievably fatal. Tied up in his breech-cloth, which hung suspended from his forehead, was about twenty-five pounds of ore. He came out safely, and the amazed manager bade him leave at once and never show his face about there again, threatening to shoot him if he did.

Another stealing trick served for a standing joke against Mr. (Helming. A very valuable specimen of silver ore was got out and handed to the manager for examination. He placed it under him, alter showing it to several gentlemen, and was busily engaged about some other matter, till a servant came along sweeping and cleaning up, and Mr. Glenning raised up and took a seat a little way off; but the thieving Mexican contrived to substitute for the specimen a different rock, of the same size, but of no value. This, when discovered, cost the poor servant a tremendous flogging.

After serving four months as wagon-master, Mr. Glenning being in want of a foreman in the blasting department, requested me to superintend it for a short time, and for two months I endeavoured to discharge that duty, though I did not like the dangerous business. It was part of my duty to measure the holes drilled by the men, which were to be eighteen inches deep.

One day, while thus employed, a Mexican labourer, who had been carelessly admitted below while drunk, was sitting down with a lot of loose powder in an open handkerchief on the ground between his legs. He began to smoke a cigarette, and dropped fire into the powder, which, in its explosion, threw him against the rocks, dashing his brains out.

A flat stone struck me in the side and knocked me close to a shaft fifty feet deep. A foot or two further and I should have lost my life. I did not consider this a healthy business and gave up my position, excusing myself on the ground of the exceeding dampness below affecting my health.

I then took charge of the wagons again. The fourth day, after renewing my trips, I was about half a mile from the mine with my teams, when the company's magazine of five hundred kegs of blasting powder, some three hundred yards from the mine, and in the edge of the town of Luce, blew up. It shattered the building over the mine, shook the hill, and down deep in the mine flung rocks upon the miners from the roofs of their drifts, killing many.

Others working in spurs at a distance from the ventilating shafts were suffocated. Altogether, eighty-five miners perished, and about sixty-five or seventy others were killed outside. The magazine was strongly built of stone and cement, but nothing remained of it except the foundation. As I felt the explosion and looked back, the smoke was bursting up like a great white cloud, in the midst of which were flying rocks. Near to me fell a human arm, probably one of the guards, as it had the cuff of a soldier's coat on it. Bottles and fragments of goods from a grocer's stand near the magazine flew past our heads. As soldiers constantly stood on guard and prohibited smoking within one hundred and fifty yards of the grounds, the cause of the explosion was and is a mystery.

After I had worked another month with my teams, I was one Sunday sitting in my room, when a Mexican came in with a beautiful piece of metallic ore, which he said he had found in a ledge and was not able to work it, but, if after looking at the specimen, I wished to work the mine, he would labour for me and sell the claim at my own price. He called again on Monday and I went with him to inspect the vein, which ran into a mountain in which there was an old Spanish mine, called the "Valenciana." This was in the edge of the city of Guanaxuato. On my showing the specimen to Fred. Glenning, said he:

"Why, that's half silver! Where did you get it?" I told him a Mexican had given it to me. He said he would assay it, and, after doing so, it proved very rich. I told him the vein was six inches wide only and very thin, but he said it was good property and I had better secure it. I immediately found the Mexican and purchased his right to the mine for twenty-five dollars, and went to the judge of the mining district and had the claim recorded in my own name.

I then hired an experienced miner and told him to put half a dozen men at work on my account. They worked on the mine some three weeks, at a cost to me of six hundred dollars, and appeared to get but little metal. One Saturday evening, after settling up, I told them to discontinue their mining as I was dissatisfied with the results of their labour. The head miner begged the privilege of working for me with the help another week at the ledge, and they kept at it day and night.

One night I was awakened about 2 o'clock by one of my Mexicans knocking at my door who wanted me to get up and examine a piece of ore they had found. He said that my head miner wanted me to send over four bottles of whisky, and come over myself if possible. I sent the whisky, then laid down my specimen on the table, and going over to the next house, called up some of my American friends, and we immediately started for my mine.

We found that they had broken into a very large "pocket" that was exceedingly rich. They had taken out over a ton of ore that was better than any I had seen in the country, and my friends congratulated me on my good fortune, pronouncing me a rich man. In the morning I requested Mr. Glenning to put somebody else in my place as I had business of my own to attend to.

The metal was a mixture of lead and silver ore, which would dissolve by a simple process, and be refined in the furnace with half the labour usually required. When the "pocket" was exhausted, as it was after a few days of labour, there was nothing left but a continuation of the old six inch vein. After refining my whole stock of ore it netted me the handsome sum of thirty thousand dollars above all expenses, including a bonus of six hundred dollars which I presented to the head miner for his words of encouragement at a dark time.

The rocky ledge proving very hard to work, as soon as the pocket was finished I made up my mind to sell out before I lost my thirty thousand dollars in blasting worthless stone. The English company had tried to buy me out, as my ledge ran in the direction of the old Spanish mine of Valenciana, and they thought it would strike that mine and prove a fortune—the Valenciana Mine had been ruined in consequence of the miners tapping water which had flooded the mine.

One afternoon I was sitting near my mine, when I was approached by Mr. Glenning, who wished to have me fix a price for my claim. After some little parley he offered me fifteen thousand dollars for the mine, and, said I, "It's your mine." I then went with him to the first judge of the mining district and made the English company a transfer in writing of the mine, the ore taken out which I had not used, and all the tools. The company paid the Mexican tax of five *per cent*, on the purchase money, and I gave them possession immediately on receipt of the fifteen thousand dollars. The company went to work at once on the mine, spending a large amount of money on it, but never realized one-half of what they paid me for it.

I now had forty-eight thousand dollars, including what I had laid up from my work, after making hand-some presents to each of my miners, for they had worked faithfully for me, and was out of debt. Making so much, and so easily, out of mining, set me half-crazy upon the subject.

Getting a compass, I went into the mouth of the English company's mine at Luce, and taking the direction of the lead, and also observing the direction of the air-shafts which tapped the mine, and also being positive that a mine hardly ever varies from its regular course as once ascertained, I went out half a mile beyond the company's limits and commenced sinking a shaft, intending to strike their ledge beyond their claim.

In this enterprise I had a partner named William Smith. As we went down we found quartz, but it was poor and as hard as a flint. Drilling and other labour was very expensive, and we now, almost in sight of the coveted prize, found that our money was out and we were helpless. I was anxious to go to Mexico and try to raise more funds and push on, but my partner's courage failed, and he was anxious to abandon the enterprise.

The English company, knowing that we were bound to strike their ledge, if we continued operations, came and offered us eight thousand dollars to discharge our men and cease work, and we sold out to them.

That was quite enough mining for me in that locality. The English company went to work forthwith, and at a depth of five yards further than where my men left off, they struck ore worth two thousand dollars a ton. They have since taken out ore to the value of several millions of dollars, at that point the mine proving as rich as the original, a mile and a half distant. The mine is owned by English lords, who have gained control over a large section of that country. They mine in half a dozen different states, keeping at their head-quarters in Guanaxuato a working capital of four millions of dollars.

If they lose a hundred thousand dollars in one place they soon make it up in another. They also carry on extensive commercial transactions, and have their own ships on the sea. They have large mining works at Zacatecas, owning two important mines there. Within thirty-five miles of Zacatecas they own a mine called the Fresnillo; one in the state of Durango, called Sombrerete, which yields immense profits, also several other smaller mines in that vicinity.

At Guadaloupe-y-Calvo they have another mine, and between Saltillo and San Louis Potosi, they work several mines, which, together, take the name of *Rial la Catosa*, meaning mining district. There the ore has been taken out leaving pillars of rock bearing metal twelve or fifteen yards in circumference to sustain the roof against the enormous pressure of the mountain overhead.

Trains drive under the mountain or into it, nearly three hundred yards to load up with ore. At Rial del Monta, a little off the road from Guanaxuato to Mexico, is another mine owned by this company, at which the silver is extracted by a blast-furnace.

CHAPTER 13

An Attack of Gold Fever

The great California gold fever had about this time (1849) broke out among the Mexicans. It was raging all around me and I became infected with the disease! I gathered together my effects and started for California. Thieves being numerous and dangerous, I put on my rough clothes, stitched my eight thousand dollars into a Mexican pack-saddle, and took the route up through Durango, by way of Zacatecas, passing through the state and town of Aguas Calientes, the most beautiful section in Mexico. The name means "hot waters," and is derived from a famous spring, coming out of the side of the mountain, which is sulphurous and hot enough to cook an egg or scald a chicken.

By its side, only ten steps distant, is a spring so pure and so cold as to make the teeth chatter while drinking. The water from the springs is carried down into the city by parallel pipes, which run along the eaves of the houses, and furnish every house with hot and cold water. The pressure is sufficient to throw the water into the air, to descend in showers of drops like rain, as it is frequently seen to do on the streets, and in yards and gardens.

In the Public Square is a large pool of cold water with a fountain always playing into it. There are public bath-houses, where for a nominal sum a man can enjoy the benefit of hot and cold water, and temper the bath to suit himself. This city has about fifteen thousand inhabitants, and is surrounded with orchards and handsome farms, and the city itself is very well built. After leaving Aguas Calientes, I went to Zacatecas, where I found the cholera was making deadly havoc among the natives. This was in the early part of 1850.

Thence I proceeded to the city of Durango, where I bought a set of cooking utensils and some other necessary supplies, put them on my pack mule, and set out on the old king's road for the port of Mazatlan, in the adjoining State of Cinaloa. The last three days of the journey was over a very crooked road, often nearly as steep as a flight of stairs, from the heights of the Sierra Madre range westward almost to the sea, through heavy forests of pine, &c, where there were no inhabitants. This road, so miserably poor, is the only highway from Mazatlan to Durango; and all the goods shipped from the former port to the interior must go over this road on pack mules as far as Durango, from which point they are often distributed in wagons.

From Mazatlan I started up the country for Culiacan, where I made the acquaintance of Don Francisco Vega, the governor of the State. I asked him, previous to starting further north, if it was dangerous to go up into Sonora, through the Indian tribes of Mayos and Yaguis, called from the rivers of those names. He said they were rather unfriendly to strangers, but he would give me a letter to the chief of the Yaguis, who commanded both tribes.

The two rivers where I was to travel were about twenty miles apart, and running nearly parallel. It was on the head waters of this River Yagui, in among the mountains on the boundary between Chihuahua and Sonora that we had that famous fight several years before with the Apaches, when we destroyed one of their villages. To the wonderfully rich country in the vicinity of that beautiful lake I have spoken of in a former chapter, it is possible that Brigham Young may move the Mormons, if they should find Utah too civilized for them and be compelled to leave for some more favoured region.

While I was at Culiacan, a peculiar incident of the cholera occurred. The people were dying so rapidly that there was no time for digging graves. Trenches were dug, the dead were carried to them in wagons and carts, thrown in and covered with quicklime. One driver took a load of bodies out of town, and among them was an old acquaintance of his, whom he tumbled into the trench with the rest, and threw on his lime.

While he had gone back to town for more bodies, this acquaintance, who was in a stupor, recovered consciousness and started on his way back to town. When the driver, who had now filled his cart and was on his way to the trench, arrived within about a hundred yards of his destination, he came suddenly upon his ghostly friend,—his supposed dead acquaintance,—and he was so badly frightened that he jumped from his cart, left it in the road, ran back to town in all haste, took the cholera himself and died the next day. I have often since that time seen "Old Jim," the supposed corpse, peddling candy in the streets of Culiacan.

From Culiacan I went on up to the town of Cinaloa, on the Cinaloa River. Thence to Villa del Fuerte, on the Fuerte River; a very swift stream, which, running from the mountains to the Gulf of California, is throughout its entire length the boundary between the States of Cinaloa and Sonora. At the mouth of the Fuerte river, which is navigable some distance for boats, is the port of Omaha, where goods are landed for the back country. I crossed this river in a canoe, swimming my mules, though the river was not high.

Thence I went to Alamos, which is on a branch of the Mayo River, about twenty miles from the main river. This is one of the richest mining regions in the State of Sonora. The mines were chiefly owned by four brothers, who were immensely wealthy. They took sides, strangely, in favour of Maximilian and what were called the Mexican Imperial laws, and when the empire afterwards went down, I learned that they were shot, and their property confiscated. Shortly after I was there, a great waterspout carried away half the town, filling up and ruining all the mines that were opened, and causing a landslide which exposed new and very rich mines.

From there I went to Rio Mayo, in the Mayo nation. The Indians of that tribe all talk Spanish. I inquired for their chief, when they answered that he lived about twelve miles distant, on the Yagui River, and asked if I knew him. I told them I did not, but had a letter for him, and had some business to transact with him. They took my horse and pack mule and fed them, treating me very kindly; and finding that I was hungry, they cooked me some supper.

After I had finished, they asked me if I knew what I had been eating, and I replied that I took it to be fish. They said it was blacksnake! It was too late then to make a fuss about it, and really I thought it the sweetest, nicest kind of food, for it was very white, and in taste resembled catfish. They had plenty of that kind of provisions, for blacksnakes of enormous size were plenty among them, and it appeared to be their favourite dish. They gave me a comfortable hut to sleep in that night, and the next morning one of the Indians escorted me over to Mateo, the chief. I found him at a nice little Indian town, on the banks of the river, in a splendid country.

He could talk Spanish, but could neither read or write. He sent for a better educated Indian who could read the letter, and who told him it was from the governor of Cinaloa. I was then treated like a gentleman, for they brought me watermelons and other fruits; and during the repast, the old chief asked me if I knew anything about medicine. Several of his tribe living nearby were down with the cholera.

An American doctor in Culiacan, a worthy physician, had given me some medicine, and I had bought some more for poor people on the road, so that I had a good supply. I told the chief I would do what I could for his sick people, and calling for a lot of mustard, the natives soon gathered a quantity of green mustard seed on the river bank. It was pounded fine, and mustard plasters put on the stomachs of the patients, some mustard tea given them, and mustard baths ordered for their feet.

This treatment perhaps saved the lives of a number; at all events, those who followed my directions recovered, and their friends could not do enough for me. I staid there two weeks, and was never better treated in my life. They had large flocks of sheep, and an abundance of fish in the river. When I left, the chief gave me a horse, and sent an escort with me to Guaymas. The Yagui is navigable sixty miles from its mouth, and for that distance is never frozen over. From its head waters the Indians bring down much gold, though they dare not venture far into the mountains for fear of the Apaches.

From this Indian village I went to Guaymas, about seventy-five miles distant. I offered to pay my Indian escort of four men, but they replied that their tribe was under obligations to me, that they had only done me a slight favour, and as their chief had not authorised them to receive pay they could not do so. Guaymas has a beautiful harbour, so protected by high hills as to be perfectly safe, and is deep enough anywhere for a man-of-war to anchor, as the shallowest place has about eight fathoms water. Back of the city is a mountain which breaks off the north wind. About twenty-five miles distant is a valuable *guano* island, from which large amounts of *guano* are shipped to England.

About seventy-five miles further north I arrived at Hermosillo. In that vicinity I got acquainted with a tribe of Indians I had never seen or heard of before, called the Ceres. They were formerly very hostile to-ward the Mexicans, and were a lazy, dirty race, living principally on the coast, and feeding mainly on sea lions, porpoises, sharks, and different kinds of fish.

When they were at war with the Mexicans, they used poisoned arrows, so virulent that whenever one of them broke the skin it was certain death. Their mode of poisoning their arrows was to get a liver of a shark or some animal, and let a rattlesnake bite it several times; then leaving it in the sun till it became perfectly green, they would stick the points of their arrows into it, soaking them in the deadly poison till they were thoroughly infected.

Hermosillo is the principal town of the State of Sonora. It contains thirty-five thousand inhabitants, is situated on a small river in the midst of a fine cotton region; it has a large steam and other flouring mills, and does more business than any other town in Sonora. It is situated about seventy-five miles from the coast, and has a beautiful temperate climate. It is a great wheat producing region, with abundance of fertile soil, and its markets abound with apples, peaches, pears, grapes, oranges, and other fruits, all grown in the vicinity. A survey has been made for a branch railroad from this place to connect with the Southern Pacific railroad.

At Hermosillo I met several Americans from California, among them Captain Ankrim, David Brown, and Thomas Smith. They said cattle were very high in California, and they had come into Sonora to buy some. As they could not speak Spanish, they hired me to interpret for them. As they represented that money could be made on cattle, and were very anxious to have me go on with them, I bought four hundred and fifty head, and putting them with those of my friends, we started with our drove of twenty-five hundred cattle for California. We had purchased good beef cattle at an average price of ten dollars per head.

At a town called Altar, near the northern boundary line of Sonora, we engaged twenty vaqueros, or Mexican herdsmen, and bought jerked beef, and bread, and *pinola* (which is ground parched corn) to eat on the way when cooking would be inconvenient. We also purchased a lot of jackasses to use in place of pack mules; eight of which I required for my use, and for my men. A number of Mexican men, women, and children, who were poor people going to California, joined our company for their own protection. We had for a guide, a Mexican who had come over the road from California to Hermosillo with the three other owners of the stock.

A part of our route lay through a sandy country, destitute of rivers or springs. On the route is a great rock, with a cavity which is so large that in the rainy season it fills up, and supplies water for travellers the year round. It was a hundred and sixty or a hundred and seventy miles from Altar, and eight miles from our last watering place. We could drink at the rock ourselves, and bring water enough for our mules, horses, and jacks; but our cattle had to go dry, and before us was a stretch of sixty miles of sandy desert without a drop of water that we knew of, or a blade of grass.

The desert was also subject to sand storms, which blew the fine sand up in clouds like a fog, and swept it over the road, obliterating all tracks, and making travelling by compass necessary. We had no fears for our jacks, for they can forage for a living. A bundle of rags, or a deck of cards is a fine lunch for one of them. The morning after leaving the watering place, there was great complaint on account of the scarcity of hats,, The jacks had been around and eaten up ten of the Mexicans broad-brimmed straw hats, besides a lot of our bread and *pinola*.

While the Mexicans were lamenting the loss of their hats, I discovered a greater loss. I missed two of my jacks, and while trying to track them, I saw the moccasin tracks of two Indians. Taking a Mexican along with me, we rode about four miles, tracking the Indians easily, and then on seeing a smoke among the hills, we dismounted,, and creeping around, saw one of the Apaches roasting a steak which he had cut from one of my jacks, which he had killed.

The other Indian had started for a stream of water close by. I told the Mexican to attend to this one, while I crawled up near the Indian by the fire and shot him in the back. He fell forward on his face into the fire, with his jackass meat. The other one escaped from the Mexican, but we secured the stolen jack that remained, and returned to camp, glad indeed to find water for our stock.

On reflection, I felt sorry that I had shot the Indian, as his theft had led me to discover water sufficient to save many of our animals, who were suffering. We sent back and picked up fifty or sixty cattle that had given out by the way, got them up and they joined the herd, when they were all safely driven to the stream of water. We remained there two days resting and recruiting the stock, and then started for Fort Yuma, on the Colorado River. We arrived there the second day after leaving the stream that saved our stock.

Upon arriving at the Colorado River, we found that the Indians had improvised a ferry boat, by making a government wagon body water tight, and we crossed in this boat, six miles below the fort, swimming our animals over. There had been a regular ferry a mile or so below the fort, but it had been destroyed, and its owners, twenty-five in number, slaughtered by the Indians, except two persons who escaped.

The men killed were Texan *desperadoes*, and their massacre was the best thing the Indians ever did. These *desperadoes*, under Dr. Craig, left Texas in 1849, and crossing over to Chihuahua, obtained leave of the governor of that state to fight the Indians for all they could take from them. The governor also furnished them with arms, ammunition, and money. Just before leaving Sonora, they assassinated some Mexicans, robbed them of their money, took as much of their stock as they needed, went on to Fort Yuma and established a ferry.

Here they carried matters with a high hand. It was not safe for a Mexican woman to cross the ferry, and after a time they extended their outrages to the neighbouring tribe of Indians, taking the women prisoners and keeping them in camp as long as they pleased. The attack which wiped out this miserable band was planned by two young Mexicans, who had attempted to cross the ferry with their wives, and had them taken from them and detained by the Texans.

The Mexicans went down the river, and the *desperadoes* supposed they had gone on their way and left their wives in their hands. But they only went far enough to find the chief of the tribe, who had suffered so horribly at the hands of the gang, and arrange for an attack on their common enemy. The attack was made as follows:

One day a number of the Indians, who were not a hunting tribe to any great extent, but lived by fishing and raising some vegetables, went into camp as usual, and mixed freely with the whites, who were in the habit of trading with them. There was a large body of Indians, together with the two Mexicans, concealed under the high bank of the river, who, on a given signal from those in camp, rushed in and with clubs and knives soon killed twenty-three out of the twenty-five whites, including Dr. Craig, with very little loss to themselves.

This was about a month before we arrived, and two or three days before the arrival of Captain Hooper at Fort Yuma, with a company of United States dragoons. No effort was ever made to punish the Indians for this uprising against their lawless miserable persecutors. A few days after Captain Hooper's arrival, the two escaped *desperadoes* came to him with a complaint against the Indians for the massacre of their companions. Captain Hooper being well posted as to their doings, clapped the two men into irons and sent them to California for trial.

We gave the Indians two beeves for helping ourselves and cattle across the river; and we laid there six days to recruit our cattle, for we found good grass in the bottoms of the Rio Colorado. While here encamped, I took the unfortunate hatless Mexicans to the sutler's store at the fort and furnished them with hats, as they had travelled all this distance in the burning sun with handkerchiefs tied over their heads.

CHAPTER 14

A Hunting Expedition

At Fort Yuma I met a very large Irish woman called "The Great Western," whom I had seen at Saltillo, when I went there with Colonel Doniphan. She was noted as a camp follower in the Mexican war, was liked universally for her kind motherly ways, and at the battle of Buena Vista busied herself in making cartridges for the army. I made myself known to her, and she was very glad to see me. She complained that Fort Yuma was the hardest place to procure any fresh supplies that she had ever seen, and begged me to sell her a beef. I sent her one as a present. She died at Fort Yuma in 1863.

One day while we were in camp, we saw a number of Indians running up the river bank towards us, manifestly in a great fright. When they got near enough to talk, they told us the devil was coming up the river, blowing fire and smoke out of his nose and kicking back with his feet in the water, and they would all be eaten up. They asked us what they had better do, and as we had not learned how to escape that individual ourselves, we could not tell them, and they hurried on to report to Captain Hooper and take his advice, which they wished given hastily, as the devil was coming very fast.

By this time the Indians were abandoning their fields and hastening to the fort from every direction. Captain Hooper did not know what they were trying to describe, but he knew that a steamboat had been ordered to come up the river from the gulf with his supplies, and going up on a hill with a spy-glass he saw the smoke above the trees beyond a bend in the river. He came down and explained matters to the Indians; but it was a long time before he could get them to venture near enough to look at the boat when she landed.

Then the men went after their squaws, hidden in the brush, and prevailed on them to come and view the steamer. She was named the *Yuma*, after their tribe, and this was the first steamer that ever run in those waters. Now three or four boats are running up that river and the Indians supply them with many products of their labour. They often laugh over their steamboat fright, and the chief especially enjoys the joke and says the white men know much more than the Indians.

From Fort Yuma we started again, going by way of New River and having to pass through a desert of sand sixty miles across, with water only at one place, and that a small pool hardly fit to drink. In passing through this desert we came upon the remains of an emigrant train, which a month previous had attempted to cross this desert in going from the United States to California.

While passing over the desert they had been met by a sandstorm and lost the road by the sand blowing over it, and had wandered off into the hills. They had finally got back into the road; but by that time they were worn out, and they perished of fatigue and thirst. In their wanderings off the road they had gone to one side and past the little pool of water, as we could see by the wagons they had abandoned. The missing of the water was fatal to them, as they had been two or three days without water, and had yet thirty miles to go before reaching a fertile region.

We could see where they had lightened their loads by abandoning goods, but still their cattle had been obliged to yield to the terrible thirst. There were eight women and children, and nine men. The body of a child had been almost stripped of flesh by the buzzards and animals, and its clothes were torn off; but most of the other bodies had their clothes on. Some of the bodies were in the road and others at a little distance, as if they had been returning to the road and they had all sunk down together exhausted, and lay there in the same position as when they fell.

A squad of soldiers from Fort Yuma overtook us at the pool, on their way to bury these unfortunate people, and we left them at their work, for we had to hasten onward as our cattle were now suffering badly. The soldiers said they should take the property of these emigrants back to the fort, and institute proper inquiries to ascertain who were their relatives and friends at the east; with what success I never learned.

We travelled that day and night, and the next forenoon arrived at a small lake at the head of New River. The next morning a difficulty arose between Dave Brown, who was one of our stock owners, and one of the Mexicans. The result was that Dave shot and killed the Mexican. We buried the poor man, and blamed Mr. Brown very much, for he had no justifiable provocation for the deed.

The Mexican herdsmen felt quite aggrieved by the affair, and asked me what could be done; but I persuaded them to wait till we arrived in California before making any trouble about it. The next water was twelve miles from this lake. Before reaching it we met a Mexican who warned us to be sure to keep our stock out of that water, or we would lose them all, as the water was very poisonous. A weed grows in the edges, and any animal eating it dies. The poison mainly comes from mineral matter, for there are green, filthy springs dripping into it, probably charged with copperas.

Along the edges of this creek were hundreds of skeletons of sheep which had perished out of a large drove that were passing over this route some time before, bound for California. A little above the creek, to the right of the road, we found a spring of good water, of which we drank and gave to our riding and pack animals; but there was none for our cattle. Twelve miles further on we came to a valley with many springs and fine grass for our cattle.

We found an American there putting up a station. We also found there a dirty lot of Indians called Diggers, who sleep in the dirt like hogs, and live on rabbits, rats, lizards, toads, snakes, and any other animal food they can get, besides eating a black, bitter kind of acorns. This was not far from Vallecito.

Four days after, we arrived in San Diego county, eighteen miles from the port of San Diego, where we staid a month recruiting our stock; and in the meantime I went down to the port to purchase supplies. After recruiting our stock we went one hundred and seventy miles up the coast to El Monte, which was in Los Angeles County. The buildings of this place looked very ancient, and the inhabitants were ignorant and vicious, caring for neither law or gospel.

At El Monte I separated my stock from that of Messrs. Brown, Smith, and Ankrim. This Dave Brown, being a regular desperado, went eight miles to Los Angeles, gambled off all his stock, got into a dispute with a Mexican over a game of cards, and shot him. He was put into jail by the Americans, partly through fear of his being assassinated. In the night a large body of Mexicans gathered, took Brown from the jail, and hung him to the top of the gateway of the prison yard.

There were in Los Angeles about an equal number of Americans and Mexicans. Lynch law was prevalent over California at that time, 1851, and the Americans made no objection to the hanging of Brown, because they knew it was just.

Meeting with an acquaintance at El Monte, I hired him to superintend the driving of my stock to San Jose, which town is a few miles from the bay of San Francisco, and about fifty miles south-east of the city of San Francisco. The drive was over three hundred miles, and I instructed him to drive slowly to keep the stock in order. Los Angeles is situated on a small river of the same name, thirty miles from its mouth, and was connected with its port of San Pedro by stages and wagons. It is now connected by railroad with its present port of Wilmington, and Los Angeles has grown to be quite a city.

After seeing my stock off, I went to a hotel in Los Angeles and there, to my surprise, met Peg-leg Smith, and Gabe Allen. After the first friendly greeting, and they had made many inquiries, I informed them I was going to San Francisco by steamer. Said Peg-leg Smith to me, "Captain, will you take me along with you?" I assented, and we got into a stage and went to San Pedro, where we went aboard the steamer *Sea-Bird* bound for San Francisco. When the clerk came around gathering up tickets, Smith was sitting with his head down, half drunk. Looking up, the clerk recognized him, and said:

"Your ticket, Mr. Smith."

"Hold on," responded Smith, "and I'll give you a ticket," commencing to unbuckle his wooden leg for a fight.

I stepped up and told the clerk that I would settle for his passage. Just then the captain came along and inquired what was the difficulty. I said, "None at all. Mr. Smith has no money and I was about to pay his passage."

"Never mind," said the captain. "He shall go free. I never charge one-legged men anything."

"Captain," said Smith, "that's good enough, let's take a drink on that at your expense," which joke pleased the captain exceedingly.

On the fourth day we arrived at San Francisco, and went to a good hotel; but it was nothing like the magnificent hotels that have since been erected there. Everything was in its infancy in 1851. A lot of government troops had just arrived there, and more were expected. Meeting with a government contractor at the hotel I asked him what he was paying for cattle on the foot, grass fed, and he answered a "bit" or twelve and a half cents a pound.

I sold him all my cattle (to arrive) at that price, and when the cattle got along a month afterwards I found, after delivering them and getting my pay, that I had sixteen thousand dollars. I did not know what to do with my money after receiving it. I considered my life more in danger than with the Indians on the plains, for the city abounded with cut-throats and *desperadoes*. I deposited the sixteen thousand dollars in Adams & Co.'s bank, for that company was banking as well as expressing at that time.

Shortly after I drew out enough to pay off my help who had

come through with my cattle, and they proposed to start on an expedition with me to the mountains to dig gold. I finally organized a party of eighteen persons, fitted up a pack mule train with pans, picks, shovels, and all the necessary outfit for gold-digging, and started for reported rich placer diggings at Camp Sonora, one hundred and fifty miles south-east of San Francisco.

We put up our tents and commenced prospecting around in the gulches. In the vicinity were many Chinamen, Americans, Spaniards, Frenchmen, and Mexicans. Some of our party told me they had found a gulch nearby which paid eight or ten cents to the pan, and upon examination I found it to be so. We immediately moved our tents up there, and went to work taking out about six thousand dollars the first eight days.

My party being all Mexicans, a little incident now occurred which raised me very materially in their estimation. Suddenly two Americans rode up to our camp, and one of them, who could speak a little Spanish, stated that he had orders from the government to collect a tax of twenty dollars from every Mexican and China-man found at work mining. I asked him in Spanish where his documents were that gave him this authority. He said his word was sufficient. I drew up my double-barrelled gun, and said: "Now, you leave here, or I'll give you documents. I've heard of your kind before." They rode away, threatening to come back and collect the tax.

I told the Mexicans to keep their arms handy by them, and do just as I bade them. Then I went to a mining justice of the peace, not far off, and asked him if there were any persons about there with authority to collect such a tax. He said there were not, but he had heard of those men and would like to get hold of them. Said I, they are out here behind your house drinking in a grocery. He said he would like to arrest them if he could get anybody to sustain him. I replied that I had eighteen Mexicans, and that I would sustain him. Then, going down to my Mexicans, who were afraid of their fives, I said to them: "You have put yourselves under my charge, and I will see you safe through everything."

There were nine Americans just below who joined us. We went up to the grocery, and, as we came near, saw the justice, who waved his hand for us to go around the house. We surrounded it, when one of the men ran out of the house, pistol in hand, and was instantly shot and killed. The other gave himself up, telling us that his name was Jack Downing. We put a rope around his neck and hung him to the limb of a tree that stood by the grocery. Before being swung off he was asked if he had anything to say, and his only reply was curses.

It was afterwards ascertained that he and his companion had a few days before murdered two Chinamen and a Mexican. The two men had four thousand dollars, which they had collected and robbed from ignorant miners. This money was deposited with the justice of the peace to pay the expenses of a mining government, which we at once set about organizing for our mutual benefit and protection.

Our little village of mining huts was a common evening resort for many persons who worked mining for some distance around. The news spread like wildfire that we had hung one and shot the other of these noted blackmailers, and the second night after the hanging, about three hundred men were assembled. We organised a mining government, with proper officers and committees, adopting a constitution and bylaws, one of the bylaws providing that no man should stay about the camp who had not some business.

I was one of a committee of four to see that these rules were enforced, and the following day we notified several gamblers and suspected thieves and robbers to leave, or stay and suffer the consequences. They left in a hurry. There-after the regular meetings of our miners' association were on Saturday nights, and our number soon swelled to between four and five hundred. Our association was also benevolent, and aided any miner who was sick, by taking care of him, cooking for him, or in contributions of money.

Several desperate characters came in from time to time; but learning our laws, and seeing the tree which served for a gallows, it looked disagreeable to them and they left. Following our example, similar societies were organized in other parts of California, as we could get no protection from the United States, its few troops being too distant and inaccessible at the instant wanted in miners' camps.

I worked there three months with the Mexicans, and when we divided the proceeds, we found that we had each made about three thousand one hundred dollars. From the mines we all went to San Francisco, and there I found in port a vessel named the Matilda, belonging to the English consul at Guaymas, bound for that port, and nearly ready to sail. As the Mexicans were anxious to return home, I saw them safe aboard, and got their money deposited with the captain, who gave it to them on their arrival at Guaymas; for I met several of them afterwards and they were highly pleased with the result of their California trip.

The day after my companions sailed I saw a good chance to speculate in sheep in San Francisco. Drawing my funds from Adams & Co.'s bank, I went to close the trade, which, unfortunately, was broken up by a third party offering more than I had done; and as I was returning to the bank to make a second deposit, I learned that the bank had just failed. Lucky for me thought I! Though I had over three thousand dollars deposited in the safe of the National Hotel, I was in no mood to lose the greater portion of my hard earnings.

I next went to see the famous quicksilver mine of New Almaden, twelve miles south of San Jose and the Soda Spring, which is a curiosity that attracts many visitors. The water boils up precisely like soda, and is taken in bottles to San Jose for drinking. The day I returned to San Jose water was struck in an Artesian well four hundred and fifty feet deep, and ten inches in diameter. The water came up with such force that if a man laid a board over the mouth and stood on it he would be raised up a foot. Four blind fish two or three inches long, were thrown out, but died immediately.

At first, a great deal of sand came up, but the water soon cleared, and San Jose is now supplied with water from this well.

Other Artesian wells were opened about this time, and a month later the waters of a certain lake, six miles long and four miles across, and fifteen or twenty feet in depth, began to dry up. The lake was situated thirty-five miles from San Jose, and in six weeks had become perfectly dry, leaving a quantity of dead fish in the bottom. In the bed of the lake was seen a huge rupture or crack that might have been produced by an earthquake at some prior period. There is now a good farm, highly cultivated, where the lake was.

In the hotel at San Jose, I overheard an old gentleman in conversation with another, speak of my father's family, and, being introduced, I found that he was Judge Murray from Missouri, and knew all my relatives. He informed me that I had a sister and a half-sister living in Napa Valley, in Napa County, California. This was great news for me, and I started forthwith to make them a visit, arriving at my sister's house the second day, and she sent for my half sister, who was married and lived about half a mile distant. It was a long time before they could believe that I was their brother; but I told them circumstances which satisfied them, and they were overjoyed at seeing one they had long considered lost. I also met many persons in this valley who were my schoolmates in Missouri,—among the rest, three sons of Ex-Governor Boggs, who had settled in the valley with their father, each owning separate ranches and keeping large herds of cattle.

After stopping in that neighbourhood a month or so, having a good time among my friends, we made up a hunting expedition, the party consisting of Governor Boggs's sons, and two schoolmates of mine who were expert hunters. We started for Russian River, mounted on pack mules, with tents, cooking utensils, and plenty of ammunition. We were very successful, killing a great many elks, bears, deer, geese, ducks, and other kinds of game.

There was a new settler on Russian River, by the name of John Cook, who came from Missouri, whose farm was devoted mainly to the raising of potatoes; and we made his place our head-quarters, going out from there in various directions. He told us one day that the bears were digging up his potatoes, and

Fatal encounter with grizzly bear

he was going to set a large trap which he had, to catch the thief. We went with him to see the tracks, and found where the fence was broken down; but the tracks I told him were not those of a bear. However, we set the trap by the fence, and left it covered up, and returned to the house.

I was busy preparing venison hams that evening, for my sisters and for Governor Boggs, as I was meat curer for the party. While laughing and chatting about our hunting adventures, and who had killed game and who had not, we heard a tremendous halloing in the potato patch. We ran out to our trap and found in it a Digger Indian! His leg was ruined in his attempts to escape. The trap was the heaviest kind of steel trap, nearly a yard across, with long, sharp teeth, and strong enough to hold a grizzly bear. I had to open it with care, for I saw that the fellow's leg was broken; and it afterwards had to be amputated at the knee. This Indian had been in the habit of stealing a bagful of potatoes occasionally, but Mr. Cook was not troubled any further with him.

We hunted there several weeks, curing four or five pack loads of venison and elk, besides some bear bacon. The second day after we started for home, we stopped at noon near a lake, where I saw some ducks, and telling the others to take off the pack saddles, I started off with my double barrel gun to get some fresh ducks to roast for dinner. I went into rushes bordering the lake that were as high as my head, having both barrels of my gun cocked, intending to shoot one before the ducks rose out of the water and then discharge the other barrel as they rose.

I was in a sort of trail and looking over the tops of the rushes at the birds, when suddenly I saw standing right before me, and not five steps distant, a huge grizzly bear! As he raised up in front of me on his hind legs, I was so frightened that I let him have both charges of duck shot in his face, and turning, I ran back as fast as possible to camp. When I got there, the boys seeing me scared, asked where my ducks were, and I replied that there was the biggest kind of a duck down near the water. The bear was tearing about, biting at the rushes, and making considerable noise.

After exchanging my shot gun for a rifle, I went back with the boys to look after him, and when we got near enough we gave him a regular broadside, which killed him. He was unusually large, and all that saved me was the double charge of duck shot, which accidentally put out both his eyes. After skinning our bear, and taking what meat we could carry handily, we started on.

Between sundown and dark we halted, and camped in the edge of some brushy scrub oak on a hillside. While we were at supper, Theodore Boggs's horse broke the bush to which he was tied, and he took him up the hill a short distance to secure him to a larger sapling. Presently we heard a fearful shriek and the growling of a bear, and knew that Boggs was in trouble. We all started for his relief, and found a large bear had him down. It was now so dark as to render it unsafe to shoot at the bear, so I attacked him with my knife, and succeeded in killing him.

We found poor Boggs horribly mutilated, his face being bitten all to pieces, and his side torn open. He was senseless when taken up, but by the time a carriage, for which we sent ten miles, arrived, which was about daylight, he was able to talk. He was aware that he could not live, but expressed a strong desire to reach home before he died. We reached home the next day, and our friend died soon after. His frightful death was a severe blow to his two brothers who were in the party. Before the carriage arrived, some of us went to look at the bear, and found her mate and two cubs by her side. The old bear was killed, and the cubs captured and taken home. Thus sorrowfully ended our excursion, which had promised so much pleasure.

CHAPTER 15

An Uprising

I stopped in Napa valley with my sisters and friends some time, when one of Mr. Boggs's sons and myself went down to San Francisco, where I met Colonel James, whom I had known in the city of Mexico about the close of the Mexican war. He was now United States attorney for San Francisco and the district. He said I was the very man he wanted to see, and offered me almost any price if I would interpret in the Land Commissioner's office, in the investigation of the false claims of several parties to Mission Dolores. He would also give me mileage and liberal wages to go over California and find evidence concerning ancient claims and titles, as the land records of each county were in a confused and very unintelligible shape.

I accepted the offer, and laboured three months, making twenty-five dollars per day, including mileage; and, among other important services, I was fortunate enough to collect such evidence as defeated the false claimants to Mission Dolores, which very valuable real estate became the property of the city of San Francisco with a confirmed and settled title.

This Mission Dolores was established by the Mexican government on real estate of its own, for the purpose of civilizing and controlling the Indians. A Catholic priest had been put in charge by the Mexican government. A Chilean and a Mexican who were in the employ of this priest were murdered, to get rid of their evidence, because, if it could be established that the Mexican Government held possession at that time, it would be fatal to the claimants under the false title.

The priest they had bribed with thirty thousand dollars to leave for Guaymas. I went down to Guaymas with an order from the Mexican consul, called on the Mexican authorities, had this priest delivered to me, and proceeded to San Francisco with him, where his testimony proved the United States title direct from the Mexican government, and the complete falsity of the pretended transfer. We were obliged to guard the priest carefully, to prevent his being assassinated.

The false claimants had a Mexican grant with an old date and the forged signature of a dead governor. The priest was well acquainted with the history of the whole transaction, as he had assisted in concocting the scheme. He was compelled on his oath to expose the knavery of these claimants, and their case was thrown out of court. I had told him, on the passage up from Guaymas, that the penalty for perjury was imprisonment in the penitentiary, which so frightened him that when he came on the stand he told the straight truth.

Just previous to his being called upon, a false witness had sworn in favour of the pretended owners; and when the priest was called into the commissioner's room to give his testimony, they stared at him in amazement, for they did not imagine that he was in the country. The priest was asked if he could point out the men who paid him thirty thousand dollars to leave the country. He pointed out those who appeared as claimants. After his evidence they abandoned the case. The papers were forwarded to Washington, and the title of San Francisco to Mission Dolores, derived by gift from the United States, was confirmed.

The witness who swore falsely was subsequently sent to the penitentiary for four years. In the early part of 1854, I had an invitation from Colonel James, and the commissioner, Colonel Thompson, to meet them at the City Hall, in San Francisco, as they were about to transact important business. I attended, and found a hall full of labourers, merchants, mechanics, and other honest men, who had met as a vigilance committee, to take active measures to put down gambling and thieving.

The meeting was secret, no one being allowed there except honest men, engaged in some reputable calling. This was on Monday night; and, after perfecting our arrangements, Wednesday morning was fixed upon for a raid on the gamblers and thieves, on which day no business was to be done, and the stores were to be closed throughout the city.

A few days before the organization of the committee, the editor of a daily paper called the *Town Talk*, had published an article which reflected severely on the gamblers and cut-throats of the city, and the next morning as the editor, Mr. King, was crossing the street, he was shot down by a *desperado* named Buckley. Wednesday morning the vigilance committee paid a visit to this Buckley, who was a notorious bully and dared anybody to arrest him. We found him asleep, and gave him no time for repentance; but the brother of the murdered editor put the rope around his neck, and we hung him from his own bedroom window in the upper story, leaving him to the gaze of thousands in the street below. He was the first man hung by the committee.

There was a vigilance committee of eight hundred, which had been organized at the other end of the city, and they, like ourselves, were divided into parties, that took the various resorts of gamblers and thieves by surprise. We hung eight that day, and imprisoned many more. We hung one man that we found in a prison cell with Yankee Sullivan; and when we took him out, it so frightened Sullivan that he committed suicide, thinking probably that his turn would come next.

It was our intention to send Sullivan back to England, where he had been a noted criminal; but we should not have hung him anyway, as he had killed no person that we knew of, and we only hung murderers. Persons guilty of smaller crimes we put in jail. This day's operations so alarmed the robbers, sports, and roughs of the city, that they fled in all directions: some to the States, some to Mexico, and others to the mountains to prey upon the miners.

We then formed what we called the City Guard, which was sustained by the popular sentiment; and the merchants once more felt safe, and business resumed its regular channels, as soon as quiet was restored. Colonel James asked me how I liked the present organisation of the city. I told him I thought it was the best organized city I ever saw in my life. There was an Italian organ-grinder at every street corner. He laughed at the remark and said there was a large number of monkeys and hand-organs in the city, but he preferred them to the thieves we had expelled.

In the latter part of 1854, I formed the acquaintance of a gentleman called Judge Jenkins. He said he had learned that I spoke Spanish, and was a good practical miner, and he wanted me to go down into Mexico with him and engage in mining; to which proposition I consented without due reflection. We started together, for the port of Mazatlan, in the State of Cinaloa, and prospected among a considerable number of mines in that vicinity, and at last purchased one for seven thousand dollars, which had been a very rich paying mine, but had filled up with water, and was now worked just enough for the owner to retain possession.

Before purchasing, I told the judge that any less than a hundred thousand dollars would be useless in working such a mine; but I would go on and expend what money I had if he was certain of raising the balance. He stated that he could get all the money we needed. He stopped there with me three months, and only furnished two thousand dollars in the aggregate, while I bought all the machinery, paid for the mine, and purchased the necessary supplies. I finally informed the judge that it would be necessary to run a tunnel into the side of the hill, three hundred feet long, to drain off the water, and thus avoid raising it by machinery. He told me to manage the matter as I thought best, and he would go back to San Francisco to get all the money we needed, and would soon return.

In about a month I received a letter from him stating that he should soon return with plenty of capital. This letter encouraged me to continue the work, and I went on and expended all my means, when, to my surprise, I received a second letter from the judge stating that his plans for raising money had failed, and he could do nothing for me.

Here I was again out of money, having spent a little over twenty thousand dollars, and the judge had spent all he had, which was only two thousand dollars. To make the matter doubly aggravating to me, now among strangers, destitute and without credit, or the power to proceed further with mining, I found that although I had expended everything I had in the purchase and working of the mine, my title would be worthless if I abandoned the mine for one month.

According to the laws of Mexico any person who took charge of an abandoned mine, and worked it, could obtain bona tide possession and ownership. I did not relish the idea of losing all my capital, and forfeiting the mine too, but what else could I do under the circumstances? Soon after, Domingo Ruby, the governor of Cinaloa, took possession of the works, spent fifty thousand dollars in completing my tunnel, struck the mine, drained off the water, took out hundreds of thousands of dollars, and was offered two hundred thousand dollars for his claim, at which price he would not think of selling. That was the second time I had been compelled to give up mining operations just on the eve of success.

I then went into Mazatlan to look for some business I could engage in without much capital, and finally bought some patent medicines and started out as a pill doctor, or physician. I had Wright's pills, Ayer's pills, and various kinds of patent medicines. I was also well acquainted with many kinds of medicinal herbs. I established myself at a town about eighty miles from Mazatlan, called Cosala. I had a great many patients there and as much business as I could attend to. I took my pay in horses, cattle, hogs, corn, or anything marketable, and was soon looked upon as a first-class physician.

When I first went there I had an open field and no competition, but after I had been there about two months, a Mexican doctor came along who had a diploma. One day, in conversation he asked me what authority I had to practice medicine. I told him that I had as much right as he had. He said he had a diploma, and he was going to have me arrested, and if I could not show a diploma, I should be stopped from practicing medicine. He had me brought before a justice of the peace, who was a particular friend of mine, who discharged me forthwith, saying I was regarded as a first-rate physician, by all his friends and neighbours; and he advised the other fellow to leave, and practice elsewhere. I had attended the justice when he was quite sick, and cured him, which was all that saved me, for the law was against quack doctors.

After getting a lot of jackasses, mules, horses, and hogs, I turned them over to a Mexican *ranchero*, to take care of on shares, and started off to seek another location, taking a recommendation from the judge. I went to a mining town about fifty-five miles north of Culiacan. I had been there about a month when I was sent for by Placa de Vega, who was sick. After curing him, he asked me if I knew anything about extracting metal from ores. I told him I was acquainted with the quicksilver amalgamating process in use at Guanaxuata, and he then employed me, and I worked for him over a year, until the latter part of 1856. His mine was poor, and did not pay expenses; and I advised him to cease operations, for I was anxious to do something more profitable.

We soon had a visitor, who was introduced to me as Lawyer Romero, of Guadalaxara, who had come to see Senor de Vega on important business, the nature of which was soon after explained to me. To understand the nature of his mission, it is important to know the condition of Mexico at that time.

Mexico was at this time a perfectly priest-ridden country. The people were in a state of abject slavery to the clergy, who not only absorbed the capital of the country, but required the greatest respect and tokens of superiority from them. When a priest passed through the streets, it was necessary for the people to fall on their knees and make the sign of the cross, or they would receive affronts from some of the soldiers who always formed the escort of a priest. They required more days for church holidays,

&c, than they allowed for business, and took heavy toll on every article raised or manufactured. They laid a heavy tax on every step in a man's existence,—baptism, marriage, and burial.

Placa de Vega, knowing my American birth, and sympathies for freedom, had sufficient confidence in me to unfold the plan of a revolution which was soon to overthrow this priestly rule. I was at Del Fuerte with him and Senor Romero on the 17th of September, 1857, the day before the revolution broke out. The president of the Republic, Mr. Comonfort, was at the head of this rebellion—this grand uprising of the people against their oppressors. The details were managed so skilfully that the liberty party had been generally organized throughout most of the larger towns of the Republic, and the day agreed upon for a *pronunciamiento* to be issued against the conservatives, or priestly party, without their knowledge, and before they could arrange a plan of defence.

A few conservatives in the city of Mexico had some information furnished them before the time set for the rising, but they were powerless before the storm that was ready to burst upon them. General Lanberg, an Austrian officer who had fought against General Scott, during the Mexican war, was in command of four hundred troops, in the city of Mexico, who sympathized with the church party. The priests offered him a large sum of money to declare for them, and influence his troops to fight for them. He took their money and promised to assist them, but President Comonfort learning the particulars, offered him a larger bribe, and he took it and declared for the liberal party when the *pronunciamiento* came out, and his troops sided with him.

The evening of the seventeenth of September, I was asked to take command of a squad of twenty men, and release fifty-eight prisoners from jail, so that they could take a part with us in the revolution. There was a grand ball in our hall of rendezvous at Del Fuerte, that evening, to allay any suspicion that the priests might have on account of seeing so many strangers pour into town and gather around one building. At one o'clock, on the morning of the eighteenth, the hour previously agreed upon by the liberals all over Mexico, the revolution commenced; and the uprising was simultaneous all through the cities of that country.

It was a dark night, which we considered favourable; half the government soldiers at the barracks had promised to aid us in disarming and subduing their comrades, if any there were who favoured the priests enough to fight for them. But at Del Fuerte we anticipated very little bloodshed, for, by a liberal supply of liquor to the soldiers we made them half drunk, and careless about guarding the barracks.

At one o'clock I started with my squad of twenty men, for the jail, with no arms except my double barrelled gun and revolver. My men had armed themselves with short clubs. On the way to the jail, I picked up several more liberals, armed with clubs, and when we arrived at the jail yard, we found the sentinel and the guard of twenty-four soldiers drunk and fast asleep. They were easily secured, and, armed with their guns, we advanced to the jail and told the prisoners what we had come for, and they were not long in rousing from their slumbers, and cheering for the liberty party.

The jail was opened, and every one of the prisoners joined our force, as did many soldiers, so that we returned to our barracks, or dancing hall, with one hundred and fifty men. This had been accomplished without firing a gun! Soon after we arrived at the hall, about three o'clock in the morning, De Vega and Romero arrived, followed by a great crowd of government soldiers and citizens who had joined our party.

Romero made a speech, telling them that the revolution was to throw off the yoke of priestly domination, and to enable the poor man to get a living without being taxed to death by the church. He then read to them the new constitution of 1857, prepared for adoption all over the republic; and when he had finished reading, the crowd all cheered and shouted in favour of the new constitution.

A military company was then formed, of persons present in the hall. De Vega and myself stepped for-ward, and Romero told them that they were to regard Placa de Vega as commander-in-chief of the forces of the State of Cinaloa, and that I was captain of that company; and this also appeared to give general satisfaction. I was then presented by De Vega with a commission to raise money for the liberal cause, with instructions to arrest any persons who would not comply with the new order of things, and be quiet and peaceable. He gave me a list of rich men in Villa del Fuerte, who favoured the priesthood, and opposite each man's name was the amount assessed against him.

My orders were to take a squad of soldiers with me, and bring back either the money or the men to head-quarters; and in case I brought the men, to keep them prisoners till the money was forthcoming. The first man on my list was a priest, who was notorious for his vicious life, and who had amassed an immense fortune from the priest-ridden people. He was on my list for twenty-five thousand dollars, and was much alarmed at seeing my men and having such an enormous demand for money made so abruptly; he denied that he had any money, but I told him it made no difference, as he was as good as the money to me, according to my orders, and he must come along.

After my men had marched him about half way to the barracks, he offered to compromise and raise five thousand dollars; but I told him that anything less than twenty-five thousand dollars would not do from him; so he walked along and was placed under a strong guard, while I went to attend to a few others who had heaped up riches out of the labour of honest people.

One man paid me a thousand dollars. All the rest I took to our barracks, which was a large building, with a large yard, or inside court; and porches, or verandahs all around; with a hundred rooms, reached only by doors from these inside porches; there being one main entrance from the street. The place belonged to De Vega's aunt, and had been built for a hotel and lodging rooms, but had been vacant for a while. My company, when all were present, numbered about four hundred, and this building was well adapted for the accommodation of the entire number.

When I arrived at the barracks with the prisoners, I found

many of my men preparing for active service by making cartridges, and cleaning up old muskets which they had collected about town. I went in with my prisoners to De Vega and made my report. The priest told him that he could only raise five thousand dollars, and the assessment was exorbitant against him.

De Vega answered: "You are worth twenty-five thousand dollars to me. You have had your way long enough; I am going to have mine awhile." He then ordered the priest to be locked up and given no tiling whatever to eat or drink till he had paid over the twenty-five thousand dollars. The other men all compromised by paying a part of their assessments down, and agreeing to pay the remainder in six days.

Early the next morning, the servant of the priest appeared with chocolate and provisions, inquiring for the "Father." We asked him what he wanted. He said he had brought the *padre's* breakfast. We told him to go back home; that the priest was not allowed to take any breakfast. The servant returned home with the news that the father was being starved to death, and in an hour a deputation of eight or ten women came to see about the matter.

They interceded for the priest, pleading earnestly for his release. Vega told them there was no relief for him whatever till he complied with the conditions. They inquired the amount demanded, and offered to raise it if they could be allowed to see the priest and obtain his consent. Vega told them he wanted no money from them, he only wanted it from the priest, and he should pay it or he would dry him up in his cell by starvation; and further added that he wanted them to leave the room and go home. They went out muttering that the curses of that priest would send us all to perdition; but we told them we should take our chances on that point.

The priest stood it out like a martyr for two days, and then begged of Vega to let him out and he would go and raise the money. Vega sent back a reply that he had no confidence in him; and told me to take six soldiers, go with Mm to his house, be sure he did not escape, and return with the money or the priest.

In half an hour we were in the old priest's cellar, where he opened an iron safe in which there seemed to be one hundred thousand dollars in gold, put up in sacks of five thousand dollars each. He handed us out the twenty-five thousand dollars, and we left him to appease his hunger and bewail his misfortunes. We took the money to Vega, who said he was very glad to learn that the priest had so much money, as he would call on him again whenever his supplies were short.

I was then ordered by De Vega to take twenty-five cavalrymen and go out in the country to levy contributions of horses and money for the liberal cause. One of the principal men on my list was Don Canute Evarro, who was wealthy, and owned a large amount of stock. He was strongly in favour of the priests, as we discovered by a conversation with him, and was much taken aback when I demanded a lot of horses and five thousand dollars in cash.

He declined to pay the cash, but offered to let the horses go; whereupon we arrested him and started him towards Del Fuerte. After going about two miles, one of the men told him how we had served the priest, which scared him so badly that he returned to the house with us, paid over the money and gave us the horses without any delay, and with a considerable show of politeness.

I was absent on this expedition eight days, and re-turned to Fuerte with four hundred horses and eighteen thousand dollars in money. De Vega congratulated me on my success, and said I was about the fittest man for general business that he had met, as I was doctor, miner, interpreter, captain, and general collector.

A servant of a rich man in the vicinity came one day to join our party as a soldier, and stated that his late master had two four pounder cannon hidden on his place. By De Vega's direction, I took a squad of soldiers and a sergeant, and went to bring the cannon to our barracks. This servant went with us as a guide, and when we arrived at the place I asked the proprietor if he had any such cannon on his premises, and he replied positively that he had not. The servant pointed out a pile of lumber, and on throwing it off we found the two cannon. I then asked for the moulds and ammunition. He said he had none. I inquired of the servant, and he said they were in a room adjoining the kitchen. The old man was compelled to show us the articles, and we bore them off to the barracks in triumph.

That forenoon, a dispatch was brought by a messenger from Sonora, to the effect that General Garcia Morales, a brother-in-law of the governor of Sonora, was coming to our assistance with a force of four hundred men and four pieces of artillery, and would arrive in a few days. He was called by the nickname of *Cotchero* (meaning in English, lizard), because he could creep up so slyly on an enemy; was a great Indian fighter, and fond of ambushes when he made them himself.

In the afternoon another dispatch was received, informing us that eight hundred of the church party were marching against us from Mazatlan. The last dispatch was from Romero, who was in sight of the enemy, having gone down to watch their movements about Culiacan and Mazatlan.

I told De Vega it was high time to begin to drill. I picked out drill sergeants, and drilling was steadily kept up until the arrival of Morales, by which time I had gathered up two hundred more recruits from the surrounding country, making our force, with the new arrival, one thousand men.

General Morales brought two twelve-pounder howitzers of American make, which had been taken from the American filibuster Crabbe, when he was murdered in Sonora. He also brought two Mexican six-pounders, which, added to my two four-pounders, gave us quite a respectable show of artillery for that country. I was appointed to take charge of the two twelve-pounder howitzers, and drill the men at the guns thoroughly, so that they might be of service in time of action.

Before sallying out from Fuerte to meet the church forces, we organised a home guard, or police force, to keep order in the town; and also put another judge in office who was a liberal, in place of one who was not. While on the march out we received another dispatch from Romero, who said he had collected three hundred more recruits, who would join us at Mocarito; and from what he could learn, our forces would then be about equal. He urged us to hasten forward, so as to effect a junction before the enemy met us.

At Cinaloa we had an acquisition of one hundred more men, and got hold of another priest, from whom Vega obtained ten thousand dollars, saying that as he was not as big a rascal as the other priest, he would let him off easier. We laid over at Cinaloa one day, for rest, and to make important changes in the government of the place, appointment of officers, and in raising a home guard for its protection. This was a place of about five thousand inhabitants.

CHAPTER 16

A Hospital Established

When we arrived at Mocarito, two days afterward, we found Romero with three hundred men anxiously expecting us. De Vega was with us, but left the fighting to Garcia Morales, whom he had invested with full command. Morales called on the citizens for carts to haul adobes and other fortifying material, and continued four days, apparently at work vigorously to intrench our position. Being satisfied that the news of these movements had reached the ears of the enemy, he ordered us all to be ready the next day to break camp and march with two days' rations.

Meantime, another hundred or more new recruits had straggled into our ranks from various quarters, and we now numbered nearly fifteen hundred men. The last evening at Mocarito, we were informed by Romero's scouts that the enemy, with sixteen hundred men, were only a day's march distant.

We therefore broke camp hastily, and Morales marched us that night about twelve miles towards the enemy, where we took a favourable position, and lay in ambush in a lot of brush and small trees by the side of the road. We laid in the brush on our faces, our artillery hidden completely from view, by green brush which we cut for that purpose. Our cavalry were in the rear of us and we intended to let their advance guard and a part of their force get past us, and then open fire on them.

Opposite to us, in the road, the advance guard of the enemy came suddenly on one of our men about daybreak, and asked him where he belonged, &c. He had been sent on an errand by an officer and had not time to conceal himself before they came upon him. While they were questioning him, a little dog that had followed us commenced to bark, and this alarmed them so that they dismounted and looked about under the trees.

Discovering the red shirts of some of our men, they endeavoured to escape; but all were shot except one, who rode back to the main body nearly frightened out of his wits. But for this little dog, our plan of ambush would probably have so surprised the enemy, that we should have killed or captured nearly all of them, as they were marching irregularly, not dreaming of any surprise, as they supposed we were still in Mocarito.

All our force now advanced two or three hundred yards, to a rise of ground which commanded the road, and, in fact, the whole plain, which was bare, with the exception of the few trees which covered our ambuscade. I planted my howitzers on a high point over-looking the road over which the enemy must come. Upon the first alarm they had retreated a short distance, and made preparations for battle; for, before that, one-half their guns were not loaded.

While they were getting ready we had ample time to complete our preparations, and soon commenced firing. The enemy had eight pieces of artillery, and we began to throw shells at each other. They commenced cutting a cactus hedge to get their artillery through, with the intention of flanking us; but a shell from us dismounted the first gun which they got through the hedge, and they changed their plan.

Advancing boldly up the road, they commenced in earnest, and musketry firing became general. The fight commenced about eight in the morning and ended at three in the afternoon. Their commanding officer was a very brave man. He charged up the hill straight to my artillery. Springing upon one of the guns, he ordered us to surrender, when one of my men shot him through the breast and he fell dead, astride of the axle of the gun carriage with his head over the gun.

Soon the enemy broke and fled. We called for our cavalry to pursue, but they had been stationed in our rear, and finding the shells bursting thick among them, they had retreated, and not one of them could be found. If the enemy had known that fact they would not have retreated in such disorder nor gone so far. On the enemy's side there were one hundred and eleven men killed and thirty-two wounded. On our side thirty-eight were killed and twenty-seven wounded, including our commander, Garcia Morales, who was wounded in the hip with a pistol-ball, and one of our artillery captains named Gumbor, was wounded in the thigh; but neither of them dangerously.

We collected our troops on the battlefield and camped there that night, and the next day buried our dead. The wounded were taken back to Mocarito, and I was detailed to establish an hospital, get it into good condition, and leave it in good hands; then I was to rejoin our forces. After getting the hospital in working order, and surgeons supplied, I levied contributions from the church party to supply our hospital with necessaries. These important duties hindered me at Mocarito two or three weeks.

Meantime the church party had made a stand at Mazatlan, at which place they had gathered; and our army, under Morales, were camped outside the town and had them besieged, with a fair prospect of capturing the entire force. They were fortified in a position that prevented them from obtaining provisions or fuel from the adjoining country; but General Morales concluded they were getting both from the coast above and from Lower California, and he was fearful it would be hard to starve them out.

While I was back at Mocarito, seeing to the hospital matters, our camp before Mazatlan had received some very welcome recruits, *viz.*: Colonel Charles Norton, Captain Ball, John Coly, William Keyes, and fifteen or twenty American and English marines, who had deserted from vessels on the coast and come in there, offering their services to the liberal party.

Anchored in the harbour of Mazatlan, about three hundred yards distant from the enemy's fort, was a merchant schooner of one hundred and twenty tons, fitted up by the church forces as a war vessel, with portholes for six pieces of artillery. They also had a beautiful brass pivot-gun mounted on deck. The vessel was named the *Itrovide*, and was of special value to the church party, so much so that we formed a plan for its capture.

Our newly arrived friends, the marines and officers had come down the coast in two small vessels of twenty tons each, which they had left six miles above Mazatlan, at a little port called Cameron. They offered to go up and get their vessels, if I would lead the expedition, and drop down on each side of the war schooner and take her by surprise. On explaining the plan to De Vega and General Morales, they scouted at the idea as ridiculous. Morales, however, soon favoured the enterprise, on learning that we only required our two twelve pounder howitzers, and a few Mexican soldiers; and if we would take the responsibility we should have what we wanted.

After dark, taking the marines and the Mexican soldiers allowed us, we went up to where the two vessels lay, put the howitzers aboard, one on each vessel, and by rowing and drifting we neared the schooner so noiselessly that we were not discovered till we had got very near to her. My vessel approaching on the left, and the other, commanded by Colonel Norton, on the right. We intended to board her at once, after the first discharge from our twelve pounders, which we had double-shotted with grape and canister.

Suddenly the man on the watch called out:

"Who's there?"

I answered, in English, "Friends, with provisions."

He said, "Anchor where you are."

"All right," I replied, rattling the chain as if letting down the anchor. It was too dark for him to see us distinctly. I wanted to get my vessel a little more abreast of them to give them a raking broadside and then grapple with and board her. With muffled oars we silently approached, when, finding the crew of the schooner aroused and gathered on deck, I discharged the howitzer among them, and we pulled in earnest for their sides, clambered up just as Captain Norton gave them another discharge from the opposite side.

Cutlasses in hand, we rushed on the few who remained on deck, nine of whom surrendered, and the remainder not killed, jumped overboard and swam for the shore. Their force numbered about thirty, and their easy capture was the result of their carelessness on watch, as they little dreamed of attack. We weighed anchor and hoisted sail, but there was not a breath of air stirring, and the schooner did not move.

We were now in an unpleasant situation, for the enemy's fort opened fire on us, and, as day was breaking, we made a good target. Our only chance was to man our small vessels and tow the schooner out of range, for their shots began to tell on us, several of our men being killed and wounded. Just as we had got her head around, fortunately a breeze sprung up, and we moved out of danger.

I had told General Morales that when our firing commenced, the enemy's troops would all come running to the beach from their intrenchments, to fire upon us, and it would be a favourable opportunity for him to capture the town by attacking them in the rear. As we moved out of the harbour, the enemy in full force were gathered on shore, even their cavalry having come down to fire upon us. It was very mortifying to see that Morales did not make the attack, which would no doubt have proved successful.

I asked one of our prisoners, a Negro, where the shells for the pivot-gun were. He brought me some fine American shells, and training the gun on some cavalry near the water's edge, I dropped a few shells among them, as well as into the fort, which had a good effect, killing a number and dispersing the crowd.

We took the captured schooner, with our little vessels, back to the port of Cameron, where we started from. Here we found a lot of our troops gathered to welcome us.

"Well," said General Morales, "you Americans beat the d—l. I wouldn't have gone with you on such an enterprise for the whole of Mexico."

Said I to Morales, with some show of anger in my question,

"Why did you not go into the city when you heard our firing and had such a good opportunity."

"I was looking at you," he replied; "expecting you would all be killed."

I told him that in war some risk must be run or nothing won.

"Now," said he, "we have them in our power. We can cut them off from provisions coining by sea or land, and we can starve them out in a very short time."

The next day, a United States man of war, the *St. Mary,* came to our port of Cameron, not being willing to anchor at Mazatlan under the flag of the church party. The officers came ashore and fraternized with our officers, and invited them aboard the *St. Mary*, and we all had a social time together.

In the meantime an American vessel, loaded with flour for San Bias, sprung a leak, and put into the harbour of Mazatlan for repairs. General Arteigo, commanding the church forces in Mazatlan, seized the flour, on the ground that the vessel had not cleared for that port. The truth was, his soldiers were in sore need of flour, as well as everything else in the way of eatables.

Captain George Lewis, the owner of the cargo, made complaint to the American consul at Mazatlan, who communicated with Commander Wells of the *St. Mary*. The result was that General Arteigo was speedily informed that if Captain Lewis was not delivered on board the *St. Mary*, at 4 o'clock the next day, with the value of his cargo, nine thousand dollars, he would come down and blow the side of their town off.

There had just arrived at Mazatlan, an English man of war, named the *Eclipse*, and the commander sent word to Commodore Wells that he had no right to make such demands. Commodore Wells returned for an answer to the Englishman, that he must mind his own business; for his part, he was only protecting the interests of his countrymen, and if the Englishman was dissatisfied with his conduct, and would anchor out at a proper distance, he could have satisfaction, for he felt competent to blow him out of the water and shell the town besides. The challenge was not accepted, however.

About 3 o'clock Commodore Wells weighed anchor and dropped down opposite Mazatlan. At 4 o'clock he opened his port-holes and shoved out his guns. The Mexicans hastily raised a flag of truce and brought Captain Lewis aboard with eight thousand dollars; but they were compelled to return and get the other thou-sand without delay. Commodore Wells then gratuitously furnished ship-carpenters, who repaired Captain Lewis's vessel, and he sailed for San Francisco, thinking his flour well sold, as he had got twice as much for it as it would have brought if he had continued on to San Bias. The American man of war soon left our port for Acapulco.

Four days after the *St. Mary* left, the bishop of Mazatlan and General Arteigo consulted with the commander of the English man of war, and bribed him, as we afterwards found, with a gift of ten thousand dollars, to take our schooner, the *Itrovide*, and a number of small boats we had captured since, while trying to run into Mazatlan with supplies, away from us. We saw the vessel approaching, and could have made our escape; but, having no suspicion, made no effort to do so, as it had been a common thing for vessels to come into our port for water.

The *Eclipse* came alongside of our schooner, hailed us, and ordered us ashore as pirates! We replied that they were meddling with business that did not concern them, and, as many of us on board were Americans, they might hear from us afterwards; but the commander insisted on our going ashore at once, and we left our valuable prize as soon as they boarded us, knowing that they were too strong for us to resist.

We had taken ten or eleven little vessels and boats that were bringing provisions to the troops in Mazatlan, and had the town nearly reduced by starvation. Among the vessels was one loaded, apparently, with copper ore. As shipments of copper were common, we did not think of looking for anything more valuable. The captain of this vessel escaped, and reported to General Arteigo that we had taken his vessel, and that the lower part of his cargo was bars of silver, which the copper ore concealed.

The bishop and general could well afford to give ten thousand dollars to get possession of this treasure, and they and their sympathizing friend, the English commander, made a good thing out of it. In about a week the English commander sent the *Itrovide* to Acapulco for supplies. Near the Las Tres Marias Islands, she sunk, and, our vessel stolen from us so shamefully went to the bottom, with sixty Englishmen on board. Of course we shed no tears over their shipwreck.

Our siege of the place still continued, and I submitted to my humble duties on shore with as good grace as possible, after being the hero of naval exploits, &c. A part of my duty was to superintend the guard and see to its being changed every six hours. Occasionally I went out with the picket-guard, and sometimes at the head of a foraging party, I was gathering supplies from the neighbouring towns.

The Negro we had found on board the *Itrovide* had joined our party, and was one night on guard when I was in charge of the picket line. The orders to sentinels were to hail all strangers with the usual "Who comes there?" and repeat it three times. If, after that, there was no response, to fire. The Negro was on guard for the first time, and I had explained to him fully how to give the challenge. About midnight I was aroused by his yelling, "Who cum dar tree times?" and bang went his gun before I could reach him.

"What's the matter?" I asked.

"Whoeber it is, I got him," said he.

The camp was aroused, and we soon discovered the cause of alarm. An unlucky jackass, browsing in the brush, had come too near to the darkey, and he had shot him between the eyes; and there he lay kicking on the ground. The next morning our quartermaster had to pay a Mexican twelve dollars and a half for his jackass.

The next day we learned that a reinforcement of troops belonging to the church party, calling themselves "the Lord's troops," had come to the relief of Mazatlan. They were under the lead of Perez Gomez, a noted Castilian. Our commander found out that only a part had arrived, and that the remainder were expected soon. General Morales now displayed his peculiar tactics again. He sent men to report in Mazatlan that we were completely demoralized, and about to retire to the mountains.

After allowing sufficient time for this report to be circulated, the bugle summoned us to pre-pare for marching, and we started about midnight away from Mazatlan towards Cosala, most of the enemy's troops pursuing us the next morning under the command of General Inguanzo. General Gomez and General Arteigo did not take part in this pursuit.

After a march of two days, we arrived at a plain between two mountains, with thick woods on both sides of the road; and here to the right and left we secreted our forces in ambush. We had received a dispatch from General Coranow, who was on the way from Chihuahua with eight hundred troops coming to our aid, that he would take this main route, and we now expected him momentarily. Still, to make all sure, General Morales had sent a messenger forward to halt Coranow's forces, some distance back, so that the Lord's troops would, after getting safely past us, find themselves attacked in front, while we sprang out from our ambush and attacked them in their rear.

The plan worked to a charm. General Coranow arrived about an hour before the battle, and stationed his force across the road and in among the trees as agreed. On came the Lord's troops in hot pursuit. Some dressed like priests, in long robes with saintly hoods, and none dreaming of danger. At a given signal, we rose and poured in a deadly volley before they could organize for defence.

Our artillery also began to play on them, when, seeing themselves surrounded, and with no way of escape, they raised the white flag and surrendered unconditionally. We got twelve pieces of artillery and all their equipments, and made prisoners of nearly all their force, which numbered about two thousand. General Inguanzo and some of their cavalry escaped; but we captured General Revoyella, the second in command, and brought him to Mazatlan, where he was sentenced to death. The church party offered a large amount to save the life of this general, but De Vega insisted on his being shot.

We returned with a force of about twenty-seven hundred, including General Coranow's command, and walked into Mazatlan without difficulty, as the troops had nearly all deserted the town on learning the disastrous results of the pursuit. In addition to this, more than half of the two thousand prisoners consented to serve on our side. Others who were stubborn we placed at work on the fortifications of Mazatlan and in covering up the numerous artificial pitfalls which the Lord's troops had constructed in the streets for our army to fall into, in case we captured their city. In each pitfall sharp stakes were driven, so that men or horses in falling would be pierced through.

General Gomez, General Artiego, and the bishop, with priests, officers, &c, escaped from the city by going on board the English man of war *Eclipse*, and sailing away, leaving the remnant of their troops in the city to escape as they could. General Gomez afterwards sailed for Spain, having married a rich wife, and preferred to leave with her for a country where there would be more safety for his head. Requisitions were made under which we were paid two months wages. Colonel Norton, Captain Ball, and myself, each received from De Vega a splendid marine sabre, worth seventy-five dollars, as a present in honour of our capture of the *Itrovide* vessel of war.

We released all the liberals that we found in jail at Mazatlan, many of whom were incarcerated in cells for no crime except that of favouring our cause.

We liberated one old man who had been arrested for selling mule-meat for beef to the half-famished soldiers (before we entered the place), but we set him free, considering the meat good enough for them, and much more desirable than starvation.

We found a fore-and-aft schooner in port, called the *Epala*, which we fitted up as a coast guard. Three captains and some others of the church party were placed on board for safekeeping. Captain Avilles, the officer in charge, came ashore with some marines one day to get orders for a cruise down the coast. The prisoners, who were not ironed, discovered the reduced number of the crew, and, rising up, they overpowered the force on board and put out to sea, making, evidently, for San Bias.

There was another schooner in port, called the *Lord Raglan*, a vessel of two hundred and fifty tons, and I proposed to Colonel Norton that we should take her with a proper force and go in pursuit, and with a twenty-four pounder which was on board, I thought we could capture or sink the runaways. On submitting the proposition to General Morales, he favoured it, and offered us the use of another schooner, the *Seventeenth*, which had just arrived in port.

Both vessels were soon under way, with one hundred and fifty soldiers on each, besides the crews. We arrived in San Bias about four hours after the run-away schooner had anchored in a basin around the point, under cover of a battery of two small guns on the hillside. I transferred fifty men to Colonel Norton, making his force two hundred, with which he was to cut out the *Epala*, while I bombarded the town.

There was a garrison there of six hundred church troops, and I did not hesitate to open fire, but blazed away with my shells at short range, and soon the custom house was in flames, and the fire spread among the palm-thatched roofs till half the town was burned. While I was thus engaged in the bombardment, Colonel Norton, with the aid of Captain Avilles, had retaken the *Epala*, killing one of the officers who ran off the schooner. The other officers succeeded in making their escape, which was very fortunate for them, for Avilles was furious in his anger toward the men who had thus stolen a march on him, and would spare no prisoners.

After the vessel had been recaptured, Colonel Norton landed his men and signalled me, as had been previously agreed upon, to follow, which I did with seventy-five men, leaving a lieutenant and twenty-five soldiers to man the gun and take charge of the vessel. Very little resistance was offered, for our united forces soon drove the church party out of town. Their loss must have been fifty or more killed, while ours was slight.

We returned to the custom house, and found the walls still standing. As they were built of adobes, and the floor of stone, nothing was burned except the roof and thin partition walls, with trifling furniture. Breaking open the safe we found five thousand dollars, which, with the enemy's two field-pieces, we carried on board as prizes. We returned to Mazatlan with our prizes, and were welcomed with salutes from our troops, who were drawn up on the beach to see us land. We were cheered for our success, and complimented by the commander, who allowed us to divide the five thousand dollars among ourselves.

Shortly after this expedition, General Coranow received orders to prepare for marching, with two thousand troops, against the Indians and Mexicans who were posted at Tepic, twenty-five miles back of San Bias. Their leader was the noted *desperado* and Indian chief Lozado, and they were fighting for the church cause. Our force was organized, and myself and Captain Brown were put in charge of the artillery. I had two twenty-four pounders and he had two twelves.

Our force was divided, part going over land, and part by water, to San Bias. There we united and marched on Tepic. When we arrived near Tepic we found there-were from four to five thousand of the enemy, mostly Indians, in the town. We opened fire on them about ten in the morning and by four in the afternoon were driving the Indians out of town, when General Coranow, our leader, received a shot through the right thigh which shattered the bone. It was the result of his rashness and imprudence, for he was with the advance, driving the Indians through the town, lancing and shooting them down in the street, when the fatal shot was fired from an upper window, and he fell.

Firing ceased then on both sides, with the Indians whipped, as we hoped. Coranow died at 9 o'clock, during the operation of amputation, which fact was kept secret from the soldiers. Next in command of our army was Cordero, a desperate villain, under whose orders firing recommenced at daybreak. We fought till 8 o'clock, when Captain Brown of the artillery fell dead at my side, with a bullet through his breast. The Indians were retreating, and we had the advantage, when a bugle sounded on our side to cease firing. I heard the bugle, but after putting my first sergeant in Captain Brown's place, I continued firing, when Cordero rode up to me, and cried out:

"Didn't you hear the bugle sound for a parley?"

"How could you expect a man to hear a bugle when cannon are firing the way they are?" I replied.

I asked Cordero what he meant by a parley. He said he was going to hold a short consultation with the Indian chief Lozado. I told him I didn't see the necessity of any truce, when we had them so nearly flogged; and he replied that he knew his business. In an hour I found out to my sorrow what the traitorous old scamp intended by his truce, for we were completely sold out, bag and baggage, to the Indian chief Lozado, for the sum of fifty thousand dollars.

By the terms, we surrendered our artillery, arms, ammunition, horses, equipments, &c., and even our side arms in most cases were taken from us. My beautiful marine sabre, presented me by De Vega, was taken with the rest, and in its place a little short thing given me, which I threw against an artillery wagon. If I had shot Cordero, when he bade me cease firing, and taken command of the force myself, we should have beaten the enemy completely, and I should have been promoted. I was tempted to do so, for I suspected some treachery, and from his villainous looks I regarded him as more fit for a prison than for the head of an army.

Cordero reserved his fine riding horse, and eighteen or twenty pack-mules to carry his money and baggage, including his own and that of General Coranow, which he appropriated as well as three or four thousand dollars in specie which the deceased general had taken along for the use of the army. He also retained an escort of fifty armed soldiers, whom he selected from our ranks, who remained friendly to him. It was suspected that Coranow had been poisoned in the amputation by the connivance of this traitor, for the surgeon employed was a citizen of Tepic and a zealous churchman.

In this engagement the enemy had lost from four to five hundred men, and our loss was about two hundred; in one sense a victory, and in another, a shameful defeat; for we now were compelled to return to San Bias and get back to Mazatlan the best way we could. There was not a horse belonging to the party; and our wounded we were compelled to leave at Tepic, to the tender mercies of cut-throats and savages.

Mournfully and silently we buried our brave commander, Coranow, and then began our weary march across the plains and over the hills, to starve upon the route, perhaps, for we were only allowed to take two days' rations out of our own quartermaster's stores. These were the liberal terms that the traitor had arranged for ns!

We kept our force from straggling as much as possible, from fear of guerrillas, and finally arrived at Acaponeta, a town of a thousand inhabitants. We were footsore, tired, and hungry, and had to sleep on the ground without blankets. I was awakened in the night by the mosquitoes, and, being very thirsty, went to a house in the distance, where there was a light, in search of water. Looking in, as I approached, I saw Cordero sitting at a long table, with his face toward me, dealing the game of *monte*, with several Mexicans sitting opposite and betting against him. He had two or three thousand dollars in gold by him on the table.

It made my blood boil to see that he had followed us, and in this gambling house was operating with the money he had sold us for. A sentinel was lying asleep outside by the door, and, looking close, though there was no moon, I discerned the forms of twenty or thirty others, who lay on the ground asleep, their guns by their sides. These I supposed to be a part of the escort he had selected from our ranks. Suddenly an idea popped into my head. I hurried back to my first sergeant, and waking him, asked him for his revolver, which he did not surrender to Lozado, having secreted it when they took our arms.

"What are you going to do?" he asked.

"Get up," said I, "and get your men up, and be very still."

"What is it?" he asked.

"Never mind," I answered. "I will soon tell you. Rouse up your men, very quick."

I soon had over a hundred of our men following me, with cat-like tread, over to the house; and on the way I hinted my plan, and told them that the infamous Cordero was actually the object of capture now; that he was at his old tricks of gambling in a house close by, &c. We stole softly up to the house and seized the guns of the guard, who were still asleep. They roused up, but seeing the yard full of their old comrades, had no disposition to raise the alarm, but felt disposed to join us.

I went into the house with five of my men, well armed, and presenting the pistol I had taken of my sergeant to the head of Cordero, I demanded his money. He had his fifty thousand dollars in the room, except several thousand he had lost at *monte* that night to the Mexican gamblers at the table. We made them disgorge, and placed them under arrest. By this time the room was full of my men, and the doors were locked.

" Captain Hobbs," asked the traitor, "what are you going to do with me, now that I am your prisoner?"

"I'll show you very quick," said I.

Taking him out into a hollow, he was shot by my order, as I was perfectly willing to take the responsibility. All our troops gathered around to see him shot, and half the inhabitants of the town, aroused by the tumult, came around to learn the cause of the uproar. By daylight nearly every man in the place had seen the corpse, and heard the story of our battle, the surrender, the weary march, and our terrible sufferings.

Hardly anyone justified the traitor; though some of the citizens of the place wondered at Cordero's folly in visiting his old gambling den; but this place was off the main road from San Bias to Mazatlan, and we turned in there for rest and provisions. Cordero must have arrived after we had laid down to sleep, in a large field outside of the village, for he would not willingly rush into our presence.

We made a demand on the inhabitants for provisions, and while at breakfast, a dispatch came from De Vega, who had heard of Cordero's treachery, requesting me to see that the traitor was assassinated before he fled the country. I sent the courier back to say to De Vega that his orders were executed even before they arrived! And sent a brief report of our condition, &c.

I also levied a contribution on the town for cattle and horses, and succeeded in getting ten head of cattle and nearly sixty horses. This was fortunate, as some of our men were worn out and were compelled to ride. We mounted as many as possible on the animals of Cordero and his guard, and made the guard walk as prisoners. I rode Cordero's fine horse, and had a sort of body guard of lame and sick soldiers riding on either side of me, on the pack-mules, that carried Cordero's baggage and the money he got of Lozado.

After a distressing march we arrived at Mazatlan, Governor Vega and Garcia Morales coming out on the road to meet us, and giving us a hearty welcome.

"Captain," said Morales "you've played one of my old tricks, on that miserable traitor." Vega thought we should have scalped him. They invited me into their carriage, and the troops came out to greet us with a band of music, and colours flying. All rejoiced that we had returned alive, even though we had bad luck. I delivered to De Vega all the property and money taken from Cordero, except what I had expended for supplies on the way. The escort of fifty soldiers were tried, but acquitted on the ground that it is a soldier's duty to render obedience to his commander.

CHAPTER 17

History of Lozado

The cause of the liberals was gaining in favour among the common people, and recruits were daily coming in. Several hundred had joined our ranks at Mazatlan, while we were absent on the expedition against Lozado. Several vessels had also been captured, and the surrounding country had been levied on for supplies of provisions and money to carry on the contest. In some of these foraging expeditions, previous to going to Tepic, I had excellent luck, and also met with some narrow escapes.

I was one day informed by Governor Vega, that a vessel was expected shortly from China, with a valuable cargo belonging to rich Mexicans of the church party living at Villa del Fuerte and Alamos, who would try to smuggle in their goods. He told me to get two field pieces on board of a schooner, take marines and soldiers and watch the coast, with a view to its capture. I told him I was no sailor; but he said Captain Ball was, and he might take charge of the vessel and I command the soldiers and marines. He offered me in addition to captain's pay, one-third of all the smuggled goods captured and delivered to him.

I consented to make the attempt, and we set sail. Soon after we left port, we fell in with a vessel from California, and inquired of her captain if they had seen such a vessel as I described. He said they had, and she was putting in toward the mouth of the Fuerte River. I gave chase, and found her opposite the smuggling port of Omaha. She attempted to escape, but a shot across her bow stopped her, and on boarding her we found it was the vessel we were in search of. She was a prize indeed, having a cargo which was worth two hundred thousand dollars, and with papers for only a small portion of it.

When the consignees of the cargo, who were on board, having come off in a pilot boat, found themselves fairly caught, they offered ten thousand dollars to be released; but I refused to do any such business. Putting a guard on board of her, I took her to Mazatlan. The consignees of the cargo went ashore when we arrived at Mazatlan, where they staid two or three days. Finally I went ashore and saw Vega. He said the business was all arranged. I said if it was all arranged it was all right, and returned to my vessel.

Shortly after, he came aboard my vessel and told me to take my soldiers ashore. I asked him about my portion of the cargo. He said I should lose nothing by him. The owners took their vessel away, and I went to see Vega again. He said they had a right to leave, for they had proper papers. I said: "That is played out, Mr. Governor. They offered me ten thousand dollars to let them off, and I am sure they had no papers." He made but little answer; I never got a cent, however, for my services, but I learned, afterwards, that Vega was bribed by the owners with a present of fifty thousand dollars. I told General Morales what our contract was, and he said it was not the first mean trick Vega had been guilty of.

It was not long before De Vega sent for me to go and take a smuggling vessel loaded with silver, which he had heard of. Said I: "Governor, you did not treat me right about the smuggled goods, and I shall not go."

He said he would order me under arrest. I told him to do so, but that it would not change my mind at all. He ordered me under arrest, but General Morales and Governor Pesquiera, of Sonora, remonstrated with him, telling him it was a shame to treat me so after the important services I had rendered. They got an order of release, but I refused to leave the barracks in which I was confined on my word of honour. I demanded a trial, though after further conversation I agreed to come out, but notified him that I should not fight any more under such leaders, and particularly under De Vega.

Soon afterwards, De Vega made a requisition for one hundred and fifty thousand dollars, to go to San Francisco, to buy arms. He got the money, went to San Francisco and never returned until the war with Maximilian, when he went to Tepic, joined the Indian chief Lozado, on the Imperial side, and is perhaps still living among the mountains of that region.

After the defalcation of De Vega, Senor Ignatio Pesquiera, the governor of Sonora, succeeded as the governor of Cinaloa; thus being governor of two states. He had a deputy in Sonora.

Soon after he was made governor of Cinaloa, Governor Pesquiera issued orders for another expedition to be organized to operate against the famous Lozado and his tribe. The shame of the former disastrous surrender still rankled in my breast, and I and my companions in arms were perfectly willing to engage in a second expedition, if commanded by faithful officers. We had received a valuable addition to our force in Mazatlan just previous to this order, by the arrival of fifteen hundred troops under General Lanberg.

Governor Pesquiera entrusted the charge of this expedition to General Lanberg, and sent with him nearly four thousand troops, including artillery and a small proportion of cavalry. Some of the troops went from Mazatlan to San Bias by land, and some by water. Near San Bias we joined our forces, and marched on Tepic. General Corona, who joined us at San Bias by water, was another new officer, and as he had a good military reputation, he was made second in command. This was the same General Corona who afterwards received Maximilian's sword when he surrendered. General Rojas had charge of the cavalry.

This Indian chief, Lozado, was a remarkable character. In his youth he was a servant, and shamefully abused by his master, who whipped his mother to death for some trifling offense. This made Lozado a *desperado* and outlaw, for he took to the mountains with a few miserable followers; and they organized a regular system of guerrilla warfare and robbery. He captured his former master and tortured him till he died.

After years of warfare, he had gathered several thousand Indians and half-breeds around him; and as they made their headquarters in the mountains, all the expeditions which had been sent against him were perfect failures. On the former occasion when we were ordered to Tepic to fight this Indian chief, his troops were gathered in the town, and we had a fair field, and should have beaten them if the treachery of our leader had not prevented.

On the present occasion, when Lozado heard of our advance upon Tepic, instead of remaining there with his tribe, he withdrew to the mountains, where he knew we could not follow him. His followers were devoted to him, and brave to the last degree. He was an autocrat,—as much so as Brigham Young. His Indians were all Catholics; and with him were priests who told these ignorant fanatics that if they fell fighting for the church they would shortly be restored to life.

In this belief, when we fought them first, these deluded savages rushed up to the muzzles of our cannon to stop their mouths with blankets and thus keep the balls from coming out. When we blew some to pieces others took their places. When our forces arrived at Tepic and found the place nearly deserted, we divided into two parties; one-half the infantry, under General Corona, marching for the mountains, with two light mountain howitzers, with orders to co-operate with the cavalry under General Rojas, who was to follow us the next day.

General Lanberg remained at Tepic for a base of operations, and to prevent the enemy from surrounding us and cutting off our retreat in case of failure. I was in charge of the howitzers, with the force of General Corona, and we cautiously advanced among the mountains to discover the favourite retreat, or headquarters of Lozado.

Upon climbing around under the summit of the Sierra de Allico, a beautiful view was presented. Here was a narrow, grassy plain, surrounded by rocky walls nearly perpendicular and towering up hundreds of feet, and at the further end of the plain it

Rancheros

terminated in a narrow canyon, or defile between the mountains. The outlet seemed to be hedged up by a sort of gate or mass of obstructions. In entering this place we had come through by a road hardly wide enough for two teams to pass, and we begun to fear that we were entrapped by our treacherous guide we had taken from Tepic.

As we turned to retreat the way we came in, huge rocks began to roll down the sides of the mountain, crushing many of our men. To add to our calamity, there was no possible chance to return through the narrow passage by which we entered, as the Indians were just above, on the hillsides, prepared to annihilate us if we did so, and had rolled huge boulders into the road, nearly obstructing it. For two days we remained there, without provisions, as our pack mules, loaded with rations, did not enter this place, being in the rear, and we could not communicate with them.

All these hours of suspense we were expecting the cavalry under Rojas to come to our aid. Finally they arrived in sight, and attacked the Indians from a point where they could drive them from the rocks above, which enabled us to clamber over the obstructions and retreat out of this prison, with the loss of twenty-four men, who were crushed to death, several mules killed, and one artillery carriage smashed in pieces. The reason that General Rojas did not get to us sooner was because he had mistaken our route and gone over thirty miles out of his way; all planned, no doubt, by his two Indian guides, who pretended to be friendly.

They escaped, or they would have been shot, as our guide was. We all returned to Tepic; and in consultation with our officers there, finally agreed to give up the pursuit after Lozado and his tribe, and return to Mazatlan, where we arrived safely and without meeting any enemy.

After remaining at Mazatlan about a month, General Morales received a dispatch from General Zaragosa, ordering him to send a force of two thousand men to join him at Sayula, and from there proceed to the siege of Guadalaxara. General Miramon had collected a large force of church troops at this place, and, by a bold stroke, General Zaragosa intended to capture that city, with all its ten thousand troops, if possible. The force was speedily organized, under General Lanberg, and proceeded to San Blas, part by water and part by land, meeting again at Tepic, as on a former occasion.

We made a forced march, our artillery and cavalry standing it very well, but the infantry suffered considerably on the route. Part of the infantry were mounted; and whenever we could make a raid on a *ranche* belonging to a churchman, and get mules or horses, we did so.

In this long march we suffered for want of provisions. One night, at a little deserted village, whose affrighted inhabitants had fled, our troops fared very comfortably, and my supper was enriched by the addition of a fat turkey, which I espied on a fence, and brought into camp. My first-sergeant in the artillery was lucky enough to capture a well-filled beehive, and our mess were in clover that night. We destroyed no property in that village, but considered ourselves entitled to all the provisions and animals we found abandoned.

We captured four priests the next day, by the aid of a liberal, who came to us and informed us where they had secreted themselves at a hacienda a little off our route. They had been operating against us, stirring up the people to organize into guerrilla parties to interrupt us in our progress. We hung two of them to a tree by the roadside, and the other two offered to join our cause and fight with us if we spared their lives. General Rojas took them at their word, and had them stripped of their robes and dressed in our uniform. One of them escaped in the night, and the other was hung as soon as General Rojas was informed of the escape of his comrade.

On arriving at the town of Sayula, we met the forces of General Zaragosa encamped near the town; and there was great rejoicing at our opportune arrival, for General Zaragosa wanted to march on Guadalaxara the following day. Uniting our forces we numbered about ten thousand, and expected some more recruits to join us before we reached the enemy's camp at Guadalaxara.

When we had been three days on the march, we met a strong force of the enemy, who had come from Guadalaxara to impede our progress, so that Miramon would have time for reinforcements, which he was daily expecting, to arrive. General Zaragosa quickly formed us in line of battle, and in two hours the enemy were forced to retreat, with a loss of three hundred killed, and nearly as many wounded.

The reason that the number of wounded was smaller usually than the number killed was that our troops were so embittered against the church party, who had been their rulers and persecutors so long, that they were unmercifully cruel in battle to those desperately wounded; and if they could not escape they fared hard, often being helped along in their exit to the spirit land by a bayonet, or shot as we ran over them in pursuit of a flying foe. In the present instance, Zaragosa ordered us to charge when they began to fall back; and we pursued them with cavalry, and seized all their artillery, eight pieces, before they could get inside the fortifications of Guadalaxara.

Our army was now in high glee, and all expected an easy capture of the city. We encamped on the held, and received several hundred recruits that night, who hearing the cannonading and witnessing a part of the battle determined to join the winning side. The next day we were before the city, and, throwing our lines around it, began that night the work of intrenching. Before we had completed our work the fight commenced, and continued at intervals for four days, with the loss of several hundred men on each side. The fifth day we were joined by Colonel Cheeseman, an old United States army officer, with a party of about three hundred Texan Rangers and half-breed Mexicans.

Firing had now ceased, and Colonel Cheeseman's advice was asked. He told General Zaragosa that he could suggest a plan of taking the city without so much bloodshed, which was, to run a tunnel from a deep ravine on the south side of the city, and close to the principal barracks. The tunnel would not necessarily be over one hundred yards in length to run under the barracks, and by exploding a mine of powder and blowing up the enemy, at night, simultaneous with a grand attack by our whole force, we should have an easy victory.

The plan suited General Zaragosa, and he gave Colonel Cheeseman the charge of the work. Three hundred sharpshooters were placed on the opposite side of the ravine, to shoot all who showed their heads above the enemy's works, and two hundred Mexicans were set at work, with picks and shovels, in the construction of the tunnel. Occasional firing was kept up, and they were closely besieged till the tunnel was finished, and the mine charged with powder. When all was ready, and our army aroused, before daybreak, and prepared for the assault, the mine was sprung.

About five hundred of the enemy in the barracks were killed by the explosion, the air being filled with flying bricks, stones, dirt, and rubbish, as well as fragments of human bodies. Our attack was well planned, and the enemy were panic stricken when they found that we were shelling every part of the city. General Miramon, who was not in the bar-racks, succeeded in escaping with six or eight thousand men and several pieces of artillery, but abandoned most of his stores and wagon trains, of which we stood in need. Their defence was spirited, considering the circumstances, for they fought us about an hour before they retreated, during which I lost twenty of my artillerymen.

Colonel O'Roscoe, after our army had entered the city, proposed to General Zaragosa to select a suitable force and pursue General Miramon. Accordingly he was placed in command of about four thousand mounted men, including several batteries of light guns, and we started and overhauled the straggling army at San Juan, cutting it up fearfully, and nearly capturing General Miramon, who escaped in disguise. Their artillery was surrendered, and many arms were taken from their troops, who were so demoralized that they fled, after an hour's fight, in every direction.

We returned to Guadalaxara after two days' absence, and found that Colonel Cheeseman had been poisoned by a Mexican woman where he boarded. It was ascertained that the priests and bishops had paid her ten thousand dollars to take his life, as they considered him a very dangerous man to their cause. The colonel was buried after a post-mortem examination had revealed strychnine in his stomach. The woman was arrested and confessed that ten priests and men in holy orders were her accomplices, having induced her to do the deed.

The next morning her head was found on one side of the street and her body on the other. The ten priests and bishops were immediately hung as accessories, one of them confessing the crime. The same day, six officers that we had taken prisoners were tried, and four were shot, while two were spared on condition of joining our ranks, as they proved that they had been impressed into fighting on the other side.

We remained here two weeks, the city presenting a very desolate appearance after the battle. Learning that General Miramon, who escaped at the battle of San Juan, had reorganized a large force, and was on his way to meet us, we made preparations for an advance against him. Our troops, numbering about two-thirds of our entire force, marched against him, confident of his speedy overthrow.

When the opposing armies met on the field we found they outnumbered us nearly two to one. General Zaragosa commanded our forces, and the fight was a tedious one, lasting two days, terminating in a loss of about seven hundred killed on each side; but we held the field and took about two hundred prisoners, among whom was General Toledo, who was shot immediately after. General Miramon withdrew from the field, and marched his army to the city of Mexico; and we returned to Guadalaxara, where General Zaragosa recruited his forces and fortified the city.

Soon after our return to Guadalaxara, Colonel Nor-ton and myself received orders to take two hundred and fifty men and return to Cinaloa. On the route we were attacked by Lozado's Indian warriors on three occasions, but escaped with the loss of seven men and one piece of artillery. The Indians outnumbered us six to one, and all that saved us was that we were all well mounted.

We arrived at Mazatlan without further molestation, and were cordially received by our old comrades and friends. General Morales informed us that we had been sent for to scour the country of Cinaloa, and bring in recruits for the liberal party, in anticipation of a decisive battle, which it was expected would soon come off at the city of Mexico, or in that vicinity. We travelled about, over the state, for several weeks, raising nearly two thousand recruits.

Wherever our troop of cavalry appeared, it was easy to pick up volunteers, and when we had raised any considerable number, we levied on horses and mules sufficient to mount them in good shape, and dispatched them to Mazatlan.

While engaged in this work, we had a severe engagement with the enemy's troops, under a leader by the name of Coghen. Our party numbered about four hundred, and we fought them at a place called Espenal, taking many prisoners and several officers, who were shot, by order of General Lanberg, after we returned with them to Mazatlan.

Coghen, however, made his escape from the field, with the remnant of his force, but was overtaken several days after, and hung, by the liberals. We remained at Mazatlan a short time, to get the recruits well drilled, and then had orders to march for the city of Mexico.

We started from Mazatlan with all the mounted force that could be organized, and all the artillery that could be spared, taking an overland route through Zacatecas, where we expected a large addition of volunteers. We were attacked by General Moreno's troops, in Zacatecas, and defeated them, with the loss of nine hundred men on their side, and about seven hundred on ours; which included several engagements, as they hung upon our rear and harassed us till we turned upon them and had a half day's obstinate fight.

They then retreated in the direction of the city of Mexico, and we pursued them till we turned off the route, to unite with the army of General Zaragosa, at Guadalaxara. Thus united, we resumed the march after a day's rest, and finally arrived with a large and imposing force, in sight of the city of Mexico.

The enemy were well fortified in the city, and were commanded by Generals Miramon, Mejia, and Marquez. We opened a fire on the city after making due preparation, and the firing was continued for four days, and terminated in a complete victory for the liberals, our whole loss being about one thousand, and that of the enemy about nineteen hundred. We found in the city vast quantities of supplies and ammunition; and we confiscated the vast property of the church for the use of the liberal party, in carrying on the war, &c.

All the priests and bishops we could find we imprisoned; and many officers captured were tried, and some of them shot, while others joined our party, some of whom fought bravely on our side. We remained in the city of Mexico, having entire control, for about six months; and under the administration of the liberals, everything settled into a state of quiet; the laws were respected, and there was general good order. Comonfort was president of the Republic, with his head-quarters in the capitol, and he was growing in favour with the church party, and universally liked by the liberals.

CHAPTER 18

Taken Prisoner

About this time war was declared by France against Mexico. The church party sided with the French, and their officers commenced raising troops to join the French army, which was soon expected to land at Vera Cruz. In this way they thought to avenge themselves against the liberal party of Mexico for their continual defeats. Some of them went to Vera Cruz with their troops to welcome the arrival of these foreign legions and offer their services.

The liberals had immediate orders from President Comonfort to organize our troops and be in readiness to oppose the French. We marched out of the city of Mexico, under General Zaragosa, to meet the invaders at Puebla on the road from Vera Cruz; and while waiting for the French to arrive we spent several weeks in fortifying the city and raising volunteers in the country around. Learning that the French were advancing on Puebla, we moved out about four miles from the city and met the enemy in an open field.

Our troops numbered fourteen thousand, and the French united with the traitors who had joined them, mustered twelve thousand. The engagement commenced about 10 o'clock in the morning and lasted until 3 p.m. General Zaragosa formed a part of his troops in a hollow square in front of an eminence or hill, and a section of artillery was placed in the right hand corner of this square, of which I had command. A little to the left of my position was a high point which the enemy endeavoured to take by a flank movement. This attempt was frustrated by some pretty sharp shelling and sundry discharges of grape and canister which drove them back.

General Zaragosa had placed in our front in a ravine or low piece of ground, about fifteen hundred men, with orders to lay close to the ground; and placed a scattering line of men in advance, and when the French made the assault these men rose up and poured in a destructive volley which gave us an opportunity to follow up with the artillery, killing a great number and causing the remainder to fall back. Twice the French advanced to gain this elevation where our light artillery were doing fearful damage in the enemy's ranks, and both times they were repulsed with great loss.

General Zaragosa finally ordered the artillery to cease firing, and the infantry, including my support, to charge in front, sending the cavalry around to attack on the flank, when the enemy broke in disorder and fled in the direction of Vera Cruz. I found after I had ceased firing that a number of my artillerymen were killed or disabled, one of whom, a sergeant, was wounded badly in the shoulder, and in my efforts to get him up and take him to a place of shelter, I was struck in the breast by a musket ball from the enemy, which broke the breast-bone; and though the ball was nearly spent, owing to the extreme distance, I found myself completely disabled for want of breath.

The ball took out a small piece, or patch from my uniform, and drove it into my breast, in front of the ball. By taking hold of the edges of this patch, I drew out the ball immediately. When our troops returned from the charge, I returned with my guns to Puebla, and the next day I went by stage to Mexico, where I was under surgical treatment six weeks. Our loss in this engagement was from five to six hundred, while the French and traitors lost over a thousand.

After being confined to my room, in the officers' quarters in Mexico, some ten days, I discovered one morning, on looking from my window, that the city was in mourning. Inquiring the cause, I learned that General Zaragosa had died in the city of

Puebla, which was sad news to me, as I considered him better qualified to command a large army than any other Mexican general. General Jose Maria Arteaga succeeded to the command of the liberal troops throughout Mexico.

Puebla was occupied by our forces and properly fortified. The French received large accessions of fresh troops and soon returned to attack the city. After a siege of about six weeks, during which there was much hard fighting, our troops were starved out. Some four thousand of them fought their way out and returned to the city of Mexico, while the remainder were forced to surrender conditionally, and after being disarmed, they were at liberty to go to their homes. Many of them, however, found their way to the capital. (This was in 1862 or 1863).

My next movement was to request to be transferred to my old field of operations at Mazatlan, for my health was poor and I preferred the air of the coast. My request was granted, and my friend, Colonel Orosca, and an escort of fifty men were allowed to accompany me, and we made our trip through the State of Durango, where we were in hopes to gather many volunteers to go with us to Mazatlan. We were several days recruiting in Durango, and several weeks elapsed before we arrived at Mazatlan. Meantime, the French had got possession of Mazatlan, coming around in war vessels.

We found our forces there much scattered and disheartened, their stock of arms and ammunition running very low. General Morales had left with a part of the troops and gone to Sonora, leaving General Corona in command. By uniting our forces, including several hundred fresh troops who came from Durango with us, we made the French some trouble, and by intrenching ourselves outside the city, we bombarded them occasionally, but made no direct assault.

We fortunately got information of a pack-mule train, soon to arrive from the mountains, loaded with silver, and destined for shipment from Mazatlan. It was an easy task for us to overpower the escort and capture the silver bars, which were worth two hundred thousand dollars. Governor Pesquiera ordered the money to be laid out for arms and supplies for our troops. A coasting vessel was procured, and General Lanberg was commissioned to take the money to San Francisco and purchase arms, ammunition, &c, for our use.

After waiting patiently several weeks, we found that he had returned with the arms, &c, and being a friend of Maximilian, and one of his countrymen, had turned traitor to us and handed over the arms and government stores to the French. Our situation was getting desperate; but we concluded to continue the siege of Mazatlan, with some hope of retaking the city, if we could cut off their supplies, which they received by water. We were already capturing all the cattle which their agents picked up back in the country, and we usually shot those of the French who were bold enough to try to run through our lines to bring in such stock.

One party of one hundred and eighty French were captured by us one day, and, as we had no use for prisoners, we shot nearly all of them. Among those that we spared was a Captain Louis Ronsey, who plead for his life, saying he was as good a liberal as any of us, but was forced into the imperial service by his connections. He gave his sword to General Corona, who took him at his word, remarking lie was the first Frenchman he ever dared to trust. In this case the clemency extended to him was well rewarded; for he fought on our side from that day till the conclusion of the war, and was a brave and trustworthy officer.

Learning that the French were about to land some troops at Altata, at the mouth of the Culiacan River, I was detailed to go with a force of five hundred men, under General Rosales, to that point. About one thousand French were landed from a man of war, and they had no idea of there being any liberals in the vicinity. They marched at once for Culiacan; and when at a small village within about nine miles, they were attacked by the liberals, who lay in ambush for them.

Our cavalry were secreted to attack them in the rear, when the fire from two small field-pieces under my charge should open in front. I had the guns posted so as to give a raking fire, as the French entered the village, and our men were scattered along on both sides of the roadway for some distance. They were totally surprised and routed, losing about eighty men killed and half their force was captured; the remnant escaping back to Altata to their war vessel. As the French held many of our men prisoners at Mazatlan, we made an exchange with them, and thus I saw again some of my old friends who were taken at the capture of Mazatlan.

From an American that we captured among the prisoners, in the last engagement, we learned that the French, at Mazatlan, had sent an order by the steamer *John L. Stevens*, to San Francisco, for rifles, cavalry, saddles, clothing, provisions, and forage. We knew of a fine coasting schooner in the river, near Altata, and finding that the French vessel had left that port with their troops, we planned an expedition to meet the *John L. Stevens* on her return trip, and seize the goods, for she had no armament, being a passenger steamer.

Our plan suited General Corona, who dispatched my friend Colonel Norton and myself with a six pounder and a suitable force of well armed men, on the mission, with strict orders to respect the rights of the passengers, if we came across the steamer. We took the schooner without difficulty and made across the Gulf of California to the port of La Paz, where the steamer was to make a landing. After cruising about several days, we espied the steamer about fifteen miles from La Paz. We had divulged our plan to the liberals of that port, who promised to aid us. When the steamer made the landing, we ran alongside, and, boarding her, commanded the captain to deliver to us all that he had on board which belonged to the French.

Great excitement prevailed on board among the passengers, as they feared that we were outlaws and robbers; but when we assured them that we only wanted the property of the French troops, that we knew was aboard, they became quiet. The captain immediately turned all the property over to us, which consisted of eight hundred rifles, many boxes of ammunition, two hundred cavalry saddles, baled hay, hard bread, salt pork, and other provisions, which were transferred to our schooner forthwith, and she was dispatched back across the gulf to Altata, where we had a force in waiting to receive the cargo.

I procured a guard of liberals from La Paz, and remained on board with one of my men and about twenty of this guard to detain the steamer, so as to give time for our schooner to land at Altata before she could possibly reach Guaymas, and enable the French to recapture the property, by sending a war vessel in pursuit. After staying on board twelve hours, and cautioning this friendly guard to detain the steamer twenty-four hours longer, I left in a small pilot boat, which our friends at La Paz furnished us, with my soldier friend for Altata.

The gulf was smooth when we started, and we thought it safe enough to attempt the passage, as my friend was somewhat skilled in managing a boat. The night following a strong gale set in, and the storm increasing, we gave up all hopes of reaching the land, for our boat filled with water as fast as we could bail it out with our hats. We let her go scudding along before the wind at a tremendous rate, for we were completely at the mercy of the elements. The gale was from the south, and we were blown ashore, after being out about forty-eight hours, at Guaymas, two hundred and fifty miles up the coast of Sonora, above Altata, where we wanted to land.

This truly was a sorry plight to be in; for the French held possession of Guaymas and the steamer would soon be here, after our friendly guard of liberals at La Paz released her. On arriving in the harbour, our boat was taken from us, and we were arrested and taken before the French commander, General Gardinelle, who asked us where we were from. I replied, "from Lower California," which was the truth. The captain of the port was a traitor, and was formerly acquainted with me, as we served together in the liberty cause against the church, but did not know that I was in the service of the liberty party now against the French; and proving nothing against us, we were discharged on condition that we did not leave town.

The French guards encircled the place, and it was no easy

matter to escape; but I knew the steamer would be likely to arrive the next day, when the story of our robbery of their vessel would cause a tumult, and we should be hung forthwith, or shot as pirates. I informed my comrade that we must escape that night or run a fearful risk; and he replied that he should remain, because the danger of running the guards was the greatest. I bade him *adieu*, and told him to secrete himself, for I should make the attempt. Lucky enough for me that we parted, for we never could have got away together.

The next morning, about daybreak, I was walking in the outskirts of the city, when I found a Mexican shepherd boy engaged in milking a number of goats. I stepped into the pen and proposed to assist him in driving his goats out of the city; also offered him a dollar to exchange his cap for my hat, and trade blankets with me, which he accepted. After we had made the change, and he had put up his milk, we started the goats for the pastures on the high hills beyond the guards, back of the city, and passed the guard without being questioned.

When we reached the top of the hill, I looked back towards the sea, and in the distance noticed the smoke of the steamer approaching; and I thanked fortune for my escape, and thanked my Creator, too, for a sufficient stock of wits to get me out of a bad scrape. I changed the cap back for my hat, telling the boy it was a tight fit. Then I started in a northerly direction down the hills, travelling towards Hermosillo, some seventy-five miles to the north, where I knew we had a force of liberals. After proceeding a few miles I came to a Mexican *ranche*, where I obtained some provisions and continued my tramp for three and a half days, till I arrived near Puebla de Ceres, almost exhausted, having crossed a country of barren plains and hills with only an occasional settlement.

I was still separated from Hermosillo by a river, which is almost dry in a dry season, but now it was so swollen with rains that I could not ford it, and there were no boats that I knew of. The people of Puebla de Ceres were unfriendly to our cause, and I dared not show myself for fear of arrest; so I remained near the river waiting for it to fall.

At the expiration of two days, the river still continued high, when I was informed by a passing Mexican mail-carrier that General Gardinelle, with his French troops, was on the march from Guaymas to Hermosillo and would arrive, probably, the next day. Here I was in another hard place; the river with its swift, muddy waters in front, and the same enemy in my rear that came near hanging me at Guaymas. I walked up and down the banks till I found a log which I thought might carry me safely over. This was my only chance, for there was no friend within hailing distance on the opposite shore.

The river was about a half a mile wide, in its swollen state, covering over a wide extent of bush and chaparral on the other shore. I divested myself of clothing, and put some papers, &c, in a large bandanna handkerchief, which I tied around my waist; then making a bundle of my clothing, in which I enclosed about twenty-five dollars, I fastened it to my head and mounted the log, which was about eight feet in length and a foot thick, determined to paddle myself across to the other shore if possible.

When about midway in the river, the swift current caused my log to roll over with me, and my bundle of clothing got loose from my head and floated down stream. Holding to my log as best I could, I succeeded in reaching a bunch of willows, growing in the stream. Here I rested a while, and then made another attempt, and reached shallow water and bushes on the opposite bank, when I easily reached the high ground. Here I sat down and contemplated my situation, which was rather a gloomy one.

My clothes and money were gone, and I knew not what to do. I had an acquaintance living in Hermosillo, a Mr. Douglass, employed in the mint, and another friend, a Mr. Hale, an American, who was a wagon-maker. After a while a Mexican boy passed nearby. I hailed him and inquired if he knew these gentlemen. He informed me that he did, and I promised to reward him if he would bring either of them to me. He returned in a short time, bringing both of my friends, who were surprised to find me in such a situation, and asked how I came in such a fix. I gave them a brief history of my misfortunes, when Mr. Douglass left me, and it was not long before he returned with a new suit of clothes.

We then in company proceeded to the hotel, where I obtained refreshments, and was soon entirely recovered from the effects of my trip. I was also furnished with an ounce of gold by Mr. Douglass. Here I was informed that there were about four hundred liberal troops in Hermosillo, under the command of Colonel Corea. I went to the colonel and informed him of my, adventures, and of the expected arrival of the French troops. He told me the governor had about eight hundred troops in the capital at Ures, and that he was going to march his troops at once to the aid of the governor.

After offering my services. I was placed by him in charge of two twelve pounder howitzers, and we started for the capital. At this crisis the French forces came in sight on the opposite bank of the river, but could not cross on account of the high stage of the water. On our way to the capital we had an attack from some seven hundred traitors and half-breeds, under the lead of a famous Indian chief, by the name of Tannery, who had raised this force in favour of the French. This occurred the night before reaching Ures, about 1 o'clock in the morning, at a Mexican *ranche* called Palma de le Noria.

I had advised our colonel to lay over here and await the approach of some cavalry, which we expected the governor to send us, as it was dangerous to proceed into the city with our weak numbers, in view of the large number of the enemy who were hovering about the capital, waiting to cut off reinforcements. The colonel, however, refused my advice and passed the *ranche* some four hundred yards, when, from among the trees and brush by the road, these Indians and Mexicans gave us a volley from their guns and rushed upon us.

The colonel and most of the men were so surprised that they broke for the woods. I had commenced firing with my howitzers when I was surrounded and ordered to surrender, and was taken prisoner with about a hundred others. The remainder of our men escaped. The prisoners were then marched to the capital, where, upon arrival, we learned that the governor and his troops had been driven from that city.

Here we were thrown into the city prison, called the "*Correccion*," where I remained about two weeks, when we were informed that the French troops, under Gardinelle, had left Hermosillo, and were on their way to Ures, the capital. Again I considered my life in danger from these murderous frog-eating French invaders, who were scouring the country to reduce it to subjection.

Once I had escaped them by running their guards at Guaymas, and again by swimming the river on a log at Hermosillo; and now I was shut up in a prison where they were sure to find me on their arrival, and my life would not be worth a "*real.*" To add to my alarm, a friendly sergeant who had charge of the prison guard, told me that the French were expected the next day.

I had a friend in Ures, a Doctor Wallace, and I succeeded in sending him a note requesting him to send me thirty-five dollars, which he immediately did; and that night I had a splendid supper, with wines and liquors sent to me by Doctor Wallace, and I invited the sergeant and corporal of the guard to sup with me, and they accepted my invitation. I then had a secret conversation with the sergeant and described to him my delicate and dangerous situation, telling him that if the French commander found me here the next day, I should be shot; and if he would assist me in escaping I would give him all the money I had. He then told me that the officer of the guard had been drinking, and that he should fill that position after 12 o'clock, and he would then assist me to escape.

At about 1 o' clock the officer was asleep. The sergeant then being in charge, he furnished me with a rifle and twenty-four cartridges. Giving his orders to change the guard, he told me in what direction to travel. Dressing me as a soldier, he took me outside with the relief guard, as if to station me on a post.

When a favourable moment arrived, he silently bade me adieu, and I started in the darkness, after placing my purse in his hand, which he received with "*mucho gracias*," or many thanks. I started northward towards Arizona whither Governor Pesquiera and his troops had been driven, doing some very tall travelling, as the danger of my being retaken was uppermost in my mind.

On the sixth day after leaving, I laid down to sleep at some old ruins not many miles distant from Santa Cruz. After starting again I had not proceeded far, when, in passing through some tall weeds and grass, I overheard some conversation which I found proceeded from seven Apache Indians. I hid myself in the grass and they soon passed by at no great distance without noticing me.

That afternoon I reached a small settlement, called Santa Cruz, my shoes completely worn out, and my feet blistered, and I was about half-famished for want of suitable food. I remained here one day and night, and, procuring a buckskin, I made myself a coarse pair of moccasins.

From the Mexicans here I learned that the governor had crossed over into Arizona. I then hired a man and a donkey to take me to the governor, who was camped in the woods in Arizona. The journey occupied nearly three days. I rode the donkey, and the man drove it, following behind on foot, occasionally spurring him up with a sharp stick, for he was the slowest beast I ever rode, and was so small that my feet nearly touched the ground.

When I arrived at the governor's quarters, I must have presented a ridiculous appearance; but announcing myself in a loud tone, the governor came out of his tent, with other friends and officers, giving me a warm welcome. Colonel Corea, who had deserted me at the *ranche* below Ures, when the Indian Tannery attacked and gobbled up those who were brave enough to stand their ground, came around to see me. He and his men had followed in the wake of the governor and were here encamped. I refused to shake hands with him, accusing him of cowardice and laying the whole blame of the disaster on him. He retired from my presence and always shunned me after that. When I narrated my hardships and hairbreadth escapes to the governor, he was surprised, and pronounced my trip a hard one and my escapes as miraculous.

I stayed with the governor four days, during which we had frequent interviews, and I advised him to seek the protection of the United States' troops at the Fort of Calibasa, which was about three days' march from his camp. Governor Pesquiera said that all he wanted was arms and ammunition to enable him to raise additional volunteers and return to the capital at Ures. I told him that Colonel Lewis, commanding at Fort Calibasa, would probably assist him with the necessary supplies; for we all knew that United States troops all sympathized with the cause of the liberals.

In accordance with my further advice, he immediately moved his camp towards Calibasa, taking his family, his officers, and all the troops; and we halted within ten miles of the fort to confer with Colonel Lewis before advancing further. We camped here that night, and the next day the governor sent me with an armed escort to the fort, to see Colonel Lewis and obtain assistance,' or, at least, get his protection, and permission to establish a recruiting rendezvous at this point.

I proceeded to the fort and delivered my message to Colonel Lewis, and we discussed matters at some length. I detailed to the colonel as well as I was able, how utterly impossible it would be for the French to establish a monarchy that would stand permanently against the will of the common classes—that Mexico aimed to be a republic, after the example of the United States, and in such an emergency as this, when the eyes of the world were viewing this contest, and regarding it as a final settlement of the question whether republicanism could succeed in a half-civilized country, we really needed the sympathy, and, if possible, the aid of our powerful sister republic.

I also pictured to Colonel Lewis how the great statesmen of the United States had generally acquiesced in the Monroe doctrine of no crowned heads on this continent, and no interference from the crowned heads of Europe. After considerable discussion, Colonel Lewis informed me that his first duty was allegiance to the United States Government; but that what I had said fully agreed with his sentiments in regard to Mexico, and if we wanted any assistance we could have it. Colonel Lewis told me to say to Governor Pesquiera that he would come out with his staff the next day, meet us on the road, accompany us into the fort, and do all in his power to make us comfortable.

I then returned and informed the governor that Colonel Lewis requested that he should proceed to the fort and he would receive him with pleasure. The following day we advanced towards the fort, and when some five miles distant we met Colonel Lewis with his staff, several of his officers, and a band of music, when I introduced him to the governor and his family. We continued on to the fort, where we found the troops formed in line to welcome us, and we met with a cordial reception. Arrangements were made for the accommodation of the governor and his family, his officers and men.

We remained here some two months; meantime, the governor and family went to Fort Tubac, some twenty miles distant on the river. The governor and wife were both taken sick and she died in four days. Her death was lamented by all the troops, who regarded her as a sort of mother, from her universal kindness and genial nature. Her body was embalmed and placed in a sepulchre in the cathedral at Tamacacari. The governor was well cared for and finally recovered. Soon after, at the request of Governor Pesquiera, I took command of five hundred troops, with orders to proceed to Sonora and attack a force of Imperialists and Mexicans that were the terror and scourge of the people in the northern part of the state; they had their head-quarters at a town called Magdalena, and were about four hundred in number.

I encamped my troops at Santa Cruz and went alone to Magdalena in the disguise of a trader or merchant, to learn the condition and situation of the enemy, where I stayed twelve hours, and then returned to my camp without being detected. We then made preparations to attack the town, and surrounding it the next night, we commenced the attack about daybreak, which resulted in the capture of all their arms and ammunition, killing about fifty and taking about sixty prisoners. Our loss was three men killed and five wounded. We also captured one hundred and fifty cavalry horses.

I then commenced getting new recruits and arming new men. I was informed that the priest of Magdalena was furnishing means to sustain the enemy's troops. I ordered this priest before me, and from citizens of the place it was proven that he had done so. I then ordered him to furnish me with ten thousand dollars for the benefit of the liberal cause in his district, or be starved in prison. After two days' confinement he concluded to pay the amount, when I released him.

Learning that the Indian fighter, Tannery, was raising troops to attack me, I organized my men as quickly as possible, having now about seven hundred, and proceeded to meet Tannery. We had a skirmish at a place called Carnaro, in a very thick piece of brush, where we fought some two hours with about equal numbers on each side, when each party became frightened and retreated, with small loss to either side.

Our panic was caused by having so many raw troops, which demoralised the whole, and they scattered over the country so badly that I was not afterwards able to collect over four hundred of them, all told, which caused me a great loss in horses, arms, and ammunition. I returned with my four hundred troops to Fort Calibasa, in Arizona, and reported to Governor Pesquiera. I found him still in feeble health, and he expressed himself satisfied with my report. In a day or two after, a mail carrier brought a dispatch stating that the French had returned to Guaymas, which was their base of supplies for the state of Sonora; also, that John Coly, my comrade who refused to escape from Guaymas with me, was finally caught and shot.

Colonel Lewis, of the fort, now informed Governor Pesquiera that he had received a quantity of arms and ammunition from the United States government, and being overstocked, we could have all we wanted, by making proper payment, &c. We also had news that General Lanberg, who had deserted our cause when we sent him for arms to San Francisco, had been appointed to the command of the imperial forces in Sonora. Lanberg was an Austrian, and a particular friend of Maximilian, who had arrived now in Mexico and proclaimed himself emperor. The war had been conducted more than a year before Maximilian usurped the reins of government, and this traitor was thus rewarded for his treachery to us. We never called him a great general, but he was often termed the Austrian butcher, for he was inhuman to prisoners.

Soon after this, the Apache Indians made a raid upon us at the fort, taking all our horses, except ten.

We then pursued the Indians several days and recaptured most of our horses. When we returned we found that Colonel Lewis had turned over to Governor Pesquiera two thousand rifles and ammunition for the liberals. Dispatches were at once sent all over Sonora, to our recruiting agents, promising them that Governor Pesquiera would return to the capital at once if the, proper forces of volunteers could be raised; and at the fort we had encouraging dispatches daily in reply, for the people were aroused; and before long we mustered three thousand troops, when we started on the march for Sonora, the governor taking command.

Before we reached Hermosillo, we got information that reinforcements, composed of two thousand infantry and a regiment of cavalry, were on the way from lower Mexico to assist our cause. At Hermosillo we met these troops, who were commanded by General Alcontra,—the cavalry by General Martinez, who was a perfect terror to the French, and his regiment was called the cavalry of the Macheteros, from the fact that they all carried short swords, or machetes, which they wielded with terrible effect; and their leader, Martinez, was a brigand, or *desperado*, everywhere noted for his rough style of fighting.

His men were chiefly outlaws, gathered from various prisons, and cared not for which party they fought so much as for the money they got. Their motto while fighting for us *was war to the death and no quarter given or asked.*

Reinforced with these troops, our army was indeed formidable, and ready for an action if the enemy appeared. About the 4th of May, 1865, being encamped two miles from Hermosillo, we were attacked by the traitor, General Lanberg and his troops, aided by a considerable party of Indians and Mexicans under Tannery, the Indian chief.

The battle commenced about three o'clock, p. m., and was finished after dark, both parties claiming the victory; but we held the position, while Lanberg retreated to Ures, the capital, with all his forces. The loss was about three hundred on each side, in killed and wounded. Among the prisoners we took was a rich Mexican, named Don Juan Enigo, who had done much to help the traitors; and as we were in want of money, Governor Pesquiera informed Enigo that he could have his liberty by paying over the sum of twenty-five thousand dollars with-in fifteen days, and if the money was not forthcoming in that time he would be shot.

Meantime we marched from Hermosillo to Rione, where we established ourselves to recruit, in preparation for a great battle which we anticipated would soon come off at the capital. Juan Enigo, in reply to the demand of the governor, said he could raise a part of the money, and pay the balance in mules; and if an officer would accompany him to his *ranche*, back almost to Hermosillo, with a proper guard, the mules and money should be forth-coming. Governor Pesquiera accepted the proposal, and detailed me with an escort of twelve men, to go on this mission.

I told the governor I thought the trip dangerous with so few men, but thinking I could raise additional men to assist us on the return, we started off. On arriving at the *ranche* of Enigo, he took us into his store and paid over the sum of eight thousand dollars in gold, and proceeding to his farm he allowed us to select two hundred mules, with which we started at once for our camp.

On our return, at about eight o'clock in the evening, we were surprised to see camp fires at a short distance from our path, which was through a ravine, and I sent a sergeant to ascertain who they were—whether friends or foes. He returned with a report that they were a scouting party of Indians, under Tannery. They were aroused by the noise of our mules, and came forward cautiously to ascertain our strength, and attack us if expedient, I decided to retreat to Hermosillo, if I could do no better.

Having several mules heavily laded with packs, I consigned their loads to a deep hollow near the road, headed the mules for Hermosillo, divided my party into two squads, giving orders that one should drive the mules with all haste to Hermosillo, while the other would stay back and detain the Indians. As the road was narrow, running through cane brake and chaparral, we could in this way keep the Indians at bay, and save the mules. As the Indians came up, I shot the horse of the leader and killed him, and then commenced giving orders as though I had a large force of men.

The noise made by the retreating mules helped on the deception, and the Indians evidently thinking there was a large force just out of their sight, beat a hasty retreat; and we were only too glad to retire in the opposite direction. About daybreak I was rejoiced to discover a small party of mounted men in the distance, who proved to be cavalrymen in the liberal cause. On meeting them, we stopped a short time for breakfast, and to discuss the news; and learned from them that they were on their way to the capital, to join Pesquiera, and that a battle was momentarily expected there. We decided to keep company with them, and join our force there.

After travelling that day in company, not without some fear of the enemy, for our party only numbered twenty-six men, we slept that night in the mountains, and arrived the next noon in sight of our forces, who were about two miles from Ures, and were engaged in a hot fight with Lanberg's troops and Tannery's Indians. The enemy were between ns and Governor Pesquiera's forces. When they discovered us they attempted to cut us off; and firing upon our party, one of our horses was shot under its rider. We took up our dismounted friend, and succeeded in getting around out of reach of the enemy's shots, and safely reached a knoll where some of our artillery were posted.

In coming so suddenly on our friends we came near being shot as enemies, but by our signs and shouting they recognised us and were glad of our assistance, and in less than five minutes we were at work. Governor Pesquiera's troops numbered about five thousand five hundred, and were commanded by Generals Garcia Morales, Alcontra, and Martinez. The enemy numbered about the same, and fought with desperation; for both sides knew full well that prisoners were no object, and it was almost certain death to fall into each other's hands.

Governor Pesquiera was fighting to get possession again of the capital, and regarded this battle as the turning point in Sonora. If defeated now he was ruined, and therefore every man was urged to do his best to gain this battle. The Macheteros under Martinez were engaged in a terrible contest with Tannery's Indians. When Morales saw that I had arrived on the field he gave me the command of two howitzers, with twenty-four artillerymen, and one hundred and fifty infantry as supports, with orders to hasten around up a narrow lane and pour in a raking flank fire on Tannery's Indians. They were mostly mounted men, and their unearthly yelling inspired the whole of the enemy's force with enthusiasm.

In starting up this lane, I used shell for awhile, then approaching nearer I used grape and canister, driving the Indians and killing large numbers. I overheard one of their officers, a Mexican, say to his men as he pointed to me: "Shoot that American captain; he is doing all this mischief." He was behind one of the cottonwood trees which skirted the road, and when he showed his head a moment later, I dropped him, at a distance of thirty yards or more, with my Texan six-shooter. I saw him fall, and what is more, I have now in use the belt he wore on that occasion.

We drove them before ns like sheep, and scattered them in all directions. On arriving at the end of the lane, I saw General Lanberg and his adjutant, both lying dead; and Martinez's cavalry just then coming up, they put a lasso around the general's neck and dragged him some distance and hung him up to the limb of a small tree so that his toes touched the ground.

A heavy thunder storm burst upon us as the enemy were fleeing, with our cavalry in pursuit, cutting them up unmercifully; and as it rained in torrents, becoming quite dark, I ceased firing, and remained on the ground till daybreak, keeping my ammunition as dry as possible, not knowing whether we should be attacked again or not.

Before sunrise, I found that we had cut the enemy all to pieces, and I received orders to return to head-quarters, and march into the city. On arriving in the city I saw that part of our troops were there already, and had got intoxicated, were breaking into houses, &c, and especially some men who joined us from Fort Calabasa were committing all manner of depredations. Orders were then given to go into barracks and make ourselves as comfortable as possible, and preparations were made to bury the dead.

Our loss in the battle was about four hundred and eighty killed and wounded. That of the enemy was nearly a thousand; and Martinez's cavalry pursued them for miles, killing many officers and men; and whenever they overtook an Indian, he was cut and hacked to pieces. On their return they hung up the dead bodies to trees by the roadside. This decisive conflict turned the tide of affairs in our favour in Sonora, and Governor Pesquiera had things his own way afterwards. Throughout the Republic, wherever the news went, it cheered the hearts of the liberals. Dispatches were sent Juarez, who succeeded Comonfort, and had been president since the disastrous siege and battle of Puebla.

The head-quarters of Juarez were at Zacatecas, whither he had been driven by the French. Maximilian had possession of the city of Mexico, having entered the country early in the year (1865), and as emperor was reigning over the country like a tyrant. The announcement of the slaughter of the Austrian traitor, General Lanberg, the friend of Maximilian, with the flower of his army cut to pieces, and the utter defeat of Tannery's Indians, made the friends of liberty rejoice throughout the nation; no doubt contributing much to the downfall of Maximilian.

Martinez's cavalry followed up this victory by scouring the state of Sonora, sweeping over it like a whirlwind; scattering the French and traitors everywhere; leaving the French no foothold except at the port of Guaymas, which was defended, in part, by a man-of-war.

CHAPTER 19

Surrender of Maximilian

To offset these successes in the northwest, Maximilian, aided by the traitor generals, Miramon, Marquez, and Mejia, had been victorious in a number of engagements in lower Mexico and the interior.

In October, 1865, an infamous decree, called the "black flag decree," was issued by Maximilian, the first article of which provides that "all persons belonging to armed bands or corps, not legally authorised, whether they proclaim or not any political principles, and whatever be the number of those who compose the said bands, their organization, character, and denomination, shall be tried militarily by the courts martial, and if found guilty, even of the fact of belonging to the band, they shall be condemned to capital punishment within the twenty-four hours following the sentence."

This decree cost Maximilian his life two years after. Under its provisions, General Arteaga, commander-in-chief of the liberals, with General Salazar, four colonels, five lieutenant-colonels, and several hundred prisoners were shot, having been surprised and captured in the state of Michoacan. This wholesale murder, contrary to all rules of civilized warfare, had the most damaging effect on the cause of Maximilian. When the news reached us in Sonora, every liberal was aroused to desperation, and resolved on vengeance.

Soon after this decree, and while we were at Ures, the capital, we received dispatches stating that President Juarez had been driven out of the country by his reverses, and forced to take shelter under the flag of the United States, at El Paso del Norte, on the Rio Grande river. Similar dispatches were sent by the president to the liberal governors of all the Mexican states, requesting them to raise money and volunteers to the extent of their ability, and unite in one common effort to drive the tyrant and usurper, Maximilian, from Mexican soil.

President Juarez secured the services of two regiments, on the American side of the river, and recrossing with them, drove the French, who had followed him nearly to the line, back into the interior; and many of them retreated in such haste that they perished on their way over the sand plains and barren hills. President Juarez established himself at Chihuahua, where he remained for a considerable time. General Escobedo was appointed by him to command the liberals in Mexico, and this officer was so successful in reorganising the army of the centre, as it was called, that after a while Juarez ventured to return to Zacatecas, which city he fortified as his head-quarters.

The next news of importance, after we had been favoured with a series of successful operations in Sonora, was that Louis Napoleon was about to withdraw the French troops from Mexico. The reason of this action of the French emperor was very easily to be seen. The civil war in the United States had closed, leaving the government in condition to enforce the Monroe doctrine, and Napoleon had been officially notified that no empire would be tolerated in Mexico; he therefore concluded to withdraw from any interference tending to the establishment of such an empire, before he found himself in trouble with the United States government.

Now, we were sure that victory, sooner or later, would perch upon our banners; and the church party trembled for fear that Maximilian would not be able to sustain himself long after the evacuation by the French.

We soon had orders for a portion of our troops to march on Guaymas, which was the only place in Sonora occupied by the enemy; and we were instructed to clear the French out of that port without delay, if we found them in possession on our arrival. On our way down we captured six officers who had fought against us in the last battle at tires.

On arriving near the mouth of the Yagui River, we learned that the celebrated Indian, Tannery, and some of his officers, had just embarked on a vessel for Lower California. We chartered another vessel, and a detachment pursued the fugitives, overtaking them and bringing them back without much difficulty. These, with the six officers taken on the way down from Ures, fifteen in all, were condemned to be shot in the back as traitors, while one French officer was shot in the breast.

The French had mostly left Guaymas before our approach, being mortally afraid of us, especially of the Machetero cavalry. Their man-of-war still remained in port, with officers and some French troops on board. There were three United States war vessels—the *St. Mary*, the *Suwannee*, and the *Cheyenne*—then near at hand on the Pacific coast, sent there to protect American interests.

One evening, while we were debating how to dispose of this French war steamer, and whether it would be feasible to blow her up by some torpedo arrangement, we were agreeably surprised to see the United States ironclad *Suwannee* arrive in port. The French vessel lowered a boat and sent officers to board the strange vessel and learn her nationality and the object of her visit. The United States commander objected to a visit at that hour from the French officers, and asked them if that was all the business they had with him.

Being answered in the affirmative, he told them that he had a notice to serve on them, which was that if that French war vessel was in the harbour the next day at four o'clock, he should open fire on her and sink her at once. The notice was all that was needed, for the next day the Frenchman weighed anchor, and departed for Mazatlan. The *Suwannee* followed closely after her to Mazatlan, where they were given twenty-four hours to remove some officers and men from that port; then the *Suwannee* followed her down the coast past Acapulco, after which she returned to Mazatlan.

The war now being ended in the state of Sonora, and there being an urgent necessity for reinforcements to go to central Mexico, to aid President Juarez, we began raising volunteers around Guaymas, for that purpose. We had a little difficulty with our cavalry general, Martinez, who demanded fifty thousand dollars of Governor Pesquiera for past services .of his regiment of outlaws. The demand was refused by Governor Pesquiera, on the ground that his men had already made a good thing out of the war; as many of them accumulated a large amount of money, for they stole everything they could lay their hands on.

Martinez threatened to steal the amount out of the Custom House if it was not forthcoming from Pesquiera; but the matter was finally compromised; not, however, till the governor had ordered out his troops, and a few drunken men of the cavalry were killed. Some months of quiet intervened, diversified with occasional skirmishes in the mountains, scouting expeditions, &c,, I then had orders to place four hundred men on board the steamer *John L. Stevens*, and go with them to Mazatlan, where General Corona held command. I remained at Mazatlan, after our arrival there, only a few weeks, before the general had a well organized force of three thousand troops all ready to start for the head-quarters of President Juarez, at Zacatecas, or of his army, under the command of General Escobedo.

It may be well to state here that while these active operations had been in progress in Sonora, under the direction of Governor Pesquiera, General Morales, and others, General Ramon Corona had not been idle in Cinaloa. He had kept the French bottled up in Mazatlan, month after month, and whenever they made a sortie beyond the fortifications, they were sure to be badly defeated. On two occasions they were terribly punished and cut up; once at the Presido of Mazatlan, and again at Palos Prietos.

General Corona commanded the expedition to Zacatecas in person; and I, as captain of artillery, was placed in charge of two twenty-four-pounders, splendid guns, and well manned by brave men. We were well mounted, well armed and provisioned; in fact, felt competent to meet the French or the Mexican traitors anywhere. Taking Tepic in our route, we came suddenly upon a force of three or four thousand Indians, led by the crafty Indian chief, Lozado, who was in favour of the imperial cause.

We attacked them, and the battle lasted the whole day, when they retreated to their favourite haunts in the mountains of Allico. Their loss was over eight hundred, while ours was not over two hundred men. We continued on to Guadalaxara, where we stopped for rest, and to gain recruits, who came in daily in large numbers, and to wait for orders from head-quarters. We soon mustered a force of four thousand well drilled men, as our recruits had all seen service, more or less. Our artillery were in capital order, but the pieces were mostly light guns, for field service, and hardly adapted for siege work.

As this narrative is not designed as a complete book of reference, nor to contain a history of all the military operations of the liberal party during these troubles, I have mainly endeavoured to give an account of matters that came under my personal observation. I knew but little of the generals who led our forces in central Mexico from the time of the siege and capture of Puebla until we had cleaned the French out of Sonora and Cinaloa. Many of the names of prominent men mentioned in this narrative may be incorrectly spelled, as I have endeavoured to give the spelling from the sound, which cannot always be correctly done with Spanish names any more than with English.

I knew by the reports that they had occasional re-verses and occasional successes or victories over the combined forces of the Mexican traitors and the foreign legions of Maximilian. I never doubted the administrative talent of President Juarez, nor the ability of General Escobedo, both of whom were nobly fitted for their positions, judging from the results. The justness of our cause, and the sympathy of our sister republic of the United States, gave us encouragement at all times, and aided the liberals in their days of darkness and discouragement.

At this time, March, 1867, Maximilian's cause was rapidly sinking. The French troops had left Mexico, and he was forced to rely mainly on the troops of Miramon and Mejia for support, and greatly overestimated their power in thinking they could uphold him. If he had followed the advice of Carlotta, his wife, and left Mexico with the French troops, it would have been far better for him. She told him before she left Mexico, that he had better leave with her, for if he stayed she feared he would never see her again, and, for her part, she would prefer to give a part of her vast property for the education of this ignorant nation, than have the empty credit of ruling over them.

The aristocratic tendencies, and the royal connections of this vain pretender decided him to make a stand and fight the liberals with the aid of the traitors and church party. Maximilian was now fortified at Queretaro, with about ten thousand troops. President Juarez had his head-quarters at Zacatecas, depending for support on the army of Escobedo, which was encamped a number of miles distant. Maximilian sent Miramon, with the flower of his army, to Zacatecas, to attack the city and capture Juarez, if possible. They had nearly succeeded in this, when Escobedo, by a forced march, arrived with his army to the relief of Zacatecas, and routed Miramon's troops, who retreated in a panic, and with great loss, toward Queretaro.

Escobedo's army, joined with some liberal troops under General Castillo, and after pursuing them about thirty miles, surrounded the imperialists, when they were nearly all killed or dispersed, Miramon barely escaping with his life, having only a feeble remnant of his followers left when he arrived at Queretaro.

Just prior to this attack on Zacatecas, General Corona had received orders to march for that place, and had been marching for two days, with all haste, when additional dispatches came, announcing the victory of the liberals at Zacatecas, and ordering ns to hasten forward to Queretaro. By a forced inarch, General Corona's force, numbering about four thousand, arrived at Queretaro, the first week in April, 1867, just in time to participate in the last grand engagement which ended imperialism on this continent. We took a position on the high ground to the south of the city, while the American Legion, under Regules, occupied the west, and General Escobedo's army were on the heights to the east and north-east of the city.

General Ramon Corona was destined to be the hero of this siege. Our position was in full view of the old convent of Las Cruces and within easy range. This was an immense stone structure with walls of great thickness, and here Maximilian made his head-quarters. The bombardment commenced in earnest and was continued for three days with little cessation. Meantime, General Corona had given me a position with my two twenty-four pounders on an eminence where every shot would tell, but he discovered and so did I, and so reported the first day that my guns were too light to batter the convent walls as I wished. He gave me orders to start for Zelaya, forty miles distant, with a strong escort, and bring two heavy siege guns, forty-eight pounders, which I did, and planted them in position. These heavy guns worked successfully, making many breaches in the walls of the convent.

General Lopez had a force of Austrians, a few French and some Mexicans defending the convent, as a sort of body-guard for Maximilian; and my heavy guns demolished such buildings as they sought refuge in. Other batteries surrounding the city were engaged in an incessant fire, destroying buildings and demolishing walls and obstructions, opening the way for the liberals, who had already gained possession of a part of the city and were often engaged in hand to hand conflicts with the imperialists in the streets.

On the fourteenth of May, about 4 o' clock in the morning, we lodged a shell in the magazine at Las Cruces, which exploded it, doing great damage and killing many. The enemy made a sortie under the lead of Miramon, intending to drive back General Corona, who, with his advance guard and a strong support of infantry, had entered the cemetery and were fighting their way to-wards the fortress of Las Cruces. After falling back a little, General Corona was reinforced and drove the enemy back into the city with great slaughter, and had nearly surrounded

Maximilian's head-quarters, when the enemy surrendered and the firing ceased. Maximilian came out of the fortress, and the white flag was displayed.

On his appearance he was approached by Colonel Green, of the American Legion, who urged him to be calm, as he was very much excited. Maximilian stood in great fear of the liberal soldiers, as well he might, when he thought of the "Black Flag Decree," and desired to surrender his sword to, and claim the protection of the commanding officer, as a prisoner of war. He was directed to General Corona by Colonel Green. As he walked on towards Corona, who, with his staff, were mounted, and were rapidly surrounding the emperor with the troops, I had a good view of Maximilian, for I had ridden up in haste and sat on my horse almost in his pathway.

As he passed me he was a little in doubt as to which was Corona, and, turning his head, he asked me to point him out. I replied in English that General Ramon Corona was the one who was mounted on the grey horse. He started in surprise at my reply, and asked me if I was an American, and I answered that I was. He then passed up to Corona, and, presenting his sword, said, "I am Maximilian. I am emperor no longer, but your prisoner." General Corona, as he received the sword, replied, "No, Maximilian, you are not now emperor, and never were."

Maximilian's troops now began the work of disarming, and our men ransacked the convent and other buildings adjacent, to find Miramon and Mejia. They seized Miramon, and would have hung him but for the interference of General Corona, who insisted that he should have a trial, according to the laws of Mexico, and be punished with other traitors in a proper manner.

Mejia was soon caught, and these three important prisoners were confined in an old convent, and kept under a strong guard. General Corona, after a conference with General Escobedo, sent a dispatch to President Juarez, reporting the results of this siege, and requesting advice in the matter. In reply to this dispatch, the president appeared at Queretaro in person; and by his di-

Execution of Maximilian

rections General Escobedo summoned a court-martial for the trial of the prisoners, the twenty-ninth of May, but which was postponed till the thirteenth of June. Maximilian, Miramon, and Mejia were sentenced on the sixteenth, and were finally shot on June 19, 1867.

When Maximilian read his death warrant, President Juarez showed him the infamous decree of October 3, 1865, under which hundreds of the liberals had been shot as soon as captured. He asked Maximilian if he signed that decree, and, if so, what he had to say in justification of such barbarous warfare. He admitted signing the decree, but said nothing in defence of his conduct. He requested a respite of his sentence for three days, which was granted, to give him time to arrange his matters. He sent for an English physician and his assistant, to make arrangements for a metallic coffin, and for the embalming of his body.

This interview was allowed on condition that myself and two other officers were present to witness it. When Doctor Jenkins and Kerford arrived, the conversation was brief. Maximilian requested them to furnish a tight metallic coffin, with a glass top, and wished his body embalmed and placed in a natural position in such a way that it could be transported to Austria. He desired that the coffin should be placed near the place where he was to be shot, as he wished to see it. He then gave Doctor Jenkins a check to pay for his services and for the coffin, and we retired. He then made his will, giving to his brother and his wife the whole of his vast property, except one hundred thousand dollars which he reserved for the wife and family of Miramon.

At 3 o' clock on the nineteenth, the prisoners were marched out of their prison, the convent of Los Capuchinos, to carriages in waiting. Maximilian was seated with a priest in one carriage, and Miramon and Mejia in another. General Escobedo ordered out four thousand troops to attend the execution, who were arranged in position at the fatal spot when the carriages and procession arrived. The place selected was in front of an old wall, in the suburbs of the city, and a seat had been provided for Maximilian, with his coffin nearby.

When he left the carriage, the priest gave him a cross to hold in his hand; and, as he approached his coffin, he examined it closely. Doctor Jenkins was present, and asked him if his coffin was satisfactory to" him, and he replied that it was. The doomed men were then placed in position to meet their fate.

Maximilian was asked what he had to say, and he asked permission of General Corona, who was standing near, to confer with the guard, who were drawn up in front waiting for orders to fire, as he desired them to shoot him in the breast and not disfigure his face. His request was granted, and he gave to the officer of the guard a gold watch, to the sergeant a gold medal, and to each man of the platoon an ounce of gold, telling General Corona to keep his sword, which he had surrendered to him before, as a present. He blamed Louis Napoleon as the cause of all his disasters. The medal he presented to the sergeant was one he had received from Victor Emanuel; and the Emperor of Austria has since paid the sergeant a large sum for it in order to get it back to Europe. All this occurred in the space of a few moments, after which he was busily occupied with the priest.

General Miramon was asked if he had anything to say. He said he was to be shot as a traitor, but he did not consider himself as such. He believed he was acting for the good of his country. Since the revolution of Santa Anna, he had seen no stable government in Mexico,—nothing but revolutions and fighting among themselves, and the country would never become peaceful until some other nation assumed control of the government. And, said he, "Now that I am about to die, remember what I say to you; for you will live to see my words prove true."

Then shaking hands with the priest, who stepped one side, the two Mexican generals were placed on seats, with their faces to the wall and their backs to the soldiers. Maximilian stood up boldly, holding out the cross and facing the executioners.

He refused to be blindfolded, and advanced two steps nearer to receive the fire. His last words were: "Poor Carlotta, had I taken your advice it would have been far better for me."

Looking directly at the file of soldiers he signified that he was ready, when they received the order to fire, and the three doomed men fell to the ground, dying almost instantly. Maximilian stood so close to the executioners that his clothes took fire, but were soon extinguished. The soldiers were ordered back to their barracks. They marched in silence, for they had witnessed a solemn spectacle. The two Mexican officers were placed in coffins, and buried in the cemetery the next day.

Maximilian's body was taken in charge by Doctor Jenkins and his assistants, and speedily embalmed; then the authorities took possession of it. Several days after this, a discussion arose in camp relative to the embalming of bodies, and a number of us had a desire to see the body of Maximilian, and obtained permission to do so. We found the countenance well preserved and very life-like. Three days after the execution, four Mexican officers, who had been secreted by some Mexican women, were discovered by the soldiers. They were summarily shot by the soldiers, as was the traitor, Colonel Mendez, the brute who ordered the shooting of the six hundred liberal prisoners. These five traitors were shot in the back without trial.

In the battle of Queretaro, which resulted in the capture of Maximilian, the enemy lost about fifteen hundred killed and wounded, and the loss on our side was estimated at eight hundred and fifty. After the battle, the appearance of the city was frightful, a large portion of the buildings being in ruins. President Juarez ordered that the three or four hundred officers and several thousand prisoners captured by us, be disarmed and allowed to return to their homes.

He then issued proclamations, re-formed his cabinet, appointed civil officers, promoted military officers for their bravery, set in motion the whole machinery of his government, and finally returned, July 15, 1867, to the city of Mexico, which he entered in triumph, amid the ringing of bells, firing of cannon, and the noisiest demonstrations of rejoicing from his countrymen. He was accompanied by a large force of mounted men, who were constituted the president's guard in the city. Most of our troops remained several weeks in Queretaro after the battle.

Some were discharged and paid off with funds received from the president, for the war was now virtually over.

CHAPTER 20

I Resign My Captaincy

Intelligence was received by General Corona that a troublesome traitor, named General Marquez, had a force in Oaxaca, capital of the state of Oaxaca, about two hundred and thirty miles south of the city of Mexico, and that he was still operating against the liberals, having no disposition to surrender. Nearly twenty-five hundred of our troops were ordered down to Oaxaca to disperse these traitors and rebels. The march occupied eighteen days, and while we were on the march, General Marquez, hearing of our approach, disbanded his troops and fled from the country.

Finding, on our arrival, no troops to fight, and many of our men being impatient to go to their homes, as the war was about finished, they mutinied and demanded their discharge and pay from our commander. He replied that he had no funds on hand to pay them. The soldiers then made a raid on the churches and several wealthy houses in the city, which contained much gold and silver. In trying to suppress this raid and restore order, one of our captains was killed. About fifteen hundred troops were engaged in this pillage, and after securing all they could lay their hands on, they deserted.

We were now left with only about one thousand faithful troops, and our General reported our condition to President Juarez. Money soon arrived, and the remaining troops were paid, with the agreement that they should remain a while longer in the service. We remained in camp near the city about a month, when we received orders to march for the mountains of Allico, to attack the Indians under Lozado, who were at this time about the only enemies in open arms against the cause of the liberals.

This march overland consumed about three months' time; but, while on the route, we received large additions to our numbers in various places, so that when we arrived at Tepic, where Lozado was posted, we mustered about three thousand troops, well armed, and commanded by our favourite, General Corona. Here we had a severe engagement with Lozado's Indians, and drove them back into the mountains of Allico. We remained in that vicinity several weeks, having frequent skirmishes with them, losing four to five hundred, while their loss was about half that number.

These Indians are so skilled in mountain warfare, and have such an advantage of position in their mountain retreats, that it is totally impossible for any ordinary army to dislodge them, or to fight them on fair terms. (I have learned recently that Lozado still holds the same position in those mountains, and is remarkable for his guerrilla attacks and frequent robberies).

I now became tired and disgusted with fighting these Indians at such disadvantages; and, feeling that I had discharged my duty towards Mexico, I resigned my position as captain of artillery, and requested my discharge of General Corona. He replied that he would be sorry to lose me, and that he had no money to pay me; that I had been a very faithful officer in the service, and deserved great praise for my bravery; and that if I would wait till he could receive a dispatch from President Juarez he would be able to pay me. I told him I knew the condition of their government, and that I did not wish to remain any longer. He replied that if I insisted on my discharge he would give it to me, which he did.

I then left for the state of Sonora, Corona furnishing me one hundred and fifty dollars for my expenses on the way. I told him that as I had spent most of my time in the service of the state of Sonora, I thought I could arrange for my pay with Governor Pesquiera, of that state. On my arrival in Sonora, I was cordially welcomed by the governor. I gave him a history of our campaign since I left him; and detailed to him the death of Maximilian, &c. He then inquired if the president had paid me for my services. I told him he had not. He said his state was badly off for money, but that he had a quantity of confiscated landed property, and if I wished that I could have it.

This property he informed me was a league square, and had belonged to a Frenchman, who took part with the French and was killed. I told him I would look at the land, and if I liked it I would take it. I examined it, and found about one hundred acres under cultivation, and concluded to take it if he could furnish me a valid title, which he said he could do, and have it free from taxes so long as I retained the property. He then gave me an order on the president, who sent me a valid title to the land in payment for my services.

Being anxious to see my old American friends, the officers at Fort Tubac, which was in command of Colonel Dunkenberger, I then left for the territory of Arizona, and contracted at Fort Tubac to furnish hay for the United States government. I received the contract from Colonel Dunkenberger and Major Vail, and by its terms I was to receive thirty dollars per ton, (gold), for furnishing the hay, delivered in the Fort of Tubac. Shortly after receiving this contract, the Apache Indians came into Tubac one night, and carried off all my mules with which I was to haul my hay, and stole most of the government horses besides.

The following day an expedition, under command of Colonel Dunkenberger, started to overtake the Indians, and I went with them. We overtook the Indians at the foot of the Santa Rito Mountain. An Indian of this thieving band, notwithstanding they had in their possession my mules and the government horses, came to us with a certificate from the officers of Fort Goodwin, claiming that he and his party were peaceable Indians.

The colonel, after reading the paper, said he was under restrictions not to fight peaceable Indians, as these had proved themselves to be by this certificate, and was undecided what steps to take, as they denied having the animals. The soldiers hooted at the colonel for his conduct, as they saw the stolen animals in the possession of the Indians, and so did I; for I knew the brand on my mules. I told him I should take the responsibility to attack them as thieves, unless he became responsible for my part of the animals stolen. This he agreed to do, and we returned to Tubac, where I resumed the work of filling my contract, being supplied by the colonel with other mules. In due time I finished the contract, hiring all the work done by Mexicans, and received my pay.

From Tubac I went to Tueson and took a sub-contract from a contractor named John Capron, for getting out timber for the United States government for use in the construction of government wagons, to be delivered at Fort Calibasa to my old friend Colonel Lewis. I was to receive twenty-five cents each for spokes, and five dollars each for hounds and tongues. I then returned to Tubac and hired seven men to go with me to the Bird mountains, near Fort Calibasa, for the purpose of getting out this timber.

I had nearly accomplished my contract, when one night our horses became frightened, and, as there were some appearances of Indians about our camp, we immediately gathered our horses and fastened them near our camp, and placed a guard for our safety. The next morning, on examining the ground around outside, I saw the tracks of moccasins in a sandy hollow. That day we took our horses with us to where we were cutting timber, and kept a sharp lookout for Indians. We worked till about 4 o'clock that afternoon, when I told my men I would go to a hollow a short distance above, where I had seen some better timber, as I wanted to pick out something suitable for a few more wagon-tongues. I took along my rifle and revolver, and advised them to keep a good lookout for themselves.

In this mountain were great numbers of wild turkeys, deer and bears, and from this source we obtained all the meat we wanted. Our other supplies we easily obtained from the fort whenever we hauled a load there. After I left the men and had proceeded some three hundred yards, I discovered, while mark-

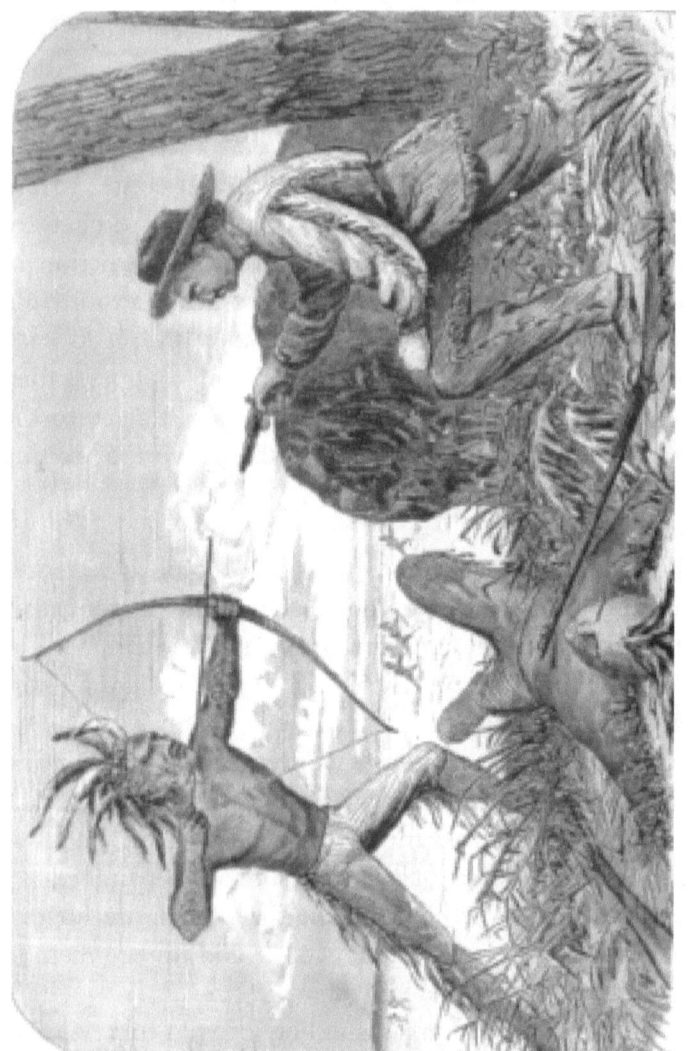

PLAYING A LONE HAND

ing with my hatchet, some good trees, that there were seven black objects to my right and rather between me and my men. At first I took them for turkeys, but soon found them to be Apache Indians.

Being so well acquainted with that species of game, I gave a war-whoop for a signal to my men; at the same time I saw two large oak trees near together, with a huge rock in front, and I hurried there for defence. Before I had got behind the rock, I was shot in the right leg, below the knee. Six buck-shot entered and lodged, as it afterwards appeared. I fell down behind the rock, but immediately raised to look at the enemy. Seeing an Indian approaching, I levelled my rifle and shot him dead.

Discovering the other six Indians coming up, I took good aim, with my large Texan six-shooter, at the foremost one, while he drew up his bow to shoot at me. I shot him between the eyes, which dropped him. He hit me with his arrow in the right cheek, near my nose, where the scar still shows very plainly. By this time my men were close at hand to assist me, and the Indians ran for their lives; but I fired again, hitting one of them in the hip, who had to be helped off by his companions.

Part of my men pursued the Indians some distance, but soon returned to see if I was badly injured. They found my leg bleeding profusely from the buckshot wounds, and I sent them after dry punk to put in the wounds to stop the blood. The arrow that struck me in the face I had pulled out, and this wound was not so bad as to occasion any alarm. They picked up the gun with which the Indian shot me, and I recognised it as having belonged to a friend of mine by the name of Scott, who lived at a cabin four miles below; and I made up my mind that they had murdered him. I asked my men if any of them had a sharp knife, and, finding them unwilling to scalp the Indians, I took the knife and undertook the job, for I wanted to show their scalps at the fort.

The Indian who shot me had very long hair, fastened up with metal rings. We started for our camp, leaving the bodies where they lay and taking the scalps. I fainted from loss of blood before getting to camp, and my men carried me to my tent, where I soon revived.

By a further application of dry powdered punk the bleeding was stopped. I sent to the fort for assistance, and before daylight the next morning about forty cavalry arrived with my messenger. I gave them directions for the pursuit of the Indians, and they found the wounded one about two miles distant, where he had dropped dead and been left by his companions, with his flesh eaten off to the bones by bears.

A snow-storm coming on, they returned to my camp, place me on a horse and started for the fort, which was some ten miles distant. After riding two miles, my wound in the leg broke out afresh, and bled so much that they were obliged to take me from the horse, and placed me under a tree, where I again stopped the blood with fine punk. My men then made a litter of poles and blankets, and carried me to the fort.

On my arrival there was much excitement on account of my fight, as the officers had great confidence in the peaceable nature of the surrounding tribes. I informed Colonel Lewis that the gun we had picked up belonged to my friend Scott, whose place was some four miles below where I was wounded; but he was rather incredulous, saying that Scott came into the fort the day before I was wounded.

On my insisting that I knew the gun, he sent a squad of cavalry to Scott's cabin to ascertain the facts. When they reached the place they found the remains of Mr. Scott terribly mutilated by knives. A Mexican boy who had been living with him was found badly wounded, but still alive. The boy was brought to the fort, as also were the remains of Mr. Scott. The boy had his leg amputated, and recovered. My wounds were getting very troublesome, and Colonel Lewis advised me to allow his surgeon to extract the shot, to which I consented.

That surgeon would have made a much better butcher than surgeon, however. He insisted on my taking chloroform, but I refused on account of the wound in my breast injuring my lungs, and I preferred to bear the pain to running the risk of taking chloroform. I was placed on a board, with my face down, four men holding me, and with an ounce ball between my teeth. The surgeon commenced by splitting my leg in the calf some five or six inches, and then with his instrument searched for buckshot in all directions. He succeeded in extracting four, when I told him I could stand it no longer.

In the operation I lost much blood, which, in addition to what I had lost before, reduced me so much that for several days I was almost insensible. When I revived I found an old Mexican woman standing by my bed, who informed me that a priest had called to see me, but I had no recollection of it. She was like a mother to me, and by her kind care I consider my life was saved. When nearly recovered, the old lady was dressing my limb one day, and, in taking off the bandage, the other two buckshot dropped on the floor. My recovery was then a sure thing, and I felt much encouraged.

An attack was made in the night on the fort soon after, and most of the animals stolen by a party of Apaches. They were pursued to their Indian village, and the property was recovered, after killing several of the Indians; and several women and children were captured and brought to the fort. Among them were two boys, about eight years old, which Major Vail took under his charge to care for. The major had two children of his own, about the same age, and these four children were in the habit of playing together about the fort. They were all playing, one afternoon, by a creek nearby, and as they did not return at their usual time, search was made for them.

About dark the searching party were horrified by finding the body of the major's little boy, who was about seven years old, terribly mutilated, his head being completely mashed by stones. Near the dead boy they found his little sister, who was nearly dead, having also received terrible blows on the head. This was the work of the two Apache vipers, who had fled for their village, fifty miles away, among the mountains.

The major sent a party in pursuit the next morning, and the boys were overhauled after two days' tracking. They were found under an oak tree eating acorns, and when they saw the soldiers in pursuit, they attempted to escape, but were overtaken and hung up to a limb of the tree. The other captive Indian children and women escaped the same night that the children were discovered murdered.

One young squaw nearly killed one of the soldiers that attempted to hinder her from escaping. They were pursued, but never caught. In all my acquaintance with Indians, I never found a tribe so mean, so contemptibly thievish, and so murderous and treacherous, as the Apaches; and the sooner the government exterminates them entirely, instead of trying to conciliate them with presents, the better. They are different from the Comanches or any other tribe I know of, as no day passes without some murder or robbery being committed by them.

Arizona territory has many gold and silver mines. The Indians have sometimes used these metals for making bullets, before they knew the worth of coin. I was an eye witness when the same surgeon who operated on me cut a gold bullet from a Mexican, who had been shot with it by an Apache. The bullet weighed half an ounce.

A short time after the murder of Major Vail's children, a Mexican woman made her escape from the Apaches. She had been a prisoner among them fourteen years, and she reported that there were large quantities of gold in the mountains where the Apaches lived. She showed some specimens of gold which she brought, weighing from one to three ounces. Some persons then employed her as a guide to these mountains. She told them it was a dangerous expedition, as the Apaches were a much stronger tribe than they were aware of.

A large party of about six hundred were gathered, however, from the vicinity of the fort to go gold hunting, and this woman accompanied them as guide. After several days' travel, as they were proceeding through a narrow pass, she and six soldiers were shot dead by the Apaches, who were concealed among the rocks. The Indians showed themselves then in such great numbers that the party of gold seekers were compelled to retreat and leave their dead. They returned to Tubac and reported that the Indians were so numerous that it was impossible to proceed to the mountains. There was an understanding between the Governor of Sonora and the commander of the United States forces at these Arizona forts, to work in harmony whenever the Apaches made a combined attack either on the Sonora side or the Arizona side, as by union they could better repel the Indians.

Soon after the return of the gold seekers, a body of Apaches made their appearance in Sonora, committing many depredations and capturing women and children. The Governor of Sonora sent dispatches to the commander of the United States troops in Arizona, appealing to him for aid, and troops were sent to his assistance immediately.

As the Sonora troops were advancing from the west, and ours proceeding to meet them, the Indians were caught between the two parties, and about eighty of them were killed and a number taken prisoners, among them a brother of the Apache chief, named Cachese. A dozen or more Mexican women and children that the Indians had in captivity were released. Cachese and the other Indians it was decided to hang at once. Cachese was singing just before we hung him, when he stopped, and cried out in Spanish: "Why do you not take a knife or a lance and kill us like men and not hang us like dogs."

Cachese was the last man hung, and when they were ready to place the rope about his neck, he caught the man who was adjusting the rope, with his teeth, tearing off part of his sleeve, when he was struck on the head by a soldier and rendered senseless, and was immediately hung.

One Indian boy, captured with them, was saved by the interference of Lieutenant Williams. He took him to Apache Pass in Arizona, where he kept him some four or five months. The lieutenant gave him a gun and ammunition as he was in the habit of going out to hunt deer, &c, and furnishing the lieutenant with game. One day the lieutenant rode a fine saddle mule out to a spring about two miles from the fort, as was his usual custom, for exercise. This young Apache was concealed behind a tree about twenty steps from the road, and attempted to shoot the lieutenant as he passed, but the gun missed fire.

Lieutenant Williams rushed up to the Indian, and, drawing his pistol, forced the young scapegrace to surrender the gun. He plead for his life, and the lieutenant bound his hands with a rope, and made him walk ahead of him to the fort. Williams was very angry, and yet very curious to know the object of the Indian boy in trying to kill him, who had been his benefactor; but when he found that he had no motive at all, he strung him up to a post in a hurry, saying that was the last Indian he would ever place any confidence in.

About this time, an emigrant train on its way from Texas through this section, had arrived at a place called Tulare Flats, when they were attacked by Apache Indians, who laid in ambush on each side of the road, each Indian being disguised by having a sage bush tied to his head. This emigrant train numbered about fifty, men, women, and children. The Indians kept quiet till the train had arrived abreast of them, when they all arose at once, and with tremendous yells frightened the teams so that they soon ran in the greatest panic.

They fired into the whites, killing all the men but two, who made their escape to Tueson. The officers at the fort at Tueson sent a party in pursuit of the Indians, who, on arriving at the place at which the train had been surprised, witnessed a horrid spectacle. Men, women, and children, most of whom were scalped, lay there with their brains beaten out; and about them were the remnants of their wagons, which had been burned.

One woman, Mrs. Mary Holliday, was found still alive with six arrows sticking in her breast, and near her were the dead bodies of her two children. She was unable to speak, and her signs were scarcely intelligible. Wagons were sent to take this unfortunate woman, the bodies of those who were killed, and what remained of their effects, to the fort, where the dead received proper burial. Mrs. Holliday lived but a short time after her arrival at the fort.

Near the scene of the fight the bodies of five Apache Indians were found, secreted in the brush. The two men who escaped gave us an account of the fight, and reported that four girls were missing from the party and could not be found, and we concluded the Indians had run them off into captivity.

Some two months after this, one of the girls made her appearance at Fort Buchanan, when she reported that two of the girls were dead, from the violence and outrage of the Indians, and, so far as she knew, the other one was still living among them. This unfortunate girl was named Emma Brown, and she was in a pitiable condition when she came to Fort Buchanan; barefoot, and nearly destitute of clothing. She gave the following account of her escape from her savage captors:

Two days before, while on the hills with a band of the Indians, she saw Fort Buchanan in the distance, and resolved to make a desperate attempt to reach it. A favourable opportunity soon occurred. The chief who had her in charge had just returned from a thieving raid of several days, and was very much exhausted. The whole band, feeling perfectly safe, had fallen asleep; and the chief, reclining with his head in her lap, was soon in a sound sleep.

Carefully freeing herself from the savage, she cast a hurried glance around her, and seeing the way clear, started on her perilous journey for the fort she had seen in the morning, determined to reach it or perish in the attempt, as she felt death to be far preferable to the life she had led for the past two months. She took the direction of the fort and travelled all night in the mountains. In the morning she discovered below her, a party of the Indians, following her. She was at this time following an Indian trail, where she had been before, but immediately stepped to one side, and secreted herself among some rocks.

The Indians passed within a short distance of her, for she could distinguish their voices easily. They did not look for her trail, as they seemed to take it for granted she would follow the Indian trail she was in, and they hurried on in the direction she had been going. More than once, as they filed past her, she gave herself up for lost, for to her excited mind it would seem that one had left the party and was approaching her hiding place; and she felt that if she was discovered it would be certain death, and very likely by a slow torture. A few days before, death would have been welcome; but now, when she had escaped from her captors, life seemed very precious to her.

As soon as the Indians passed her, she started up the mountain, out of their route, and secreted herself among some rocks which overlooked her former hiding place. Here she dreaded an encounter with some wild beast, for the place was wild and rough; but she preferred death in that form rather than recapture. In a short time she discovered the Indians (about fifteen in number) returning. Coming to the place in the trail where she had left it, they dismounted from their horses and searched in all directions, and in doing so, passed around the rocks where she had first secreted herself.

From here she had been very careful to walk on stones or rocks to her present hiding place, and they were unable to track her. She remained in her hiding place until the Indians had left, and gone back to their camp; then with desperate energy she resumed her flight towards the fort, where she arrived utterly exhausted, as she had been two days on her weary march without food or sleep. Her feet were bound up with pieces of the last skirt she had, for the Indians had kept her barefooted for fear she might escape. Her clothing consisted simply of a chemise, well worn and ragged from contact with the brush as she passed along. Her way to the fort had been through a country abounding in small scrubby prickly pear bushes, which had destroyed her clothing, and her feet were so filled with the thorns that it was some days before they were all removed.

She was taken in charge by the wife of Major Wells, at the fort, and was confined to her bed, in care of the physicians, more than a month before she recovered. During this time she was often delirious, shrieking in her agony: "They have killed my father, and mother, and two sisters; don't let them kill me."

It was true that her parents and sisters were killed in the massacre, and she was left alone in the world. When she had regained her health, she was sent by the officers at the fort, who supplied her with clothing and money, to San Francisco, and from thence to Galveston, Texas, where she had an uncle, the only relative she had living.

This kindness of these United States officers is only one instance among many that have come under my observation in the western country, and at the frontier outposts. They invariably treated the poor captives that were wrested and saved from the hands of Indians, with the greatest kindness, whether they were Mexicans or Americans, and supplied them with funds and clothing, medical attendance, and everything, free *gratis*, never asking or accepting any remuneration; and I believe their generosity to the unfortunate is not generally known, but it is worthy of being known throughout the world, for it is unparalleled, and beyond all praise.

CHAPTER 21

My Uncle's Massacre by Moromons

A few weeks after the events narrated at the close of the last chapter, a large party of Apaches appeared in the state of Sonora, committing all manner of depredations, and were pursued by the Mexicans into their own country. There they had an engagement, and most of the stock that had been stolen was recovered, and about eighty Indians killed. A small party of Mexican women and children that had been taken from Sonora by the Apaches, escaped by their shrewdness; for during the light they secreted themselves in the brush, and as the Indians ran, they remained concealed till the Mexicans were close upon them.

Among the prisoners released was Miss Holliday, who was captured by the Indians at the same time as Emma Brown, at the massacre of the emigrants, an account of which has been given. She was a daughter of the woman found by the soldiers who went to the relief of the train. Governor Pesquiera, of Sonora, sent word to the fort to notify the officers of her escape, and to inform them that she was under his protection.

The officers made up a purse for her relief, and sent it to her by a messenger, and instructed him to ascertain from her whether she wished to return to Texas. She returned the money to the officers, by the messenger, with many thanks for their kind offer and sympathy, and added that as her relatives were all dead, having been killed by the Indians, she had no home to go to, but as General Alcontra, the commander of the Sonora troops, had saved her life and requested her hand in marriage, she had accepted his kind offer and would soon go to housekeeping. This woman is now living happily in Ures, the capital of Sonora; and the last I heard of her she had three children, and was wealthy.

My wounds were now so far healed that I was able to walk about some; still, I suffered much from some undiscovered difficulty in the limb. I proceeded to Tueson for a change of medical treatment, and placed myself under the care of a noted surgeon named Lord, who appeared to understand my troubles. My leg continued badly swollen, and I was taken with chills and fever, when Doctor Lord informed me that I must leave that part of the country or lose my life.

It so happened that a government train was at Tueson, bound for Los Angeles, California, and I received permission to accompany it. I was placed under the care of the chief wagon-master, whose name was Caton. The day I left Tueson I had my horse, saddle, and bridle brought around and put in care of the wagon-master, for I was not able to ride him, but was placed in a wagon, on a cot hung by the four corners.

Soon after leaving Tueson I saw a poor Mexican walking along beside the wagon, carrying his blankets on his back. I called him to me, and on inquiry found he was going to California. This I thought an excellent opportunity to make an arrangement that would be to our mutual advantage. So I told him I was in need of a man to wait upon me somewhat, daring the journey, and if he would do so, he could put his blankets in my wagon and ride my horse; and if this was not an equivalent for his services, I would pay him what was right. He seemed very much pleased with this, and I ordered my horse turned over to him for his use.

Alas, for the depravity of Mexican nature! Since I saw him mount my horse, when turned over to him I have never beheld him, nor received the services to be rendered; the only equivalent for the horse and trapping being a badly worn blanket he put in my wagon.

One month and nine days after we started from Tueson I arrived in Los Angeles, California, and soon found a good surgeon, to whom I stated my case, and placed myself under his care. On the way, I had been failing in health, and the journey had made my limb much-worse, and it was now in a state of high inflammation. He examined my limb, and said a portion of my shin bone was broken, or slivered off by the shot, which accounted for its not healing, and that it should be extracted. He performed the operation, and took out a piece of bone some three inches long and of very irregular shape.

I suffered much during the operation, but under his subsequent judicious treatment the swelling was reduced and the inflammation cured, and I immediately began to improve in my general health. It was some time before I could walk, however, and by that time the physician's bill, with my expenses for board and attendance, had made sad inroads into the money I had on my arrival at Los Angeles.

I here met, one day on the street, Nathan Martin, whose life I had saved when he was captured by the Comanche Indians. I had not seen him since he left with the Indians for Mexico, thirty-one years before, and had supposed him dead. He informed me of the particulars of his escape, and invited me to go to his house, for he resided in El Monte, a few miles distant. I accepted his invitation and had an agreeable visit.

I also met here a cousin of mine, Alexander Hobbs, who informed me of the assassination of my uncle and his family, in the Green Meadow massacre, by the Mormons, in Utah Territory. He said it was his determination to kill every Mormon he came in contact with, when he had an opportunity, in revenge for the murder of our uncle and his family. He also informed me that Brigham Young was now riding in the same carriage in which my uncle's family were at the time of the massacre. When I heard him say that, my blood boiled, for I could not bear the thought of old Brigham converting my uncle's fine family carriage into a Mormon turnout for the transportation of the old beast and his concubines.

At this time Mormons were in the habit of coming into Los Angeles with long trains of wagons, every spring, for the purpose of procuring supplies. There was at this time one of their trains, of about one hundred wagons, in town, nearly ready to leave for Salt Lake. It was discovered that they had a number of mules, which they had probably stolen from the government, which had been branded U. S.; but the marks had been obliterated by burning over the place with a hot iron.

In consequence of this, the United States officers took some two hundred of their mules from them, confiscating them as government property, which the Mormons strongly protested against, but they could not prove any title to the mules. Their train then left for Salt Lake, by the way of Fort Goodwin. Nine of the Mormons did not accompany the train. They remained in Los Angeles some two weeks, and during that time succeeded in stealing eighty-five mules from a Mr. Towns, who was a stage contractor on the Overland Route.

The same day the Mormons left with the mules, word was sent to a vigilance committee at El Monte, about twelve miles distant, on the road to Salt Lake. We raised about thirty men and started in pursuit of the villains. I soon struck their trail, and we followed it to the mountains, and soon found that we were close upon them, as their dust showed plainly as they ascended the road over the mountain.

Being in charge of the party, I divided it, and sent one-half of the men, under the lead of my cousin, around the mountain to head off the Mormons as they descended the opposite side. My men pursued them to the top of the hill, and began the descent, over a rough road, over which we could see the mules were forced with some difficulty by the Mormons. We kept in their rear till they had reached the foot of the hill, where my cousin's party were concealed, when both parties attacked them, and all but one surrendered, and he in trying to escape was shot, and his horse killed under him, both falling dead.

Those who surrendered begged hard for their lives; but there was no mercy in our party for such thieves, and my cousin told them to make their peace with God in a hurry, and think of Brigham Young for the last time, for we had no time to waste over them. We hung them all on the trees by the roadside, and, waiting only long enough to see them fairly dead, we started for Los Angeles to return the mules to their owner.

On returning to Los Angeles with the property, the owner, Mr. Towns, was delighted to recover the animals, and paid us well for our services. Everybody was anxious to know what we did with the Mormons, and we replied that they would hear quickly enough, from the Mormons at San Bernardino, a town near where we hung them, which was full of Mormon inhabitants. It was found afterwards that they were greatly enraged when they discovered the bodies of their friends hanging on the trees, and took them down and buried them with great pomp and ceremony.

Being now fully recovered from my wounds. I caught the prevailing excitement of that country relative to gold digging, and went with two men. named Brown and Bennett, to the Chain Mountains of California prospecting. We had with us our pack animals and provisions. These mountains abounded with game. bear and deer being plenty. One afternoon I had been out alone prospecting about a mile and a half from our camp, and as I was returning I saw two small grizzly bear cubs. I looked in all directions to see if the old bear was around, but could not discover her.

I then concluded to shoot one of the cubs, but knowing how the grizzly will resent any injury to its young. I looked first for a place where I could make myself secure in case of danger. I shot one of the cubs with my rifle, breaking its shoulder, when it commenced a great outcry, which brought the old one to its assistance. I was not long in climbing a high rock nearby. nor in discharging my revolver at her. for I had no load in my rifle. I wounded her badly with my six-shooter, but did not kill her, nor disable her enough for me to venture down from the rock, so I remained there all night.

The bear made several attempts, during the night, to reach me, but being weak from her wounds could not do so. When it was light enough to see the animal I finished her with another shot, and killed the remaining cub, its mate having died during the night. The cubs were fat, and weighed perhaps a hundred pounds each, but the old bear was poor and unfit for eating. Bennett and Brown hearing the firing in the morning, came running up and found me skinning one of the cubs. They looked on in amazement at the sight of the three bears, and said they had heard the tiring in the evening and had been very anxious on my account.

We finished skinning the bears, and carried the cubs and skins to our camp. I had a good appetite for bear meat that morning, and we made a capital breakfast from one of the cubs, after which I told my companions that I should take a nap, for I had stood guard all night, and they could go out and do the prospecting that day.

I slept till three o' clock, and then arose and cut up my meat for drying and curing. My friends soon returned, and Brown reported that he had discovered a lead mine. He showed me some of the metal and asked my opinion of it. I tried it by smelting some of it in my ladle for running bullets, and found it contained some silver. He then said he thought our fortune was made. We went together and examined the ledge, and found it a vein of lead and some silver intermixed.

It was nearly four feet wide and over a foot thick, and we judged that it ran into the mountain some distance. I told Brown that we had better have the property recorded in our names, and he proceeded at once to Los Angeles, sixty miles away, for that purpose. On the fourth day he returned and said he had made the record for us jointly. Mr. Bennett and myself supposed he had done so, as our agreement at the outset was to share our discoveries and profits equally.

The next day after Mr. Brown returned I found a prospect of gold, in the head of what is called St. Gabriel's canyon. A few days after this, Mr. Bennett said he was going out to kill a deer if possible. He started away about three o'clock, and in an hour we heard a report of a gun a short distance off. I told Mr. Brown that our friend had found game nearby, and we went to see what he had shot. We found him shot through the body, the ball having entered near the navel and come out at the small of the back.

As he was still alive, he gave us an account of the manner in which he was shot. As he was walking through the brush, on the lookout for game, and not paying attention to his footing, he stumbled and fell, the fall causing the discharge of his gun. We carried him to camp, and he asked me what I thought of the wound. I told him he must prepare himself for the worst, but we would do all in our power for his comfort.

At the same time I sent Brown to the nearest settlement for medical assistance for our friend, though Bennett said it was of no use for he should soon die. Brown went after a physician and some friends, leaving me alone with the dying man. He lived about an hour after Brown left us, and I passed a miserable night alone in those dreary mountain wilds with the body of my dead friend.

There I sat with no light, save the flickering glare of a fire I always kept burning in front of the cabin, to keep away the wild beasts. It seemed as though Brown would never return, and it was the longest night I ever experienced. I have passed many nights in situations that would not be called desirable by nervous or timid people, but never one that seemed go awful to me as this night alone with death.

About daylight, Mr. Brown, with several persons including a doctor, arrived from Qui Qual Mungo, a small town about twelve miles from our camp. Finding that our friend was dead, they advised that he be taken to their village and properly buried, which was done; and the funeral services at Qui Qual Mungo were attended by a large number of sympathizing strangers. Just before his death, Mr. Bennett told me that he willed me his gun and two pack animals, and also his interest in the mine which we owned in company. He said he had a brother, William, living in San Luis Obispo, California, to whom he requested me to write, and inform him of the circumstances and manner of his death.

He further said that I would find in his carpet-sack about one hundred dollars, which he wished me to use as far as necessary in defraying the expenses of his burial. He attempted to tell me something about a check, but he was so weak that he could not make himself understood. With the money found among his effects I paid his funeral expenses. I offered to pay those who had assisted us in removing him from our camp to the village, &c, but they refused any compensation.

After our partner's death our camp was so lonely that we concluded to go to Los Angeles, taking with us all our effects, and those of our deceased friend. On our way Mr. Brown said he was aware that Mr. Bennett had some money over and above the expenses of burial, &c, and wanted to know what disposition I was going to make of the property, urging that it be divided between us; for, said he, "his brother never need know of it, and *dead men tell no tales*."

I told Brown I was not in the habit of doing business that way; and stated that what was left would go to Mr. Bennett's brother at San Luis Obispo, for I had written to him and expected he would meet us at Los Angeles. On our arrival at Los Angeles I received a letter from Mr. William Bennett, in answer to one I had sent him, informing me that he would soon arrive at Los Angeles, and perhaps by the next stage.

At the hotel where we stopped I asked Brown to show me the record, or certificate of record, of our lead and silver mine, that we had been assured by him was recorded in the office at this place in favour of all three of our party. He replied that it was among his papers, and that he would show it at some other time. I then became suspicious that he was not a trustworthy man, and proceeded to the miner's recording office to make inquiries respecting the matter, and found that Mr. Brown was in the employ of a New York company, and had secured the mine in the name of the company and himself, leaving myself and Mr. Bennett out altogether.

I then returned to the hotel and told Mr. Brown I wished him to get his papers and show me my own and Mr. Bennett's interest in the mine. He said he would before he went to bed.

He then left the hotel and did not return till quite late,—after I had retired.

Early in the morning a servant came to my room and told me a gentleman wished to see me down stairs. On going down I met Mr. Bennett's brother, who said he had come to Los Angeles in reply to my kind message, and wished me to relate all the particulars of his brother's death, &c. I then gave him, in detail, all the facts, narrating our experience in the mountains, and the unfortunate accident that had broken up our party and deprived his brother of life.

I took him to my room and showed him his brother's clothing, money, pocket book, papers, letters, &c, and also told him his brother left one hundred dollars, and I had it ready to give him, excepting the amount I expended in his burial. I also told him that his brother had verbally willed me his interest in the mine, his gun, his two pack mules, and the remainder of the money, after deducting expenses; but that he was so near his end when he did so that I had no writing to that effect, and should claim nothing; the property was all at his disposal.

He told me my conduct in the matter had been such that he was satisfied I was honest, and he had no doubt the facts were as I stated: that he did not wish the money, and requested me to keep it and also the pack mules. In looking over his papers he found a check for five hundred dollars on Wells, Fargo & Co., of San Francisco, which explained what Mr. Bennett attempted to tell me of a check just before his death. He retained the check, papers, and clothing, and thanked me heartily for the kindness I had shown his brother. I told him of the rascality of Mr. Brown in regard to our mining affairs.

After we had finished our breakfast Mr. Brown came in, and I informed him that as soon as he had eaten his breakfast I wished to talk with him. I kept a sharp lookout for him, and finally saw him attempt to leave by an opposite door. I called to him, when he came and took a seat with Mr. Bennett and myself. I then told him I considered him anything but a gentleman. He asked me what induced me to say so. I told him I had been to the miner's recording office, and from what I had learned there I considered him a d——d rascal.

At this he started from his seat and seized a knife which he carried concealed in his breast pocket, and I pulled out my six-shooter, with which I struck him on the head and knocked him down, the blow causing the discharge of one of the chambers, carrying a ball through a large mirror behind the bar, shivering it to atoms. I then gave him several kicks, when I was seized by Mr. Bennett and the barkeeper, and my pistol taken from me. In striking him I cut a large gash over his right eye, the mark of which he will carry to his grave.

I was then inquired of by the barkeeper and several others as to the trouble between us, when I informed them it was a private matter, of no consequence to anyone but ourselves, but that Brown deserved severe punishment. The barkeeper said the glass cost him forty dollars, which amount I at once gave him. Mr. Brown and myself were then taken before the authorities and tried, which resulted in fining me ten dollars for using an unlawful weapon, and in fining Mr. Brown forty dollars, as he drew his weapon first and commenced the affray.

Mr. Bennett paid my fine, and after the bystanders and the guests of the hotel had been informed of the facts of the case they fully justified my course, and said if they had known he was such a knave, they would not have interfered to save him. Brown got his wound sewed up, and soon left town in disgrace, for the news had spread all over the city.

Mr. Bennett returned to San Luis Obispo, and I remained about a month at Los Angeles.

Chapter 22

Death Valley

About the year 1868, there was a great excitement in regard to the Owen's River mines, in Inyo District, California. I packed my mules with provisions, a pick and shovel, with pans and other outfit, and started for Owen's River, in company with a train of wagons bound for the same destination. The owner of the train was a French Canadian, by the name of Nadieu. The wagons were loaded with provisions and supplies for miners at Cerro Gordo. We arrived at Owen's River, which I found a hard country, twenty-two days after leaving Los Angeles.

We stopped at a place called Lone Pine, some eighteen miles from the Cerro Gordo mines. As this was a very elevated country, the snow was so deep the wagons could not ascend the mountains. The provisions were carried up the mountain on pack mules, and with my mules I accompanied them. On my arrival at the Cerro Gordo mines I saw no way of feeding my mules, and, therefore, sold them to Mr. Nadieu. I then dug out a large hole in the bank, and fixed up a rude habitation.

Here I became acquainted with a number of Mexicans, one of whom had discovered the mines in this vicinity. These mines were discovered in the following manner: A Mexican by the name of Pablo Flores, who was a prisoner among the Pah Utah Indians, discovered some green rocks and lead ore. A short time after he had found these metals, the Americans had a fight with the Indians at Owen's Lake, when he made his escape. He showed the Americans specimens of the metals, which led to the discovery of the Cerro Gordo mines.

All the metals in this vicinity are worked by smelting, or by the tire process. I soon commenced work for Belshaw and Elder, in the erection of a smelting furnace. After the furnace was completed I continued in their employ in smelting the ores. These metals contain arsenic and other poisons. In working these metals there is made what is called a flux, which is a composition of lead, silver, iron, and cinder or dross, which is placed in a furnace and smelted, and then run into pigs or bars, composed of lead and silver.

The pigs are then shipped to San Francisco where the lead is separated from the silver. A ton of these pigs yield nearly a thousand dollars in silver. The lead is worth about five and a half cents per pound there, and just about covers the expense of transportation to San Francisco, and the expense of separating and refining.

I continued in this business until I became paralyzed from the effects of the poison in the smoke, when I was placed in the hands of a physician, and by the time I was able to resume work I had expended all my funds. I then became acquainted with a man by the name of Honn, a Dutchman, who told me he came here from Salt Lake by the way of Death Valley, which he considered a very rich country in the way of minerals, and proposed to me to go with him and prospect that country. I told him I had no means, to which he said all he wanted was a couple of pack mules or jacks, and provisions, for which he could furnish the means.

He agreed that we should share equally in whatever we found, and said if we were successful in prospecting, he had a friend who would furnish anything we might want for mining, provided we would give him a share. We then bought two jacks and loaded them with provisions and mining utensils, and started for Death Valley, in company with a man named Hunter, who joined us the day we left.

The region about Death Valley is, for the most part, very mountainous, but in some sections are found deserts of sand sixty miles in width. During the year 1852, an emigrant train in passing through this section, attempted to go by way of the valley, as they stood in great fear of the Indians who infested the mountains. But they ran from one danger into another. In crossing this desert they lost their way, and with one exception all perished.

The man who survived, whom we met, gave an account of a rich silver mine, which was discovered by one of the men who perished. The man who found this mine made a gun-sight of a piece of the metal, which gave to the mine the name of "Gun-sight Lode." We tried to induce our informant to accompany us to this mine, but he declined, saying he had passed through enough in that section already, and never wished to return there.

As the account of the richness of the mine was very nattering, we decided, after learning its location, to find it if possible. On our arrival in the valley we found the remnants of the train and the skeletons of the party, in a locality which agreed with the description given us, as did the location of surrounding mountains in the distance. In prospecting we found many kinds of minerals, but the country was destitute of water and wood, the mountains being composed of ledges of rocks. But the mine we were unable to find.

After searching in vain for eight days, finding but little water, my feet became so lame that I was able to walk only with great difficulty. My friends left me at a small pool of water which we fortunately found; and, taking with them provisions and water sufficient for two days, started on a prospecting trip to a mountain which appeared about twenty miles distant, saying they would return the next day if possible.

I remained at this pool four days, my friends not making their appearance. My anxiety on account of my friends, who were now two days behind their time, was intense, as I feared that even if they did not perish from lack of food and water, they might be massacred by the Pah Utah Indians, as I knew they frequented that vicinity. I also felt that I was in no condition to defend myself if attacked by Indians.

On the morning of the fifth day I went to the top of a high hill to take an observation, and from there I discovered a man coming over the sandy plain below. I started to go to him, and found on reaching him that it was my friend Honn, who was nearly dead from hunger and thirst. In answer to my inquiries, he said he had left Mr. Hunter three or four miles back so exhausted, that he was unable to go further. I then took Mr. Honn into camp, and gave him food and drink. These men in going out prospecting had refused to take the jacks, for fear they might not find water sufficient for them, and they might perish, thus leaving us no means of escape from that barren country.

While I had been gone, two hours, the jacks had been into our camp and eaten up most of our flour, which placed us in no enviable situation. Mr. Honn, after eating, immediately fell asleep, and I took some provisions and a canteen of water and started in search of Mr. Hunter, taking Mr. Honn's tracks as a guide. In my anxiety, I did not stop to get the jacks, but started on foot. I found Mr. Hunter asleep, with his gold pan under his head.

When I aroused him from his slumber, he looked wildly at me, and attempted to escape; but I caught him and endeavoured to quiet him. He soon recognized me, and made inquiries for Mr. Honn. I told him he was all right and in camp. He then said, "For God's sake, have you any water." I gave him the canteen, which contained about three pints. He grasped it, and in his eagerness would have drank it all, had I not taken it away from him, when he begged that he might drink all he wished. I told him he must eat something, and when he had done so I would give him more.

After eating I gave him a small quantity of water, and he became more calm and rational. He then told me that in returning from the mountain, where their search had been unsuccessful, they had become bewildered, and not feeling at all sure that they were going in the right direction, he had given himself up as lost. As soon as he felt able to walk to camp we started on our return, and when about half way there, I allowed him more water and food. We arrived safely in camp about sunset.

We found our friend Honn still sleeping soundly, and Mr. Hunter had a good night's rest, as he slept soundly till morning. In the morning I told them we should be compelled, for want of provisions, to return to Cerro Gordo as soon as they were able to travel. Our stock of flour had been reduced by the raid made on it by the thieving jacks, to about six pounds, and this had been somewhat injured by them. As Cerro Gordo was over a hundred miles distant it was necessary for us to start as soon as possible, in order to reach it before our provisions gave out.

We retreated from this desolate place (appropriately named Death Valley), and arrived finally at the mountains just below Cerro Gordo and found the snow and ice so plenty on the mountains that our animals could not easily ascend. We told Mr. Hunter if he would remain where we then were with the jacks we would endeavour to reach the mining camp at the top of the mountain and return with provisions, which he consented to do. All we had to leave with him was a small piece of bacon and some ground coffee. The jacks were able to survive on tall bunch grass and small brush.

Mr. Honn and myself reached the top of the mountain that night, about 9 o'clock, wading through the snow in some places to our waists. After much suffering from cold and hunger, by midnight we reached Cerro Gordo, or the camp of miners. Mr. Honn being rather fond of whisky, commenced indulging freely, for he was nearly frozen; and both of us were after a while warmed up and thawed out with hot drinks furnished by these hospitable miners who had given us up for lost.

Early in the morning we obtained a sack of flour, some bacon, and other provisions that we could easily carry on our backs, and some matches, for we knew that we should be detained at the foot of the hills until the weather changed, and started on our return to Mr. Hunter. We had each obtained a bottle of whisky, and Honn was so careful of his that he carried it in his hand.

He was a little unsteady from the effects of the "thawing out" process of the night before, and, in descending a steep place, his foot slipped, and, as the sack of flour on his back made him top-heavy, he fell, and rolled heels over head some thirty feet. The bag of flour caught in the brush, tearing it and spilling part of the precious contents.

Honn brought up against a pine tree, and holding up his bottle, on which he had bestowed most of his care, he remarked that he had saved the best part of his load. I gathered up what flour I could, and told him I thought the flour of the most importance, but he preferred the whisky. We then made our way down the mountain as best we could, and finally found Mr. Hunter, who was overjoyed to see us. I made a fire in our little camp stove, wet up some of the flour and baked some biscuits, which, with our other fixings, made us a capital meal.

We remained here several days, our jacks getting recruited in a small ravine below where there was no snow and the bunch grass was plenty. We now commenced to work oar way up the mountain sides with our jacks, for the snow had rapidly melted and settled, and then frozen stiff, so we could get our beasts along. In due time we arrived in camp at Cerro Gordo, where we were looked upon almost as having returned from the grave.

We had discovered fourteen ledges of different kinds of metals, silver, gold, and copper, and brought specimens of each with us. These we now had assayed, and they were pronounced rich; but the locality was such, the country so desolate on account of the scarcity of wood and water, we could get no parties to interest themselves in our discoveries.

Soon after our return, a Pah Utah Indian came to Cerro Gordo with a very rich specimen of gold. He could talk Spanish a little, and told me if I would give him some presents he would show me where the gold was. I then asked my friends Hunter and Honn if they would accompany me with the Indian. Mr. Honn was ready to go, but Mr. Hunter, on ascertaining that from all I could learn from the Indian, the mine was probably on the borders of Death Valley, said he had seen all he wished to of that country, and would not return there if the whole country was a solid mass of gold.

I then took the piece of gold which the Indian gave me, and had it assayed, when it proved very rich. I took the Indian to a store and asked him what he wanted, and he said some calico, tobacco, a pipe, and some beads, which I gave him. We then bought provisions enough to load our two jacks and another a friend of mine gave me, and started to find the gold ledge which the Indian told us it would require ten days to reach.

The first eight days of our journey passed without any particular adventure. On the ninth day, when we awoke in the morning, our Indian was missing, and I never saw him afterwards. I told Honn that the Indian having proved false, we had better go on as we were so near Death Valley, and do the best we could at prospecting. He thought the Indian had started off for his tribe, to inform them of our position, and feared that they would soon be down on us in force to murder us.

I told him we had two Henry Rifles, which would give us thirty-two shots, and two six-shooters with twelve shots more, making forty-four shots, and that those Indians only had bows and arrows, and that we could cope successfully with them, and we had better proceed, hoping to find gold enough to make our trip profitable.

We started soon after breakfast, taking along a ten gallon keg of water, and followed an Indian trail till about 4 o'clock, when we suddenly came across a squaw of the Pah Utah tribe, who was digging palm-roots, which is the principal food of that tribe. On seeing us she was badly frightened, and fell on her knees, making signs for us not to kill her. I then took her by the hand, and, raising her up, showed her our water keg, and made signs to ascertain if she could tell us where we could obtain water. She then started, and following the Indian trail, showed us a small spring. Here we encamped for the night.

Immediately after showing us the water she wanted to leave us, and I made signs for her to remain and she should have something to eat. When I offered her some food she took it in silence, but would eat nothing till Mr. Honn and myself commenced eating, when she had more confidence and began to eat. After supper Mr. Honn and myself lit our pipes and commenced smoking, when she made signs that she wanted to smoke, and I politely offered her the pipe, when she puffed away and blew the smoke out of her nose several times, then returned me the pipe. After this she appeared more contented and remained with us that night, being provided with a blanket, &c.

I told Mr. Honn I deemed it prudent for one of us to remain on guard, and he thought the same. I there-fore kept awake till after midnight, when he relieved me, and stood guard till nearly morning, when we were aroused by our jacks running towards us much frightened. At first we thought the Indians were upon us, and, jumping up, we seized our rifles and prepared to give them a warm reception; but the howling of wolves around us convinced us that there was no cause of alarm from Indians just then. Although wolves may not seem very desirable neighbours, we felt much relieved when we found what frightened our animals.

After breakfast we were about resuming our march, when I made signs to the squaw to learn where we could find the next spring of water. She pointed forward in the direction of the Indian trail, making signs to the sun, so that I understood we could reach water before sunset. I had with me some curiosities for Indians, such as beads, red handkerchiefs, finger rings, &c, and I gave her a sample of each, for which she appeared grateful, and we then allowed her to depart. She started for a mountain a few miles distant and we packed up and journeyed onward.

After going nearly fifteen miles we came to a small stream of water, which was in Death Valley, but it was so bitter as to be unfit for ourselves or animals. After looking around for some time I found a spring of good water, near which we encamped for two days. In prospecting there we discovered places which yielded eight cents perhaps to the pan but no rich ledge as we expected.

Here we were surprised by the appearance of two Americans who rode into our camp, one of whom had an arrow sticking in his left shoulder. His name was William Wilson, and that of his companion was John Patterson. They stated that they, in company with two others, come into this valley prospecting, as an Indian had shown them some rich specimens, which he said came from this vicinity.

They had been visited at their camp, which was about ten miles below us, by a party of Indians, who had showed them some nice specimens of silver and gold, making signs that they were obtained at a mountain a few miles off, and offering to show them the way to these rich diggings. Two of the men left with the Indians, expecting to return the next day. The following day the two men left in camp were attacked by a party of Indians, and hastily mounting their horses, they had escaped, leaving all their effects, and providentially had seen our camp and joined us.

They said the two missing men were brothers, by the name of Copeland, and that they feared the Indians were traitors and would assassinate them. After I had cut out the arrow head from the man's shoulder, they concluded that it was best to return to Silver Peak, where there was a miners' settlement called "Belmont flat," and get help to re-turn to their camp and search for the Copeland brothers. Belmont was distant nearly eighty miles, and as they knew the route, and that there was water in three places, Mr. Honn and myself decided to pack up and accompany them, for the situation began to appear dangerous if we remained behind.

We arrived safely at Belmont, and found it quite a settlement. We organized a party of twenty-four men, with pack mules, provisions, &c, and started back to Death Valley in search of the missing men. We searched in every direction in the valley and in the mountains where the Copelands went, but could see no traces of them, except the campfires where the Indians had been.

After several days of anxious search, we went to the camp where the two men were attacked, and found that all the property left there by them had been carried away; also found one dead Indian covered up with brush, who was very likely killed by a shot from one of the men who escaped. The Indians wisely kept out of our sight, for our party of twenty-four were well armed.

Being satisfied our search was of no avail, Mr. Wilson said he would be revenged on the Indians for the loss of his friends. He had brought some strychnine for that purpose, and mixing some of it with a sack of flour, and one of sugar, left them as a present to-the rascally redskins if they should happen to return there. The whole party now concluded to go back to Belmont and obtain provisions and mining implements to work several mines or placers which we discovered. While at Belmont an old Indian came into the place and reported that the Indians toward Death Valley were dying rapidly of cholera.

The same party of twenty-four men soon returned to Death Valley taking the old Indian with us, and we found quite a camp of dead Indians laying around not far from where the poisoned provisions were left. We then told the old Indian to show us the two missing men or their bodies or suffer instant death, and he led us along the hillsides to a place where we found good water, and we encamped that night near the spring. Here the Indian made an attempt to escape, but was shot and killed by a man on guard.

The next day we continued on in the same direction the Indian was leading us, and soon came to another Indian camp where there were nine more dead Indians. From here we went to the "bitter water creek " at the foot of the hills, where Mr. Honn and I had discovered good gold indications, which turned out so well that we remained there several weeks, when, finding our supply of water failing, and our provisions giving out, we returned to Belmont.

An excitement was now raging here relative to minerals in the White Mountains, and all who had any-thing to say spoke well of the wonderful quartz of the mountains, with its occasional veins of almost pure metal. Mr. Honn and myself packed our jacks with provisions and started for the place, full of hope and excitement. On our arrival we found several prospecting parties already at work, and before long we discovered a few scattering veins of silver ore not over two or three inches wide and very thin.

They were rich enough, but were imbedded in hard rock which could not be worked without stamp mills, crushing apparatus, &c. I then went to Independence with a small party to get some of my specimens assayed, leaving Mr. Honn to take care of things and continue prospecting. At Independence they pronounced some of my specimens as yielding five thousand dollars to the ton of rock, which simple announcement made a great stir in that vicinity. There was an English stock company here operating in mining with machinery, and they offered me two hundred dollars to show them where I obtained my specimens, to which I consented, as I had no means to work a mine in the way it would be necessary to work this.

With two of the English company and several employees I started for the White Mountains, and after eight days reached the mines and showed them the small veins of silver, which pleased the English gentlemen, for they concluded, that though small and unimportant, these veins led somewhere to the mother vein, which would prove of great value. They sent to Independence for machinery and tools, and employed me as foreman over twelve Cornish miners to superintend the work at one hundred dollars per month, and provisions found, while my friend Honn took a contract for getting timber from the mountain for house-building.

I advised the company not to expend much capital in buildings nor in working the mine, but they thought they knew best. They worked the mine about three months, and laid out in all two hundred thousand dollars before they gave up that it was a non-paying concern. They admitted as they abandoned it, that my advice should have been followed.

Mr. Honn and myself returned to a place called Lone Pine, on Owen's River, eighteen miles from Cerro Gordo. Lone Pine is not far from Owen's Lake, a remarkable body of water which always remains at the same height, Owen's River and various smaller streams empty into this lake, and there is a peculiar oil-worm that inhabits its waters, and, drifting ashore in large numbers, they are used for food by the filthy Indians in the vicinity.

Scientific men have analyzed the water and pronounced it strongly charged with borax, and it is considered beneficial in cutaneous diseases to bathe in it freely. After bathing in it, however, it is necessary to wash in pure water, or the skin will peel off as if burnt. In washing clothes it requires no soap, but clothes washed in it must be rinsed in pure water or they will be destroyed. On this lake a small steamer, and afterwards a flat boat were launched, for taking supplies across to the miners; but in six months the steamer was rendered unserviceable by the action of the water.

After we had been in Lone Pine a while, the Pah Utah Indians grew very hostile, and we formed a company of the miners for protection. About this time we received information that a family had been murdered by the Indians at a place called Hayway Meadows. We started immediately for the scene of the massacre, and found the woman and two children of the family killed. The husband was not at home at the time of the massacre, and three hired men who were working there ran away.

The woman defended herself until the Indians set fire to the house. We found her body lying in front of the house with three arrows sticking in her breast, and the children's skulls were crushed. We buried the remains of the woman and children, and soon discovered the three men servants returning from their concealment on the hills, who told us in what direction the Indians had gone.

One of the men was slightly wounded in the back of the neck by an arrow. I told them they ought to be ashamed to run and leave a woman under such circumstances; but they said that they urged her strongly to flee with them, but she refused. We then started off in pursuit of the Indians, who numbered over a hundred, and we had fifty-six men in our party, all mounted. We overtook them near Owen's Lake, where, being surprised by us, they were mostly driven into the lake and over half of them shot or drowned.

A few made their escape and the remainder we captured and took to Fort Independence, and turned them over to the United States officers. One Indian girl was found buried in a sand bank where she had secreted herself so nicely that only her nose and chin were visible. We recovered some two hundred and fifty dollars in gold from the Indians, also the clothing they had stolen from the murdered family.

When the unfortunate husband returned and found his wife and children slaughtered, his grief made him desperate. His name was Wright, but he has been wrong ever since, as many of the Indians have found to their sorrow, for with a crazy zeal he fought everything in the semblance of an Indian, whether friendly or not, whenever he had an opportunity. I restored him the gold and the clothing they stole from him, when he smiled on me with grateful looks for my services, and with fearful oaths vowed to have his revenge.

Finally he was arrested by the United States officers for killing friendly Indians, and confined at Fort Independence as insane; but death came to the poor man's relief in a few months, for his last days were spent in mad ravings and bitter cursings of the Indian race.

Not long after we had routed these Pah Utahs, a party of Mexicans were on their way to Saline Valley for salt, when they were attacked, and all but one killed by the Pah Utahs. This man came into Lone Pine and reported the massacre, when I started with my company in pursuit of the Indians, the escaped Mexican going with us as a guide. On arriving at the place of attack we found nine dead Mexicans; and three dead Indians were found nearby buried up with stones. On the third day of our pursuit we overtook the Indians and hemmed them in at the base of an almost perpendicular mountain, where they could not escape.

We killed fifteen of them, when the remainder, numbering over two hundred men, women, and children, surrendered.

When the chief gave himself up he said he was anxious for peace with the whites. He could speak Spanish tolerably well, and told me his name was "Big Foot." We took away their bows and arrows and a few guns they had with them, and marched them as prisoners to Fort Independence.

The Pah Utahs then concluded a treaty of peace with the officers at Fort Independence, the chief promising to call in all his warriors who were out under different leaders. In the meantime they had attacked a place called "Hog Rogers's Ranche," near the foot of Owen's Lake. When the news reached us, I left with my men, accompanied by this chief, he promising to call off his men and deliver them to the officers at the fort. On our arrival at the *ranche*, Rogers and his dog (who was a powerful and vicious animal) had killed three Indians, and the others had left.

This man Rogers was a noted *desperado*, and as soon as he saw the Indian chief with me he raised his rifle and shot him dead. I then, to satisfy the tribe, took Rogers prisoner, and carried him back to the fort, leaving two men in charge of his *ranche* till he could have his trial. He was tried by the officers and bound over to keep the peace. There was another Indian at the fort calling himself second chief, who was then promoted to head chief, and they gave him the name of Joe Bowers. Bowers succeeded in uniting the scattered warriors in the neighbourhood of the fort, and was furnished a passport from the officers for his safety among the whites.

When they were all gathered they were placed on a reservation near Fort Independence, where they now are, I presume, and to the best of my knowledge have remained friendly ever since.

Chapter 23

The Execution

A short time after the treaty with the Pah Utahs, a man calling himself Delaney, and claiming to be a Methodist preacher, came to live with Hog Rogers, and entered into partnership with him for the purpose of fencing a farm at the foot of Owen's Lake. After being with him some three months, Rogers was missing. Teamsters going up and down the road made Rogers's house their stopping place for refreshments, and in answer to their many inquiries concerning his absence, Delaney told them he had gone to the mountains prospecting.

After a time, the teamsters found the *ranche* deserted, and suspecting foul play, they told the circumstances to the miners at Lone Pine. A party of six, including myself, immediately set out for the *ranche* to investigate the matter, and on our arrival at the place found it deserted, as there was no living being there, except Rogers's faithful dog, his hogs, and poultry. The dog, who was a large and ferocious animal, stood guard over the house, and would not let any of the party enter; and we could not make up our minds to shoot or injure the faithful creature.

After trying in vain to coax him so as to let us pass, I secured him with a lasso, and tied him to a post. This faithful guarding of the house convinced us that if Rogers had been foully dealt with it was by no stranger, as the dog was his constant companion. We searched the house and stables, but discovered no clue to the mystery; but on returning to the house, I saw, under the edge of the bed, a blood stain. We then took up two of the floor planks and found the dead body of Rogers, who had been shot with a pistol ball through the head. The body we took up and buried decently, and returned to Lone Pine, and reported the facts to the authorities.

I was then appointed deputy sheriff, and as there was no doubt of Delaney's guilt, was sent in pursuit of him, with two good friends who volunteered to assist me. About one hundred miles from Lone Pine, we heard of a man answering to his description who had passed through a small mining town called Tail Hold. We followed on to a place called Visalia, hearing nothing further of him, and had nearly given up finding him; but on going about two miles further, we came to a grove where a camp-meeting was being held, and stopped to make some inquiries for the man.

Here we found him, preaching to the people from the stand. I could not be mistaken in the man, for I had often seen him at Lone Pine and at Rogers's *ranche*. I made my way to the stand, and, placing my hand on his shoulder, informed him that he was my prisoner. Recognizing me as coming from the vicinity where his crime was committed, he attempted to draw a pistol from his pocket. I had my hand on my revolver when I touched him on the shoulder, and I at once struck him on the head with it, knocking him down.

Great excitement now existed all over the camp ground, the brethren asking me for what reason I was treating a brother in that manner. I then ran my hand in his breast pocket and secured his small revolver, which I held up to the astonished gaze of the people, and asked them if it looked very ministerial to be preaching with such a weapon in his pocket, and informed them that I had a warrant for his arrest as a thief and murderer.

They asked Mr. Delaney if he knew me, when he answered that he had seen me at Lone Pine, in Inyo County. I placed him in charge of my two friends while I went to my saddle-bags to get a pair of strong handcuffs, which I placed on him. We then started for Visalia with the prisoner, as the brethren by this time saw that they had been deceived by him, and would not interfere to save this wolf in sheep's clothing. At Visalia he was handed over to the authorities and placed in jail.

The next morning I took the prisoner in charge and our party started for Lone Pine. When we had reached the outskirts of the town, he informed me that he had some money and some clothes at the house of a Methodist preacher, and begged permission to return for them. We went back and got the clothes and live thousand dollars in gold. This man was very indignant at having been so deceived, and told Delaney he had been the cause of breaking up the camp-meeting, and had done vast injury to the cause of religion, and inquired what he had been guilty of. Delaney excused himself by saying a false charge had been gotten up against him, but he should vindicate himself and return there to make matters straight. I told the preacher that he could bid Delaney goodbye, for in all human probability he would not come back there.

We then resumed our journey to Lone Pine, and got as far as Portersville that night, where I was obliged to put the prisoner under a strong guard, as there was no jail in the place. The next morning the guards in-formed me that Delaney made desperate attempts during the night to remove his handcuffs and escape. On learning this, I went to a blacksmith's and procured a pair of shackles and placed them on his ankles.

For greater security and speed, I put the prisoner and the money on board the regular stage for Lone Pine, and took my seat opposite him, while one of my assistants sat beside him, and our animals were led by the other assistant behind the stage. The morning we left Portersville I discovered that the prisoner had a knife which had escaped my notice in the search I made of his person; this I immediately took possession of.

Before arrival at Hog Rogers's *ranche* Delaney offered me the five thousand dollars, and as much more which he claimed that he had buried on Rogers's premises, if I would allow him to escape. He told me the other five thousand dollars were buried at the corner of the spring house. I informed him that I would see about his offer when we had dug up the other money.

At Rogers's place we found my friend, Mr. Honn, and two other men, whom the authorities had placed there in charge. I told Delaney to show me the place where the money was buried, and he did so. My friend Honn, finding a spade, dug it up. With the money were one gold and two silver watches. One of the silver watches had been stolen from a Mr. Nadieu, who had stopped at Rogers's house over night. The money being mostly in silver coin, it was too heavy to be carried by him when he left.

Mr. Honn now informed us that Rogers's dog had lain on the grave of his master since he was buried, only leaving it occasionally to get food. Mr. Delaney secretly asked me if I was not going to allow him to escape, in consideration of so much, money, &c., and I answered his impudent proposition by saying I was a sworn officer, and bound to do my duty. We arrived at Lone Pine, which was some twenty miles from the ranche, at eight o' clock that evening.

When I was handing the prisoner over to the authorities there was great excitement through the place, people collecting from every direction, shouting "Hang him! Hang him!" They succeeded in getting a rope around his neck, dragging him a short distance; but I defended him, and appealed to the crowd to preserve order, at the same time cutting the rope by which he was being hauled on the ground. A squad of soldiers who were at Lone Pine here interposed to assist me in my duty and took charge of the prisoner. Delaney then confessed that he deserved death, but that he wished to make a confession before he died.

The excitement continued through the night, some of the miners being very boisterous and demanding his execution without delay, telling Delaney that his time had come. I handed over to the authorities the money, watches, pistol, and knife, taken from the prisoner, excepting the gold watch, which I told them I would keep till I found the owner; and also told them that the silver watch found with the money belonged to Mr. Nadieu, as his name was on the inside of the case, and Delaney had confessed to me that he had stolen the watch from him. My fees and those of my assistants were paid out of this money.

The following day Delaney had his trial, and confessed that he had killed Mr. Rogers for the purpose of securing his money, which he had ascertained was concealed under the hearthstone in his house. He said also that Delaney was not his name, but that his real name was Smith; that he was born in Indiana, and had been married four times. He requested three or four days' time in which to write a history of his crimes, which was granted him by general consent; for the public mind there had become quite interested in these developments, and felt disposed to let the villain unburden himself and free his mind by confession.

The chief points of his confession were as follows: When he was twenty-one years of age, his father was hung, in Posey county, Indiana, for shooting one of his neighbours. To avoid the obloquy which attached to him as the son of a murderer, he left home soon after his father's execution, and made his way to Springfield, Illinois, where he married a respectable girl by the name of Knox, with whom he lived about six months, and getting possession of her property, about ten thousand dollars, left her and went to Little Rock, Arkansas, where he lost all the money, except five hundred dollars, in gambling.

Here he again married a respectable girl, and after living with her about six months, he obtained some three thousand dollars from her in cash, when he left her and went to New Orleans, and there married a French Creole girl. From New Orleans he went to Fort Leavenworth, taking his wife with him. Here he said his wife left him, as she had fallen in love with a United States officer. He remained in that vicinity some time, with the determination of killing her, but she was so closely guarded he was not able to accomplish his purpose.

From Fort Leavenworth he went to Salt Lake, where he said he married a Mormon girl, and after robbing her of what money she had, he went to California. During the time, from his leaving home, he had changed his name four times, and thought himself unfit to live longer. He confessed that the gold watch I had in my possession belonged to Edward Hatch, a man that he had killed in Virginia City, Nevada, under the following circumstances: They were at work together about four miles from Virginia City, mining, where he killed Mr. Hatch, and buried him in a shaft which they were excavating. He had taken his gold watch and about four thousand dollars in money which Mr. Hatch had in his possession.

He wished me to write to Mrs. Hatch (for the murdered man left a wife and two children) and inform her of the fate of her husband, which must have been the cause of much anxiety to her, and also of the fate awaiting his murderer. This I promised to do. After this murder, he made his way to Lone Pine, where he became interested with Hog Rogers in fencing a farm; and his career from that time is known to the reader.

When he was taken out to be hung he requested the privilege of speaking to the persons assembled. He said his career had been a sad one from his youth up. He had commenced with deception and stealing, and now was about to suffer for murder. He acknowledged that his sentence was just, and that he deserved death for his many crimes. He ended his address by urging all present to be warned by his fate.

He then bade them all goodbye, and in another moment, the rope being adjusted about his neck, strong hands turned the rude windlass that was in use there for hanging up beeves when slaughtered, and was now used in place of a gallows, and after a little struggling, all was over with this hardened criminal. After awhile the body was taken down and buried.

Some four days after this I met my friend Mr. Honn, from Rogers's *ranche*, and he told me that Rogers's poor dog, Jack, had died from grief, and that he had buried him by the side of his master. Rogers's real name was John, but he had received the name of Hog Rogers for stealing hogs some years before, and he took pride in being familiarly called by the name the teamsters had given him.

The authorities at Lone Pine advertised extensively in the United States and Mexico for heirs to Rogers's property, but no one appearing to claim it, the money found by the confession of his murderer, and the proceeds of his real estate, which was sold at auction, were used for building school houses in that vicinity.

CHAPTER 24

The Last of the Gang

California, as is well known, was, in its early history, made a place of refuge by thieves, gamblers, and *desperadoes* of all classes; and like Texas in its infancy, it suffered much from the lawlessness of many who went there as speculators and miners. This element in the population rendered necessary those vigilance committees which sprung up in a night, all over the state; for in the newly and imperfectly organised government, there was too much delay in dispensing justice to this class of rascals.

In the course of my California experience I have seen many villains brought to their deserts by these committees, and have aided in ridding the country of many of them; and for my part in these acts I have never felt the least regret, as I always felt sure they were guilty of the crimes of which they were accused, even if all the proceedings at their trial were not in accordance with the customs of the Eastern States.

One of the worst bands of *desperadoes* that ever infested California was one led by Joaquin Murietta and a man called Three-fingered Jack. The latter of these took special delight in torturing and murdering Chinamen.

This Joaquin Murietta was made the *desperado* he was by the villainy of some of the characters spoken of at the commencement of this chapter. He was a Mexican who arrived in California in 1851, with his wife, and discovered some rich gold diggings in Mariposa county. He had accumulated all the gold he could tie up in a buckskin, when four American *desperadoes* came to his claim and ordered him to leave. He went to his cabin for his effects and was followed by the Americans. They took the gold, which they found in the possession of his wife, and then insulted her, at which Murietta became enraged and drew his pistol to defend his wife, for they had commenced to abuse her shamefully. He was then seized by three of the ruffians, taken from his house and tied to a tree, where they flogged him. He begged of them to kill him but not to torture him and abuse his wife in that manner.

After the whipping they released him, and warned him to leave the country by a certain date or they would kill him. He left the mine and went to a mining place about five miles distant, where several Mexicans, some of them his friends, were at work, and related to them the story of his wrongs, at which they were very indignant. With his friends, he returned immediately to his old camp and killed three of the fiends who had so abused him and his wife.

Had he been satisfied with thus taking speedy vengeance on those who had caused his misery, no one could have said a word in his condemnation. But at that time there was a strong feeling of hostility existing between American and Mexican miners, and he swore vengeance on all Americans, on account of the deeds of these outcasts. That same night he left Mariposa, with his wife, and started for St. Joseph, some of his Mexican friends accompanying him.

At St. Joseph he became acquainted with Three-fingered Jack, and they formed a business connection as desperadoes and robbers. They, with several Mexicans, then returned to Mariposa county, where he killed the remaining American who was concerned in robbing him. Murietta then persuaded an Indian of the Yagui tribe, who was an accomplished cut-throat, to join his party; and they succeeded, in a short time, in killing and robbing a number of Americans.

The gang soon numbered some twenty-five or thirty men, and their custom was to kill and rob all Americans they met on the road; but on meeting a Mexican they would furnish him with horses or money if he was destitute.

At one time they robbed Wells, Fargo & Co's Ex-press, on its way from the camp of Sonora, and captured about sixty thousand dollars in gold dust. This happened in Calaveras county. In the stage were four passengers and the driver, who were all killed with the exception of one girl. She was brutally outraged by Murietta and left to her fate. The stage horses were taken by the party. The girl was soon discovered by some teamsters who were passing and taken to Calaveras, where she had a brother residing, by the name of John Morgan. When she informed her brother of her sad condition, he offered a reward of a thousand dollars to anyone who would show him Murietta, the perpetrator of the villainy.

Murietta hearing of the reward, went into Calaveras one night and going to Morgan's house, with his pistols in hand, told him that he understood he had offered a reward to anyone who would show him Murietta. Mr. Morgan said he had made such an offer, when Murietta presented a pistol to his head and told him he was the man and had come to claim the reward. Morgan handed him the thousand dollars and asked him if he had any further demand to make. Murietta said: No, he only wanted the reward; but that if Morgan said anything in regard to the matter he would burn the town before morning. Murietta was disguised by heavy false whiskers, as he had a number of different disguises which he changed as he went into different places.

Before daylight that morning he visited a gambling house which was in operation in the town, where the game of *monte* was going on, and learning that there were some twenty thousand dollars in the concern, he bet for some time against the game, losing considerable money.

None of the gamblers recognized him in his disguise. When he rose to leave they urged him to stay, as he appeared to be a good customer. He said he would return shortly with more money, and if he had luck he would break the bank. He soon returned with his party and walking up to the man who was dealing the game, said to him, "Now your bank is broke," and shot him dead. Two men sitting near the dealer shot Murietta in the breast, but as he wore a chain armour under his clothing, the balls had no effect. Three of the gamblers were killed, and three others made their escape.

Murietta and his party took all the money they could find, and left the place in a hurry. Those citizens who were up early in the morning saw a party of horsemen fleeing from the town in all haste, but were not aware that it was the gang of Murietta until Morgan appeared and told how the bandit leader had coolly abstracted one thousand dollars from him during the night. This in addition to his sister's disgrace, now made him desperate.

The next heard of Murietta was about seventy-five miles from Calaveras, where he and his party entered a Chinese camp, and surprising them in the night, robbed the poor astonished Chinese of all their gold dust and valuables, while Three-fingered Jack amused himself by killing and mutilating a number of them. From this camp they went to St. Joseph, where Murietta had left his wife. In 1854, Murietta and the party, emboldened by their successes, made a tour by night through central California, doing all manner of mischief; breaking open stores, robbing banks, and shooting innocent people on the highways.

The United States officers in California sent word, or published a notice, to Murietta that if he would deliver himself up to them his life would be spared, as they thought he had some reason for doing as he had done. He replied to them that he never would surrender as long as life was left him; that he thought the Americans had treated him like a dog, but that he did not care so much for, as for the treatment they had shown his wife; that it was his determination to kill as many Americans, and commit as many depredations as possible. He claimed he had been an honest man up to the time of the abuse heaped on himself and wife by the four Americans. His party still continued killing and committing the grossest crimes. The authorities offered a reward of nine thousand dollars for Murietta dead or alive.

A company of twenty-five men was now organized by Michael Burns and Mr. Love, for the capture of Murietta. They followed the bandits for many months, but they had fortified themselves strongly in the mountains, coming down frequently to make raids upon trains and villages, always being able to return with their plunder to the mountains.

After a long and unsuccessful search, Burns and his party met a Mexican boy who had been herding sheep on the mountain, and had come down into a settlement for provisions. They inquired of this boy if he knew of any party secreted in the mountains. He said he had noticed men and horses in a little valley in sight of where his sheep were grazing.

They hired this boy to return and pilot them up the mountain; and upon reaching the place from which he had seen the party, he pointed to a little vale between the mountains and showed them twenty-five or thirty horses feeding. Burns's party were well armed with rifles and revolvers, and being sure of their men if they used judgement, they cautiously descended towards the camp, which they could plainly see in the brush, and surrounded it without being discovered. Burns was a good shot, and he wanted the pleasure of shooting Murietta himself; for he knew him, when he was not disguised.

Circumstances favoured the attacking party. The band had just returned from a successful raid, and were all seated about a table, celebrating their good fortune. But for the fact of their being thus noisily engaged, Burns's party might not have succeeded as well as they did in surrounding them unobserved. The signal for the attack was to be the firing of Burns's gun. He gave the signal by taking good aim at Murietta's head, putting in a ball near his left eye, which killed him instantly.

The remainder of his party, which was composed of twelve men, were also killed, with the exception of Three-fingered Jack, who jumped on a horse and attempted to escape, but being closely pursued, was overtaken. He turned on the men in pursuit, firing several shots at them from his revolvers, wounding one man in the side. They then called on him to surrender.

His reply was that he preferred to be shot rather than hung, and he would not surrender; he was shot and fell dead from his horse. They cut off his hand which had three fingers on it, as an evidence of his death, and taking it with them, returned to where Murietta was killed; and cutting off his head took it with the hand of Three-fingered Jack to San Francisco.

Their arrival in the city created a great excitement, and many doubts were expressed as to its being the head of Murietta. Finally, to satisfy all doubts and enable the captors to claim the reward, the wife of the bandit chief was sent for. She was stopping with friends at a place called Johnstown, and on her arrival she said if it was the head of her husband they would find a scar on his left cheek. An examination showed the scar as she described it. When the head was shown her, she pronounced it her husband's. The reward was then paid over to Burns and his party. The head of Murietta and the hand of Three-fingered Jack were preserved, and are still in San Francisco.

Murietta's wife stated that he had been strictly honest up to the time they were so maltreated by Americans; adding that for her part she regretted that he had not killed more than he did. During this interview she said that she intended to return to the state of Sonora, where her husband's father and mother resided, when the authorities inquired whether she had means to reach Sonora. She said she had; but if destitute she would not accept anything from an American. A few days after this she left San Francisco by vessel for Sonora.

A number of Murietta's band were not with him at the time of the attack of Burns, but were in the mountains, scattered in small bands, with a large number of horses and mules. When their chief was killed they attempted to make their escape to Mexico as stock drivers, but were overtaken in Los Angeles county, and nearly four hundred head of horses and mules taken from them. In this encounter eleven of the gang were captured and hung, but several made their escape; among those who were hung was a man called Bloody Bill, but whose right name was Jack Downing.

He was a hardened wretch, and had no such show of reason for his conduct as Murietta had. Before being hung he was asked what he had to say, when he replied that he had killed a dozen better men than any of his hangmen, and that he intended if he had not been caught to kill a dozen more. His captors waited to hear no more of his brutal speech, but hung him instantly.

Word was sent to Fort Yuma, on the Colorado River, of the escape of some of this part of the gang, and the officers cautioned to be on the watch for them. It was soon found that two of them were drowned in attempting to cross the Colorado, but the rest succeeded in reaching the state of Sonora. The governor of that state had received a dispatch from the United States officers stating that such a party were in his territory, and by a little strategy they were captured and hung, with one exception.

Among them were two leaders, called Lame Floris and Curly-headed Chihuahua. These two men confessed where they stole most of the horses and mules, and stated that when they were obliged to flee from the mountains in California with their animals, they left in such haste that they could not dig up about thirty thousand dollars in gold which they had buried in different places. Curly-headed Chihuahua was therefore spared awhile, for he promised to accompany a party to show them where the money was, if the authorities would save him from the gallows.

To this the governor agreed, and a company of fifteen mounted men of the governor's guards started with this *desperado*, having orders to keep a sharp lookout for him, and reached the mountains, secured the gold, and returned with it safely, delivering it to the governor of Sonora, who deposited it in the treasury for safe keeping until some proper claimants should appear.

During the absence of this party to the mountains, the governor received information that this band of robbers had stolen from his sister-in-law, in California, over a hundred brood mares, mules, &c, which so enraged him that when they returned with the gold, he told this curly-headed scoundrel that he should be saved from the gallows, as agreed, but he should be shot immediately; for he was too dangerous a man to be turned loose to organize, perhaps, another band as formidable as the previous one. He was therefore taken out and shot, before he had time to rest himself from his long and weary ride.

The governor informed the authorities in California of the recovery of this large amount of gold, which had been stolen by Murietta's party, and that any person who brought sufficient proofs of ownership should have their part of it. One Californian brought proofs that he was a sufferer to the amount of several thousand dollars, which the governor paid to him; but a large part of the money was never claimed, for the reason that the owners were murdered as well as robbed.

The governors of Sonora and California entered into a mutual agreement, and published an order, that until further notice no man should be allowed to pass from one state to the other without a written permit duly signed by the proper officers. This was considered absolutely necessary to facilitate the arrest of roving murderers and highway robbers, of which the country was then full.

After this order was put in operation, murders and robberies became less frequent, for those who were caught and found guilty, either by a vigilance committee or by a justice of the peace, were immediately hung.

Chapter 25

The Attack

The United States government wished to make a survey of the almost entirely unknown country about Death Valley, and to lay out a route from Fort Independence, in Inyo County, California, to Fort Mohave, and an expedition was ordered for that purpose. The commanding officer of this expedition, Captain Andrew McFarland, heard of my experience in that desolate region, and wished to engage me as a guide, offering me very liberal terms. I told him I was not acquainted with the entire route, but that if he wished my services I would do the best. I could for him. I told him I only knew the route to the vicinity of the Bitter water in Death Valley, but thought from what I knew of the country I could guide him through.

We started from Fort Independence with eighty-five soldiers, and took with us the Pah Utah Indian chief, Joe Bowers, and another of his tribe, who were now friendly with the whites.

On our arrival at Bitter water, the Indian, Joe Bowers, told me he could show us water some twenty-five miles distant, to which place we proceeded and found it. He then told me that we should arrive the next day at a mine where there had been about fifteen Americans assassinated. On our arrival at the place he designated, we found a mine where work had evidently come to a sudden standstill.

We found a tunnel about sixty feet in length, with a pile of about twenty tons of lead, &c, lying in front of it. There also was a blacksmith shop, with an anvil remaining. Bowers removed all doubt we might have had of the fate of the men who had worked this mine, by taking us to a shaft about fifteen feet deep, into which he said their bodies were thrown. By means of a rope, I descended the shaft and found the skeletons of the miners. We did not disturb the remains of these unfortunate men, but filled in the shaft sufficient to bury them.

Bowers said that these miners who were from Arizona, had been killed by some of his tribe under lead of Big Foot, the chief, who it will be recollected, was killed by Hog Rogers. The Indians were in the habit of trading with the miners for liquors and dry goods, which gave them an opportunity to learn their strength and habits, and also disarmed the miners of any suspicion they might have on seeing a number of Indians in their camp.

A plan was formed by Big Foot to murder and rob the party. Bowers, feeling for the whites, stole from camp one night and told them they had better leave the place, for if they remained they would all probably be murdered by Big Foot and his party. As near as he could understand them, they replied that they had no fear of Big Foot, as they had confidence in his professions of friendship.

One afternoon when the Indians went among them, apparently for trading purposes, they surprised and killed all the Americans, except one, who made his escape. This man's name was John Hughes; and, as Bowers was somewhat acquainted with him, as he spoke Spanish, he made an effort to save him, and prevented the Indians from pursuing him. The Indians took away all the property in the camp, even to the leather covering of the blacksmith's bellows, with the exception of four or five bottles of quicksilver, some picks, shovels, and the anvil.

Joe Bowers here informed us that he could remain with the expedition only two days longer, as in that time we should arrive within the limits of another tribe of Indians called the Digger Indians, who were hostile to his tribe. For the two days he continued with us he showed us water on our route, and at the end of that time took me on to a mountain peak and showed me in what direction to find Fort Mohave. He pointed to an Indian trail over the mountain, and told me to follow it.

On returning to camp, Captain McFarland gave him an order on the proper officers at Fort Independence for his pay as guide, and also a certificate that he had proved true to us. He was presented with a mule packed with provisions sufficient for his journey, and started with the other Indian for Fort Independence, telling us that hereafter we would find water sufficient on our way.

We travelled twenty-five miles in the direction indicated by Bowers, and reached the Digger tribe of Indians, and encamped by the side of a beautiful stream of water among the hills. The Indians were friendly, and I found one half-breed Mexican among them who could speak Spanish, and who agreed to guide us to Fort Mohave.

On the second day of our encampment, while the captain was engaged in making a survey of the country, and a map of our travels, &c, the Indians invited us to join with them in hunting rabbits, which little animal abounded among those hills, and was a favourite article of food with them.

Their mode of capturing the rabbit is to place a net, some one hundred yards in length, made of willow strips and bark, with wings on either side, of brush, &c, as an obstruction. The Indians go out in all directions and scare up the rabbits, running them into the net, the meshes of which are of a size to allow a rabbit's head to pass through.

In this way they become entangled and are killed with clubs. If any escape from the net they are pursued, and then follows an amusing scene, as the Indians in throwing their sticks and clubs often hit each other's legs, killing the animals only after an exciting chase. When they accumulate a sufficient number of rabbits, they make a fire of sage brush, and other wood, throwing in the game just as it is caught, and when cooked, eat the entire animal. It is perhaps unnecessary to say that we did not join in the feast.

After remaining in camp three days, having sufficiently rested ourselves and animals, we left for Fort Mohave, the half-breed Indian accompanying us, as guide. We arrived at the fort after several days of further travel, having gone forty miles of the distance without seeing any wood or water.

We took this route as it was much shorter than that by the Indian trail, and gave us a better crossing of the Colorado river. Captain McFarland calculated the distance from Fort Independence to this fort to be four hundred and fifty miles. The country we had crossed lays between the Sierra Nevada mountains and Arizona.

We had been at the fort eight days, when the man Hughes, who had escaped at the time of the massacre at the mine shown us by Joe Bowers, came in with a party of twenty-five or thirty men, he had made up at Prescott, Arizona, to return with him and work the mine, which he represented as being very rich in silver and lead. This mine, which was discovered by a Mexican, is called the Plomoso mine, the name signifying leaden. Our captain made arrangements for our return to Fort Independence by way of the mine, as this man Hughes told him he could give him much valuable information.

After remaining several days longer at Fort Mohave to recruit our animals, we packed up and started on the return trip. The mining party had preceded us, and on our arrival at the mine, we found them procuring some very rich metal. We stopped there a few days, looking about and prospecting, when Hughes said if we would go with him he would take us to a mountain where he had heard there were some very rich ledges, but which he had not explored on account of the hostility of the Indians who lived in that section. Captain McFarland decided to accompany him, and we started for the mountain; to which, on our arrival, we gave the name of "telescope mountain," from its being very high, with the top covered with perpetual snow. The sides of the mountain are covered with trees, called *pinon*, and are inhabited by a tribe of Indians who are entirely uncivilized.

The *pinon* tree bears a nut about half the size of a chestnut, which is used very extensively as an article of food by the Indians. It grows in a pod or bur, which contains twenty-five or thirty nuts, which are quite oily. We found large piles, containing many bushels of these burs or pods, covered by branches of trees and leaves. The nuts are prepared for eating by covering over these piles with dirt and setting the heap on fire, thus keeping a smouldering fire to bake and soften the shells of the nuts. When the shells are nearly reduced to charcoal, the kernel of the nut can easily be taken out, and they are eaten with great relish by the Indians. We prospected this mountain for many days in different directions, and found eighteen ledges containing gold, silver and lead.

From this mountain we went in a southerly direction, and came to a mining place which had been worked. Here we found some bones of men and a few mining implements, and in the vicinity were four wild horses, which we drove into a deep hollow, where, by the help of the soldiers, I secured them with a lasso. We returned from this deserted mine to telescope mountain, where our friend Hughes left us and returned to his party.

Captain McFarland selected this vicinity as a reservation for the United States government, deeming the land valuable for mining purposes. Our provisions having become scarce, we hastened onward to Fort Independence. The day after leaving the mountain, we reached Death Valley, where we found some Indian camps, their fires still burning, but no Indians in sight. On going to a stream of water nearby one of these camps, I discovered an Indian boy about four years-old lying on the ground, in a small bunch of rushes.

As soon as he saw me he started to run, but I caught him and carried him to camp. He was quite wild and would neither talk, cry, or eat. After being with us two days he came to his appetite and took some food. We took a supply of water and crossed the desert ninety miles without seeing any springs. In this trying journey we lost four horses, that perished from want of water. On our arrival at the opposite side of the desert, we saw signs of water, and by digging procured a good supply for ourselves and remaining animals. We camped at this place several days, and named it "Grape Vine Canyon," on account of the great number of wild grapes in the vicinity. In eight days after leaving this canyon, we arrived at Fort Independence.

On our route the Indian boy made several unsuccessful attempts to escape, and on our arrival at the fort I gave him to a lady, who named him "Good Luck." Some eight days after our arrival at the fort, the mother of this Indian boy arrived and claimed the child. The lady, Mrs. Hughes, employed the squaw to live with her as a servant, and sent the little boy to school, where he learned English rapidly. The last I knew of them the squaw and child still remained with Mrs. Hughes.

After being paid off for my services as guide and interpreter to Captain McFarland's expedition, I stayed about the vicinity of the fort a short time to recruit my mules. During my stay here I made the acquaintance of five men who were about to start, with a Mexican guide, for a mountain about one hundred and fifty miles distant, in the direction of the Colorado River. They stated that the mountain abounded in minerals, and showed me some specimens, said to come from there, which were very rich. I concluded to go with them, and we started, well mounted and well armed, for we felt that with a party so small as ours, it was necessary to take all precaution for our safety.

We arrived at the mountain and prospected several days, finding some ledges of silver and copper ore. We killed four ibex or mountain sheep, and dried the meat to take with us in a further exploration. We proceeded towards the Colorado River a day, and, finding nothing, returned to Slate range, where I saw some mineral ledges and coal. From thence we proceeded towards the Hot Springs.

These springs are near a small lake, and we discovered their locality long before reaching them from the column of steam which rose in the air. When we came to one spring it was boiling like a pot and considerable sulphur was below it, having been deposited by the water running from the spring. My mule chanced to step into the water soon after it left the spring, and his unusually quick movements in getting out of it satisfied me it was warm, to say the least.

About twenty yards from this spot was a spring of pure cold water. At these springs and vicinity I found many curiosities of different kinds. Four or five miles from the Hot Springs we found a mountain or hill some three hundred feet in height, which is almost a solid mass of matter that resembles a green or dark coloured glass bottle, and we concluded to call it the "Glass Mountain." The appearance of the ledges and entire surface indicated volcanic action at some former period.

As we were getting short of provisions, we concluded to go at once to Lone Pine, which place we reached in safety. We remained at Lone Pine two weeks recruiting and laying in provisions, and then with several others we started for a mining camp called Yellow Pine, near the town of Colorado. Here we found nearly one hundred and fifty miners at work in the different ledges. In prospecting here I found a ledge of silver imbedded in rock so hard I could not break it profitably, and sold it out to a party from San Francisco for four hundred dollars. It proved to be a valuable mine. I remained here a while carrying water with my two jacks to the miners, which netted me about five dollars per day.

This added one more to the instances where I had made a discovery of very valuable mines, which I was not able to work for want of capital, which the reader, who has followed me through this narrative, will recollect. My experience has been similar to that of most miners who worked with little capital. At times I have been very successful, and would seem to be on the road to fortune; but after exhausting that claim, my profits would all be melted away in prospecting before I found another paying claim. But capitalists, men with means to procure the necessary machinery for working mines similar to the one just mentioned, have made immense fortunes, where a man without capital could not have made enough to keep soul and body together.

While at Yellow Pine I heard of some mines that were paying large profits in the edge of Lower California, about two hundred miles distant, and with a party started for them. Arriving there we found where the mines had been worked, and we encamped near a small stream of water in the vicinity.

On looking around I found the bodies of two dead miners, whose broken skulls indicated the work of Indians. From the appearance of the bodies I judged that they had been killed only a few hours. I returned to the men and advised preparations for defence. Placing our provisions and mining implements in a favourable spot, we cut down small trees and piled around them for a temporary breastwork in case of attack. We prepared our supper early, so as to have no fire at night to attract the attention of any Indians that might be in the neighbourhood.

After supper we were surprised by a Mexican woman coming into our camp in great excitement. She said she came from a small camp of Mexican miners, a short distance below us. The night preceding, a party of Indians, belonging to the Maricopas tribe, came into their camp, pretending to be friendly. When they had an opportunity they rose and attacked the Mexicans, and she fled from the camp, in her fear not waiting to see what became of her husband and child. She had remained secreted all day, and on coming out of her hiding place at night had fortunately seen our camp.

The next day, about sunset, her husband came into our camp from New River, about thirty miles away, the nearest settlement, with forty Americans and Mexicans he had been there to get to aid him in his search for his wife and child. Her husband was very glad to find her safe in our camp, and inquired where his child was. She told him she could not find it, and that the Indians must have killed it or taken it off with them.

On learning that I had had some experience in hunting Indians, he asked me to join in the pursuit for the recovery of his child, but I replied that it was too late to start that night, and that we had better bury the two dead men, which we did. He said their names were "Louis" and "Antoine"—that they were French Canadians, but he knew nothing of their relatives, or whether they had any. They had been allowed to work in their mine to make their party larger in case of attack.

The next morning early I accompanied his party in pursuit of the Indians, leaving my party to guard the camp and take care of the provisions and animals. We struck their trail, and about 3 o' clock that afternoon I discovered smoke a short distance ahead of us. I told the others to remain where they were, and I would go up among the rocks and ascertain their position and strength, and signal to them to come on, if prudent; if not, I would return.

After satisfying myself that we were more than a match for the Indians, I beckoned to my companions to come on cautiously. When they had crept up close to me, I pointed out to the father of the lost child his little innocent sitting not far from the Indians, who were gathered around a fire feasting on a mule which they had killed, and were cooking by roasting pieces over the fire. I told them if I was to command the party they must obey orders, to which they consented.

My orders were that we should crawl still nearer, fire on them, and then rush in on them at once. After crawling about fifty yards further, we all fired, taking care not to hit the child. I selected for my man one standing with his back toward me, and who was toasting a piece of mule meat for the child. My ball struck him in the small of the back, and passed through his body into the fire, scattering the brands.

A friend near me fired on two Indians who were cutting out pieces of the mule, and, as both of them stood in range, the ball killed both. Five other Indians were killed at the first fire and several wounded. As we rushed upon them they fled, leaving the child, who was soon caught up in the arms of its father. When the Indians reached the top of the hill, they stopped and halloed to me in Spanish, telling me they were friendly Indians. I inquired of what fort they claimed protection. They replied of Fort Yuma. I then asked what they were doing in this part of the country, to which they made no reply.

The chief, who was standing on a high rock, showed a paper, which he said was given him by a United States officer, and which would show that they were friendly; adding, that he should go to the fort and tell how we had killed his people. The Mexican, who had recovered his child, raised his rifle and shot the lying chief dead; saying to me, he will give no information now. This talk and showing of the paper was only a ruse to gain time for the remainder of his Indians, who were not far off, to reach them, when they would attack us.

In half an hour after, on our return, we were attacked by about one hundred and fifty Indians, and one Mexican of our party was killed. We fought and retreated back to our camp, when, being joined by the remainder of our party, we drove off the Indians, killing a number and wounding many. The meeting of the mother and child was very affecting. After having lunched hastily on cold meats, we went to work and built a rock fortification, or breastwork, five feet high, of rough stones piled up carelessly, but it answered every purpose.

In the party that came with me from Colorado district, California, were two men named Jones and Patterson, who were my especial friends; and we three had much influence over the others. We planned many arrangements for the company, among the rest a kind of supply party, or express escort, to get provisions, &c, from the nearest settlements.

After constructing our breastwork, which seemed capable of protecting double our number, we considered that by posting sentinels we should be enabled to work the mines without danger from attack.

The next morning we were startled by a Mexican receiving an arrow fired by some unseen party. We sprang for our guns, and some ran behind the breast-work, but no Indians could be seen in the brush, nor could we find any after searching in all directions.

About 3 o' clock that same afternoon, our camp was further strengthened by the arrival of about twenty-five Mexicans and Americans, which made us number in all eighty persons, and we felt quite secure afterwards. We were now ready to commence mining, and we formed a sort of partnership, each to share equal-

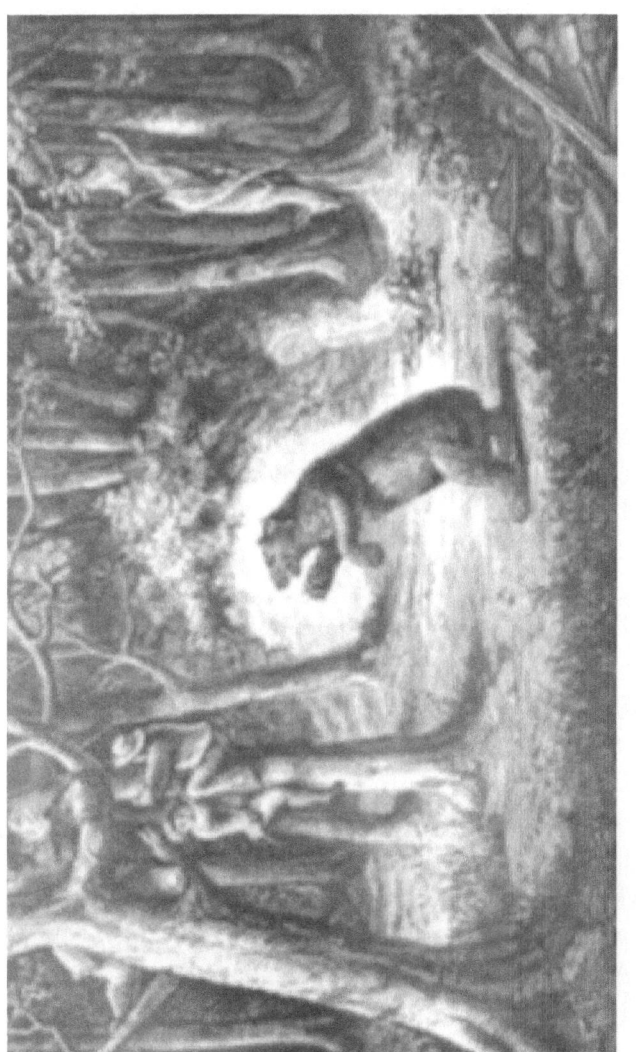

AN UNWELCOME VISITOR

ly in the profits of the whole, to be divided at the close of each month. As our company was about equally divided—Mexicans and Americans—it was thought best to make two working parties, one of each nation, to avoid any trouble that might arise if they were in too close companionship.

We worked in this way for a month with very good success, as it was found at the end of that time that we had made eighty thousand dollars. This sum, according to our agreement, was divided among the company, giving to each man one thousand dollars. The news of our success was soon spread abroad, and, as the result, large numbers of miners soon made their appearance, attracted by the supposed richness of the mines. The advent of honest miners was all well enough, but the news also brought ail undue proportion of gamblers, thieves, and cut-throats.

Seeing this unfortunate rush of villains, and knowing that we were in greater danger from them than from the Indians, I conferred with, my friends Jones and Patterson, in relation to leaving the place before we got into difficulty or lost our gold. They agreed with me that we had better leave, especially as the mines would not yield so much the next month as the first, for the surface gold was nearly exhausted and the shafts were getting deeper and growing more difficult. They asked me if we should return the way we came, and I said by no means, for all the *desperadoes* were taking that route in coming here, and if they saw us returning north, would be likely to infer that we were loaded with gold dust, and try to assassinate us; or we might be followed by some of the new comers.

We concluded to leave suddenly in the night, and by a different route. We started before daybreak for the mountains, travelling slowly with our mules for three or four days, prospecting by the way. At the end of this time we came to a nice gulch, or hollow, where the appearances were favourable for gold digging. Game of all kinds abounded in the vicinity, and we concluded to remain and camp there a few days to prospect for gold, also to secure some meat. I told Jones and Patterson if they would go out prospecting, I would go out and kill some deer. They started out to see what they could find, and in a short time I succeeded in killing two deer, which I dressed, and was busy cooking a good supper from one of them, when my friends arrived. They reported that the prospect of gold was slim, and they did not think it advisable to remain.

After eating supper, we hung the remainder of our venison on some low trees, and made up our beds for the night. This is a very simple operation, and consists of spreading a blanket on the ground, placing a rifle under one side, and a revolver under the end designed for the head of the bed, to protect them from dew or rain, and have them within easy reach in case of need. After completing our chamber work, we seated ourselves about the fire, smoking and talking till about 9 o'clock.

We were just congratulating ourselves on our escape from the outlaws, when I heard a crackling in the brush, near where we had left the mules. I suggested that there might be a grizzly up there, but Jones said it must be the animals, and we paid no further attention to it, but kept on talking, when suddenly an enormous bear, probably attracted by the smell of our venison, sprang into our camp, between us and our arms, and faced us.

We were not long in giving up our quarters to our unwelcome visitor, and Jones and Patterson made all haste to get into one tree, while I took to another. The bear then very coolly walked up to our meat, and as he appeared to have a good appetite, did not leave enough of it for a man's breakfast, when he turned and laid down in the middle of one of our beds, and composed himself for a night's rest. From our elevated position we could look down on him, but it was with no kindly feelings.

About daylight he got up, stretched himself, and started for some water. Now was our opportunity, and we were not slow to improve it. Hastily descending from the trees, where we had been compelled to pass the night in a way that did not tend to increase our regard for our visitor, we seized our rifles and cautiously pursued him. We came upon him, drinking at a small stream a short distance from our camp, when Jones shot him through the neck, and I hit him just over the eye, which killed him instantly. We dressed him on the spot, taking from him sufficient steak for breakfast, in place of the venison steak he had stolen from us, and prepared the remainder of the carcass for future use.

After we had eaten our breakfast, we laid down and slept till afternoon, when I went to look after our mules. I found my jacks missing and did not find them till I had searched two days, when I brought them into camp. They were so frightened by the bear that they wandered off farther than I ever knew them to stray before. In my travel after my jacks I saw several species of bears, grizzly, black, and cinnamon, but they were not nearby and I concluded not to attack them.

During my absence my friends had killed a deer, and I enjoyed my supper of venison steak very much, as my appetite was good. I told them I considered that we were in greater danger from bears in this vicinity than we were from the *desperadoes* we left at the mining camp, and to my mind it seemed like jumping out of the frying pan into the fire. So we agreed to pack up and leave these pests, and go where we need not be on the lookout for bears day and night. We left early next morning and travelled three days, in which time I think we saw more game in the way of bears and deer, than I ever saw before in my life.

CHAPTER 26

Amalgamation Process

After going a short distance, we came across a wild steer, and I told my companions that we must be nearing some settlement. The steer was frightened, and left at the top of his speed. We journeyed on till evening, when, seeing a stream of water, we, camped for the night and prepared supper. Soon we heard the barking of a dog, and on looking around discerned a light in the distance, which seemed to come from some house. Jones wanted to saddle up and go towards it, but I persuaded him to remain where we were till morning.

Early in the morning, after eating, we proceeded in the direction of the light we had seen the evening previous, and came to a very large and thrifty looking Mexican *ranche* and stock farm. When we arrived the people were milking the cows, and on seeing us became frightened and ran to the house, but they soon returned and inquired our business. Among them was an old gray-haired man, who asked us what nation we belonged to. The reader must bear in mind that we had on our mining suits, with hat-brims nearly the size of a small umbrella; and with our revolvers hanging in our belts, and rifles slung over our backs, we must have presented a terrifying appearance to civilized people.

We answered the old man, who seemed to be the owner of the place, and looked old enough to be a rival of Methuselah, that we were Americans, travelling towards the coast in hopes of finding a seaport town or settlement of some sort. He replied that he had heard of Americans but had never seen one before. Probably few people had ever seen just such looking Americans as we were.

We conversed freely in Spanish, and told him not to be frightened in the least, for we should not harm him or his family, but would like to buy some milk if he could spare it. He said he never sold anything to travellers, but that we were welcome to anything on his place. He invited us into the house, and showed us a room where we could make ourselves comfortable, and offered to send us some milk at once. He sent us three wooden bowls and three wooden spoons, a bucket of milk, and a sack of *pinola*, which is a kind of meal made by pounding parched corn in a mortar.

We told the old man we would like to remain with him a few days to recruit our animals. To this he readily consented, and when the time came for us to leave he insisted that we should tarry longer. As he insisted upon it, we remained about a month, the old man enjoying my Spanish conversation, and delighted to hear of our adventures.

The old man gave us an invitation, after we had been there some time, to accompany his family in gathering prickly pears. We willingly accepted the invitation, for the old man had some interesting daughters who desired us to go as much as he did. He told us not to touch the pears, but to let his servants pick them, as they had the tools to do it with, but we could not do it with our hands. My friend Patterson thought he would try and gather a few, and did so.

Attempting to taste one he got his mouth so full of prickles that he was busy that day in getting them out. We got back to the house towards evening, having passed a very pleasant day. One day, in riding out some miles from the house with our aged host, I had my rifle along. The old man said he had seen guns before, but never saw one used, and was very anxious that I should show him the effect of a shot. A deer started up within long range, when I shot him through, much to the astonishment of my companion. We tied the deer to my saddle and returned

Mr Jones in a deer-trap

to the house.

The manner of catching deer in that country is with a spring-pole and a snare. One evening Mr. Jones invited one of the daughters to take a walk with him into the woods to look around a little, and have some private conversation; for both of my friends had picked up considerable Spanish, and could talk with the girls. Suddenly Mr. Jones found himself elevated in the air about ten feet, and hanging by one leg, having accidentally stepped his foot into one of these spring traps.

The girl by his side screamed, but could not extricate him; and Patterson and myself, who were strolling about at no great distance, hearing the noise went to his assistance. On our return to the house, the joke was too good to keep, and we gave the old man a full description of the affair, at which he laughed heartily, and asked Jones if he did not think these spring traps better than guns, as they saved using powder.

Our host invited us one day to take a ride and look at his stock. The cattle were to be gathered from the plain, driven into a large field which was enclosed by a high fence, and such as required it caught and branded. This is an annual custom in that section, and at this time all new cattle and such of the increase of the herd as have arrived at a proper age are branded. He inquired if I understood using the lasso. I told him if he would give me a good horse and the right kind of a saddle, I thought I could help him some. He furnished me with these and a lasso, and I started with the old man and his servants, while Jones and Patterson remained at home, chatting with the women, because there were no more outfits of riding saddles, lassos, &c.

We succeeded in bringing in about one thousand head, of all ages, and getting them inside the enclosure, when the gate was shut and the work of lassoing commenced. The old man was very much surprised when he found that I could lasso as many as any of his servants. Jones and Patterson stood looking through the fence to see the sport of lassoing and branding the cattle, and going up to them I saw the girls were with them, gazing with pleasure at our success.

One of the girls said I might be an American, but they had never heard that Americans were acquainted with that business. I had to explain to them that evening all of my four years' captivity among Indians, and how I used the lasso among them as well as in Mexico afterwards.

A peculiar looking building adjoining the old man's residence attracted my curiosity, and I asked him what it was for. He replied that he built it as a church, and invited us to look inside. We entered, after removing our hats according to custom, and saw that it was very nicely fitted up with crosses, representations of the Virgin Mary and saints, statues, flowers, candles, and everything usually found in such chapels.

I asked him how they performed the marriage ceremony in that part of the country. He said he had an old Indian priest who had received the power to marry and perform some services, having been instructed in Latin somewhat, and invested with authority sufficient at least for that purpose. For his part, he thought he could marry parties as well as priests, for mutual love and consent were the main points; the rest was of small consequence.

After we had retired for the night, Mr. Patterson made the remark that he thought he should have to employ the old Indian priest to marry him to one of the girls. This was such a surprise to me that I asked him if he was in earnest or joking. He said he meant it, but did not know how to approach the old man on the subject; but as far the girl was concerned, she was willing enough, he knew! I asked Patterson if it was not a pretty short acquaintance, when he laughed and said it was, rather, but they had improved every minute and made rapid progress in their courtship.

He thought the risk on his part was trifling compared to the girl's, and there was nothing like trying, anyhow. He thought the girl would marry him out of pure love, for he confessed there was nothing attractive about his appearance. He begged me, as I could talk Spanish better than he, and had more influence with her father, to say a good word for him the next morning after he had mustered courage to ask his consent, which I agreed to do.

After breakfast, he approached the old gent on the subject, to which he replied that if the girl was willing, and Patterson would agree to stay there and live with him, he had no objections. I was taken aside by him and asked if I knew Patterson's history, and whether he had a wife already. My answer was that I knew nothing of him except for a few weeks, but liked him and believed he was an honest man; also, that he had often represented to me that he was a single man.

The Sunday following was fixed upon for the marriage, and on that day they were duly united. The old Indian who pronounced them man and wife was about as brief in his ceremonies as he was unintelligible, for his language was a compound of several tongues, *viz*.: Indian, Spanish, and Latin; but the bride and groom were apparently impressed with the important fact that they had undergone some strange transformation!

We had a fine dinner served, and after that a dance, which was enlivened by occasional sips of domestic wine, some of which was so old that the year of its manufacture was forgotten. For music we had the services of two Indians, one of whom played on a flute made of a sugar cane, and the other had a fiddle of his own construction, made more for wear than for fine music—particularly wear of the nerves. We tried to keep step to the music, but owing to the grape juice or the quick motions of the musicians, we made rather con-fused work of it. The dance was concluded by mid-night, at which hour Jones and I retired to our room to consult in regard to the policy of resuming our journey, and to mourn the loss of our genial and clever companion, Patterson.

The next day we announced that our visit among our hospitable friends was about to end, and we were obliged to leave. The old gentleman insisted that we should remain with him, but we told him we had more important business to attend to. He requested us to stay until he could furnish us with provisions for our journey, as it was a long distance to a seaport where communication by steamer with California was possible, and advised us to go to La Paz, at the southern part of the peninsula of Lower California, as he had understood the California steamers touched there. Accordingly we staid two days longer, during which he had a beef killed, and prepared from it a quantity of dried strips, which, with many other things, he presented us for our comfort on the way.

The morning we left he presented us with two line saddle horses, with the remark that it was foolish to travel on mules or jacks in a country where horses were so plenty. We offered to pay for the horses, but he said we were welcome to them. He also gave us directions for the route to La Paz, which was about three hundred miles distant, for we were not far from the centre of the peninsula of Lower California.

We then bade our friend Patterson and the family good bye, leaving our mules with Patterson and mounting our new horses, and leading our jacks, we headed due south for La Paz, which port we reached in eight days, suffering considerably for want of water on the route. On reaching La Paz we found revolutionary disturbances among the Mexicans there, one party sustaining and the other opposing Governor Dominguez. He learned of our arrival and invited us to co-operate with him in his cause, but we declined on the plea that we were there for a day or two only and should leave by the first steamer.

As there was no steamer in port, and we thought it dangerous to remain there, we went northerly on the coast of the Californian Gulf to a small port called Incenal, where we saw many Indians and Mexicans engaged in pearl diving, and some of them possessed a faculty of remaining under water for a long time. One of the divers was caught by a shark, and I saw him devoured. I purchased two pearls from the divers, paying twenty-five dollars for them, one of which was about the size of a common grape.

Here we changed our minds about going to California, and concluded to cross the gulf to Guaymas, in Sonora, and visit my old friends. We were partly influenced to this decision by seeing the captain of a small vessel, who was bound for Guaymas and urged us to go along with him. We had some difficulty in getting our animals on board, but the captain and crew finally succeeded. Arriving at Guaymas and getting acquainted there with the commander of an English vessel in port, I sold him my two pearls for two hundred and fifty dollars. We remained in Guaymas several days, visiting some of my friends, then proceeded towards the interior of the state, stopping awhile at a mining camp called Brunces.

At these mines they extract the silver from the lead by smelting the whole in a furnace, running in into pigs, after which the silver is easily separated. Other ledges in the vicinity, where the silver is mixed with the rock, are worked by the amalgamation process. In this process the ore and rock are first pulverized and mixed with quicksilver and water, when the whole is well worked together by being placed in a vat and stirred up by a wheel or rotary machine, when the metals settle to the bottom and the refuse passes out with the water when drawn off, when the silver and quicksilver are gathered into a cloth and pressed, which partly separates them. The operation is completed by heating the remainder quite hot, when the silver rises to the top.

From here we went to the Pimos Indian village, which is a collection of adobe houses. They are square, and the door or entrance is in the roof. On the edge of the roof, all around, is a wall pierced with portholes for defence. They enter the house by a ladder, and when they reach the roof they draw the ladder up after them. This tribe is industrious, raising corn, wheat, and vegetables; they are small in stature, quite dark in colour, and flat nosed, but friendly and hospitable.

Nearly all of these Indians speak Spanish. Their chief amusement is in playing ball, using a large India-rubber ball weighing seven or eight pounds. In playing, when the ball bounds they strike it with their hips instead of a club. We stopped several days with the chief, whose name was Mattio, and he made us welcome, taking no pay for his hospitality. When we were preparing to leave, he asked us which way we were going, and when

I replied to the Opoto village, he said it was unsafe for us to go without an escort on account of the Apaches, and furnished ten of his warriors to accompany us. He also furnished abundant provision for our journey.

About midway between the two villages we encountered a dozen Apache Indians who were driving about twenty-five head of cattle and several mules and jacks. We fired on them and killed two of their number, the rest fleeing and leaving their animals in our possession. We hurried on with our captured beasts for fear of some larger force of Apaches who might pursue us. Arriving at the Opoto village, our Indian escort reported that we had two Apache scalps, which caused a general rejoicing throughout the village. We were then taken to the house of the chief, and our stock put in a pen, when we received from him a cordial welcome; for he was hostile towards the Apaches, and was rejoiced to see their scalps.

The chief said they must have a dance over the scalps that night, and asked Jones and myself, with our escort, to join them. At the dance they produced some liquor which they called *mascal*, which is made from a plant that grows similar to a cabbage, which yields a fruit which is pounded and the juice extracted and fermented by placing in rawhide vessels which are hung in the sun. We divided the cattle and mules taken from the Apaches, with the Indians who accompanied us, and told the chief to kill two or three of our cattle for the feast that night, which was done.

A large fire was built up near the dancing ground, and the dressed beeves were placed nearby. When anyone wished to eat they would cut pieces from the beef and roast it for themselves by holding it over the fire on sticks. The two scalps were elevated on tall poles in the centre of a ring, around which they danced. Several hundred Indians—men, women, and children—were dancing at the same time, which afforded Jones and myself much amusement.

By midnight the majority of the party were drunk, and at one o' clock Jones and I went to bed; but when we arose in the morning the dance was still going on and nothing left of the two beeves except the bones, much of the meat having been wasted. The chief, by our direction, had two more of our beeves killed.

We made some coffee for breakfast and gave the chief some, which he said was the first he ever tasted; he called it very fine. This feasting and dancing continued three nights, and at the end of it our friendly escort said they must return to their village. When asked how much we should pay them for their services as escort, they said they were well paid by the division of the captured animals, and started on their return perfectly satisfied.

The Opoto Indians are friendly to whites, but are not civilized to any great extent, and they dwell in caves or rude huts. They are inferior in appearance, with low foreheads, the hair growing down near the eyebrows. They raise very little grain, living chiefly by hunting. The chief inquired if we were Americans, and when told that we were, he said the Mexicans had represented that Americans were a bad people, but they must be mistaken, for he thought if we were a fair sample they were the best people he ever knew. He showed me some fine gold in a goose quill, and said it came from rich mines in the limits of his tribe, but he kept the matter secret for fear of being overrun with the Mexican miners. His tribe had learned the value of gold by being able to purchase clothing and supplies with it from the Mexicans.

We bade this chief *adieu*, and presented him what remained of our share of the cattle captured from the Apaches. We were held in high esteem by him before we made him this present, but afterwards he was anxious to do all he could for us; and when we started towards Arizona Territory, he furnished an escort of twenty men, who were very willing to accompany us, to the next tribe of Publanos. After presenting us to the chief of this tribe, who received us very kindly, our escort returned.

In this trip, after leaving Guaymas we had two objects in view: one of which was to reach Fort Buchanan in Arizona, ultimately, and then return to California, revisiting certain mineral ledges I had discovered in my former travels. Another object was to make an exploration among certain friendly Indian tribes, on our way to Arizona Territory; and our route in northern Mexico was thus necessarily circuitous, for we often went out of our way to see some new tribe, or visit some new mines we heard of. As we were not burdened with cares of family or property, we shaped our course according to our inclinations, going wherever there was a prospect of finding anything entertaining.

We visited the Publanos, as we heard much in their favour from the Indians we had left. We found them an agricultural people, with a nice village, catholic church, &c. They raise corn, wheat, and vegetables; have some peach, apple, and pear orchards. They have many mills, for grinding their grain, which are very rude, and are propelled by mule power, the grain being fed to the mill by the hand of a squaw.

One of these mills will ordinarily grind about two bushels of grain per day; but this amount can be increased somewhat, in case of necessity. These Indians are copper-coloured, with roman nose, and high foreheads, showing intelligence in their features and actions; and many of them speak Spanish, and some have blue eyes. They have a justice of the peace, independent of their chief, whose emblem of authority is a gold headed staff.

When a trial is to come off, an assistant of this justice carries the staff to summon the parties to appear before the court. The sight of the staff is in effect the same as a warrant. When the parties are all assembled evidence is heard and cases decided according to the testimony. I saw four Indians shackled at the ankles sweeping the streets, under sentence of this justice, in punishment for disobeying laws of the tribe. These Indians are called quite honest in their business dealings, and we had a pleasant visit with the chief for a day or two.

As in the case of the other tribes we had visited, the chief urged us to stay longer, when he found we intended to leave, and on our departure furnished us with a party as escort and guides to our next stopping place. After the escort was provided we packed our animals and went to Magdalena, a Spanish town, where we found the Mexicans indulging in the ceremonies of Saints' week.

They had a great procession, at the head of which was a priest, followed by four young ladies carrying a figure representing Christ on a bier, and beside it another figure representing the Virgin Mary, also borne by young ladies; and each one in the procession was carrying a lighted wax candle. At short intervals the procession halted, when all would kneel and repeat their prayers. The march through the town occupied about three hours, when they all returned to the church, where they deposited the figures of Christ and the Virgin Mary within the altar.

The ceremonies, varying with each day, lasted from Monday till Sabbath morning. No one was allowed to eat meat during the time, no bell was allowed to be rung, all amusements or indulgence of the passions was strictly forbidden, and no one was allowed to ride or use an animal in the streets. A party of men paraded through the town armed with sabres, knives, and other weapons, to enforce the orders of the church. On Friday the figure of Christ was placed in a coffin, in the altar of the church, and the coffin covered with wreaths and bouquets of flowers, where it remained until ten o'clock in the morning of Sabbath day, when it was taken from the coffin and placed in its position to show that he had risen from the dead, at which hour all the bells in the place began to ring, and the people commenced shouting and singing with joy.

Just then a figure representing Judas Iscariot was brought out and mounted on an ass. A rope was stretched across the street and the effigy was hung to it, amid the shouts of the populace. The figure was filled with fireworks, which, by some slow fuse arrangement, finally exploded and blew the thing in pieces, which was the grand finale of these religious ceremonies. When this was over, the Mexicans commenced horse-racing, cock-fighting, drinking, gambling, dealing *monte*, and playing all manner of games, which lasted for another week.

My friend Jones and I enjoyed ourselves for these two weeks looking on as spectators. The latter week we attended several *fandangoes* or dances, and made some acquaintances.

We met here two Americans, named White and Mulligan, who told us of a mountain district near the Arizona line called Plancha La Platus (meaning iron and silver), where they had been with a small party, but had been driven off by Indians. They stated that the mountain abounded with minerals, including silver ledges. On inquiry we found that several Mexicans in Magdalena knew of the mines, and had been to the mountain; but they were also driven off.

White thought we had better raise a party and go there; and as Jones and Mulligan were ready, I consented to join them, and we hired twelve Mexicans as guides and escort. Jones and I had eight pack animals, which we loaded with supplies and started off, our party numbering sixteen, all armed, and ready for mining or fighting Indians. On arriving at the place, we found plenty of lead and iron, with occasional silver ledges.

At the foot of the mountain we discovered some ancient ruins, indicating that the mines had been worked formerly. We also found some wild cattle and hogs. We encamped inside of some old walls, and arranged the place for our defence in case of attack. After perfecting these arrangements I took my rifle and went out in search of game, and found a fat wild cow, which I shot. While dressing her I heard a noise on the hill nearby, and on looking up I saw twelve Apache Indians driving and leading about forty head of horses.

I hid behind a rock and they did not discover me, though they passed within a hundred yards.. When they were out of sight I returned to camp, where I procured help, and went back and secured my beef, and brought it into camp. Afterwards I kept a good lookout for Indians. In prospecting in this vicinity I saw several shafts which had been worked, and found metals of different kinds, making selections of many choice specimens. Some ledges appeared to be nearly pure lead. We had been here eight days, when the Mexicans said they could not risk staying any longer for fear of the Indians.

The Apaches had a regular trail which passed near our mines, and they had murdered all miners that they came in contact with. We had seen skulls and other human bones in that vicinity, and the sight of them made the Mexicans rather fearful. We therefore returned to Magdalena, where our specimens were tested and pronounced valuable, some yielding as high as two thousand dollars per ton.

I wrote to the governor of Sonora, saying that if he would furnish troops we would return and work the mines, and divide the profits with him. In reply, he wrote that he would see if it was possible, and inform me in the course of a month. In about two weeks he wrote me that he had not the troops to spare, as there was a revolution or political rising in some parts of his state, which called for all the troops he had. We saw no way of organizing a force of citizens sufficiently strong to defend ourselves against three or four thousand Apache warriors in the district we left, therefore we disbanded our company.

Myself and friend Jones then started for Fort Buchanan in Arizona, taking no escort this time, as the route was much safer and there was considerable travel from Magdelena to Fort Buchanan. Still we kept on the alert for Apaches, who often attacked travellers by this route. The Apaches are the only tribe I ever had a lasting dislike to. This may be partly the result of being so long associated with their enemies, the Comanches, but the principal reason for it was their low treachery, for one never knew when to believe their assurances of friendship. At all events, I dreaded a meeting with them, unless I had some support, more than with any other tribe.

On our way we stopped over night at Santa Cruz, where the Mexicans told us the Indians were plenty, ahead of us, and advised us to be on the watch for them. At our next camping place, while I was cooking supper, a Mexican girl, about fifteen years old, came suddenly upon us. We started up in surprise at the appearance of this half-naked, barefooted girl. She said she had run away in the night from some Indians who had captured her.

She was washing clothes at a small stream, near her home, about thirty-five or forty miles distant, when two Indians stole carefully up and carried her off. When she saw the smoke of our fire she hesitated about approaching; but seeing from our appearance that we were not Indians, she had concluded to throw herself on our protection and ask us to assist her in reaching her home, where she had a widowed mother, with no brothers or sisters.

She feared her mother would be suffering great anxiety on account of her absence. We gave her some food, and, as it was early in the evening, we repacked our animals and started with the girl for San Antonio, a mining place about ten miles distant. Here we placed the girl under the charge of Mrs. Hatch, whose husband was foreman of the smelting works. The girl said she belonged at Sycamore Ranche, and, Mr. Hatch, after providing her with clothing and necessaries for her comfort, concluded to send her home the next day with a proper guard, and requested me to accompany them.

A party of eight mounted men volunteered to go with me and the girl to her home, which we reached without seeing any Indians. The mother of the girl had nearly despaired of ever seeing her again, and her meeting with her child was very affecting. She was so grateful for the part I had taken in her return, that she urged me to take one of her mules as a present. This I at first declined to do, as I wished no reward for what I looked upon as an act of simple humanity; but when I found that she was deeply grieved by my refusal, I accepted it. She had a large amount of stock, and since the death of her husband had carried on a very successful business of stock raising, by the help of Mexican servants.

We returned to San Antonio after receiving the blessing of the old lady, and the warmest thanks of the daughter, who appeared to be very well bred and quite a modest girl. At the mines we were advised not to proceed to Fort Buchanan alone, as two men like us would be in great danger of attack from Indians. Hearing that government soldiers, were expected to arrive soon from the fort with supplies for the miners, we waited a day or two and returned with them to Fort Buchanan.

On our arrival at the fort a report came in that ten or twelve men, women and children had been assassinated by the Apaches on the St. Peter's river. Jones and myself were invited by Major Cremona of the fort to accompany a party of twenty-two citizens and a squad of soldiers, led by him, in pursuit of the murderers. On reaching the place a shocking sight presented itself. The people were murdered and scalped, and their property and stock taken away.

We followed the trail of the Indians two days, when Major Cremona proposed to give up the pursuit for fear the party would suffer for want of rations before they got back to the fort. I objected to returning, saying that he had small sympathy for the dead or their friends, to stop now when we were so near the Indians; for I was sure they could not be far in advance of us, as they had to drive the cattle they had stolen, and we were well mounted. I added, that when we overtook them, the cattle would furnish us sufficient food; and if the worst should happen, I could eat mule meat, as I had done before.

The citizens of our party felt the same in regard to the matter as I did, for they felt that they were not safe if such raids by Indians were allowed to go unavenged. But my reasoning did not convince the major, who felt unwilling to expose his men to the chances of starvation, and returned with them to the fort. Jones and I then held a consultation with the citizens, and they said they were willing to follow me anywhere. We resumed the pursuit, and within an hour came up with an ox that had become tired out, from which we procured meat enough for our wants and pushed on.

At night we camped near a small stream of water, our party being much exhausted, and prepared supper, making a fire in a deep hollow to avoid being seen by the Indians if they were near. After eating, I ascended a hill nearby, and saw a few miles ahead, several camp fires. I returned to camp, and reported the location of the Indians, when the party agreed with me that our best plan was to allow our animals to feed till about midnight, and then by making a circuit, get in advance of the Indians and attack them as they came up, as they would not be expecting any foes in that direction.

This plan was successfully carried out, as we got in advance of them about a mile, and posted sentinels to warn us of their approach. About daylight our sentinels came in and reported the Indians near. We then secreted ourselves, and waited till the cattle and horses had passed us, and as the Indians, who were carelessly following them, not dreaming of attack, came abreast of us, we poured a volley into them, killing seven and wounding several more.

One of the wounded Indians fell from his horse, having a bullet through his thigh, and one of our men, named Joe Carroll, rushed upon him, when the Indian raised up and shot Carroll in the breast with an arrow, wounding him severely; but Carroll had strength to kill the Indian. There were about thirty-five or forty of the Apaches, and those not killed by our first fire escaped through the brush. We pursued them about a mile, but only came up with one who was wounded, and I despatched him with my revolver. We returned and collected the cattle and horses, after which I told the party we ought to return in haste, for we might be near the Apache nation.

We scalped the Indians, though some of the party said it looked barbarous; but I kept on scalping, saying that business men always took receipts, and I wanted something to show our success. Taking the nine scalps and getting poor Carroll mounted on a pony, we set out on our return to the fort as rapidly as possible. Having to drive many cattle, it was slow travelling for a wounded man, and I urged the necessity of someone going to the fort for assistance, and a surgeon, so as to meet us half way, but no one dared venture to make the trip.

I drew the arrow head from Carroll's breast, when he began to bleed freely, and only lived to reach the place where the massacre occurred, where we buried him on the banks of the St. Peter's river, with the bodies of the murdered citizens. We had recovered over sixty head of cattle, mules, and horses, and having got them so far on our journey, felt sure of reaching the fort in safety, which we did the next day.

The officers at the fort were surprised to see us re-turn with the stock. They asked me all the particulars of the fight, which I gave in detail, and showed them the nine scalps, which the commanding officer gazed at in surprise, and he invited Jones and myself to take supper with him. While eating with him, he asked us to give him the scalps, as his command of the fort would expire in a month, and he wished to take them with him to California. I told him he was welcome to take them, if he would publish the truth, and credit us citizens with the honour, instead of saying that his soldiers did the work. He promised to do so, and on his arrival at San Francisco he kept his promise, publishing the names of our party in the papers, a list of whom I had given him.

In the course of our conversation at the fort, I told him that if the United States government would give me a contract to procure Apache scalps at fifty dollars each, and allow Jones and me to pick our men from the citizens and hunters in those parts, it would be better policy for the government than sending troops into that region. It is not probable that such a course will ever be pursued by the government, as it would be looked upon as barbarous in the extreme by those who still have faith that they can be conciliated and civilized. But those who hold to this opinion do not know the Apaches as I do. There is not one particle of honour in the whole tribe.

Chapter 27

Sunday Amusements

In about a week after we arrived at Fort Buchanan a brother of a man who was murdered by the Apaches, and who owned most of the stock, came and claimed them. We delivered him all except ten head, which belonged to another citizen that was also killed at the time. He offered us a part of the stock for our services, but Jones and I declined any compensation. As for the rest of our party, they had scattered and were not near the fort. He then insisted on our taking a fine pair of matched mules which he drove with his team. Those mules brought us five hundred dollars at the fort, and we divided the money, Jones and I taking a part, and the remainder was given to such citizens of our party as we could find.

Hearing of some gold diggings at a place called Penalto, where the mines paid well, Jones and myself and two Mexican guides set out with supplies for the mines. Arriving at Apache Pass, at the government station, the officer in command asked us where we were from, and where bound. We told him from Fort Buchanan, at which he was surprised, because ours was the smallest party he had lately seen that came through without trouble. He said the United States mail carrier had been killed by Indians the day before, within five miles of his station.

At his request we consented to remain with him for a short time to await the arrival of a mule train with machinery for the mines we were about to visit. In two days the train arrived, headed by Stephen O'Choas, the owner of the teams, and a partner in the mines. In the train were twenty-four wagons, loaded with tools, machinery or supplies, with ten mules to each wagon. The third night after leaving Apache Pass, the train was attacked at Willow Creek by Apaches, who succeeded in running off eighteen mules. I proposed to Mr. O'Choas that we should pursue the thieves; but he objected on account of the delay, preferring to lose the mules.

Finally we arrived at Penalto, where we found a great number of miners, some at work, and others prospecting. Jones and I went to work, but barely paid expenses; as surface mining, which at first paid remarkably well, had about given out, and the gold could not be found in any paying quantities, except in ledges, which must be worked by companies possessed of capital, with quartz machine crushers, and all the necessary appliances. The place was rapidly filling up with desperate characters, intent on plunder.

I told some of the miners that a vigilance committee should be organized to preserve order, which suited the honest part of the miners, and they held a meeting for that purpose, organized a society, and commenced operations immediately on one desperado named John Jenkins, who had committed two murders. He was arrested and hung on a tree at once. Another man who had robbed a miner of four hundred dollars worth of gold dust, was caught and compelled to restore the money to the man he had robbed, and as he received bruises in the fight he had with the villain when he robbed him, which disabled him for a fortnight, we also demanded for the miner his expenses and remuneration for his lost time.

Then ten minutes was allowed this thief to quit the place for good, or be hung. He begged for a mule or horse as he was lame, when a miner, out of pity, gave him a worn out jack that was turned out to die, and he moved off in great fear, requesting us to make due allowance of time if the old bob-tailed jack should happen to balk with him before he got out of the place.

After the crowd had seen this one off, we went around the place and gave notice to the gamblers and all persons who did not make their living honestly to go to work or leave the camp within twenty-four hours. A part of them left and the others went to work, and after this the camp was more quiet and few disturbances occurred. These Penalto mines lay east of Apache Pass, between Mesilla and El Passo del Norte. Jones and myself remained here about six weeks, when I met a French Creole, a trapper, who was called Monsieur Louis. He informed me that he had about fifty traps, and everything required, and was on his way to the Gila River to trap beaver, which were very plenty there. He said he did not like to go alone, and if Jones and I would join him, we would share alike in what we caught, which he was confident would pay us better than mining where we were.

Here a change of adventure was open to us, and we did not hesitate long in accepting the Creole's offer, but packed our animals with provisions and ammunition, and were off with him for the head waters of the Gila River. Arriving there we found encouraging signs of beaver, and camped awhile, having some success, for I knew how to bait the animals with a scent composed of several ingredients. I told the Creole that the fur was inferior, as the climate was too warm. After catching about forty and curing the skins, we left for the Colorado, where we found great numbers of beaver, but the skins were as poor as the others. After remaining about ten clays, we had caught one hundred and fifty beaver, and dressed the skins, which we added to our former lot, and baled some of them up, intending to ship them to market.

The last evening we spent here, an old Indian squaw came into our camp and pretended to be very hungry. I had my suspicions that she was a spy, and had come into our presence to learn the numbers and strength of our party, and report to her tribe that they might judge whether it would be safe to attack us. I gave her what she wanted to eat; and then she proposed to leave; but I told her she must remain over night, and we made her as comfortable as possible.

During the night she attempted to escape, but Louis levelled his rifle and bade her lay down. She sat down by the fire and cried, which convinced me that she had a party lying in wait to attack us. We kept a close watch over her till morning, when we finished baling our furs, packed our animals, and started for Prescott mines in the Mohave Indian nation, the Frenchman acting as guide. We mounted the squaw on a mule, and tied her on to prevent her escape. When we got near Prescott mines, when we thought we were out of danger from her friends, we let her go, giving her some provisions to last her on her tramp homeward.

At Prescott we found rich mines and silver ledges, worked by a large company; but no good surface diggings nor sight for us to remain. We therefore proceeded with a party for Fort Yuma on the Colorado River. On our way we saw a fine country, with rich soil, which was fast being settled by Texan emigrants. On our way we passed through the village of the Maricopus Indians, on the Gila River, who were a very friendly people, and reached Fort Yuma without any mishaps or skirmishes with the enemy.

On our arrival at the fort we learned that a vessel was expected soon to arrive from San Francisco, and decided to wait for it, thinking it would afford us an opportunity to send our furs to market. When the vessel arrived we placed our furs in charge of Mr. Hooper, who supplied the fort monthly with provisions from San Francisco. He offered to take our furs to San Francisco, dispose of them to the best advantage, and bring or remit to us the proceeds at Fort Yuma.

While at the fort, General Banning and Colonel Keller came there on their way to Sonora to confer with the governor of that state on important business. Finding that I was well acquainted with Governor Pesquiera, they offered me good pay to accompany them as an interpreter and guide, which I accepted. I told my friends Louis and Jones to remain at the fort till I returned from the trip, which might occupy a month, to which they consented; for they wanted to see the result of the fur shipment, and it would be several weeks before any returns could be got.

I went with the general and colonel in a four horse stage. Feeling somewhat alarmed on account of the stage robberies on that line, we were well provided with revolvers, and I took along my favourite rifle. After the first day's journey our route lay through a sandy desert, where water was a scarce article for ninety-five miles; and we were obliged to carry enough, in leather bottles or kegs, to keep ourselves and horses from dying with thirst. We also took provisions and some forage.

In crossing this desert, it is dangerous to lie down, as almost every bunch of sage-brush contains a rattle-snake. It was a long and tedious ride through the sand, but when we reached Dalton station, we laid over to recruit a little, and started with a change of horses for Ures, the capital of Sonora. The next station after leaving Dalton was Altar, where they told us it was dangerous to travel further, without protection, from Apaches and robbers.

The general therefore hired eight mounted Mexicans as an escort, to accompany us to the capital, where we arrived in safety and were glad to find good hotel accommodations after our fatigue and peril. I went that evening to see the governor, and received a very hearty welcome from him. I informed him that General Banning and Colonel Keller were there from California, and wished to have an interview whenever it would be convenient. He made an appointment to meet them the following day at his office.

The next day when we were assembled in his office, I introduced my friends, and the governor was so pleased with the nature of their business that he brought out several bottles of champagne, and the interview became a very social one. They invited the co-operation of the governor in the establishing of a port at some favourable point just below the mouth of the Colorado on the coast of Sonora, for the convenience of the interior trade with Arizona and upper Mexico.

The governor assured them he would do all in his power to further their plans and wishes; and added, that when he was driven from his own country into Arizona he had been treated very kindly by the Americans, and it was through their influence he had regained his position; and that he felt under obligations to return their kindness. He said I was a witness to those matters as I was a captain in his artillery and interpreter for him at the time. He said the opening of the port did not rest with him, but that he would send a dispatch to the President of Mexico and inform him in writing of the advantages that would accrue to the state of Sonora, and do all in his power to bring about the desired result. General Banning and Colonel Keller were perfectly satisfied with this, and said that was all they could ask of him. The governor gave a splendid ball that evening, and invited us to attend, which invitation was thankfully accepted.

The following day preparations were made to proceed to the proposed port to make examinations, with an engineer named Captain Polamus, who was brought on by General Banning. This was on Saturday—the governor told them that he was to have a bullfight on the following day (Sunday), and invited us to remain to witness it, and the general and party finally concluded to remain. The fight commenced about 3 o'clock, p. m., and six high spirited bulls were fought.

A bullfight amphitheatre is large enough to seat an audience of three or four thousand people, with a large circular pit in the centre, which is separated from the outside or circle of seats by a safe wall, so that none of the audience can be harmed by the infuriated beasts. One bull at a time is let into the enclosure or pit, where ten persons are standing, dressed in fantastic colours. Three of these gladiators are mounted on horses, one of them armed with a lasso, and two of them with spears or lances. The others are furnished with red flags, which serve to exasperate the bull. The spears are used on him for the same purpose. The lasso is used in case the bull gets any of the men into too close quarters, to pull the animal away from his victim.

When at last the bull has become perfectly enraged the bugle is sounded, and a man, designated as the captain, steps into the arena with a red flag and a sharp two-edged sword. On showing the flag the bull makes directly for him, when it is his business to dodge him, and, at the same time kill him, by running him through the heart with his sword.

After the bull is dead, a pair of mules, covered with red blankets, with harness and bells on them, are led in, and they draw out the bull to make way for the next combat, which immediately follows; and thus the fight continues amid the cheers of the audience until all the bulls, except one, have been killed.

Frequently they have a wild beast, a bear, or lion for example on hand (as they had a California lion in this case). The cage containing the lion is hauled near the centre of the arena where there is a strong post. The lion has a long chain fastened about his neck and the other end is secured to the post for safety. There is a red cloth on the lion's neck, and, when all is ready, the last bull is driven into the amphitheatre.

I never heard such a noise from any assemblage as came from that crowd when that bull made a rush for the lion, which was not a very large animal, but a very ferocious one. This fight lasted at least for half an hour, and the bull was horribly cut up; but after tossing up his antagonist in the air several times, and getting him worried out, he finally got him down and gored him to death, which ended the bullfight. After this the bulls that had been killed were dressed, and the meat fed out to convicts in their prisons.

The governor inquired how our party, especially General Banning, liked the bullfight. The general replied that he considered it rather barbarous, but the governor excused it by saying that the people demanded such excitement, and it was their amusement instead of theatres.

Next morning, being furnished with provisions and horses, also an escort of soldiers provided by the governor, we left for the place of the proposed port. The governor, with a band of music, accompanied us a short distance, and wished us success as we separated.

We at length arrived at our destination, which was at Port Lobas, or in English, Port Wolf, which, at first sight, gave promise of being one of the finest harbours on the Sonora coast. We had with us a canvas boat, and in this the engineer examined the harbour and found plenty of water for the largest ships; and we also discovered that it was a safe refuge for vessels in case of storms. The waters also abound in fish of different kinds.

We remained here four days, making examinations; and discovered a beach where, after removing six inches of sand, was a mass of alum salt. We found it by seeing a place where some persons, probably Indians, had cleared off a quantity of sand and taken out the salt. On our third day there, some thirty Indians came into our camp, who said they were of the Ceres tribe. The soldiers of our escort confirmed their statement. These Indians live entirely on sharks, sea lions, and fish.

That afternoon, while Captain Polamus was out in the woods, he was bitten by a rattlesnake. He came into camp terribly frightened, saying he was a dead man. On inquiry I found that he was bitten in the instep. I pulled off his shoe and tied a cord very tightly above the wound, and cut the wound a little to let it bleed. I hurried off one of the Mexicans to hunt up some snake-weed, telling the captain not to be frightened for I could cure him. I searched for the snake and killed it, bringing the reptile into camp about the time the Mexican returned with the snake-weed, which was found growing in abundance in the vicinity.

Making a strong tea of the weed, Polamus drank probably a quart of it, and having pounded and mashed a lot of the herb, I made a poultice of it, placing it over the place that was bitten, which had by this time swollen considerably. I opened the snake, took out his liver, cut and spread it on the poultice over the wound, and bound it on tightly with a part of the split body of the snake, when the sharp pains began to decrease and the green poison commenced oozing out.

The captain's ankle did not swell above the place I tied the cord around, and at 12 o'clock that night I removed the bandage, and asked him how his foot felt. He replied that it was numb, but we considered that was in consequence of the tight cord which I now loosened some. He said it was fortunate that I was along with them, otherwise he believed he should have died very soon.

In the morning he appeared quite well, and said he felt no

ill-effects from the bite; so I removed the poultice and bandage, and rubbed some gunpowder into the wound, which was the last thing done for it. The captain then wished me to show him some of this weed, which I did, and he picked a quantity of it, so that he would know it again, should he have use for it. This running vine or weed has a small blossom that resembles a rattlesnake's eye. I was once bitten by a rattlesnake myself, and was made acquainted with this remedy by a Comanche Indian, who cured me. It is always found in a country where rattlesnakes are numerous.

After making all the preliminary surveys for a landing place, wharf, &c., and finding the harbour free from reefs or sunken rocks, we prepared to return.

This port is due west from the town of Altar, and about one hundred and twenty miles from it. We were three days returning to Altar, where the general dismissed the escort of soldiers and presented them a hundred dollars, which they at first refused, saying they were under pay from their governor; but the general insisted on their taking it as a present, when they received and divided it among themselves, starting off the next morning for Ures, the capital, while our party took the stage for Fort Yuma.

On the route, after two days of travel, our stage driver stopped and said there was a party of men ahead, on the right side of the road. I told him to halt there till we could ascertain who they were and learn their objects; and immediately we all got our weapons in readiness for defence. On getting out of the stage, I noticed the men making for the road, advancing slowly towards us, and I cautioned the passengers again to prepare for them.

These robbers, eight in number, rode up to within fifty or sixty yards of us, when we ordered them to halt. They wore masks, and looked at us a moment, as we had our rifles levelled at them, appearing undecided whether to attack us or not. Presently the leader inquired the way into Mexico. I told them in Spanish that they were already in Mexico, and they knew it well, but if they didn't retreat and get out of our way in double quick time, they would find themselves on the road to a hotter climate.

The leader now ordered them to advance, and at the same time I shot at him; but his horse threw up his head and received the ball between his eyes, dropping dead. General Banning then fired at the dismounted man and killed him, which caused the rest to scatter. We went to the body, and, on pulling off the mask, found him to be a half-breed Indian. In his belt were two fine revolvers, which I took possession of.

This attack was about twelve miles from St. Domingo, which place we intended to reach that night. It may seem strange that a stage should be attacked in daylight by a band of robbers; but this was the only chance they had, as the stages on this route did not travel nights on. account of the numerous robberies which had been committed on them. We left the horse and rider where they fell, and pushed onward. On arriving at St. Domingo, the general asked me what he had better do relative to the shooting, and I advised him to report it to the authorities. He left the matter entirely in my hands, saying he was not acquainted with the Spanish customs or language.

Finding a magistrate I gave him an account of the attack and its result, when he asked how many robbers there were; and when he found there were eight of them, he asked for a description of the man killed. When I had told him all I was able to, he replied that it was a noted robber of the plains for whose capture, dead or alive, a reward of five hundred dollars had been offered by Governor Pesquiera. He wished me to present his compliments to General Banning, and say to him that he had rendered a charitable service to the people of that section by killing the villain. He then ordered a wagon, with an armed escort, to go out and bring in the body if it could be found.

When the party returned they brought the body and also the saddle; and after the magistrate had given them an inspection, he pronounced the man to be the same notorious thief and murderer he had suspected. He was quite pleased to know for a certainty that the country was rid of this villain, for he had committed many murders in that vicinity, and invited our party to breakfast with him, urging the general to wait a few days and get returns from the governor, with the reward; but this proposition was declined on account of the delay. I tendered the pistols to the magistrate, but he insisted on my keeping them for my services.

The next night we arrived at Dawson's station, on the borders of the sandy desert, which we all dreaded to cross. For about ninety miles the ground is incapable of producing much but rattlesnakes, with other reptiles and vermin. There is no grass, water, or timber in sight, nothing but sand and sage-brush. When the wind sweeps across this desert, the sand is blown like snow, and fills up the travelled paths; and, in consequence, travellers lose their way and perish. Persons acquainted with it have a land mark for a guide, which is a high mountain that can be seen from all parts of the desert.

The top of the mountain is dark in appearance, and it is therefore called Black Head Mountain. I have crossed this trackless waste four times, but never admired the trip. On the east side of the mountain is a tribe of Indians, called the Papago's, which in English is Potato. The name is derived from the wild potatoes or artichokes which are found there in abundance, and which form a principal article of their food. They are as good marksmen as any Indians I ever saw, with the exception of the Comanches. They are employed by many of the farmers and stock raisers of Arizona to assist them, and are quite an industrious, peaceably disposed tribe.

After remaining at Dawson's station long enough to rest and recruit ourselves and horses, we laid in a good supply of water and provisions, with grain for the horses, and resumed our seats in the stage, wondering what new surprises were awaiting ns in our weary ride across the desert. We had no adventures until we were about midway across the desert, when, as we were travelling slowly in the night, for it was quite dark, our lead horses became frightened. I got out of the stage, and, peering through the darkness, discovered a body in the track of the road.

On lighting a lantern, I found that the man was perishing for want of water; and after giving him some, he revived, and we managed to get him on top of the stage. After giving him some food he inquired for his comrade, but he could remember but little of him after he laid down to sleep.

His companion had strayed from the road and perished; but we took this man along to Port Yuma, where he was recognized as a noted thief, who, with his partner, had run away from California with stolen property, and after swimming their horses over the Colorado river, they had vainly attempted to cross the desert. The authorities at Fort Yuma took him in charge, and sent him back to San Francisco, where, as we understood afterwards, he was sentenced for a long period to the penitentiary.

General Banning paid me, on our arrival at the fort, five dollars per day for the time I had been with him, and Captain Polamus offered me one hundred dollars for my services at the time he was bitten by the rattlesnake. This I declined to accept, but he insisted, saying he thought it a pity if his life was not worth a hundred dollars. After remaining a few days at the fort, the general and his party returned to California.

CHAPTER 28

A Brutal Dogfight

On arriving at Fort Yuma I found my friends, Jones and Louis. Mr. Hooper had returned from San Francisco with the discouraging news that he could only obtain one dollar each for our beaver pelts, on account of the poor quality of the fur, which put a stop to our trapping for beaver any more that season. It was lucky that I had money, for my friends were rather destitute, and at the fort our supplies cost us as much as they would in New York, for no quarter-master of any post is allowed to scatter the property of the government.

While at the fort we heard of the finding of a dead body on the road, which answered to the description given of the comrade of the thief we restored to life. We did not feel particularly grieved to hear of his death.

While at the fort I learned the particulars of a grand humbug, in the shape of a silver mine, of which Colonel Samuel Colt, of Hartford, Connecticut, was induced to become one of the chief proprietors. The company was composed of New York and California speculators. The mine was located about thirty-five miles, in a westerly direction, from Tubac, in Arizona. Bars of silver were sent to Colonel Colt, with a statement saying that they came from this mine, and purporting to give the quantity of silver that a ton of ore would yield.

A scientific man was employed to make assays of the ore. He reported to the overseer that the ore was not one-tenth part as rich, as represented, but lie was bribed to keep quiet about the matter, and not publish his assays; for, as they said truly, the stock was selling well in the New York market, and if the mine did not pay in one way, Wall street, New York, would make it pay in another. Colonel Colt was innocently led into the speculation from false representations respecting the richness of the lodes.

A friend of his who was living in California informed Colonel Colt that the mine was a humbug in season for him to dispose of his interest for about one hundred thousand dollars. Though the mine was worked for several years afterwards, it never paid expenses, and was eventually abandoned. The speculators who started it made a good thing, but the stockholders suffered, losing all they invested.

Near this silver mine another fraud was perpetrated, in the way of gold mining. A party of Americans were prospecting for gold, when some Chinese came along, looking for some mine to purchase. Some of the Americans took the Chinese party away to some diggings that did not pay very well, while the rest remained to prepare the ground so as to show some rich diggings when the Chinese came back. The Yankees dug into the side of a bank and mixed fine gold dust with the loose earth, and then loading their guns with powder mixed with gold dust, fired away at the bank where they had been digging.

They were all prepared to receive the Chinese when they returned. After the Chinese had washed out two or three pans of earth they had about eight dollars in gold as the result. Then they offered the Americans ten thousand dollars for the claim, which was accepted and the money paid over. That was what is termed salting a mine The sale occurred about sundown, and the Americans left before the new owners had time to discover the trick.

The Chinese worked the claim till they got out about two ounces, which was just about the amount the Yankees tired into the mines in salting them. Becoming discouraged soon after, they gathered up their rice and tea and started for Tueson, the capital of Arizona territory. When about half way on their journey the Apaches attacked them, killing the entire party,—ten in number. The Chinese are fine subjects for scalping, as the hair is shaved close near to the crown of the head.

The same party who killed the Chinese also killed a Mr. Pennington and his two sons, about two miles from where they killed the Chinese. The Indians were then pursued by the troops at Tubac. They had gone to a mountain called St. Oreto, where a party of Mexicans and Americans were at work getting timber for a saw mill. The Indians came across two Mexicans who were herding a drove of thirty yoke of oxen. They killed the Mexicans and a part of the cattle, and passed on to where the party were at work attacking them boldly. They met with strong resistance, and the fighting was kept up five hours.

Mr. Rickman, the head man of the working party, was shot in seven different places, but survived. Nine. Indians were killed, and the remainder fled in haste just as the troops from Tubac arrived. The working party informed the troops that the Indians had just left, and offered to accompany them in the pursuit, but the captain of the party said his rations were nearly exhausted and he should return to the fort. Mr. Rickman accompanied the troops. On their return to the fort, the party stopped and buried the two Mexicans and ten Chinamen that had been murdered by the Apaches. In due time the company arrived at the fort, and reported their doings.

This is a fair specimen of the way the Indians were dealt with by the government troops at that time, and from reports, I see the same policy is continued. After one of their barbarous massacres, they were pursued for a short distance and then allowed to escape, instead of being followed up, at all hazards, and punished as they deserved.

A short time after the return of the company of pursuers to the fort, a train of wagons was on its way from California to Tueson, *via* Fort Yuma. At Fort Yuma the wagon-master, Mr. Davis, was taken sick, and I was employed in his place, to take the train to Tueson and return. My friends, Jones and Louis, were also engaged to accompany us by Mr. Alexander, the owner of the teams, who had a large contract with the United States government for freighting supplies from the coast to the interior. Our train was composed of twelve wagons with ten mules each. About midway between Fort Yuma and Tueson is a place called Pecacho, near a black mountain, where we camped for the night.

In the morning I went out and told the men who had guarded the mules during the night to come in and get their breakfasts, while I remained to watch the mules. I was sitting down enjoying my cigarette, when I observed a commotion among the mules, and looking further saw two Apaches, who had separated a portion of the mules and were driving them off. Catching up a Spencer rifle, lent me by Davis, I shot one through the back, and the other attempted to escape, but I dropped him with a ball through the hip.

The teamsters came running to see what was the matter. On seeing the wounded Indian they dispatched him; after which we harnessed up and moved forward hastily, knowing that other Apaches were close by. We arrived at Tueson without further trouble, but we had not been there long before some Indians came there and complained that I had killed two of their tribe, who were friendly.

I was immediately ordered under arrest by the officer at the barracks; but Mr. Alexander soon arrived and inquired into the matter, and went to see the commander of the troops. He returned with the commander, when I was asked if I shot the Indians and my reasons for so doing. I confessed that I did, and should do the same thing every time. The colonel said those Indians had obtained a certificate from him, a few days before guaranteeing to them United States protection. I asked the colonel if he gave them any authority in that paper to capture mules and run off with them.

He was quite indignant at my asking him such a question, and inquired if I meant to insult him; I disclaimed any such intention, but said that I had shot them in the act of stealing Mr. Alexander's mules, and if he wanted to keep me under arrest he could do so, but he would do it at his peril, and I should demand a large sum for each day of my detention, enough at least to cover all his back pay, and all he could make for some time to come. He concluded that I had better go and say no more about it. After this, while I stopped at Tueson, this colonel, whose name was Thompson, treated me with marked politeness and courtesy.

In the streets of Tueson, which is quite a town, or city as they call it in Arizona, I happened one day to meet an acquaintance named Michael Burns. He had come from the mountains about six miles distant where he, with a friend of his, named Johnson, had been engaged on a contract burning charcoal. He showed a bullet hole through his hat, and said that he and his companion had been attacked by Apaches, and Johnson had been killed. He had come to Tueson for assistance, but said he should prefer citizens rather than United States troops, for they had lost a lot of cattle, and soldiers did not go far after Indians to recover the property of citizens.

I made up a party of eighteen citizens and teamsters and started off, with Burns for a guide. We found Johnson's body, pinned to the ground by a scythe which he was using in cutting grass at the time he was killed, and he was badly mutilated and scalped. We buried Johnson's body, and then hurried forward in pursuit of the Indians to revenge the death of Johnson and recover the stolen cattle. We overtook them the third day encamped in a hollow, where they were waiting for another party, who had been on a raid in a different direction, to join them, and fell on them suddenly, killed seven and captured one, and the remaining five or six escaped.

We also secured Johnson's scalp. The captured Indian was made fast to a mule, and, with the cattle, we returned to Tueson. Sometimes the Indian, who was bound hand and foot, was under the mule's belly, and sometimes he would fall off and be dragged some distance by the ropes which bound him, which made his seventy mile journey any thing but agreeable. On our way back we met a small party of a dozen Indians on their way to join the party we had routed. They were driving a number of horses and mules they had evidently stolen. When they saw us coming, and discovered we were too strong for them to engage with, they broke for the mountains, leaving their stock, which we gathered up and took with us on our way to Tueson. Before arriving there we met a party of soldiers sent out by the colonel, who feared we were in trouble, as we had been absent nearly a week.

When we arrived at the barracks we hung the Indian captive, and buried Johnson's scalp decently, after showing it to Colonel Thompson. Colonel Thompson, who saw us hang the Indian, asked who was in command of the party. I told him I was, and that I had done this as a favour to Mr. Burns, whose friend was killed and stock taken off by the Apaches. Colonel Thompson asked Burns why he did not call on the troops for assistance instead of citizens. Burns replied that he liked the way Captain Hobbs and his friends followed the Indians, it being so different from paid soldiers, who generally gave out when their rations became short.

The following morning Colonel Thompson sent for me to call at his office. He received me cordially and inquired if I was the Captain Hobbs who had been with the Comanches, and also a companion of Kit Carson, of whom he had heard several speak favourably. I told him I was; when he said that had he known me before he never should have arrested me for killing the Apache thieves. He asked me to excuse him, and offered me employment as a guide and interpreter among the Indians and Mexicans, to aid him when they made incursions outside.

I told him, as I had formerly told another United States officer, that the only contract I would take from the United States with reference to Indians was to bring in Apache scalps at fifty dollars each. He replied that my proposal was unreasonable, for his troops were there for the purpose of maintaining good order, and keeping the Indians friendly. I bade him goodbye, and the next day Mr. Alexander's train was ready, when I had to take charge of it on the return to Fort Yuma, Burns accompanying us. Arriving there, we found Mr. Davis, the former wagon-master, had recovered, and I resigned my position, was paid off, and the train proceeded to California. Besides receiving one hundred dollars per month from Mr. Alexander, I received a present of two hundred dollars from him for killing the two Apache thieves who attempted to run his mules off.

My friends Burns, Jones, and Louis remained with me at Fort Yuma, where we stayed a few days waiting for something new to turn up. After awhile I fell in with a friendly Mexican who told me that many persons were leaving for the new gold diggings at a place called Cow Hills, on the Colorado River. By his favourable representations our party were induced to go there, first being supplied liberally by the quartermaster of the fort with all needful provisions. When we arrived at the gold diggings we found more people than gold. All the paying claims were worked by parties that would not sell out, and there was a small show for us, so we decided to hunt game and sell it to the miners.

Our course was to go back into the country, killing deer, rabbits, and other game, which were plenty in the mountains, and bring it in on our animals. We sold readily all the deer we could kill at twenty-five cents per pound, and rabbits at one dollar each. We followed this several weeks, killing in that time one hundred and ninety-six deer, a very large number of rabbits, and one black bear, which paid us each five hundred and forty dollars,—a larger sum than was realized by most of the miners. At the end of that time the miners began to leave, as the profits were getting decidedly small, and of course our occupation of supplying them with game was gone, and we were again deliberating what course to take, or where to journey.

After due deliberation, our party determined to cross the mountains of the Sierra Nevada range, and go to San Diego, on the Pacific coast, to kill game for the San Francisco market. After a ride of thirteen days we reached the vicinity of San Diego, and commenced killing ducks, geese, and small game, not far from the coast. We procured an old tame ox and took him about in places where ducks and geese were plenty, firing over his back, which he was used to. In that way we could approach very near to the game, as such game were accustomed to the sight of cattle. We sold our game at San Diego for about a month, when Burns and Louis went to San Francisco to act as our consignees for the sale of larger game, such as bear and deer, which we knew were plenty back in the mountains fifteen or twenty miles. If the market was good we intended to hire help and ship game in large quantities.

Jones and I saw them off on the steamer, and then returned to the hotel in San Diego, where to our great surprise we met our old friend Patterson and his wife, from Lower California, whose marriage I have previously mentioned. Of course we had a good time that night. Patterson said his father-in-law had done well by him since we left, and that he had got the whole family now tolerably Americanized. He had come by steamer to San Diego to procure a supply of goods for the family, and wanted us to return with them and stay a while; but we thought best to decline for the present. They stayed several days at San Diego, and we enjoyed their society very much.

In about a week or ten days we received a letter from Burns, saying, common sized deer were worth twenty-live cents per pound in San Francisco, and that there was good sale for bear meat at nearly double that rate. After Patterson and wife left by steamer, we went back with some hired help to the mountains in pursuit of game. By the assistance of our Mexican friends we found good hunting ground for deer and bears. We sent game to the wharf at San Diego by our Mexicans for shipment per steamer. The first trip they carried one small grizzly bear and five deer. Our business was profitable till the weather became too warm for shipment of fresh meat, when we went higher up the mountains and dried our venison and bear meat, writing to Burns that we would soon be in San Francisco.

After a good run of luck we came down to San Diego with our animals loaded with valuable skins, dried meat, &c, which we delivered at the shipping ware-house, and placed our mules and jacks in the care of the owner of St. Isabel's Ranche, near

San Diego, and took the steamer for San Francisco with our bales of hides and dried meat.

On our arrival there we met our friends Burns and Louis, who were on the lookout for us. Our bear hides, deer skins, and dried meat sold for eighteen hundred dollars, which was better than some of our mining experiences. While we stopped in San Francisco, we learned that there was to be a dog-fight for two thousand dollars a side, at the Mission Dolores, about three miles from the city. We concluded to attend; but it was the first, and I trust the last dog-fight that I shall witness of that sort.

The fight was between two English bulldogs, one owned by an Englishman and the other by an American. A short time after the fight commenced, the Englishman claimed that the Yankee's dog had a foul hold. The American denied it, when the Englishman stepped into the ring to separate the dogs, but received a blow from the Yankee that sent him sprawling on the ground. The Englishman jumped up and shot the American dead; his friends then returned the Englishman's shot, killing him also; and during the fight four men and one dog were killed, which ended the performance, and was all I wished to see of such sport.

While I was in San Francisco I heard of a huge grizzly bear that was on exhibition there some years previous, which weighed eleven hundred pounds. It was brought from St. Joseph district, and was about to be shipped eastward. For the particulars of its novel capture I am indebted to some worthy gentlemen who saw the animal while on exhibition in San Francisco. P. T. Barnum, of Barnum's Museum, offered to pay eight hundred dollars, for a grizzly bear, caught alive, that should weigh one thousand pounds, or more.

A Yankee, named Cobb, who was in California at the time this proposition was made, began to look about him to see if he could not secure the prize. He chanced to hear that for a long time a bear had been making raids on the ranches of Peter Quivey and a Mr. Wilson, near St. Joseph, and carrying off a great deal of their young stock. From the size of the animals carried off, and the trail made by the bear, it was evident that he was of unusual size. Cobb at once went to see Quivey, who showed him the trail by winch the bear came on to his premises. Cobb sunk a pan into the ground, near this trail, and taking advantage of the known fondness of bears for sweets, poured into it about two quarts of molasses.

On the morning following the baiting, they found the pan licked clean. Cobb, thinking he now saw his way clear to capture the brute and secure the prize, set men at work in St. Joseph to make a strong cage to hold the bear when caught, in the meantime continuing the rations of molasses. When everything was in readiness for his reception, the regular rations of the bear were varied one night, by adding to the molasses two or three bottles of brandy. On going to the pan in the morning, Cobb and his friends found it cleaned out as usual, and at a short distance from it they found the bear lying perfectly stupefied.

It was now an easy matter to secure the brute. Mr. Cobb commenced by placing over his jaws an iron muzzle, for safety, in case he should recover too soon, and then tied his feet securely. A two-horse wagon was driven from Mr. Quivey's, and bruin loaded into it—this loading requiring eight men—when he was driven to Mr. Quivey's, where the cage was waiting to receive the prisoner. When he was fairly in the cage his muzzle was removed and his feet untied; but one of his fore and one of his hind legs were chained to the cage, in such a manner that on his becoming docile they could be easily released. Water was then thrown on him to bring him out of his stupor.

When he was restored to consciousness his efforts to liberate himself were frightful. He even bent, in his frenzy, some of the iron bars to his cage, which were an inch and a half in diameter. It was about a week after his capture before the bear would take any food; but after that time he appeared to resign himself to his fate and make the best of the situation. Wells, Fargo & Co., as the agents of Mr. Barnum in the matter, paid Cobb his eight hundred dollars, and employed him to accompany the bear to New York, by the way of Panama. The bear was kept in the museum until it was destroyed by fire. Mr. Barnum has often said to his friends, that the bear and sections of the big trees, both California curiosities, formed one of the greatest attractions he ever had in the museum.

The preceding story I have inserted in these pages, considering that I received it from reliable authority, and that it would interest my readers, as it did me, for I have often captured grizzly bears in my experience, but never with molasses and spirits, for I preferred a good rifle.

CHAPTER 29

Deserted by Our Guide

It was in the summer of 1869, when our party, having stayed in San Francisco several weeks, and, being tired of the monotony of hotel life, returned by steamer to San Diego, where we found our mules fattened up and in good condition for travelling. I asked Burns and Louis if we should return to the mountains for game, which idea pleased them; but at Jones's suggestion we concluded to go back to the San Bernadino Mountains, about one hundred and fifty miles to the north of San Diego, on a trip of exploration.

We travelled slowly, killing game on the way, and after a week's travel, camped at the foot of the mountain near a spring where feed for the animals was plenty. There was no lack of game, but the signs of gold were slim enough, the gulches and ledges barely showing the colour occasionally.

Burns started out about 3 o'clock the day after our arrival, to get a shot at a bear, if possible. I urged him to wait till next morning, when I would accompany him, for it was late to go alone, and he was rather inexperienced in bear hunting; still he insisted on going by himself. After supper, as Mr. Burns did not return, we became very uneasy about him. I lit pine torches, elevating them on a pole, and fired my rifle several times to guide him in returning; but we not no answer. It was not prudent to search for him that night, it being quite dark, and we should not be able to follow his trail; but early in the morning Jones and myself started to find him.

We followed his track two miles or more, then fired blank cartridges, when we could just hear him answer us. We found him in a small tree, with a grizzly bear and two cubs lying at its foot; but the bear was badly wounded so that she could not rise. Still Burns was afraid to come down, for his gun was laying near the bear's head, and he had stayed up in the tree all night, and he suffered so with the cramps that he could hardly move. We shot the old bear, and so relieved Burns from his disagreeable position.

We skinned the animal and left the carcass, which was too poor to eat; but we picked up the cubs and carried them to camp. Mr. Burns said that in future he should take my advice, and not start out hunting so late in the afternoon. He had a good appetite for his breakfast, after which he had a long sleep, while Jones and I went out prospecting.

We found a wild turkey roost, which we told our comrade of when we returned, and it was arranged to have a grand turkey shoot when the moon should be at its full, which would be in a few nights. We moved our camp to within a mile of the turkey roost, got wood and leaves together under the trees where they alighted, and everything in readiness to kindle the fires. Then when the moon shone out full, one night, and the turkeys could be seen in the tree tops, we kindled our fire to get a clearer view of them, and succeeded in killing fourteen nice ones.

The light of the fire blinds and confuses the turkeys, thus making them an easy prey. Having no success in finding gold, we decided to leave that section, as we had a fine stock of choice provisions now for a tramp. The next day, in travelling around to the north of the mountain, we discovered some horses and cows feeding in an enclosed lot, which indicated that some *ranche* must be nearby. A little further on we came to a Mexican *ranche* near a stream. The people there were frightened and ran from us as we approached, but were soon quieted when we addressed them kindly in Spanish.

We told the woman that we were friends who merely desired to rest there awhile, and inquired for her husband. She replied that he was away in the fields looking after his stock. She told us we could put our things on the porch of the house and rest ourselves, while she sent a child for her husband to return.

Our pet bear cubs pleased the daughter of this lady, who gave them some milk, which made them act quite lively and playful. As they were some trouble to us, and starving for want of suitable nourishment, we gave them to the young lady, who promised to bring them up with the best of care. About dinner time the husband and his brother returned, meeting us with a cordial welcome. We presented him two of our wild turkeys, which placed us on a very friendly footing.

In the course of our conversation he remarked that it was a long distance to the nearest settlement, and when I inquired why he located so far from any neighbours, he said it was on account of his hatred towards lawyers and new settlers. In explanation of this reason he said that he owned a nice farm and home for his family in Los Angeles county. Unfortunately for him a portion of his land showed signs of being rich in gold. A party of Americans came along and squatted on some of his mineral lands, and he gave them notice that it belonged to him; but they cared nothing for his legal rights, and persisted in remaining on his grounds.

He finally went to law about it, and the first lawyer charged him an enormous sum for advice and procuring a writ of ejectment, which he paid down; but after much delay, he lost his case in the first trial, which result he was confident was obtained by bribery by the Yankees. Costs for appeals, continuances, and legal services became a regular bore, and he packed up his effects, leaving the property and his lawyers in disgust, with the determination to get isolated so far from society that no man would covet his property or undertake to dispossess him. We told him to have no fears of our laying any claim to his lands, for our party couldn't content themselves long enough in one place to even plow the ground for a crop.

We remained there several days examining the surrounding country, finding plenty of game in the way of antelope, deer, bears, wild turkeys, &c. Our host told us that he had lost many young calves and much other stock by bears, but he was not able to prevent these depredations, or catch the animals. He asked me if we could contrive any way to rid him of these pests; adding that he once lassoed a bear, but he broke the lasso and came near killing him and his horse, when he fled for his life and had not attempted to catch any since.

I told him if he would give me some pieces of timber I would make a trap, baiting it with fresh meat, and set a spring gun which would be apt to kill any thing that came that way. I put the trap on the bear's accustomed trail, loading the gun with several balls, and the next morning one of the brutes was found dead in the trap. The gentleman offered me a beef for the favour I had done him, but I declined it, telling him he had my sympathy for his previous bad luck.

Before leaving our friendly host we asked him the distance to Fort Mohave, where we intended going.

We knew the direction of the fort, and intended to travel by the compass. He was not posted in the geography of the country, but said there was a wagon road about twenty miles to the northward which led from the coast eastward through the interior of Arizona to Salt Lake, over the sandy plains. We left for Fort Mohave by going to the north till we struck the road spoken of by our friend, and following it as far as it took us in the right direction, reaching the place with-out encountering the Indians.

On our way to the fort, we met a vigilance party returning to Los Angeles, having been out in pursuit of a horse thief, whom they had overtaken and hung. They had also hung a man travelling in his company, on the supposition that he was an accomplice, but it afterwards appeared that he was an innocent man, a merchant at Salt Lake, and had been to Los Angeles to purchase goods. On his way home he had fallen in with this thief, and not knowing his character, had kept along with him for the sake of his company.

This case was rendered still more lamentable from the fact

that the murdered man left a wife and four children. I have been in pursuit of a good many criminals, under direction of vigilance committees, but never would consent to the harming of any man till his guilt was proved, beyond the shadow of a doubt; and had this party pursued the same course with the stranger, and held him a prisoner till they could have learned something in regard to him, an honest man would not have been sacrificed, and the vigilance committee would not have felt remorse, caused by their hasty action.

On our arrival at Fort Mohave, the commander asked where we came from, and we briefly recounted our travels, not forgetting to tell him of the Mexican *ranche* where we stayed a week with the man who desired to get out of the reach of society.

From Fort Mohave we left for the White Pine silver regions, taking along a friendly Indian guide, who pretended to know the whole route; but we relied partly upon the compass. Fort Mohave lies east of the San Bernardino mountain, on the Colorado River, and we were travelling northward, through a portion of Nevada. On our journey we picked up many stones of various colours, some resembling the California diamond, and others looking like a ruby.

By the aid of our guide, we usually found water and feed for our animals where we camped at night, and though we saw small parties of Indians, at a distance, several times, we were not disturbed. When about half way on our journey, our guide left us, and made his way to a party of friendly Indians in the vicinity, obliging us afterwards to travel by compass.

The night our guide left us, as we were sitting around our fire, we were surprised by the appearance in our camp of a young girl about twenty years of age, and nearly destitute of clothing. She commenced talking in an Indian language that was unknown to me. On looking closely at her, I thought I could discover, through the paint on her face, the features of a Mexican, and spoke to her in Spanish, when she replied in the same language, and gave us an account of how she came to be there. She said that a number of years before, her father's house had been attacked by Indians, and the whole family, with the exception of herself, had been murdered.

Her life had been spared at the request of the chief's son, and since that time she had been compelled to live with him as his wife. The tribe, which numbered in all about two hundred and fifty, were encamped a few miles from us. They had seen us at times for three or four days, and when they saw our camp fire so near to them, had sent her to find out about us, thinking we might be Mexicans and she could, by listening to our conversation, ascertain our plans.

She had appeared so well contented with them, thus throwing them entirely off their guard, while she watched for an opportunity to escape, that they had no fears of her attempting to leave them. When she found that we were Mexicans or Americans, she decided to make herself known and consult with us as to the best method of attempting her escape. She did not wish us to attempt her rescue, as she feared our party was so small we should get ourselves into trouble.

I told her I had had considerable experience among Indians, and had never left a captive among them from any fear of consequences, if I attempted to release them. On inquiring what weapons the tribe used, she said they had no firearms, their weapons being only bows and arrows, spears and clubs; when I told her I thought we could protect her without danger; at all events, we were willing to make the attempt. In this decision Bums and Louis both agreed with me. As her clothing had become badly worn, Burns presented her with a pair of pants and a flannel shirt, and as he was a small man, his clothing fitted her very well.

In the morning we got away from our camping place as early as possible, and pushed forward at as great speed as we could, for we felt very certain that the Indians would soon be in search of their scout. In this we judged correctly, for we soon saw them lurking on our trail, but taking good care not to get within reach of our rifles. We were well supplied with ammunition, and had no fears of being attacked, except in the night, and we took every precaution to guard against that.

After being followed in this way for two days, I became impatient at being obliged to keep such a close watch on the movements of the Indians, and determined, if they came near enough to give me a chance, I would fire on them, which would either bring them down upon us or relieve us of the annoyance of their company. Shortly after I came to this decision, I saw one of the party in advance of the others, and near enough to be in range of my rifle.

I asked the girl who it was, and she replied that it was the son of the chief, with whom she had been compelled to live. I then inquired if she had any objections to my killing him, and she replied that she had not, when I fired and, owing to the great distance, killed the pony, instead of the rider; at which the whole party retreated over the plain, and we saw no more of them. We then thought best to make as much haste as possible, as we did not know what effect the shot might have on our pursuers, until we arrived at Hamilton, a small settlement in the White Pine region, finding wood and water convenient for camping places, and killing game on the way.

At this mining place we found kind friends, and one old lady who took a deep interest in the Mexican girl, and furnished her with suitable clothing. After washing the paint from her face, and dressing her after the manner of civilized people, she made quite a genteel appearance. Here we rented a miner's cabin, and went to prospecting for a mine, the girl offering to do our housework, though she made it her home with the old lady. I showed the coloured stones to a New York man who was there, who purchased them of me at good prices, and inquired of me where I found them and whether they were plenty.

On my telling him they were, he wished us to return with him, but we told him the desert over which we passed was not very inviting to a man used to luxuries, and we could not think of returning. We remained here two weeks, but finding no rich prospecting, we decided, as provisions were high, and forage for our beasts very scarce, that our best course was to leave. The old lady who furnished the clothing, asked the Mexican girl to remain there with her; but she refused for several reasons, but the main one she kept secret, which was a fondness for our friend Burns, as near as I could judge.

We headed for Mono Lake in company with a party who were going there with two hay wagons to get forage. Arriving at Mono Lake, we saw in the hills opposite several excavations or large rooms dug out of the hillsides, one of which we camped in, as it was about fifteen by twenty-five feet, the walls being mainly of solid rock.

Mono Lake is about four miles long and three miles wide, and is fed by hot and cold springs. There is a small settlement of forty or fifty inhabitants who live by farming and by the sale of hay, which is abundant in the vicinity. I was informed by a gentleman living there by the name of Scott, that a daughter of Kit Carson was buried nearby. At my request he pointed out her grave to me, when I employed a man to build a fence around it, as a mark of respect to, and in memory of her father, with whom I had been pleasantly acquainted.

I remembered seeing this girl often, when she was about eight years old. She was a daughter by Kit's first wife, who was called the Pine Leaf and was of the Blackfoot tribe. This girl was called the Prairie Flower, and was born at Bent's Fort on the Arkansas river. Her mother died when she was ten years of age. The girl then lived in Colonel Bent's family till she was sixteen years old, when she married a man by the name of George Stilts of St. Louis, Mo., and went to California with him in 1849. Stilts was a reckless man, and turned out to be a regular desperado. After travelling about in California with her husband a while, she left him, and went to Mono Lake with a gentleman and his family, and died there. She was a noble looking woman, of mixed complexion, black eyes and long black hair, and could excel most men in the use of the rifle.

After seeing her grave properly fenced, and recruiting our animals, we started for Silver Peak, which is a high mountain covered at the top with perpetual snow. Here we saw valuable silver mines, worked scientifically by a large company from New York. The quartz rock is transported from the mountain to the crushing mills in the valley below, several miles distant. We saw one twenty stamp mill there which crushed over forty tons of the rock per day, and they said it yielded sometimes fifty dollars per ton!

We left here for Virginia City, Nevada, and the first day out overtook a Dutchman on foot, carrying on his back a shovel, pick, and large gold pan, two blankets, and some provisions. We asked where he was from, and he answered from "Dat miserable Vite Pine shettlement." As we had an extra pack mule, we offered him the use of it to pack his things on; but for some reason he refused it, saying he ought to suffer some hardship for being such a fool as to come out there. He came up with us at night where we were encamped, and stopped with us. His feet were blistered, and he looked so worn out that we gave him some coffee, which revived him. In the morning we persuaded him to use my jack and ride on top of his things.

After carrying this load some three or four miles, the donkey, which had no bridle on, in going into a stream of water to drink, elevated his hind feet and sent the Dutchman over his head into the water. Striking on his back, with a part of his traps falling on his head, he would have made a laughable sketch for an artist. Crawling out of the water and picking up his goods, he began raving and cursing the donkey in all the languages he knew. He began stripping off his clothing to dry in the sun, and begged me to unload the rest of his luggage and trumpery off that donkey, swearing that it was the last animal of that kind he would ever get on to. We took off his things, bade him goodbye, and left him to his own devices, and arrived at Big Pine on Bishop's creek that evening.

From Bishop's creek we went to Aurora, where we stopped a day, and then proceeded to Virginia City, where we prospected for a few days, leaving the Mexican girl at a boarding place, where she could get rested from the fatigue of her travels. We found one claim which we recorded and sold for seven hundred dollars.

One evening, our Mexican girl, (I say our, for we all felt a deep interest in her,) remarked in presence of our party, who were at supper, that she wished to speak with me aside, to ask my advice. She said in the interview that Burns had proposed to marry her, and, as she had no relatives to go to, and regarded me as a friend and father to her, she wished to ask me if Mr. Burns would not prove a suitable husband, and inquired how long I had known him, &c. I recommended him as a good-natured, truthful man, and advised her, if she liked him well enough, to marry forthwith. Then calling in Mr. Burns, I asked him, before her, whether it was his intention to marry her; and he replied that it was.

I announced then to Jones and Louis that important business was on the docket, for Burns and the girl were to be married on the coming Thursday, (this was on Monday,) and asked them if they would consent to spend the seven hundred dollars for which we sold out our claim, on the bride and bridegroom, so as to have a wedding that would become the dignity of our party, and leave some spending money for the happy couple.

They willingly consented, leaving it to me to plan the whole thing and see that nothing was lacking. I agreed to get the outside garments for the bride, and gave her money to purchase what she needed to complete the outfit. I happened to find a good silk dress at a ladies' furnishing store, all made in style, which, with some slight alterations, fitted charmingly. When she came bustling from her room into the parlour of our hotel to show Burns and me the fit of her new dress, the day before the marriage, she appeared so happy that I felt rewarded for all my pains on her account. She showed by her pleased actions, however, that it was the first silk dress she was ever the owner of.

The marriage ceremony was performed in the hotel parlour by Judge Hanner, an old friend of mine, who resided in the place. We had as good a private dinner as Virginia city could furnish, and after dinner a dance, which the guests of the house kept up till 3 o'clock next morning.

We remained at the Virginia City Hotel several days after the wedding, and then proceeded to Grass Valley, in company with the newly married couple, where we found great numbers of Chinese, and a splendid mining camp. A company were building flumes for bringing water for mining purposes from one mountain to another, a distance of thirty miles or more. The cost of the water works was over a million dollars to the company. The parties who constructed the water works made more money than the miners, for they sold them the water at the rate of three dollars per day for what would run through an inch pipe. We remained at Grass Valley three weeks, purchasing of some of the miners their gold dust at fourteen dollars per ounce, and selling it to the express company at from seventeen to eighteen dollars.

We left here for the San Joaquin River, where we found line lands for agricultural purposes, grazing lands, &c. After remaining several days in the vicinity, finding many kind people scattered through that section, who were all doing well at farming, Mr Burns concluded to settle down upon one hundred and sixty acres of land as a squatter. We stayed with him till we had helped to build him a log cabin with the assistance of some neighbours, and then bade him and his wife farewell. He still resides on the same place, living happily with his wife, and has accumulated considerable property.

Chapter 29

A Visit to the Comanches

While we were at San Joaquin settlement, a party of Mexicans and Chileans came along, and, noticing that they were all remarkably well mounted, I inquired where they were going. They said to the head waters of the San Joaquin river, at Tulare Lake, to catch mustang horses and other stock which they had heard were running wild there. They invited us to accompany them, and Jones and I accepted the invitation; but Louis left us and went to San Francisco.

We went to Tulare Lake and found the report about the horses there to be no exaggeration. We spent some time in constructing a huge pen, three hundred feet square, built of posts set in the ground close to each other, and which were nine feet high after setting. From the entrance of the pen wings were constructed each way for half a mile, the fence forming them being high enough to turn the animals into the pen.

The horses would go back from the lake a dozen miles or so for good grazing ground, and return galloping to the lake occasionally for water, sometimes in straggling order, and sometimes in a compact body. Our men were so stationed, at long intervals, on each side of the trail, as to close in behind the animals and thus keep them going in the direction of the pen, if they showed any disposition to go back on coming in sight of it.

Our plans succeeded beyond our expectations, as the animals rushed into the inclosure at full speed, filling it up with a variety of ponies, mules and horses, when the entrance was closed up and they were secured. The next business was to lasso the animals, and break them to lead, which we could do at our leisure. One gray stallion in the herd attracted my attention, and I lassoed him, and after some difficulty got him outside the pen and tied him firmly to a tree, where I left him till morning that he might expend his strength in trying to get loose.

In the morning I found he had dug a hole in the ground by pawing with his fore feet, large enough to bury himself in; and he appeared rather worn out by his exertions. The whole party were now busy lassoing and breaking the animals, some by one process and some by another. A Chilean, who had a great deal to say about his experience in horse taming, offered to ride my stallion for me to break him; but I had no faith in his boasting and feared he would get hurt if he attempted it, and declined his offer, preferring to ride him myself.

After some handling I mounted him, when he threw himself with me on him four times, but I was always on his back when he rose. I had him soon conquered so that he was quite docile under the saddle; but the Chilean soon after got badly thrown by an obstinate mule, and after that said but little of his experience in horse-taming.

After a week or more, we got the animals so that we could lead them by the side of our gentle ones, and returned with them as far as St. Joseph, where the stock was fairly divided and the party separated. In the division there fell to Jones and me about twenty head, which we took to our friend Burns's place, where we remained till we got them broken—some to the saddle, and some of the heaviest to harness, for work.

After several weeks' patient labour, I got the gray stallion, spoken of before, and which fell to me in the distribution, so well broken, that I sold him for four hundred dollars. He proved a very valuable animal, and afterwards won two races on the Mission Dolores course near San Francisco. The remainder of our stock Mr. Burns agreed to take good care of on his farm, and we were to give him one-half the increase for his trouble.

While we were staying with our friend Burns at the San

Joaquin settlement, a messenger came into the place from Soda Lake, with a statement that an emigrant party from Texas, were there in a pitiable condition, as they were very short of provisions, and had had their horses run off by Indians. Previous to losing their horses they had got off the direct route, and had wandered about so long that the provisions taken for their journey had given out.

A contribution of animals and provisions for the relief of the emigrants was soon made up, and a relief party of ten persons volunteered to accompany the messenger. The citizens who had contributed the articles requested me to take the lead of the party and push on with all haste to the sufferers. We travelled as rapidly as possible, and when we arrived within about ten miles of the place where the emigrant wagons were, we met a number of the party, who had become impatient at the delay in the return of their messenger, and had wandered away from the others, in their efforts to find some settlement. We gave them food, and they returned with us to their friends.

On our arrival at the wagons, the scene was affecting. The whole party were suffering for food, and crowded anxiously about us. Their joy and gratitude at finding that we were well supplied with provisions for them, was more than sufficient to repay us for any trouble we had been at in reaching them. After giving our horses time to eat and rest a little, we harnessed them to the wagons and started for San Joaquin settlement. The emigrants, who numbered in all about seventy-five had not decided on any definite place to settle, but naturally wished to see the people who had so quickly responded to their cry for help.

On our return journey we procured a quantity of provisions at a government station, called Taycon, where the commander, Colonel Allen, treated the party kindly, furnishing all they needed. We got the train through in safety to San Joaquin settlement, where the entire party were so pleased with the country that they decided to take up land in the vicinity, either by purchase or otherwise.

Mr. Burns took great interest in these people, assisting them materially in the selection of lands, and picking out pleasant locations; for he desired them as neighbours, and in due time they all settled near him. The country around abounded in game, the waters of the river with fish, so that all these people had to buy was flour, clothing, and groceries. They are still residing in that vicinity, and have nice farms and are doing well.

Jones and I remained at the settlement about a month longer, when we made a contract with an agent of a New York company to go to the Sierra Nevada mountains prospecting for metals. The emigrants tried to dissuade us from the undertaking, urging us to settle down beside them; but finding us determined to leave, they offered to raise a purse for our benefit as some compensation for our services in their behalf.

We declined their proposed gift, telling them they would find a use for all their spare funds, and that they were welcome for what we had done for them, as it was nothing more than we should do for other parties in like circumstances, without expecting any reward. Among the emigrants was a widow, who offered to make a present of herself to me for life; but I declined that offer also, telling her I had a wife already among the Indians, which seemed to take her by surprise. We left all our animals with Burns, except two riding horses and two pack mules.

The agent who employed us offered to pay us a certain salary, besides all our expenses, and give us in addition a one third interest in what mines we might discover. He was to pay also the entire expense of working any mine that we found, which proved valuable. When we arrived at the mountains we commenced prospecting as soon as we had pitched our camp.

The next day I discovered a silver ledge, which I deemed valuable, and, according to custom and regulation, I posted up a notice to cover the claim in behalf of the New York company. We remained in this vicinity three months, and during that time discovered and marked fourteen ledges of different metals, *viz*.: gold, silver, and lead, one of which had a trace of quicksilver.

On our return to Visalia, the nearest county seat to the mountains, we had these ledges recorded in the name of the New York company, reserving for ourselves a one-third interest. Then we returned to our friend Burns and the settlement of our new friends, the emigrants, on the San Joaquin.

The agency of the New York company was in San Francisco, and as Jones was pretty well used up he desired me to go and report there what we had done.

I went by boat to San Francisco, showed my specimens at the company's office, where they were assayed, and pronounced equal to the average California mines. They informed me that their company had purchased a large interest in the Washoe mines, which had proved worthless, and in consequence their company had become insolvent; but that in a short time a new company would be formed out of the ruins of the old one, with plenty of capital, when they would examine the ledges we had discovered.

I told them that did not suit me at all, and I wanted the privilege of selling out to other parties, if they could not pay me, and also to go on with mining according to agreement. They finally said if I would wait a month, if at the end of that time they were not in shape to comply with my terms, they would release me from the contract and allow me to sell out to any other parties. I agreed to this, and went back to my friend Burns, where I waited a month, and then received from the agents of the company a communication releasing me from the contract, and making over to Jones and myself all their interest in the mines.

After consultation with Jones about the matter, I found that he was quite indifferent about working the mines with me, on our own account, for he said he had been prospecting nearer home, and had found a Texan widow who was quite willing to marry him, and he said he thought he had better settle down on a farm with her and go to raising mules and horses. This was the same widow that had offered herself to me as a partner on a former occasion. The result was that they were soon married and settled on a farm near our friend Burns. This was the third partner I had lost by matrimony.

Feeling desolate and forsaken, I concluded to take up one

hundred and sixty acres of land near my friends, which I covered by land warrants, received for services under Colonel Doniphan, and which I still hold, considering it my home. On the land I erected a comfortable house, and put some stock on the place, hiring a family to occupy the house and take charge of the farm.

I then resolved to make another visit to my Comanche friends, and, bidding my old comrades adieu, started with one horse and a pack mule across the White Mountains through the Apache country, heading for Alberquerque in New Mexico, thence easterly to Little Red river between New Mexico and Texas, where, from my knowledge of Comanche habits, I might hope to find some of them at this season of the year. I soon struck a trail of a Comanche war-party returning from a raid into Mexico, and, finding it fresh, followed it up until I arrived at the camping ground of the nation, where I was warmly received by my old friends and relations, and found that no great change had taken place since my last visit. I stayed for some weeks with them enjoying the hunting and feasting, and will here describe some feats of horsemanship which I have omitted in the previous chapters.

There is one warlike feat in which all the Comanche warriors are trained from their infancy. As the man is dashing along with his horse at full speed, he will suddenly drop over the side of his horse, leaving no part of his person visible, except the sole of one foot, which is fastened over the horse's back, as a purchase by which he can pull himself to an upright position. In this attitude he can ride for any distance, and, moreover, can use with deadly effect either his bow or fourteen-foot lance.

One of their favourite modes of attack is to gallop towards the enemy at full speed, and then, just before they come within range, they drop upon the opposite side of their horses, dash past the foe, and pour upon him a shower of arrows directed under their horses' necks, and sometimes even thrown under their bellies. All the time it is nearly useless for the enemy to return the shots, as the whole body of the Comanche is hidden behind the horse, and there is nothing to aim at save the foot just projecting over the animal's back.

Sometimes the Comanches try to steal upon their enemies by leaving their lances behind them, slinging themselves along the sides of their steeds, and approaching carelessly, as though they were nothing but a troop of wild horses without riders. A quick eye is needed to detect this ruse, which is generally betrayed by the fact that the horses always keep the same side towards the spectator, which would very seldom be the case were they wild and unrestrained in their movements.

Every Comanche has one favourite horse, which he never mounts, except for war or the chase, using an inferior animal upon ordinary occasions. Swiftness is the chief quality for which the charger is selected, and for no price would the owner part with his favourite steed. Like all uncivilized people, he treats his horse with a strange mixture of cruelty and kindness. While engaged in the chase, for example, he spurs and whips the animal most ruthlessly; but as soon as he returns, he carefully hands over his valued animal to his women, who are waiting to receive it, and who treats it as if it were a cherished member of the family.

The mode in which the Indians supply themselves with horses is worth a brief description. In various parts of the country the horses have completely acclimatized themselves, and have run free for many years, so that they have lost all traces of domestication, and have become as truly wild as the buffalo or antelope, assembling in large herds, headed by the strongest and swiftest animals.

It is from these herds that the Indians supply themselves with the horses which of late years have become absolutely necessary to them; and in most cases are captured in fair chase after the following manner. When a Comanche wishes to catch a fresh horse, he mounts his best steed and goes in search of the nearest herd. When he has come as near as he can without being discovered, he dashes at the herd at full speed, and, singling out one of the horses, as it gallops along, hampered by the multi-

COMANACHES CATCHING WILD HORSES

tude of its companions, throws his lasso over its neck. As soon as the noose has firmly settled, the hunter leaps off his own steed (which is trained to remain standing upon the same spot until it is wanted,) and allows himself to be dragged on by the affrighted animal, which soon falls, in consequence of being choked by the leathern cord.

When the horse has fallen the hunter comes cautiously up, keeping the lasso tight enough to prevent the animal from fairly recovering its breath, and loose enough to guard against its entire strangulation, and at last is able to place one hand over its eyes, and the other on its nostrils. The horse is now at his mercy. In order to impress upon the animal the fact of its servitude, he hobbles together its forefeet for a time, and fastens a noose to its lower jaw; but within a wonderfully short period he is able to remove the hobbles, and to ride the conquered animal into camp. During the time occupied in taming the horse, it plunges and struggles in the wildest manner; but after this one struggle it yields the point, and becomes the willing slave of its conqueror.

The rapidity with which this operation is completed is really wonderful. An experienced hunter is able to chase, capture, and break a wild horse within an hour, and to do his work so effectually that almost before its companions are out of sight the hitherto wild animal is being ridden as if it had been born in servitude. The native hunter, cruel master though he generally is, takes special care not to dampen the spirit of his horse, and prides himself on the bounds and curvets which the creature makes when it receives its master upon its back.

There is only one drawback to this mode of hunting. It is impossible to capture with the lasso the best and swiftest specimens. These animals always take command of the herd, and place themselves at its head. They seem to assume the responsibility as well as the position of leaders, and, as soon as they fear danger, dart off at full speed, knowing that the herd will follow them. Consequently they are often half a mile or more in advance of their followers, so that the hunter has no chance of overtaking them on a horse impeded by the weight of a rider.

A new method of horse-taking has been invented since the introduction of firearms. This is called "creasing," and is done in the following manner. Taking his rifle with him, the hunter creeps as near the herd as he can, and watches till he fixes on a horse that he thinks will suit him. Waiting till the animal is standing with its side towards him, he aims carefully at the top of the neck and fires. If the aim be correct, the bullet just grazes the neck, and the horse falls as if dead, stunned for the moment by the shock. It recovers within a very short time; but before it has regained its feet, the hunter is able to come up with the prostrate animal, hobble, and secure it.

This is a very effectual method of horse-catching, but it is not in favour with those who want horses for their own riding, because it always breaks the spirit of the animal, and deprives him of that fire and animation which the native warrior prizes so highly. The horses that are generally brought into settlements to sell are those that are obtained by "creasing." Experienced purchasers, however, do not care much about such animals. Creasing is, moreover, liable to two disadvantages. The hunter is equally in danger of missing his mark altogether, in which case the whole herd dashes off, and gives no more chances to the hunter; or of striking too low, in which case the horse is killed on the spot. I once killed a splendid stallion in this manner, the ball going an inch below the right spot.

After a few weeks of these diversions with the tribe, my old restlessness returned, impelling me once more to set out for California. I therefore bade my friends *adieu*, and taking advantage of the departure of a war party whose route would take me some way on the road I wished to travel, I started with them and accompanied them to a place near Paso del Norte, where I parted from them to pursue my lonely path through Arizona, by way of Mesilla and Prescott, passing through the Apache country without having my hair "lifted" by those enterprising and peaceful savages. This might be owing to their forbearance, but possibly, my own vigilance contributed somewhat to that result.

I reached San Bernadino, a Mormon settlement in Los Angeles county, California, thence took a north direction by what is called the coast range to Fort Tejon. Upon arriving at what is called Tejon mountain, I laid by for a few days to recruit my animals, who were pretty well worn out. While there I lived among several Mexican shepherds who kept large flocks of sheep and goats, and learning that they were troubled by the nightly visits of a grizzly bear who loved mutton, "not wisely, but too well," I offered to rid them of him.

We built a scaffold near the scene of his depredations, and, placing a sheep convenient for him, I took up my position on the platform at nightfall and waited for him. In an hour or two he made his appearance, and commenced his supper, but a shot from my rifle disturbed his repast and disquieted him very much. A second shot restored his tranquillity, by taking away his breath, and the shepherds were enabled in a measure to get square with him upon the mutton account, by making a feast of him. After remaining with these hospitable people eight days, I returned to my home in Tulare county.

Chapter 31

Decide to Settle Down

A short time after my return from my visit to the Comanches, I was sent for by the commander at Fort Tejon to act as guide for a surveying party to be, sent by order of the United States government to explore the route across the desert from the Sierra Nevadas to Fort Mohave, Arizona. I had thus officiated once before and did not relish the job, though I finally accepted it. I told Colonel Allen of the fort and the chief engineer that the country was not worth exploring, and that there would be great danger of suffering on the route from scarcity of water and forage. The surveys had to be made, they said, any way, and with a party of twenty-four we succeeded in reaching Fort Mohave after enduring some hardships and abandoning one of our wagons, which was afterwards recovered.

While at the fort I met some of the tribe of Indians who had formerly held in captivity the Mexican girl who was married to Burns, and they recognized me as the man who had taken her away from them. These Indians had become friendly, and had settled on a reservation near the fort. They inquired after the girl, and I gave them the particulars of her marriage to my friend Burns.

They could not be reconciled, however, to my taking away the girl so summarily, especially complaining of that shot of mine which killed the leader's horse, and said they considered me a bad man. On the return the surveying party took a southerly route, heading for San Diego, through the coast mountain range, which route was comparatively pleasant, abounding in game, plenty of water, &c. We went to San Francisco, where I was paid off, and remained a while at the Eldorado hotel.

While in the city I met, one evening, Doctor Perfonton, who was years before connected with a noted gang of robbers, but who now was residing in the city and editing a paper, mainly devoted to scandal. Our interview was not pleasant for the following reasons. Many years before, when his band of thieves were at the height of their power, robbing and murdering indiscriminately, I had the pleasure of assisting in the extermination of the band.

A rich Mexican merchant, named Charvis, was on his way from New Mexico to St. Louis with a train of wagons and a large amount of money, for the purpose of purchasing goods. The train was met by this gang of Perfonton's on the plains, at a place known as cow creek, and, excepting Mr. Charvis and one of his teamsters, the whole party were brutally murdered. Mr. Charvis was spared a short time to make him disclose where the money was concealed, and after the money was found he was murdered also.

The teamster, who escaped, made his way to Fort Leavenworth, where he reported the massacre and obtained a party of soldiers to go in pursuit. I happened to be out hunting on the head waters of the Pawnee Fork, with a party from Bent's Fort, when the soldiers from the fort came along and told us of the destruction of the train; and when they found that we knew the country, requested us to go with them and assist in finding the murderers.

After four days' search, aided by the teamster for a guide, we met this band of robbers, who little dreamed of an attack by government troops. They attempted to escape, but I shot Perfonton's horse from under him, and a soldier shot one of the band named Asbury, when the party surrendered. The money was mostly recovered, over one hundred thousand dollars, and the robbers taken to St. Louis, tried and hung, with the exception of Doctor Perfonton, who escaped the gallows by turning state's evidence, and was sent to the penitentiary, from which, after staying two years, he was pardoned.

The money retaken from the robbers was given in charge to Colonel Owens, a friend of the Charvis family, who was a leading man of the Santa Fe trade. Colonel Owens went forward with the teams to St. Louis, purchased the goods, and sent back the train and property to Santa Fe, under the management of Doctor Conley of Booneville, Missouri. Charvis's widow employed the doctor to sell out the goods and take charge of her property; after a year or two they were married, and settled on one of the largest stock farms in New Mexico. Mr. Charvis was a man universally respected, and the murder of himself and friends produced much excitement. Doctor Conley lived about eight years after his marriage, and left a son who is being educated in the college at Santa Clara, California.

To return to my interview with Perfonton at the Eldorado Hotel, in San Francisco. When he saw me standing conversing with a party of gentlemen, he eyed me for some time; and when a favourable opportunity presented, inquired if we had not met somewhere before. I asked him if he remembered how I shot his horse on the plains after the murder of Charvis and party; which caused him to turn deathly pale, and he begged me not to expose him. He said he was now leading an honest life, and was managing the publication of a paper.

I told him to have no fears of my exposing him, so long as he behaved himself; but should he pursue the opposite course, he might expect me to reveal his former character. I often met him afterwards in San Francisco, but he never was easy in my presence. He died in Oakland a few years ago, leaving a family; and I am not aware that anyone in those parts ever found out his true character or connection with the aforesaid murders.

After remaining a short time in San Francisco, I returned to my friends Jones and Burns. Our Texan emigrants proved good neighbours, and were breaking their lands, putting in crops, &c.

My farm in the vicinity, not being large enough for a stock *ranche*, I purchased land adjoining, and decided to stock it with sheep. A friend of mine living at some distance, sent me word to come and see him about sheep, as he had nearly four thousand head, and circumstances compelled him to offer me a part of them on shares. I agreed to take two thousand to care for, and give him half the wool and half the increase, returning him also the original number at the end of two years.

The first season scarcely any rain fell in that section, and I was obliged to take them to the Sierra Nevada mountains and hire them pastured in order to keep them alive. When the rainy season came on I got the sheep back to the San Joaquin valley, where I kept them till the two years had expired, when on settlement with Mr. Caruthers, I had about two thousand head of sheep and lambs for my share.

Leaving my flocks in the care of my uncle and proper herdsmen, I have since been employed in various trips over that country. One of these trips was as guide with a Mr. Ray, over the Sierra Nevadas, with a large flock of sheep which he was taking to Virginia City, Nevada. We started the first of July, and the fourth, at night, while camped under a large old sycamore tree, a heavy shock of an earthquake rattled the large limbs down upon us, killing Mr. Ray and wounding two of the Mexican shepherds.

Mr. Ray's son, who was sleeping near his father, was uninjured, and I escaped with a few bruises; but one of our wagons with provisions was nearly wrecked. I returned to Poterville (Mr. Ray's residence) with his body, in company with his son. The sheep were left in care of the servants who were acting as shepherds, till our return, then we proceeded onward toward Virginia City, and I left them, when they got over the mountains and could do without my services.

On my return home, I took a new route, through the mountains, passing a mining camp at what was called Green Horn settlement, where I had a friend Eugene, a Frenchman, who kept a miner's store. He was glad to see me, as he had been robbed the night before of four thousand dollars worth of gold dust by a band of four robbers, who had made their escape; and he offered me one thousand dollars reward for the recovery of the property.

I raised a party of eight men and followed them.

About thirty miles from the settlement they had stolen some stage horses from a station, and one hundred and fifty dollars in money from the proprietor. Then they had gone on to Walker's pass, at Indian Wells, and stolen more horses. Here we were informed that the thieves were pretty drunk when they left that place. We tracked them to a place called Desert Springs, where they had robbed a house of seven hundred dollars, and a gold watch belonging to a lady. Continuing on their track we came up with the rascals, where they had stopped for rest over night; and when they saw us they opened fire on our party, killing one of our horses. We returned their fire, killing three of them. We captured the other one, and recovered all the stolen property.

We returned with our prisoner, taking the same route we had come over, in order to restore the stolen property to the rightful owners. At Desert springs we returned the watch to the lady; and the seven hundred dollars to the owner, Mr. Johnson, and a pair of fine horses they had taken from him; and he in gratitude made us a present of two hundred dollars.

So we proceeded homeward, returning to each sufferer their property they had been robbed off, till we arrived at Green Horn settlement, where we restored the four thousand dollars in gold dust to the Frenchman, who was made perfectly happy by our success, and paid us the one thousand dollars reward.

Our arrival with the prisoner was soon noised abroad, and while we were eating supper with Eugene, and giving our miserable horse thief the last food he would ever taste, of crackers, &c, in the store, where we had him securely bound and guarded, we were disturbed by cries from a mob outside of, "Bring out the robber," "Hang him," and soon they found him, got a rope about his neck, dragged him to the nearest tree, where they hung him up and left him.

He said before being hung that he belonged to a respectable family, but bad company in Virginia City, Nevada, had proved his ruin. He was short of money there, when he was approached by his three late companions, (one of whom was only sixteen years old,) and invited to join them in their travels, which he consented to, as they had plenty of money, and offered him all he wished. He said the sixteen year old boy we had killed in his party, was the worst character in the lot, being perfectly desperate, and urging the rest on to murder and robbery.

This *desperado* was, in some respects, like many others I have seen executed under similar circumstances. No matter how perfectly recklessly they may have exposed their lives in their raids and fights, many of them, when they saw the rope and rude gallows for their execution, would cry and beg for their lives to be spared, as earnestly as a woman.

From this settlement I returned to my place in Tulare county, and made up my mind to attend to the business of stock raising, leaving the wild, roving, adventurous life I had led for so many years, for it hardly paid to be exposing my life to hunt for gold or robbers. At all events, at my period of life it certainly seemed safer to settle in Tulare county and take care of my stock, which was rapidly increasing, and needed my attention.

After coming to this conclusion, I spent several months in selecting and purchasing cattle for the San Francisco market. I was also often employed by large stock raisers in that vicinity, in lassoing and catching wild cattle, for branding, and for the market. My old experience with the lasso was of great service in this line of business; for no wild bullock could escape me when I had a good horse and a good lasso.

On one occasion, being out on the plain a few miles from Visalia, I saw a carriage containing a lady and her two daughters going at a tremendous rate towards a rough, stumpy piece of land, where the timber had been cut off; and seeing at a glance that their horses had become frightened, and had left the road, I put spurs to my horse and galloped near them, when I threw my lasso over the near horse's head. This stopped the carriage just in time to prevent them from going to destruction among the stumps a few rods before them.

The ladies were much alarmed, and told me how their horses became frightened by some object in the road, and desired me to drive them into Visalia, which I did, after fastening my horse behind their carriage. On driving them to their residence in the town, I discovered that they were the wife and daughters of Mr. Douglass, one of the leading merchants of Visalia.

The husband and father, when he heard of the danger they had been in, and had escaped from only by my hand, was very much moved and wished to make me a present, in token of his gratitude. This I declined, telling him I never considered myself entitled to any reward for aiding, or saving the life of any one in danger. I was abundantly rewarded for this act by the friendship of Mr. Douglass, as ever since that time he has been one of the best friends I have had in California,

In the San Joaquin valley there are numerous settlements, and many towns of considerable size; but occasionally in that country a wild animal will appear that seems a connecting link with the period before the country became settled. On one occasion I was out lassoing cattle with a Mexican, and had no arms, except a butcher knife. On returning homeward I came in contact with a stray elk, which I made up my mind to capture. He was a tough customer, with horns spreading near six feet; and when I rode up to him he looked quite savage and showed light as soon as I threw my lasso over his horns, bringing him to a standstill.

He was running when I threw him, but on regaining his feet he made for me and my horse, presenting a frightful appearance, his hair all turned the wrong way, and in his rush grazed the horse with his horns. My Mexican friend caught him with his lasso by the hind feet, when the elk was thrown to the ground. My trained horse kept my lasso tight on the animal's horns, while the Mexican held him by his hind feet, giving me a chance to dismount and cut his throat, which was a good job, considering the fleetness of such animals and the difficulty of their capture.

This elk was of large size, and his horns I preserved and still keep them at my *ranche*, near Visalia, as a memento of a desperate struggle with an elk, and an ornament over my doorway to show to visitors who happen to call upon me.

Among other employments I engaged to fill a sub-contract

for three hundred and fifty head of cattle for a beef contractor for Fort Tejon, to receive my pay when the contract was filled. I was successful in this undertaking, and made money on the job, satisfying all the parties concerned and supplying good beef.

After this I returned to my *ranche* and made some heavy purchases of sheep for the San Francisco market, which ventures always proved profitable. In that vicinity it is an easy matter to collect a few thousand sheep, as there are many stock raisers that can spare from five hundred to one thousand, and scarcely miss them. I sold my sheep in San Francisco to wholesale purchasers, and might have built up a prosperous trade if I had remained at the business, but circumstances prevented me.

LASSO FIGHT WITH THE ELK

CHAPTER 32

Robbery of a Mule train

I find, on looking over the proof sheets of the foregoing pages, that by some means I have omitted to give an account of some of my adventures, which I think will prove of interest to the reader, and have thought best to give them in a chapter by themselves without regard to the time or order in which they happened.

At one time I was in Zacatecas, out of employment, and looking for a job, when the agent of a company running stages from that place to Agua Calientes, some seventy miles distant, wished to engage me as a driver of one of their stages, for a short time, till they could fill the vacancy caused by the death of one of their drivers. This route was infested by thieves, and robberies of the stage and passengers were quite frequent. I remained in this employment about five months, during which time the stage was robbed several times by armed Mexicans. So long as the drivers did not expose the robbers, their lives were safe enough; but in case of exposure their death was certain,—in consequence of which the driver's policy was to keep silent.

For several weeks my stage was not attacked, but then came a series of robberies. First a priest and several students were on their way to the city of Mexico, as passengers, and they had considerable money in their possession. Before leaving Zacatecas the students procured three or four bottles of brandy, which they used rather freely, and after going a few miles they remarked that the route was infested with robbers, but being well armed, they told me they feared no danger. From their hilarious manner I inferred that they rather courted an attack, and told them to be on the alert, for they would all need their weapons, provided the robbers should pounce upon us suddenly. After changing horses at the second station from Zacatecas and proceeding some three miles from that point, sixteen robbers made their appearance at the side of the road and rushed upon the stage, calling upon me to halt and deliver what was valuable in the stage.

I halted without waiting for the argument of a rifle ball, when the robbers pointed their guns into the stage windows and ordered the passengers to surrender their valuables. The brave young students turned white as sheets, and, instead of using their pistols, gave up everything demanded, even to their loose clothing.

One of the robbers remarked that it was too bad to rob the priest. Among the party was a small Castilian, who appeared to be their leader, who said the priests were the very ones he preferred to rob, as they got their money easy; and he would have no conscientious scruples about robbing an angel if he got a chance. He made the priest hand over his money, watch, medal, and all his clothes, except his shirt and drawers. The robbers espying the brandy bottles, drank up the liquor, and said it was the best party they had struck for some time. They then ordered me to proceed, cautioning me to keep perfectly still about the matter, or I should forfeit my life

We then went forward, and for several miles I did not hear a word from my nearly naked passengers. When I looked back on them they were gazing into each other's faces in mute astonishment. I ventured finally to remark that their feelings must have changed somewhat in regard to guerrillas, and politely asked them why they did not shoot the robbers, as I had heard them say they should do if attacked.

Their excuses were various; but the truth was they were no exception to the rule I have found general, that all braggarts are arrant cowards when danger overtakes them. On our arrival at the end of my route, I was obliged to drive the stage to the rear of the stage house to enable the passengers to reach a room by a private way so they could procure some clothing before appearing in public.

The same evening I met some of the party of robbers in the billiard room of the hotel. They spoke to me, asking if I wanted any money, offering me plenty if I would accept; saying, that if I kept quiet all would be well, but otherwise I should be assassinated forthwith. I refused to take any of their ill-gotten gains; but not wishing to offend them, I excused myself by telling them I was well supplied.

A short time after this a conductor of a mule train started from Zacatecas for Tampico with half a million dollars worth of silver, having a large escort to guard the treasure. When about fifty miles from Zacatecas, they were attacked by one hundred and sixty-five robbers, and during the fight eleven of the troops of the escort and seven of the robbers were killed. The troops were defeated and escaped, but sent back to Zacatecas for assistance. The silver was packed on mules and the robbers started the train for the mountains to secure the treasure.

About five hundred cavalry were despatched from Zacatecas to overtake the robbers, and recover possession of the train. When the troops came in sight of the robbers they found them halted at the foot of the mountain. When they saw the cavalry in pursuit they cut open a part of the silver sacks and scattered it over the ground, then hurried up the mountain side, fleeing in all directions.

As the troops came to the silver strewn on the ground, they dismounted from their horses and commenced a general scramble to gather it up, thus giving time for the robbers to get away with most of the treasure. Before the officers could rally the troops, the robbers had arranged for their defence in a narrow pass in the mountains, where they resisted the advance of the cavalry successfully, obliging them to give up the chase and return without the silver they had saved, and it was never recovered.

The stage I drove was attacked a second time on the route

in a secluded, desolate spot, by a dozen or more robbers. In the stage were nine Englishmen, with several thousand dollars in their possession. They were well armed, with guns and pistols, and when the robbers appeared and ordered me to halt, with their guns pointed towards me, I held up; but the Englishmen told me to drive on or they would shoot me, which placed me in no enviable position. I kept on till the one of the lead horses was shot, which so entangled the team that I was obliged to stop, and one ball penetrated the rubber cloth in front of me, doing no other damage.

The Englishmen now jumped from the stage, shot one robber dead, wounded another, and killed or disabled two of their horses; after this warm reception the robbers fled in haste. I could not help noticing how differently those Englishmen conducted themselves in danger, from the way the bragging Mexicans had done, when my stage was attacked on a former occasion. I had heard them make no boasts of what they would do if attacked, nor express any desire to see the band that would dare attack them; but although they said little, when the time came, they acted.

The Englishmen took the wounded man prisoner, and prepared to hang him if he did not confess who his companions were. He was drawn up three times before he would make any confession. He finally said the whole band was composed of more than a hundred men, giving many of their names. We took him along to the next station and handed him over to the authorities, who sent him back to Zacatecas. He confessed that the chief clerk of the stage route was one of their party, and had kept the band posted in regard to the shipment of valuables, or the transit of money. After the arrest of this wounded man the clerk suddenly disappeared with about sixty thousand dollars which way in the stage house.

The wounded man made these confessions on condition of his life being spared. His arm was amputated and good medical attendance secured. He told of money buried in different places. In an old mine was found a sack containing ten thousand dollars, which was let down the shaft by a rope. He informed us of a house in Zacatecas, where was found a large quantity of plunder, such as clothing, watches, jewellery, saddles, blankets, &c, which the gang had there secreted, the house being in the outskirts of the city, and the front part used as a drinking saloon kept by one of their party.

The authorities took this property and hung the keeper of the den with a number of his confederates. I now resigned my occupation of stage driver, telling the company that it was too dangerous to suit me. They tried to have me continue, offering me large pay; but I positively refused to stay longer. When the wounded man had recovered from his amputation, the first time he ventured into the street he was assassinated by one of his old companions.

From the wild, rough nature of some of the mountain districts east of Zacatecas, it is easy for organized bands of robbers to secrete all the booty they can capture, and many a train of mules, loaded with silver from the mines in the interior, has been waylaid and robbed on its way to the city of Mexico, or to the coast.

There was a little mountain village called Xerez to the west of Zacatecas, where the inhabitants, almost to a man, including the priest, were concerned in robbery or in the concealment of stolen property, and got their living by this means. Nature had furnished them with admirable facilities for defence, as the only approach to the village was by a narrow, crooked path or trail, running in some places directly under ledges of rock, towering above hundreds of feet, so that the roadway was easily obstructed; and if a party persisted in pursuit, they could roll down heavy rocks upon their pursuers. A party of soldiers who were once following a band of robbers through this narrow pass were almost annihilated by the masses of rock which came crashing down from the heights above.

At one time, while in the employ of an English mining company at Durango, I came near losing my life by the treachery of supposed friends. I had been sent in charge of a pack train, with

Novel Barricade

an escort composed of a Mexican sergeant and fifteen soldiers, to one of the company's mines at Guadaloupe-y-Calvo, to bring in seventy-five thousand dollars worth of metal. When we were ready to start on our return trip, a party of English and American miners who were about to leave the mines for Durango, proposed to accompany me.

To this arrangement I consented, after having ascertained that they were honest men. When we had accomplished about half the distance, and were encamped for the night, a Mexican boy, who acted as my servant, warned me privately of a plot between the sergeant and the troops to kill me and the English and Americans, with a view of stealing the treasure. I immediately informed the English and Americans (who were all armed,) that our lives were in danger from a set of vagabond traitors, who had conspired against us, and asked if they would assist me in conquering them., to which they readily consented.

The soldiers were at some distance from us, cooking supper, with their guns stacked; and we approached them familiarly, in such a way that their suspicions were not excited, till they saw us surround the stacks of arms, and then it was too late. We fired into them, killing two, when we secured and bound the others, hand and foot. We then sent the boy to a mining town, ten miles distant, for help. The magistrate came with twenty-five men to our assistance, and sent the train forward under their protection to Durango.

When we arrived with our prisoners they were tried, and the sergeant and corporal were hung, the others being sentenced to labour on the streets five years, with ball and chain attached to their ankles. The Mexican boy told the truth, for they confessed their crime, and he was rewarded by the company with a present of five hundred dollars.

I was sent at another time to one of the company's mines at Bueno Sara, with a pack train of ten mules, besides seven mounted friends to assist me and for protection. Our business was to get an English lady and her daughter, with their baggage, and bring them to Durango, where her husband was awaiting her.

On our return from the mine to Durango, while we were crossing a plain, where there was no shelter of any kind for the ladies, we were attacked by about forty Apaches. We saw the Indians coming towards us, when they were quite a distance away, and, as we had no natural shelter, it became necessary to devise an artificial one. The baggage was hastily removed from the mules, when they were cast and their feet securely tied. This served a double purpose, as it effectually prevented a stampede and enabled us to use them for purposes of shelter. The cast mules and baggage were arranged in a circle, within which we placed ourselves, and behind this novel breastwork we awaited the attack of the Indians.

When they charged upon us, they were entirely exposed to our fire, while we, by keeping close to the mules and baggage, could not be harmed by their arrows. When they came within range, we opened fire on them, and killed several, beside wounding some of their animals, when they retreated, carrying their dead and wounded with them. None of our party were injured, but we had two mules killed. Our singular breastwork had saved our lives, and we resumed our journey and arrived safely at Durango.

The lady's husband, Mr. McIntire, gave us a hearty reception, and was much astonished to hear of our perilous adventure with the Indians. He said he never would have thought of such a means of defence, and I hardly think he would, for he was an assayer at the mint and did not know anything about fighting Indians; but he did know how to order a splendid supper for us, and he afterwards made me a present of five hundred dollars, saying he considered he was indebted to me for the preservation of the lives of his wife and daughter.

At the annual fair at San Juan de los Lagos, which I attended in the latter part of the year 1841, (see chapter 4, where the place is called San Juan,) among the various amusements were several bullfights, some of which were very ludicrous, and as I am not aware that they have ever been mentioned in any book of travel,

I will give a description of one of them here. In the centre of the arena a greased pole was erected, the top of which was crowned with sundry prizes of money and clothing, very tempting to the poorer "Greasers" who were welcome to take them down, while at the same time a wild bull was at liberty to enjoy himself in the arena by knocking them down.

A considerable number of Mexicans went for the coveted goods, and the bull, as was his privilege, went for them. Sometimes the "Greasers" would succeed, by clustering around the pole and climbing upon each others' shoulders, in nearly reaching the prizes, when the bull would make a wild rush at the lower strata of struggling humanity, and knocking out the under pinning, of course the superstructure would descend with considerable more celerity than comfort, amid roars of laughter from the audience. By perseverance under difficulties, however, the top of the pole was at last reached by one of the contestants, and stripped of the prizes.

The last bull that was brought into the ring had his horns sawed off, or blunted, and a string of silver coin upon a strong wire was fastened from one horn to the other, and anybody who chose and was smart enough could *take the bull by the horns* and help himself to the money. Of course the animal objected to having any liberties taken with his head, and treated his persecutors with divers and sundry "horns' which "elevated" many of them in a surprising manner.

Finally, by persistent worrying, they succeeded in getting hold of him in sufficient numbers to throw him down, and when the wire was wrested from his horns a funny scramble ensued for the possession of the money. All hands let go of the bull for that purpose, who regained his feet, and smarting under the indignities which had been heaped upon him, executed sundry bull-rushes among the struggling crowd, knocking them right and left, and giving the Mexican silver a remarkably lively circulation. This was a rather rough sport, but was highly enjoyed by the spectators.

At another time I was in New Mexico, stopping at the foot

of the Taos Mountain, hunting with a party all through the mountains for game. We had many adventures with bears, and one day I come near losing my life by a grizzly. I had shot a small deer and a wild turkey, and was proceeding to camp, when my favourite dog, which I had owned for some months, scented game in another direction and started for it. I followed him, and soon discovered two small bear cubs, which I foolishly fired on, without noticing the old she bear, which was close by.

I wounded one of the cubs, when it commenced to cry, and the old one was upon me before I could reload my rifle. In the tussle which ensued, she struck me on the left leg, just at the knee. I had on a pair of strong buckskin pants, but her claws penetrated them and tore the tough leather-like cotton to the bottom of the leg, at the same time tearing my knee fearfully.

All that saved me was my dog, who attacked the bear in the rear, when she turned around quickly and caught the dog, and nearly squeezed him to death. While the bear was thus engaged, I drew my tomahawk from my belt and settled it deep in her brains, killing her just in time to save the dog. The wounded cub I then despatched, and rolling the other in my hunting shirt, I made my way to camp, carrying him safely home.

I succeeded in taming this cub, and in time he became a great pet, and was a general favourite with the hunters. As he grew up he showed remarkable intelligence and aptitude for tricks. I taught him to wrestle with me, and sit up at my order; and he and my dog soon grew to be great friends, playing together by the hour; but he would never tolerate any other dog near him, and once he split open the head of a strange dog who attempted to be too familiar with him. He would frequently accompany me and the dog on hunting expeditions; but as he was fat he had to lag in the rear, going out, but when we turned toward home he would take the lead and keep it.

On one such occasion I had become interested in the pursuit of game, and did not realize how late it was till it began to grow dark, when I found I was a long way from home. I started to retrace my steps, but it was soon so dark I could not discern the landmarks, and I commenced preparations for camping out till morning. I noticed the bear appeared very uneasy, going a short distance toward home, looking back, and then coming up to me.

After this had been several times repeated, I decided to follow him, when he started in the direction of home, and continued his course, without the least hesitation, till he brought me there, apparently knowing the way as well in that pitchy darkness as by daylight. I called him "Cuff," and he knew and would answer to his name as well as any dog. I finally sold him for ninety-five dollars to Bensler & Kelly's circus, which was travelling through New Mexico.

A few months afterwards I lost my noble dog in a fight with a species of panther, or what is called in that country a California lion. This animal is not, more than half the size of an African lion, but resembles it very much in some respects, the head and neck being shaggy and large and the body tapering small towards the tail; it has also the same long claws and great strength of limb.

I had become known all around Santa Fe as having been successful in several encounters with bears and other wild animals, and one day I had an invitation from a stock raiser to go with him to his *ranche*, some thirty miles from Santa Fe to track, and kill, if possible, a California lion that had been destroying his small stock. I took along my dog, who was afraid of nothing, and very keen scented. After our arrival at the place, I had to wait several days for the panther to make his appearance so as to enable me to get a fresh trail.

Finally he was seen early one morning in a pasture eating a small colt which he had killed. My dog was uncommonly large, and always ready for a fight, so in company with several friends, who followed with rifles to see the sport, the dog led the way, with me in close pursuit. The animal after eating all he could of the colt, had retired a few hundred yards to the brush, where he had lain down to sleep, and was awakened by the approach of the dog who was ready to spring on him.

On seeing us so near, the savage brute undertook to escape,

by climbing a tree; but the dog caught him by the leg, and they rolled over on the ground, biting and tearing each other terribly, the dog having a firm hold upon the panther's neck. At last the dog's side was torn open by the long claws of the animal, just as I fired a charge into the head of the infuriated panther, which was a lucky shot, as he was just ready to turn upon me.

The poor dog was too far gone for me to save him. I bound up his wounds as well as I could, and carried him back to the *ranche*, but he lived only a few moments after reaching it. The neighbourhood generally turned out to see the carcass of the animal I had shot, and sympathized with me in the loss of so noble a dog. After giving him a decent burial and receiving seventy-five dollars for my job, I returned to Santa Fe, feeling thankful for the preservation of my life, but gloomy at parting from the dog. In our hunting expeditions after this the dog was very much missed, as it was very unusual to find one that would attack as ferocious animals as he would.

At one time I was fortunate enough to win a small bet and rid a mining village of a bore, at the same time. There was in this village, as is usually the case, a small store, where the miners would get together after their day's work was over, and exchange stories and items of interest with each other. One of these parties was always talking of ghosts, and their appearance to men. I became tired of so much in the same strain from him, and determined to put a stop to his ridiculous talk.

So one night, when he was in the midst of one of his tales, I very abruptly told him I did not believe his statement, nor in ghosts at all. This, it appeared afterwards, was just the statement he had been trying to get someone to make. So he appeared quite indignant at having his word doubted, and offered to bet me five dollars that I could not walk around an old graveyard, which was back from the store some distance, without seeing a ghost and running from it.

It was a dark night, but I concluded to accept his wager, and, staking our money, I started alone on my walk, with a man following some distance in the rear to see the result and note whether I made a circuit of the haunted yard. I secured a good cudgel at the start, and when about half way around the yard the ghost, sure enough, made his appearance. I stalked boldly up to it and pounded away till I made it cry murder and everything else calculated to bring assistance, till the arrival of help, when a lantern revealed the countenance of the man I had bet with. After giving him an extra blow or two I let him go, cautioning him to leave the place for good, or stop his ghost yarns. It cured him effectually of his attempts to sell people, and made him quit the neighbourhood as soon as he got over his bruises.

Conclusion

In the foregoing pages I have endeavoured to give an account of a portion of my adventures in a life of more than usual peril and excitement. I was induced to publish this account by the earnest recommendation of many friends. It has been written out, as I have had time, entirely from memory, as I never kept a diary of events, never thinking that I should publish my experiences.

For this reason, I have been unable to give exact dates in all cases; but as the object I had in view, was not to publish a history of the country where I have been, but to relate personal adventures, this will not prove, I hope, any drawback to the interest of the reader. As far as the narrative relates to my transactions, I have confined myself to the literal facts.

In looking back over my life, I find that although I have not, perhaps, always obeyed the Golden Rule, yet it is a great satisfaction to me to think of the numbers of my fellow beings I have been instrumental in saving from death and misery at the hands of savages, and from the horrors of starvation.

And now, that my labours in this direction are completed, I shall probably retire to my California home, and devote myself to stock raising. Hoping that this narrative may prove of interest to the reader, I will say—goodbye.

www.ingramcontent.com/pod-product-compliance
Lightning Source LLC
Chambersburg PA
CBHW021955160426
43197CB00007B/145